Happily Ever After

Sharing Folk Literature With Elementary and Middle School Students

Terrell A. Young
Washington State University
Richland, Washington, USA
EDITOR

INTERNATIONAL
Reading Association
800 BARKSDALE ROAD, PO BOX 8139
NEWARK, DE 19714-8139, USA
www.reading.org

The International Reading Association attempts, through its publications, to provide a forum for a wide spectrum of opinions on reading. This policy permits divergent viewpoints without implying the endorsement of the Association.

Director of Publications   Joan M. Irwin
Editorial Director, Books and Special Projects   Matthew W. Baker
Managing Editor   Shannon Benner
Permissions Editor   Janet S. Parrack
Acquisitions and Communications Coordinator   Corinne M. Mooney
Associate Editor, Books and Special Projects   Sara J. Murphy
Assistant Editor   Charlene M. Nichols
Administrative Assistant   Michele Jester
Senior Editorial Assistant   Tyanna L. Collins
Production Department Manager   Iona Muscella
Supervisor, Electronic Publishing   Anette Schütz
Senior Electronic Publishing Specialist   Cheryl J. Strum
Electronic Publishing Specialist   R. Lynn Harrison
Proofreader   Elizabeth C. Hunt

Project Editor   Shannon Benner

Cover Design   Donna A. Perzel

Library of Congress Cataloging-in-Publication Data
Happily ever after : sharing folk literature with elementary and middle school students / Terrell A. Young, editor.
    p. cm.
Includes bibliographical references and indexes.
 ISBN 0-87207-510-9
 1. Folk literature--Study and teaching (Elementary)--United States. 2. Folk literature--Study and teaching (Middle school)--United States. 3. Multicultural education--Activity programs--United States. I. Young, Terrell A.
 LB1583.8.H36 2003
 372.64--dc22

2003018329

Contents

SECTION THREE
Sampling Folk Literature Across Cultures

SECTION FOUR

Celebrating Folk Literature in the Classroom

Preface

Terrell A. Young

Folk literature, also called traditional literature, represents a substantial portion of the trade books published today for children and young adults. This literature is well represented in book awards such as the Newbery and the Caldecott, in many district and state reading curricula, in published literary anthologies and basal readers, and in university textbooks about children's literature. Yet, no single volume focuses entirely on the full breadth of this wonderful genre and on the teaching of it in elementary and middle schools. This collection is an attempt to fill that void.

Happily Ever After: Sharing Folk Literature With Elementary and Middle School Students first provides teachers with foundational understanding of the folk literature genre. Next, their understanding of the subgenres is developed through the scholarly treatment of each one. In their treatment of folk and fairy tales, fables, myths, legends, and tall tales, the authors present a fabulous array of activities for immersing students in the literature. Then, they introduce teachers to a rich mosaic of folk literature representing many different cultural groups and peoples. Finally, teachers see how folk literature can extend their students' literacy and love of reading through a range of classroom applications spanning the full range of the language arts.

This book is appropriate for preservice and inservice use by teachers and/or librarians pursuing course work in children's literature. Beyond its use as a textbook in formal courses, though, this book also can serve as an excellent personal reference tool for K–8 teachers, administrators, and teacher educators. Finally, this book is ideally suited for use in school district staff development activities.

The book is divided into four sections. The first provides an overview of traditional literature. The chapters in the second section take a closer look at the subgenres of folk literature, helping readers to better understand folk and fairy tales, fables, myths, legends, and tall tales. The third section deals with traditional literature across cultures and includes thought-provoking chapters dealing with African, Asian, European, Jewish, Latino, Middle Eastern and South Asian, and Native American folk literature. Section four looks at how teachers might use folk literature in their classrooms through comparing versions and variants of a single tale type, collecting oral folklore and adapting it to the written form, drama, and writing.

Section One

In chapter 1, I build a foundation for the study of folk literature by defining the genre and presenting the benefits for students when teachers share folk literature in the classroom. Then I introduce readers to folk literature's subgenres and conclude with a brief presentation of common folk motifs.

Section Two

Folk literature's many subgenres present a treasure trove of opportunities for teachers and students. It is sometimes a challenge to categorize folk literature; many collections include a range of the subgenres. Some books have the word *legend* or *myth* in the title when the story is clearly a folk tale (refer to chapters 2, 4, and 5 for more about folk tales, myths, and legends). This section of the book, then, seeks to further define fables, myths, legends, and tall tales, as well as folk tales and fairy tales. Yet, readers will see that classifying the traditional story challenges even the experts. I believe it is more important to share the stories than to classify them with total certainty.

Talented professors, teachers, authors, and librarians paint the landscape of traditional literature in exploring the subgenres in this section. In chapter 2, Anne Marie Kraus unravels the world of folk tales. Nancy J. Johnson and Angela Sorgatz Vroom explore more fully the role of fables in the classroom in chapter 3. The authors share a plethora of current fables, along with numerous activities to help students experience the joy of reading and writing fables. A cogent discussion of mythology for children follows in chapter 4, in which Sam L. Sebesta and Dianne L. Monson share how the canon of mythology now expands beyond the traditional Greek, Roman, and Norse retellings. Darcy H. Bradley helps readers to better understand legends in chapter 5, and the boisterous world of hilarious hyperbole opens up to readers in chapter 6 by Linda M. Pavonetti.

Section Three

Young people today are fortunate to have the opportunity to experience folk literature from the many cultures that make up our world. Such study provides them with insights into the beliefs, values, and lifestyles of the various cultural groups. Section three illustrates the diversity of tales across cultures. This section begins with Deborah L. Thompson's introduction to the rich literature of Africa in chapter 7. Chapter 8, by Belinda Y. Louie, focuses on the wealth of stories from Asia. In chapter 9, Ellen A. Greever and John Warren Stewig illuminate readers' understanding of tales from Europe. Evelyn B. Freeman presents Jewish tales of great poignancy and wit in chapter 10. Chapter 11, by Lynn Atkinson Smolen and Victoria Ortiz-Castro, presents the story heritage of Latin America, the Caribbean, and Latinos in the United States. Marcia Baghbans's chapter 12 acquaints readers with the wit and humor of the Middle East and India. In chapter 13, Debbie A. Reese demonstrates the need for retellers of Native American traditional stories to remain true to the culture.

Section Four

A wealth of classroom applications in this book will facilitate student response to folk literature. Ann Sloan and Sylvia M. Vardell illustrate how variants of a popular tale can enhance student learning in chapter 14. Many teachers begin with oral folklore before moving into teaching the more frequently used folk literature, and chapter 15 by Nancy L. Hadaway highlights how teachers can engage their students in the study of folklore. Drama provides a natural response to folk literature in chapter 16 by Judy Sierra, which showcases ideas for allowing students to respond to folk literature through drama. Next, Laura Tuiaea describes a unit that she uses to involve her students in creating their own "fractured fairy tales" in chapter 17. Finally, Jane E. Kelley helps readers consider folk tale themes and values in chapter 18.

Throughout *Happily Ever After*, authors help readers better understand folk literature and its place in the curriculum. More important, they project a sense of how much students enjoy experiencing folk literature, introduce readers to the richness of many different cultures' folk literature, and offer ideas for how to use the stories in the classroom to pique students' imaginations. In essence, the book is a guide for helping teachers and students experience the "happily ever after" magic found in folk literature.

Acknowledgments

Any book of this magnitude relies on the support, expertise, time, talents, and generosity of many wonderful people. I wish to express my gratitude to the authors of the many chapters in this volume. This book is a tribute to their efforts, scholarly expertise, and passion for folk literature. It is also important for me to recognize the tremendous support I received from the editorial department of the International Reading Association. Matt Baker saw merit in the proposal, calmed my fears in the most difficult moments, and, with Shannon Benner, shepherded the book to its completion. Both Matt and Shannon exemplify great editorial skills with their brilliance, insight, and ability to blend the work of 24 authors into a unified work—yet maintain distinct voices. This book is much better because of their direction. The proposal reviewers also made many helpful suggestions, and I wish to offer my sincere appreciation for their efforts. Jonathan Young spent hours searching the Internet to identify authors and illustrators for the reference lists. I want to especially thank him for sacrificing beautiful spring days to help with this project. The children's trade book publishers not only produce exciting folk literature for our reading pleasure and study but also allowed us to reproduce many book jackets that enrich the book and increase its overall appeal. Their generosity is indeed appreciated.

My university colleagues have contributed greatly to my career. I wish to thank Nancy Hadaway and Sylvia Vardell for their continued support, encouragement, and efforts to push my thinking forward. I have truly benefited from all of our collaborations. The people I work with on a day-to-day basis at Washington State University greatly enrich my life. I wish to acknowledge Valarie Akerson (now at Indiana University), Stephanie Bauman, Helen Berry, Deanna Gilmore, Larry Gregory, Judy Morrison, Amy Roth McDuffie, Marisol Rodríguez-Price, Carol Stape, and Bette Ward for making my work environment pleasant, productive, and professional. They have taught me that the grass is actually greener in eastern Washington's desert than on the other side of the fence!

My family has been a constant support to me throughout my life. I want to thank my mother, Patricia Young, and my siblings, Janet Coats, John Young, Lisa Moeder, Stacey Briggs, Jennifer Glynn, and Lori Young. Finally, I owe a great deal to my wife, Christine, and our terrific children, Jonathan, Natalie, Emilee, and Jeffrey. Their love, support, friendship, and patience keep me grounded in what is truly important and make "happily ever after" a reality for me.

TAY

Contributors

Marcia Baghban
Professor of Elementary Education
Queens College, City University
    of New York
Flushing, New York, USA

Darcy H. Bradley
Editor
Richard C. Owen Publishers
Bellingham, Washington, USA

Evelyn B. Freeman
Campus Dean and Director
The Ohio State University at Mansfield
Mansfield, Ohio, USA

Ellen A. Greever
Assistant Professor of Information
    Studies
University of Wisconsin–Milwaukee
Milwaukee, Wisconsin, USA

Nancy L. Hadaway
Professor of Curriculum and Instruction
University of Texas at Arlington
Arlington, Texas, USA

Susan Hepler
Children's Literature Specialist
Alexandria, Virginia, USA

Nancy J. Johnson
Professor of English/Language Arts
    Education
Western Washington University
Bellingham, Washington, USA

Jane E. Kelley
Assistant Professor of Children's
    Literature and Literacy Education
Washington State University
Pullman, Washington, USA

Anne Marie Kraus
School Library Media Specialist
Roosevelt Elementary School
Iowa City, Iowa, USA

Belinda Y. Louie
Associate Professor of Education
University of Washington, Tacoma
Tacoma, Washington, USA

Dianne L. Monson
Professor of Children's Literature
    Emerita
University of Minnesota
Minneapolis, Minnesota, USA

Victoria Ortiz-Castro
Former Bilingual Teacher
Postgraduate Student in Literary
    Linguistics
University of Strathclyde
Glasgow, Scotland

Linda M. Pavonetti
Associate Professor of Children's
and Young Adult Literature
Oakland University
Rochester, Michigan, USA

Debbie A. Reese
Postdoctoral Research Associate
in Educational Policy Studies
University of Illinois at
Urbana–Champaign
Champaign, Illinois, USA

Sam L. Sebesta
Professor of Education Emeritus
University of Washington
Seattle, Washington, USA

Judy Sierra
Author and Folklorist
Oakland, California, USA

Ann Sloan
Doctoral Candidate in Library
and Information Studies
Texas Woman's University
Fort Worth, Texas, USA

Lynn Atkinson Smolen
Professor of Literacy Education
University of Akron
Akron, Ohio, USA

Angela Sorgatz Vroom
Elementary School Teacher
Whatcom and Skagit County School
Districts
Bellingham, Washington, USA

John Warren Stewig
Professor of Education Emeritus
University of Wisconsin–Milwaukee
Milwaukee, Wisconsin, USA

Deborah L. Thompson
Assistant Professor of Education
The College of New Jersey
Ewing, New Jersey, USA

Laura Tuiaea
Language Arts/Social Studies Teacher
Chief Joseph Middle School
Richland, Washington, USA

Sylvia M. Vardell
Professor of Literature for Children
and Young Adults
Texas Woman's University
Denton, Texas, USA

Terrell A. Young
Associate Professor of Literacy
Education
Washington State University
Richland, Washington, USA

Introducing the Folk Literature Genre

CHAPTER 1

Unraveling the Tapestry: An Overview of the Folk Literature Genre

Terrell A. Young

This introductory chapter will invite and persuade readers to explore the broad genre of folk literature. Teachers often are unaware of the breadth of this genre, but it is exactly this scope that offers such a rich source of learning possibilities. The following questions are addressed in this chapter:

What is folk literature?

What are the benefits of using folk literature in the classroom?

What are the many subgenres of folk literature?

Why are the same stories told across cultures?

What are some of the motifs commonly found in folk literature?

What Is Folk Literature and What Are Its Functions?

Also known as traditional literature, folk literature is essentially the canon of tales or stories of a people, passed down orally through many generations. Folklore—referring to a variety of oral lore including greetings, jokes, remedies, stories, etc.—emerges from the folk, or grass roots, culture and becomes folk literature when it is recorded in written form. Generally, stories of folk cultures cannot be traced to one single person. Such tales were initially spread by word of mouth, and each reteller left a faint impression on the tale by crafting the story anew to fit the audience and the setting. These changes also reflected the teller's attitudes, values, insights, and artistic gifts (Rosenberg, 1997). Moreover, many of these tales were further altered when retold in written form. For instance, Charlotte Huck explains in an author's note her changes to *Toads and Diamonds* (1996), in which the sweet Renée's words are accompanied by flowers and jewels while her selfish and cruel sister's words are accompanied by toads and snakes. Huck places limitations on Renée's gift because "to speak flowers and jewels for the rest of [one's] life would be a curse and not a gift. It also seemed important that Renée be accepted for her own true self" (n.p.).

Folk literature addresses many needs of people. Russell (2001) notes four such needs:

1. The need to explain the natural world in the absence of scientific information;

2. The need to articulate our fears and dreams, thus making them accessible and manageable;

3. The need to impose some order on the apparent random, even chaotic, nature of life, thus helping us to understand our place in the universe; and

4. The need to entertain each other, as well as ourselves. (p. 149)

We can add a fifth need: the need to transmit values to children and youth. For this reason, folk literature has been referred to as the "cement of society" (Durkheim, 1933). The stories provide group members with common experiences that reinforce desired values and moral lessons. For example, Michael Lind's retelling of the Comanche tale *Bluebonnet Girl* (2003) extols the value of personal sacrifice for the good of the group. In *Tanuki's Gift* (Myers, 2003), a tanuki (a small raccoon-like animal) helps a Buddhist priest see how friendship is worth much more than gold. Thus, folk literature has many benefits to people as individuals and as a society. Moreover, it has great potential for students in elementary and middle schools.

What Are the Benefits of Using Folk Literature in the Classroom?

Many types of traditional literature are available to today's students; they can read and listen to the entire range of folk literature, from riddles and rhymes to fables, fairy tales and folk tales, myths and legends. Most basal readers and literature anthologies include selections from traditional literature. Ironically, tales once told only orally are now found published in picture book format, with rich illustrations to cue the reader to important story elements and to provide visual cultural details (Hadaway, Vardell, & Young, 2002).

This genre provides engaging reading material for students, because folk tales are generally short stories that can be read quickly. This brief format is ideal for English-language learners who may lack the English proficiency to tackle lengthier and more complex reading assignments. Plus, young students delight in the way folk literature tends to capture oral qualities in print (such as in Verna Aardema's use of onomatopoeia in her retelling of the Liberian tale *Koi and the Kola Nuts* [1999]), and they readily join in as the teacher reads the tale. A chorus of student voices echoes the sounds of sandals scuffing upon the path (*ras, ras, ras*), the little snake slithering (*wasa-wusu, wasa-wusu*), the crocodile's tail lashing (*belong-belang, belong-belang*), and the chopping of the mango tree (*pim-pen, pim-pen, pim-pen*).

In an ideal world, all young children would come to school steeped in hours of nursery rhymes and other tales. Such experiences not only help children see consequences of actions, but they also provide children with a sense of story (Sierra, 1996). From even the simplest tales, children learn the elements of a good story: character, plot, setting, and theme.

Book cover from *Aesop's Fables* by Jerry Pinkney. Copyright © 2000. Used by permission of North-South Books.

Trade book versions of folk tales are also a way to help students understand the personal dimension and the standards of behavior of a culture, and at the same time they are a way to reduce stereotypes (Bosma, 1992). "Folklore contains references to a society's values: what the people value; what they laugh at; what they scorn, fear, or desire; and how they see themselves" (Young & Ferguson, 1995, p. 491). In the words of Rudolfo Anaya (1999), "Stories help us understand and appreciate other people and they hold many valuable lessons" (p. 16).

Traditional literature also provides students with a frame of reference to bring to the literature and cultures they will later encounter. Many allusions to traditional literature appear in longer works of fiction and nonfiction (Norton, 1990). Indeed, many fantasy stories echo literary patterns found in myths and legends (Blatt, 1993). Students can find many protagonists who lack important information about their births, set out on quests to correct wrongs, have access to magic in their fights against evil, and, once successful, return home to help others. Even the Harry Potter books are rich in mythological allusions, as noted in chapter 4 of this book.

Finally, folk literature can effectively complement the various curricular areas. For example, one fifth-grade teacher reads pourquoi tales (etiological folk tales with explanations of how things came about) to her students when they learn about animal camouflage and adaptation in science class. A high school geography teacher uses folk literature as an entry point when introducing his students to various regions and countries. A history teacher reads aloud Carmen Agra Deedy's *The Yellow Star: The Legend of King Christian X of Denmark* (2000) when introducing her students to Nazi-occupied Europe. Even mathematical principles can be illustrated by using folk literature, such as exponential growth in Demi's *One Grain of Rice* (1997b).

Given the many instructional benefits of folk literature, teachers need to consider using this genre more frequently. Therefore, the next section of this chapter examines what traditional story types can be included in the classroom.

What Does the Study of Folk Literature Include?

Traditional literature includes a wide range of published variations, including fables, myths, legends, tall tales, and folk tales. Indeed, even the category of "folk tale" includes pourquoi tales, trickster tales, fairy tales, literary tales, and fractured fairy tales whose authors are known. This is a very popular niche in the publishing market, and many artfully written and beautifully illustrated versions can be found that can have immense appeal across the grade levels. The best examples reflect careful study of the root culture so that the language and illustrations accurately reflect the story's culture for the reader. *Mufaro's Beautiful Daughters* (Steptoe, 1987), for example, is an outstanding example of a "Cinderella" tale with illustrations inspired by the flora and fauna of Zimbabwe, and yet it reflects a universality in character and theme that appeals to even secondary students.

Table 1.1 illustrates some of the unique differences in the major subgenres of published traditional literature. Such an organizational graphic aid can help students to classify the tales under study by drawing their attention to the essential characteristics of each story. In addition, this graphic can assist students in their efforts to create their own stories.

Traditional literature has served to educate listeners/readers about the creation of the world, the history of its people, and the moral values a particular culture holds dear. Over the years, fables, myths, legends, tall tales, and folk tales have evolved as distinct literary vehicles with these specific purposes.

Fables

Fables are often short stories featuring animal characters who teach young people lessons with stated morals, often with mixed results. Both Russell (2001) and Savage (2000) point out that children frequently miss the intended message of the morals presented in stories. Yet, students enjoy the fables for their clever animal characters and conflicts, even though parents often wish their children would internalize the morals.

The best-known fables are those said to be written by Aesop, a slave living in Greece between 620 B.C. and 560 B.C. Examples of these fables abound in collections: *Aesop & Company* (Bader, 1991), *The Aesop for Children* (Winter, 1994), *Aesop's Fables* (Pinkney, 2000), *Fables From Aesop* (Lynch, 2000), *The Lion & the Mouse and Other Aesop's Fables* (Orgel, 2000), and *A Sip of Aesop* (Yolen, 1995).

Table 1.1
Comparing Subgenres of Traditional Literature

	Definition	Characters	Setting	Teller's Belief
Fable	Very brief story that points clearly to a moral or lesson	Often personified animals	Backdrop: "Once upon a time..."	Not told as fact
Myth	Symbolic story created by an ancient people to explain their world	Deities and others endowed with supernatural powers	Backdrop: "In the beginning..."	Told as fact
Legend	Traditional narrative of a people, often based in historical truth	Historical figures with fictional traits and situations	Backdrop: "When Arthur was king..."	Told as fact
Tall Tale	Exaggerated narrative of characters that perform impossible feats	"Larger-than-life" historical or fictional people with superhuman strength	Backdrop: "I reckon by now you've heard of Davy Crockett..."	Not told as fact
Folk Tale	Fairy, human, or animal tale passed down by word of mouth	Flat, stock characters; may be human or animal	Backdrop: "Long ago and far away..."	Not told as fact

Adapted from Bosma (1992), Goforth and Spillman (1994), and Lukens (1999).

The Ant and the Grasshopper (Poole, 2000) is an example of the many Aesop's fables available in picture book formats. Pat Mora's retelling of the Mayan fable *The Race of Toad and Deer* (2001) begs to be compared with Aesop's "Tortoise and the Hare" story.

Although students are familiar with Aesop's fables, other fables exist as well. Jean de La Fontaine, a French poet living in the 17th century, retold fables in beautiful verses. One example of La Fontaine's fables is *The Fox and the Stork* (McDermott, 1999), in which a stork finds a way to outwit the fox who tricked him. Another is *The Miller, the Boy, and the Donkey* (Wildsmith, 1990), in which a miller who tries to please everyone eventually decides he should have made up his own mind in the first place. The Jataka Tales are Indian fables dealing with Buddha's animal rebirths before he became the "Enlightened One." Jataka tales can be found in Martin's *The Hungry Tigress* (1999) and Demi's *Buddha Stories* (1997a).

Chapter 3 offers many recently published fables, along with classroom applications for teaching with them.

Myths

Virginia Hamilton (1988), the Newbery Award-winning author, explains,

> Myths present themselves as truth and as accounts of actual facts no matter how different these facts or truths may be from our ordinary, "real" experience. There are myths that are sacred or religious. In all of them, there is the feeling that the unusual or divine events are inevitable. (pp. ix–x)

Myths explain, among others things, the creation of the world, how light was separated from darkness, and the origin of seasons. They tend to focus on the "big picture" of the natural order of things. People generally consider myths of their own cultures to be true (Rosenberg, 1997).

Students also can find that different cultures have explained these phenomena in different ways throughout the ages. For example, creation stories from around the world can be found in Virginia Hamilton's *In the Beginning* (1988) and Ann Pilling's *Creation* (1997). Through these works, teachers can encourage their students to compare creation stories across cultures.

Greek, Norse, and Roman myths continue to fascinate young people today, as they have for years. These stories are often hero myths that present the grand adventures of the gods without seeking to explain anything. Greek and Roman myths can be found in Aliki's *The Gods and Goddesses of Olympus* (1994), Robert Burleigh's *Hercules* (1999), Kate Hovey's *Arachne Speaks* (2001), Jan Mark's *The Midas Touch* (1999), Doris Orgel's *We Goddesses* (1999), Anne Rockwell's *The One-Eyed Giant and Other Monsters From the Greek Myths* (1996), and Jeanne Steig's *A Gift From Zeus* (2001). Norse myth collections are found in Mary Pope Osborne's *Favorite Norse Myths* (1996) and Neil Philip's *Odin's Family* (1996). Greek, Roman, Norse, and other myths from around the world are also available in general collections such as Philip's *The Illustrated Book of Myths* (1995) and Mary Hoffman's *First Book of Myths* (1999). Pat Mora's retelling of the Mayan myth *The Night the Moon Fell* (2000) provides an explanation of how the stars were placed in the night skies.

Many teachers find the small collections and picture book versions of myths more readable for their English-language learners and struggling readers than what is often encountered in literature anthologies. Students also are intrigued at the parallels between the supernatural powers of the gods of mythology and the superhuman abilities of the cartoon and television heroes of popular culture, such as Superman, Batman, the X-Men, etc.

Mythology often includes sacred or religious text and, as mentioned previously, is believed to be true by the teller. Thus, stories from the Judeo-Christian tradition, such as the Old Testament stories in *Moses* (Fisher, 1995) and several accounts of the Noah's Ark story (Cousins, 1993; Gerstein, 1999; Janisch, 1997; Kuskin, 2001; McCarthy, 2001), contribute to this subgenre. New Testament stories also abound, such as *Young Jesus of Nazareth* (Mayer, 1999b). *Iblis* (Oppenheim, 1994) is a story from Islam and the Muslim world, and *Hanuman* (Jendresen & Greene, 1998), a powerful Hindu story of a monkey hero, comes from one of India's most sacred texts, the *Ramanyana*.

The number of Noah's Ark variants invites comparison. Moreover, students can carefully analyze illustrations of the various retellings to develop and enhance their visual literacy. The variants also can be compared to flood myths from other cultures, such as Maria Elena Maggi's version of the Kariña myth *The Great Canoe* (1998) from Venezuela.

See chapter 4 for further exploration of the mythology subgenre.

Legends

Legends share stories of the heroic deeds of historical figures—usually saints, kings, or heroes. The people in legends often actually existed, but their lives and deeds may be embellished in the retelling. Unlike other folk literature, legends are usually associated with particular times and places in history (Rosenberg, 1997). Robert San Souci's retelling of *Fa Mulan* (1998) is a notable example of a legend based on a historical figure. Mulan's fictional glorious deeds continue to inspire people, although little is known about her real life. Disney's movie version *Mulan* draws children's attention to and helps them understand the book, which is generally regarded as culturally authentic. Other popular legendary heroes include Robin Hood and King Arthur; their stories are found in such books as *Robin of Sherwood* (Morpurgo, 1996), *Young Arthur* (San Souci, 1997), and *Excalibur* (Talbott, 1996). Mariana Mayer's *Women Warriors* (1999a) introduces many legends and myths about women. Older, more proficient readers may enjoy Salina Hastings's retelling of the legend *Sir Gawain and the Loathly Lady* (1985). Students revel in predicting the solution to the question King Arthur must solve in order to save his life: "What is it that women most desire?"

See chapter 5 for further discussion about legends and their place in the curriculum.

Tall Tales

The perfect complement to geography or social studies is tall tales, which are often set in specific regions; they are exaggerated narratives containing oversized, boisterous characters; humorous actions; and picturesque language. Children can sit spell-bound as they listen to stories of Paul Bunyan, Mike Fink, John Henry, Febold Feboldson, and Pecos Bill. Their stories are available in many excellent collections (see Osborne, 1991; San Souci, 1991; Walker, 1993) or in delightful picture books such as Julius Lester's *John Henry* (1994) and Rosalyn Schanzer's *Davy Crockett Saves the World* (2001). Students can write hyperbolic stories more readily with these out-rageous story models.

Many students will have enjoyed hearing tall tales with male protagonists, but most are unfortunately not as likely to have heard the stories of women in tall tales (Young & Ferguson, 1999). Bess Call, Annie Christmas, Sal Fink, Slue-Foot Sue, Sally Ann Thunder Ann Whirlwind Crockett, and Angelica Longrider offer intriguing stories for sharing with today's students. These larger-than-life women can be found in Virginia Hamilton's *Her Stories* (1995), Anne Isaacs's *Swamp Angel* (1994), Steven Kellogg's *Sally Ann Thunder Ann Whirlwind Crockett* (1995), and Robert D. San Souci's *Cut From the Same Cloth* (1993).

Book cover from *Sally Ann Thunder Ann Whirlwind Crockett* by Steven Kellogg. Copyright © 1995. Used by permission of HarperCollins Publishers.

Tall tales, often set in the United States, provided early American settlers with inspiration as they settled new frontiers and met the challenges before them. Yet, tall tales are not unique to the United States. Aaron Shepard's retelling of *Master Man* (2001) provides readers with an excellent example of a Nigerian tall tale. In this story, Shadusa, a very strong man, learns of his wife's great wisdom when he encounters two men with incredible strength who create thunder while fighting to determine who is the real Master Man. Other international tall tales include Margaret Mahy's *The Seven Chinese Brothers* (1990) and Claus Stamm's *Three Strong Women* (1990).

Chapter 6 documents the development of tall tales in the United States.

Folk Tales

Folk tales—animal, human, or fairy stories passed from generation to generation through the oral tradition with unknown authorship—exist in an abundant variety. This section will look briefly at pourquoi tales, trickster tales, fairy tales, literary tales, and fractured fairy tales. See chapter 2 for further explanation of the "how and why" of folk tales and fairy tales.

POURQUOI TALES. Many pourquoi or etiological folk tales intrigue students with their odd explanations of how things came about. It may be animal appearance or behavior as in *How Chipmunk Got His Stripes* (Bruchac, 2001), *How Turtle's Back Was Cracked* (Ross, 1995), and *How the Rooster Got His Crown* (Poole, 1999). Others shed light on human behavior and customs as in *How the Ox Star Fell From Heaven* (Hong, 1991), which illustrates why people eat three meals per day, and *The Birds' Gift* (Kimmel, 1999), which explains how the tradition of pysanky eggs (the batik Ukrainian Easter Eggs made by drawing wax patterns on eggs before dipping them in dyes) began in Ukraine. It is important to note that some pourquoi (and trickster tales) are classified as myths depending on the teller's belief.

These tales will be addressed in chapters 2, 4, 7, 8, 9, and 11.

TRICKSTER TALES. A very popular international folk story motif is the trickster tale, which humorously portrays protagonists who use wit, pranks, deceit, and mischief to triumph over their more powerful foes. Yet tricksters do not always prevail, for they are often victims of another's trickery. Sample trickster tales from around the world include *Jabutí the Tortoise* (McDermott, 2001), *Tops & Bottoms* (Stevens, 1995), *Maui and the Sun* (Bishop, 1996), *Mr. Pak Buys a Story* (Farley, 1997), *Anansi and the Magic Stick* (Kimmel, 2001), *The Pot of Wisdom* (Badoe, 2001), and *Jump on Over!* (Harris, 1989). Immigrant students may well know trickster tales that have not yet been written down, and they may be willing to share these in class.

Trickster tales will be discussed in chapters 2, 4, 7, 8, 9, 11, and 12.

FAIRY TALES. Many people are surprised when they learn that fairy tales do not always include fairies. The name *fairy tale*, also called wonder tale, evolved from *faerie tale*, with *faerie* being an Old French word meaning enchantment or magic (Goforth & Spillman, 1994). Thus, fairy tales always contain some form of enchantment or magic. Huck, Hepler, Hickman, and Kiefer (2001) point out that

> part of the appeal of the fairy tale is the secure knowledge that no matter what happens, love, kindness, and truth will prevail—and hate, wickedness, and evil will be punished. Wonder tales have always represented the glorious fulfillment of human desires. (p. 235)

Current collections of fairy tales include *Fairy Tales*, retold by Berlie Doherty (2000), and *The Fabric of Fairy Tale*, retold by Tanya Batt (2000). Many picture book versions of popular fairy tales such as those of Cinderella, Beauty and the Beast, Sleeping Beauty, and Snow White and the Seven Dwarfs are available. A beautiful example is found in Paul Zelinsky's lavishly illustrated retelling of *Rapunzel* (1997).

Disney's movie versions of the stories of Cinderella, Snow White and the Seven Dwarfs, and other fairy tales often set the standard for what students come to think of as the "real" version. It can thus be an interesting learning experience to watch a video version of "Cinderella," for example, and then compare it with picture book versions such as those illustrated by Marcia Brown, Susan Jeffers, or Nonny Hogrogian (Hadaway, Vardell, & Young, 2002).

Chapters 2 and 18 of this book offer further insight into fairy tales. Chapter 14 shares how teachers can engage their children in a lively study of fairy tale variants.

LITERARY TALES. A modern adaptation of traditional folk literature is the literary tale that has roots in the oral tradition. These works are distinctive in that they have known authors who write in the traditional folk style.

For instance, Hans Christian Andersen is the author of "The Ugly Duckling." Yet even literary folk tales are retold; Jerry Pinkney recently adapted and illustrated *The Ugly Duckling* (Anderson, 1999b) and *The Little Match Girl* (Anderson, 1999a). Moreover, the text in Naomi Lewis's retelling of *The Emperor's New Clothes* (Anderson, 1997) literally dances with the spectacular paintings by Angela Barrett, whose illustrations set the tale in pre-World War I Europe and capture the essence of the setting and people.

FRACTURED FAIRY TALES. Many students thoroughly enjoy the "fractured" fairy tale, in which authors create new literary tales by altering or mixing up the characters, setting, points of view, or plots of more traditional well-known tales. These parodies are best appreciated when students have encountered the original tales first. Jon Scieszka, a former teacher, is a master at writing fractured fairy

Book cover from *The Pot of Wisdom: Ananse Stories*, written by Adwoa Badoe, illustrated by Baba Wague Diakite. Copyright © 2001. Used by permission of Groundwood Books.

tales. His *The True Story of the Three Little Pigs* (1989)—which is written from the wolf's point of view—remains a classic in this subgenre. Students also enjoy his story collection *The Stinky Cheese Man* (1992) and his parodies of Aesop's fables in *Squids Will Be Squids* (1998). Other popular examples of fractured tales are Michael Emberley's parody of "Red Riding Hood," *Ruby* (1992); Fiona French's *Snow White in New York* (1986); Bob Hartman's *The Wolf Who Cried Boy* (2002); Kathryn Lasky's *The Emperor's Old Clothes* (1999); Paul Rosenthal's *Yo, Aesop!* (1997); Diane Stanley's *Rumpelstiltskin's Daughter* (1997); and Audrey Wood's *The Bunyans* (1996). Teachers will find it valuable to compare the fractured versions with their traditional European antecedents.

Chapter 17 presents the story of how a middle school teacher guided her students in creating their own fractured fairy tales.

The range in length and reading levels found in published folk tales makes them a good choice for the most diverse classes. Young children and those learning English as a second language benefit from the repetition and predictable language patterns found in many folk tale examples (Hadaway, Vardell, & Young, 2002). For instance, *The Bossy Gallito* (González, 1994) is a cumulative tale in which language and actions are repeated over and over. The rooster soils his beak pecking corn from mud and wants the grass to clean it for him. Eventually he visits the sun and begs, "Please, dear Sol, dry the water who won't quench the fire who won't burn the stick who won't hit the goat who won't eat the grass who won't clean my pico so that I can go to the wedding of my Tío Perico!" This repetition supports young readers' early reading attempts. For example, the teacher can take each phrase within the cumulative pattern and record it on cards that are distributed to groups of students. As the phrase comes up in the story, students can hold up the cards so their class-mates can read along. Because the phrases are repeated, the opportunities for building oral proficiency, as well as word recognition and comprehension, increase.

Folk tales also can be used with older students. One fifth-grade teacher reads from Virginia Hamilton's *The People Could Fly* (1985) so her students can better understand how the slaves expressed their fears and hopes to one another. For older students, teachers can combine this book with an examination of the following website for even richer study: From Remus to Rap: A History in Theory and Practice of the African-American Storytelling Tradition (www.yale.edu/ynhti/curriculum/units/1992/4/92.04.06.x.html; this site provides exposure for secondary-level students to African American traditional culture).

Students enjoy hearing and reading folk literature, and various extension activities can enable students to respond to stories through art, drama, movement, and games. These instructional activities are fun, but more importantly, they facilitate comprehension and promote response.

Folk literature offers teachers many instructional options for today's students. Indeed, teachers who use folk literature in their classrooms report a high level of student engagement and enthusiasm.

Why Are Similar Stories Told Across Cultures?

Some basic story lines transcend national boundaries (Sierra, 1996). For example, students delight in the similarities of *Little Red Riding Hood* (Hyman, 1983) from Germany and *Lon Po Po* (Young, 1989) from China. Also, story variants are passed through the oral tradition with similar plots and motifs. Variants of "Cinderella," for instance, are found all around the world, with more than 500 variations from Europe alone (Dundes, 1988; Yolen, 1988).

Two theories exist to explain why traditional variants can be found across cultural, political, and ethnic boundaries. The first, polygenesis, suggests that the stories developed across cultures to address needs and desires common to all people. Monogenesis, on the other hand, promotes the notion that each story was first told in one area and gradually spread to other parts of the world. An example of monogenesis is found in the Anansi tales that originated in western Africa and spread to the Americas through forced migration. Eventually some of these tales evolved into the Brer Rabbit tales of the southeastern United States.

What Are Some of the Motifs Commonly Found in Folk Literature?

Motifs, the smallest elements of tales, are found throughout folk literature. Indeed, a single tale may have many motifs embedded within it. Teachers use their knowledge of motifs to encourage students to compare and contrast traditional variants across cultures (Huck et al., 2001).

Many common motifs exist in traditional literature. The numbers three and seven frequently appear in tales such as "The Three Bears" and "Snow White and the Seven Dwarves." Magical and supernatural helpers (fairies and fairy godmothers) come to the aid of good and deserving characters who often suffer abuse from cruel family members—possibly wicked stepmothers. Trickery, spells, magical objects, quests, foolish bargains, wishes, and transformations also find their way into traditional narratives. Russell (2000) notes that some motifs

> are accompanied by powerful visual images by which we readily identify many folktales—a glass slipper, a bean stalk and a talking harp, a spinning wheel, a poisoned apple, a bloody handkerchief, a red riding hood. These stark visual elements give tales their enduring strength. (p. 161)

Teachers and librarians can learn more about folk motifs by reading the two volumes of Margaret Read MacDonald's *The Storyteller's Sourcebook: A Subject, Title, and Motif Index to Folklore Collections for Children* (see MacDonald, 1982; MacDonald & Sturm, 2001). MacDonald's resources make it possible to find children's books that employ the same motifs or tale types.

Conclusion

Folk literature, the collected and transcribed oral tales of a people, is particularly suited for today's students. Indeed folk stories may be one of the ingredients necessary for children to find delight in books. The acclaimed author Madeleine L'Engle

(1989) refers to Fromm's *The Forgotten Language* when stating "the only language that transcends time, culture, people, and race is the language of fantasy, fairy tale, and dream.... [I]t stretches us, opens doors to new ideas, will not let us be content with easy answers" (p. 131). Teachers and librarians can open doors to literary connections, humor, intrigue, and wonder through experiencing and responding to folk literature.

REFERENCES

Blatt, G.T. (1993). High fantasies: Secret openings to the ring of myth. In G.T. Blatt (Ed.), *Once upon a folktale* (pp. 181–192). New York: Teachers College Press.

Bosma, B. (1992). *Fairy tales, fables, legends, and myths: Using folk literature in your classroom*. New York: Teachers College Press.

Dundes, A. (1988). *Cinderella: A casebook*. Madison, WI: University of Wisconsin Press.

Durkheim, E. (1933). *The division of labor in society*. Glencoe, IL: Free Press.

Goforth, F.S., & Spillman, C.V. (1994). *Using folk literature in the classroom: Encouraging children to read and write*. Westport, CT: Oryx.

Hadaway, N.L., Vardell, S.M., & Young, T.A. (2002). *Literature-based instruction with English language learners, K–12*. Boston: Allyn & Bacon.

Hamilton, V. (1988). *In the beginning: Creation stories from around the world* (B. Moser, Illus.). San Diego: Harcourt Brace Jovanovich.

Huck, C.S., Hepler, S., Hickman, J., & Kiefer, B.Z. (2001). *Children's literature in the elementary school*. New York: McGraw-Hill.

L'Engle, M. (1989). Fantasy is what fantasy does. In J. Hickman & B.E. Cullinan (Eds.), *Children's literature in the classroom: Weaving Charlotte's web* (pp. 129–133). Norwood, MA: Christopher-Gordon.

Lukens, R.J. (1999). *A critical handbook of children's literature*. New York: Longman.

MacDonald, M.R. (1982). *The storyteller's sourcebook: A subject, title, and motif index to folklore collections for children*. Detroit, MI: Gale.

MacDonald, M.R., & Sturm, B.W. (2001). *The storyteller's sourcebook: A subject, title, and motif index to folklore collections for children, 1983–1999*. Detroit, MI: Gale.

Norton, D. (1990). Teaching multicultural literature in the reading program. *The Reading Teacher, 44*, 28–40.

Rosenberg, D. (1997). *Folklore, myths, and legends: A world perspective*. Chicago: NCT Publishing Group.

Russell, D.L. (2000). *Literature for children: A short introduction* (4th ed.). New York: Addison Wesley Longman.

Savage, J.F. (2000). *For the love of literature: Children & books in the elementary years*. New York: McGraw-Hill.

Yolen, J. (1988). America's Cinderella. In A. Dundes (Ed.), *Cinderella: A casebook* (pp. 294–306). Madison, WI: University of Wisconsin Press.

Young, T.A., & Ferguson, P.M. (1995). From Anansi to Zomo: Trickster tales in the classroom. *The Reading Teacher, 48*, 490–503.

Young, T.A., & Ferguson, P.M. (1999). "Move on over, boys!" Women in tall tales. *Northwest Reading Journal, 8*, 10–12.

CHILDREN'S BOOKS CITED

Aardema, V. (1999). *Koi and the kola nuts* (J. Cepeda, Illus.). New York: Atheneum.

Aliki. (1994). *The gods and goddesses of Olympus*. New York: HarperCollins.

Anaya, R. (1999). *My land sings: Stories from the Rio Grande*. New York: Morrow.

Andersen, H.C. (1997). *The emperor's new clothes* (N. Lewis, Trans., & A. Barrett, Illus.). Cambridge, MA: Candlewick.

Andersen, H.C. (1999a). *The little match girl* (J. Pinkney, Illus.). New York: Phyllis Fogelman.

Andersen, H.C. (1999b). *The ugly duckling* (J. Pinkney, Illus.). New York: Morrow.

Bader, B. (1991). *Aesop & company* (A. Geisert, Illus.). Boston: Houghton Mifflin.

Badoe, A. (2001). *The pot of wisdom: Ananse stories* (B.W. Diakité, Illus.). Toronto: Groundwood.

Batt, T.R. (2000). *The fabric of fairy tale: Stories spun from far and wide*. Cambridge, MA: Barefoot Books.

Bishop, G. (1996). *Maui and the sun: A Maori tale*. New York: North-South.

Bruchac, J. (2001). *How Chipmunk got his stripes: A tale of bragging and teasing* (J. Aruego & A. Dewey, Illus.). New York: Dial.

Burleigh, R. (1999). *Hercules* (R. Colon, Illus.). San Diego: Silver Whistle/Harcourt.

Cousins, L. (1993). *Noah's ark*. Cambridge, MA: Candlewick.

Deedy, C.A. (2000). *The yellow star: The legend of King Christian X of Denmark* (H. Sorensen, Illus.). Atlanta, GA: Peachtree.

Demi. (1997a). *Buddha stories*. New York: Henry Holt.

Demi. (1997b). *One grain of rice: A mathematical folktale*. New York: Scholastic.

Doherty, B. (2000). *Fairy tales* (J. Ray, Illus.). Cambridge, MA: Candlewick.

Emberley, M. (1992). *Ruby*. Boston: Little, Brown.

Farley, C. (1997). *Mr. Pak buys a story* (B. Huang, Illus.). Morton Grove, IL: Albert Whitman.

Fisher, L.E. (1995). *Moses*. New York: Holiday House.

French, F. (1986). *Snow White in New York*. Oxford, UK: Oxford University Press.

Gerstein, M. (1999). *Noah and the great flood*. New York: Simon & Schuster.

González, L.M. (1994). *The bossy gallito/el gallo de bodas* (L. Delacre, Illus.). San Diego: Harcourt Brace.

Hamilton, V. (1985). *The people could fly: American Black folktales* (L. Dillon & D. Dillon, Illus.). New York: Knopf.

Hamilton, V. (1988). *In the beginning: Creation stories from around the world* (B. Moser, Illus.). San Diego: Harcourt Brace Jovanovich.

Hamilton, V. (1995). *Her stories: African American folktales, fairy tales, and true tales* (L. Dillon & D. Dillon, Illus.). New York: Blue Sky.

Harris, J.C. (1989). *Jump on over! The adventures of Brer Rabbit and his family* (B. Moser, Illus.). San Diego: Harcourt Brace Jovanovich.

Hartman, B. (2002). *The wolf who cried boy* (T. Raglin, Illus.). New York: Putnam.

Hastings, S. (1985). *Sir Gawain and the loathly lady* (J. Wijgnaard, Illus.). New York: Morrow.

Hoffman, M. (1999). *A first book of myths: Myths and legends for the very young around the world* (R.W. Langton & K. Kimber, Illus.). New York: Dorling Kindersley.

Hong, L.T. (1991). *How the ox star fell from heaven*. Morton Grove, IL: Albert Whitman.

Hovey, K. (2001). *Arachne speaks* (B. Drawson, Illus.). New York: Simon & Schuster.

Huck, C. (1996). *Toads and diamonds* (A. Lobel, Illus.). New York: Greenwillow.

Hyman, T.S. (1983). *Little Red Riding Hood*. New York: Holiday House.

Isaacs, A. (1994). *Swamp angel* (P.O. Zelinksy, Illus.). New York: Dutton.

Janisch, H. (1997). *Noah's ark* (L. Zwerger, Illus.). New York: North-South.

Jendresen, E., & Greene, J.M. (1998). *Hanuman* (L. Ming, Illus.). Berkeley, CA: Tricycle.

Kellogg, S. (1995). *Sally Ann Thunder Ann Whirlwind Crockett*. New York: Morrow Junior.

Kimmel, E.A. (1999). *The birds' gift: A Ukrainian Easter story* (K. Krenina, Illus.). New York: Holiday House.

Kimmel, E.A. (2001). *Anansi and the magic stick* (T. Stevens, Illus.). New York: Holiday House.

Kuskin, K. (2001). *The animals in the Ark* (M. Grejniec, Illus.). New York: Atheneum.

Lasky, K. (1999). *The emperor's old clothes* (D. Catrow, Illus.). San Diego: Harcourt Brace.

Lester, J. (1994). *John Henry* (J. Pinkney, Illus.). New York: Dial.

Lind, M. (2003). *Bluebonnet girl*. (K. Kiesler, Illus.). New York: Henry Holt.

Lynch, T. (2000). *Fables from Aesop*. New York: Viking.

Maggi, M.E. (1998). *The great canoe: A Kariña legend* (G. Calderon, Illus.). Toronto: Groundwood.

Mahy, M. (1990). *The seven Chinese brothers* (J. Tseng & M. Tseng, Illus.). New York: Scholastic.

Mark, J. (1999). *The Midas touch* (J. Wijngaard, Illus.). Cambridge, MA: Candlewick.

Martin, R. (1999). *The hungry tigress: Buddhist myths, legends, and Jataka tales* (R. Wehrman, Illus.). Oxford, MA: Yellow Moon.

Mayer, M. (1999a). *Women warriors: Myths and legends of heroic women* (J. Heller, Illus.). New York: Morrow.

Mayer, M. (1999b). *Young Jesus of Nazareth*. New York: Morrow.

McCarthy, M. (2001). *The story of Noah and the Ark* (G. Ferri, Illus.). New York: Barefoot.

McDermott, G. (1999). *The fox and the stork*. San Diego: Harcourt Brace.

McDermott, G. (2001). *Jabutí the tortoise: A trickster tale from the Amazon*. San Diego: Harcourt.

Mora, P. (2000). *The night the moon fell: A Mayan myth* (Domi, Illus.). Toronto: Groundwood.

Mora, P. (2001). *The race of toad and deer* (Domi, Illus.). Toronto: Groundwood.

Morpurgo, M. (1996). *Robin of Sherwood* (M. Foreman, Illus.). San Diego: Harcourt Brace.

Myers, T. (2003). *Tanuki's gift: A Japanese tale*. (R.G. Roth, Illus.). New York: Marshal Cavendish.

Oppenheim, S.O. (1994). *Iblis* (E. Young, Illus.). San Diego: Harcourt Brace.

Orgel, D. (1999). *We goddesses: Athena, Aphrodite, Hera* (M. Heyer, Illus.). New York: Dorling Kindersley.

Orgel, D. (2000). *The lion & the mouse and other Aesop's fables* (B. Kitchen, Illus.). New York: Dorling Kindersley.

Osborne, M.P. (1991). *American tall tales* (M. McCurdy, Illus.). New York: Knopf.

Osborne, M.P. (1996). *Favorite Norse myths* (T. Howell, Illus.). New York: Scholastic.

Philip, N. (1995). *The illustrated book of myths: Tales & legends of the world* (N. Mistry, Illus.). New York: Dorling Kindersley.

Philip, N. (1996). *Odin's family: Myths of the Vikings* (M. Foa, Illus.). New York: Orchard.

Pilling, A. (1997). *Creation: Read-aloud stories from many lands* (M. Foreman, Illus.). Cambridge, MA: Candlewick.

Pinkney, J. (2000). *Aesop's fables*. New York: Sea Star/North-South.

Poole, A.L. (1999). *How the rooster got his crown*. New York: Holiday House.

Poole, A.L. (2000). *The ant and the grasshopper*. New York: Holiday House.

Rockwell, A. (1996). *The one-eyed giant and other monsters from the Greek myths*. New York: Greenwillow.

Rosenthal, P. (1997). *Yo, Aesop! Get a load of these fables* (M. Rosenthal, Illus.). New York: Simon & Schuster.

Ross, G. (1995). *How turtle's back was cracked: A traditional Cherokee tale* (M. Jacob, Illus.). New York: Dial.

San Souci, R.D. (1991). *Larger than life: The adventures of American legendary heroes* (A. Glass, Illus.). New York: Doubleday.

San Souci, R.D. (1993). *Cut from the same cloth: American women of myth, legend, and tall tale* (J.B. Pinkney, Illus.). New York: Philomel.

San Souci, R.D. (1997). *Young Arthur* (B. Henterly, Illus.). New York: Doubleday.

San Souci, R.D. (1998). *Fa Mulan* (J. Tseng & M. Tseng, Illus.). New York: Hyperion.

Schanzer, R. (2001). *Davy Crockett saves the world*. New York: HarperCollins.

Scieszka, J. (1989). *The true story of the 3 little pigs by A. Wolf* (L. Smith, Illus.). New York: Viking.

Scieszka, J. (1992). *The stinky cheese man and other fairly stupid tales* (L. Smith, Illus.). New York: Viking.

Scieszka, J. (1998). *Squids will be squids: Fresh morals, beastly fables* (L. Smith, Illus.). New York: Viking.

Shepard, A. (2001). *Master man: A tall tale of Nigeria* (D. Wisniewski, Illus.). New York: Lothrop, Lee & Shepard.

Sierra, J. (1996). *Nursery tales around the world* (S. Vitale, Illus.). New York: Clarion.

Stamm, C. (1990). *Three strong women: A tall tale from Japan*. New York: Viking.

Stanley, D. (1997). *Rumpelstiltskin's daughter*. New York: Morrow.

Steig, J. (2001). *A gift from Zeus: Sixteen favorite myths* (W. Steig, Illus.). New York: HarperCollins.

Steptoe, J. (1987). *Mufaro's beautiful daughters*. New York: Lothrop, Lee & Shepard.

Stevens, J. (1995). *Tops & bottoms*. San Diego: Harcourt Brace.

Talbott, H. (1996). *Excalibur: Tales of King Arthur*. New York: Morrow.

Walker, P.R. (1993). *Big men, big country: A collection of American tall tales* (J. Bernardin, Illus.). San Diego: Harcourt Brace.

Wildsmith, B. (1990). *The miller, the boy, and the donkey*. New York: Oxford University Press.

Winter, M. (1994). *The Aesop for children*. New York: Scholastic.

Wood, A. (1996). *The Bunyans* (D. Shannon, Illus.). New York: Blue Sky.

Yolen, J. (1995). *A sip of Aesop* (K. Barbour, Illus.). New York: Blue Sky.

Young, E. (1989). *Lon Po Po: A Red Riding Hood story from China*. New York: Philomel.

Zelinsky, P.O. (1997). *Rapunzel*. New York: Dutton.

Exploring the Subgenres of Folk Literature

CHAPTER 2

The How and Why of Folk Tales

Anne Marie Kraus

The term *folk*—as in folk tale, folk dance, folk art, folk music—implies an art whose origins rest in the creativity of common people, and whose propagation relies on the passing on through personal sharing, all within a cultural context. Within the structure and limits of the form lie endless possibilities for embellishment, variation, and wondrous artistic experimentation. This chapter attempts to capture a sample of folk tales in their astonishing variants as they have been passed on, first through the oral tradition, now through the advances in children's book publishing. Anyone's definition of folk tales may justifiably encompass more or fewer tale types than those discussed here; however, the following tale types are joyfully explored in this chapter: pourquoi tales, trickster tales, fairy tales, transformation tales, noodle-head tales, and cumulative tales.

Within these labels, there is often overlap; for example, a trickster tale or pourquoi tale may include an essential transformation element. Such is the delight of folk tales; we use these categories to help us gather them, but ultimately they cannot belong to any one of us. These stories go out into the world for all to enjoy. As stated in a traditional ending to many African tales, "This is my story. If it be sweet, or if it be not sweet, take some and let the rest come back to me" (Aardema, 1994, p. 30).

Thanks to the abundance of children's books published, many cherished tales are finding new audiences. Tales that would have been lost, or kept in relative obscurity, now wait for us, replete with stunning illustrations. What an opportunity (and duty) we have to bring the old wisdom and joy of folk tales to new generations of children. Children *need* to become familiar with these tales, both for reasons of cultural literacy and for a broader perspective on the world. To look at the wonders of nature

Portions of this chapter were published previously in the author's books *Folktale Themes and Activities for Children, Vol. 1: Porquoi Tales* (Teacher Ideas Press, 1998) and *Folktale Themes and Activities for Children, Vol. 2: Trickster and Transformation Tales* (Teacher Ideas Press, 1999). Used with permission of Teacher Ideas Press.

through the window of a pourquoi tale, to recognize and predict the patterns of a trickster, to imagine the "what ifs" through a transformation tale—these are the expanded worlds awaiting children through the world of folk tales.

Pourquoi Tales

"In the beginning..." or "Back in the old times, when the animals and the people spoke the same language..."—thus begin numerous fascinating stories of the origin of the world and its creatures. *Pourquoi tale* is the term given to stories that explain how things came to be. These stories come from people who have spent time pondering the wonder, the complexities, the details, the awe-inspiring power of nature. *Pourquoi*, the French word for *why*, is used for the body of tales sometimes called "origin" stories or "how and why" stories. These tales range from explanations for huge phenomena—the sky, the Earth, human beings, death—all the way to small details of animals' physical markings—the cracks on Turtle's back, Rabbit's split lip, the colors of birds' feathers (Kraus, 1998).

Tales pondering the larger, more cosmic issues, such as the beginning of life on Earth, often are referred to as creation myths or creation stories. Creation stories are immersed in a culture's philosophical and religious belief systems, for example, the Native American tales of Earth resting on Turtle's back. To some extent, this belief-based orientation is true also of pourquoi tales. With all these tales, it is important to present them to students with reverence and respect, not as "quaint" or superficial explanations of the natural world, made up in the absence of science. Indeed, these tales are filled with scientific understanding, and they often contain gentle lessons about the consequences of one's actions. Pourquoi tales often contain a transformation sequence, for example, a human turning into a mountain or a star. Although there is certainly overlap between creation myths and pourquoi tales, the exploration in this chapter will focus on pourquoi tales, stories that explain the origins and characteristics of animals, landforms, astronomical formations, weather, art forms, traditions, and more.

Animal and Insect Characteristics

An easy and delightful way to get students started with pourquoi tales is to read about the antics of the animals resulting in some characteristic marking that endures to this day. In Joseph Bruchac's *How Chipmunk Got His Stripes* (2001), a little brown squirrel teases Bear once too often. Bear swipes at the escaping squirrel, leaving claw strokes that mark him as Chipmunk. This tale, well suited to younger children, contains gentle lessons about behavior. A Vietnamese tale that is good for older students is "How the Tiger Got Its Stripes" in *Children of the Dragon* (Garland,

2001). "Why Bear Has a Stumpy Tail" in Hamilton and Weiss's *How and Why Stories* (1999) is a well-known tale from many cultures. "Roasted Ears" in *Is My Friend at Home?* (Bierhorst, 2001) tells why Coyote's ears are short.

Stories of birds and insects are fascinating in their creativity. Virginia Hamilton's *When Birds Could Talk and Bats Could Sing* (1996) is a handsome collection of eight African American tales illustrated by Barry Moser. These tales include explanations of Cardinal's color, Hummingbird's sounds, and Buzzard's bald head. *Insect Facts and Folklore* (Kite, 2001) pairs brief tales with detailed information about 12 insects. "Why Firefly Carries a Light" explains that Mosquito keeps chasing Firefly with his dagger (stinger), therefore Firefly carries a torch to keep watch for him. The humorous Yoruba tale, *Zzzng! Zzzng! Zzzng!* (Gershator, 1998) tells of a time long ago when all of creation was pairing off, so Mosquito went looking for someone to marry. After many frustrating refusals, Mosquito returns to Ear to remind him that she is always around. "The Ant and the Bear" in *Spirit of the Cedar People* (Lelooska, 1998) explains why ants have a skinny waist and also why we have daylight and dark every day.

Landforms

Many of the pourquoi tales of landforms are somber, colored by high drama or tragedy. A tale of struggle may end with a character being transformed into a mountain or a landscape being ravaged. Carol Vogel's *Legends of Landforms* (1999) relates 14 dramatic Native American tales of the events that shaped the Earth. Landmarks include the Grand Canyon, the Hot Springs of Arkansas, Mount Shasta, and the Badlands. This book pairs each tale with the geologic history of the formation of these land monuments. The story of "Mateo Teepee" (the name preferable to the more widely known Devil's Tower, disrespectfully named by white explorers) describes a breathless chase scene. Seven maidens are pursued by grizzly bears. Just at the moment of capture, the rock they jump onto begins to grow toward the sky. The angry grizzlies continue to leap and claw at the giant rock; their claw marks can be seen to this day on this tall, bold rock. This book's level of sophistication makes it a good choice for middle school students.

A similar scene of rock growth appears in Robert D. San Souci's *Two Bear Cubs* (1997b). The two young cubs wander away from their mother, and the rock they are resting on grows to become El Capitan of Yosemite National Park. Kathy-Jo Wargin tells two gentle tales of Michigan's landscape. The wistful *The Legend of Sleeping Bear* (1998) tells of a brave mother bear who helps her two cubs escape fire by swimming across Lake Michigan. The cubs tire and drown, to return as the two Manitou Islands; the mother, ever watchful on the shore, becomes Sleeping Bear Dune.

Wargin's *The Legend of Mackinac Island* (1999) tells how the turtle Makinauk becomes the island, with the help of animal friends who dive down to bring up earth for his back.

Eric Kimmel's Aztec tale *The Two Mountains* (2000b) tells of the secret love between the son of the sun god and the daughter of the moon goddess, and their tragic transformation into mountains. Another somber transformation is told by Michael Caduto and Joseph Bruchac in *Keepers of the Earth* (1989) and by Bruchac in *Native American Stories* (1991). "Loo-Wit, the Fire Keeper" tells of recurring fighting between brothers and tribes. Loo-Wit, a peaceful woman who shares her fire, becomes the object of fighting and is eventually transformed into a mountain for many years. But she still has fire, and when the people do not take care of the Earth, she explodes as Mount St. Helens. Another pourquoi tale of volcanoes is *Pele and the Rivers of Fire* (Nordenstrom, 2002). Pele, the volcano goddess, travels from Tahiti to Hawaii. Each place that she stops becomes a new volcanic island.

The Mien people of Laos, known for their unique embroidery, have a delightful explanation for the peaks and valleys in the land. *Piecing Earth & Sky Together* (Day, 2001) tells the story of a brother and sister who come down from heaven to make the earth and sky. The brother makes beautiful shimmering blue cloth for the sky, and the sister embroiders the plants and animals of the land on her cloth. When they are done, the pieces do not fit together, so the sister takes up her needle and she pulls and pushes peaks, gorges, hills, and valleys until they fit together.

Stories of the Sky

Numerous pourquoi tales explore phenomena of star constellations, the movement of the sun and moon, and the cycles of day and night. In the Yoruba tale *The Coming of Night* (Riordan, 1999), night belongs only to the underwater world. When the river goddess sends her daughter to marry the earth chief, the sun is relentlessly hot and bright. Finally, the river goddess sends Night in a sack, bringing the relief and the coolness of the dark. The Nigerian tale *The Day Ocean Came to Visit* (Wolkstein, 2001) explains why the sun and moon had to leave their homes on Earth and why they now live in the sky. *The Son of the Sun and the Daughter of the Moon* (Huth, 2000) is a Saami tale about the love between the Moon Daughter and a Brother of the Northern Lights. The Polynesian tale "Maui and His Thousand Tricks" in *When the World Was Young* (Mayo, 1995) tells of a time when daylight was much too short. Maui and his brothers snare the sun and make him promise to travel more slowly across the sky. "The Great Bear Hunt" in *Turtle Island* (Curry, 1999) describes the Fox (Native American) story of the three hunters who are forever chasing after the bear, as stars in the eastern winter sky.

Ten tales of the moon are told in Rina Singh's *Moon Tales* (1999). "Anansi" tells the West African story of Anansi and his sons; he wishes to possess the glowing silver ball but ends up tossing it into the sky for all to share its light as the moon. "Hina" is a Polynesian tale of the woman who makes beautiful tapa cloth. This remarkably feminist story tells how Hina chooses a life of solitude over the domination of a demanding husband. She walks upon a rainbow to the moon, where she can be seen to this day. Geraldine McCaughrean's *Starry Tales* (2000) contains 15 tales for older readers, including explanations of why the moon is visible in the day, why the moon is less bright than the sun, and why there is lightning before thunder.

Weather Tales

Tales of weather explain the origins of storms, thunder, rainbows, and seasonal changes. The Vietnamese tale "The Legend of the Monsoon Rains" in *Children of the Dragon* (Garland, 2001) tells of an implacable Lord of the Seas who returns yearly to try to win a princess he cannot have, so he sends torrential rains and winds in retaliation. *The Boy Who Wouldn't Obey* (Rockwell, 2000) is a Mayan tale of Chac, the god of rainstorms, and a boy who steals Chac's tools with disastrous results. *The Twelve Months* (Martin, 2000) describes the origins of the weather and seasons as coming from 12 brothers deep in the woods.

Carole Vogel's *Weather Legends* (2001) pairs 10 folk tales with nonfiction essays on weather phenomena. "Rainbow" is a Papago (U.S. southwest) tale of the love between a boy and a girl. "Wind" explains that a huge bird known as the Storm King flaps his wings to create storms and winds in the northeast Atlantic. Other topics in Vogel's collection include the pourquoi tales "Snowstorms and Changing Weather," "Seasons," and "Indian Summer."

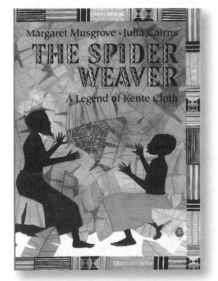

Illustration by Julia Cairns from *The Spider Weaver: A Legend of Kente Cloth* by Margaret Musgrove. Published by the Blue Sky Press, an imprint of Scholastic, Inc. Illustrations copyright © 2001 by Julia Cairns. Used by permission.

Origins of Arts and Traditions

Not only do pourquoi tales explain characteristics of nature, they also explain the origins of various artistic expressions and traditions. *The Spider Weaver* (Musgrove, 2001) explains the origins of West African Kente cloth making. Paul Goble's *Storm Maker's Tipi* (2001) gives the legend behind the traditional painting designs on a Siksika tipi. *The Birds' Gift* (Kimmel, 1999) tells of the first pysanky, the intricately decorated Ukrainian eggs. *The King's Secret* (Farley, 2001) is the story of the creation of Korea's hangeul alphabet.

Other Pourquoi Tales

The variety of pourquoi tales seems infinite. Stories of plants, foods, the salty sea, survival—these are just a few more topics explored by these tales. Patricia Powell's *Blossom Tales: Flower Stories of Many Folk* (2002) contains short tales of the origins of flowers. The book includes tales from Hawaii, England, South America, and Italy. The Comanche legend *Bluebonnet Girl* (Lind, 2003) explains the origin of the bluebonnet flower in Texas.

The Ojibwe tale *The Legend of the Lady Slipper* (Lunge-Larsen & Preus, 1999) is a touching story not to be missed. Disease strikes everyone in the village, so a brave girl walks through bitter winter snows to get medicine. On her return trip, she loses her moccasins, and her bloody path is marked in the spring by the lovely moccasin-shaped flowers. "Why Peaches Are Sweet" in *Is My Friend at Home?* (Bierhorst, 2001) tells the Pueblo story of a dinner shared by Dove and Bee. Bee puts honey on the peaches to make them sweet. In return, Dove gives Bee some of her feathers. That is why peaches are sweet and bees can fly. Although primarily nonfiction and activity-based, the book *Oceans: An Activity Guide for Ages 6–9* (Castaldo, 2002) includes tales to explain why the sea is salty and the origin of whales.

Many pourquoi tales relate how an essential element for survival first came to the people (or the animal people). *Snail Girl Brings Water* (Keams, 1998) is a Navajo story about how the precious commodity of water first comes to the arid desert lands of the American southwest. *Fire Race* (London & Pinola, 1993) tells how Coyote steals fire for the animal people, with the help of his friends' teamwork.

For additional pourquoi tales, see *Folktale Themes and Activities for Children, Vol. 1: Pourquoi Tales* (Kraus, 1998), especially the chart in chapter 4 that indexes tales by theme and topic.

Activities With Pourquoi Tales

The nature of pourquoi tales makes them best suited to students in grades 3 through 8. Although the mood of pourquoi tales ranges from light and humorous to dramatic and somber, the psychological aspects of these tales require a degree of maturity for students to appreciate them. These stories usually end with a message such as, "that is why the colors of birds' feathers [or bears' tails, or the shapes of mountains or star constellations] are the way they are today." This requires maturity on the part of the listener/reader to understand that this is a story explanation within a cultural context. It is neither 100% "true," nor is it "fake" (as children state it) in that it is ridiculous and therefore to be dismissed. It speaks of certain truths, and teachers should teach students to revere both the story and the culture for the insights presented in the story.

Young children (grades K–2) may enjoy a pourquoi tale, but they will invariably blurt out their pressing need to know, "Is that *true*?" Young children are constantly working at sorting out what is fact and what is fantasy. They will readily accept a fairy tale and its magical qualities because children have an active fantasy life, and a fairy tale falls clearly on the fantasy side. But a pourquoi tale, to some degree, falls "between the cracks" of fantasy and truth. By third or fourth grade, you can begin to discuss with students the idea that these stories come from the deep wisdom of a culture, that they have certain truths in them, and that the listener/reader may take from them whatever truths he or she wants. It is wise to ask children after reading a pourquoi tale, "What messages or lessons might we learn from this story? What feels true about this story?"

Pourquoi tales can be used to create an entire reading unit for study. The reading level of many picture book editions is appropriate for third and fourth grade, but some of the lengthier story collections are more suitable for middle school readers. Paperback availability makes it possible to purchase multiple copies of selected tales for reading groups or for guided reading. Following is a suggested general sequence of a thematic reading unit. For a more detailed lesson plan, complete with examples, see Kraus's *Folktale Themes and Activities for Children, Vol. 1: Pourquoi Tales* (1998).

1. Whole-class introduction: read-alouds, discussions, and charting or Venn diagramming
2. Reading groups: multiple copies of titles in a variety of reading levels and student journal responses
3. Cooperative groups: Small groups of students read clusters of tales grouped thematically or topically (for example, three stories about weather, two stories about plants) and cooperatively fill in Venn diagrams.
4. Extensions: Students write their own pourquoi tales, dramatize tales, and perform shadow puppet theater.

Venn diagramming is an excellent method of developing higher order thinking skills, and pourquoi tales present the perfect opportunity to use them. One of the astonishing aspects of pourquoi tales is the appearance of universal themes across cultures. People separated by miles and hemispheres have created related stories about the coming of sunlight, the tails of animals, the shaping of mountains. Each story is unique, yet there are some things in common. When these patterns of recognition start popping into students' minds, it's time to organize and formalize these thoughts with a graphic organizer. A two- or three-circle Venn diagram, quickly drawn on large chart paper, provides the perfect setting for a class discussion in which children can point out all the common and unique elements in the stories. Here are some story groupings that can provide lively comparison discussions:

Mountains/hills: *The Legend of Sleeping Bear* (Wargin, 1998), *Two Bear Cubs* (San Souci, 1997b), and "Mateo Teepee" in *Legends of Landforms* (Vogel, 1999)

Islands: *The Legend of Mackinac Island* (Wargin, 1999) and "The Hawaiian Islands" in *Legends of Landforms* (Vogel, 1999)

Moon: *The Day Ocean Came to Visit* (Wolkstein, 2001), "The Rabbit and the Moon Man" in *Moon Tales* (Singh, 1999), and *The Son of the Sun and the Daughter of the Moon* (Huth, 2000)

Weather: *Master Man* (Shepard, 2000), *The Boy Who Wouldn't Obey* (Rockwell, 2000), and "The Legend of the Monsoon Rains" in *Children of the Dragon* (Garland, 2001)

Because many of these tales ponder the phenomena of nature, they pair very nicely with science and social studies lessons. For any social studies unit on a country or culture, the addition of pourquoi tales provides a deeper cultural insight and also often provides information on the animals or landforms of the region. The same is true of science units based on the topic of study. A useful book to connect older Native American practices with modern science is Fern Brown's *American Indian Science: A New Look at Old Cultures* (1997). This nonfiction resource points out the deep scientific knowledge and practices among many Native American tribes, dispelling any misconceptions about Native American stories not being rooted in scientific knowledge. There are also some science-based books that already have done the job of pairing pourquoi tales with scientific information:

Insect Facts and Folklore (Kite, 2001)

Legends of Landforms: Native America Lore and the Geology of the Land (Vogel, 1999)

Weather Legends (Vogel, 2001)

Oceans: An Activity Guide for Ages 6–9 (Castaldo, 2002)

Why Seals Blow Their Noses: North American Wildlife in Fact and Fiction (Swanson, 1992)

A Grand Canyon Journey (Anderson, 1997)

Trickster Tales

Brer Rabbit escapes again, with a satisfied chuckle. Raven transforms himself, steals the sun through deceit, and brings sunlight to all living things. Anansi gets himself another good meal, without the effort of gardening or cooking. Coyote tries unsuccessfully to steal food, yet he keeps turning up to play mischief on others. Trickster tales are part of the folk tradition of nearly every culture of the world, carrying themes and motifs in common. These entertaining stories are successful with all ages but are particularly appealing to younger children.

A trickster is a character who uses his wit and cunning to outsmart another individual, tricking him or her into achieving the trickster's goals. He is usually smaller or physically weaker than his opponent, and he gains his advantage by using "brains over brawn." A trickster's characteristics span a wide range of personality traits, from negative (greedy, lazy, ill-mannered) to positive (helpful, playing tricks for the benefit of others). Because a trickster often behaves badly, these tales, although primarily entertaining, also communicate lessons about moral values in society.

Some tricksters are considered culture heroes. Culture heroes are legendary characters who have powers beyond those of their peers. They are given credit for providing essential elements to the cultural group, such as the sun, land formations, fire, weather, and even cultural values. Yet these tricksters are not gods; they may have some superhuman powers, but they are not deities.

This aspect of the culture hero takes on special significance in the case of Brer Rabbit and other African American tales. Africans captured and brought to America under the brutal conditions of slavery took their stories with them, and despite their oppression they continued to nurture their storytelling traditions. This creativity led to the creation of Brer Rabbit tales, which, to the casual notice of white oppressors, were simple stories for entertainment. But to the storytelling community of African Americans, they were stories that embodied the spirit of the trickster: the triumph of the oppressed. The Brer Rabbit character became a metaphor for the slave who was tricking the so-called master (often Brer Fox, Brer Wolf, or Brer Bear) with his superior wit.

Part of the appeal of the trickster is that he is often smaller, or in a position of less apparent power, than the trickee. We immediately identify with this position, having all felt unempowered in various situations ourselves at one time or another. Jane Yolen notes, "Every culture seems to treasure the cunning of the underdog" (1986, p. 5).

African Tricksters

A delightful way to get started with trickster tales is to read stories of Anansi the spider, prankster of numerous West African tales. The Anansi stories retold by Eric Kimmel and illustrated by Janet Stevens bring laugh-out-loud humor to audiences of all ages. *Anansi and the Magic Stick* (2001) is the story of magic gone amuck. Lazy Anansi steals a magic stick that performs chores, but he uses it irresponsibly, with disastrous results. Kimmel's *Anansi and the Moss-Covered Rock* (1988) is the quintessential sketch of the food-stealing trickster. In this story, Anansi gets tricked back by a timid little bush deer. The Kimmel and Stevens author-illustrator team also has produced *Anansi and the Talking Melon* (1994) and *Anansi Goes Fishing* (1992a). In Pat Cummings's *Ananse and the Lizard* (2002), Ananse learns the name of the chief's daughter by spying, but he loses the contest to marry her. For more Anansi tales in collections, try *The Pot of Wisdom: Ananse Stories* (Badoe, 2001).

Other animals play the role of tricksters in African tales. *Crocodile and Hen: A Bakongo Folktale* (Lexau, 2001) is in easy-reader format. This African tale tells of a crocodile that repeatedly tries to eat Hen, but she keeps calling him "brother," and he gets so confused he cannot bring himself to eat her.

Book cover from *Trouble* by Jane Kurtz. Illustrations copyright © 1997 by Durga Bernhard, used by permission of Harcourt, Inc.

Native American Tricksters

The main trickster characters in Native American stories are Coyote and Turtle, but other animals may play the trickster role, too. Four of the stories in *Is My Friend at Home?* (Bierhorst, 2001) are Coyote tales, showing him as a gentle trickster, sometimes the victim of the trick. In "Roasted Ears," Badger convinces Coyote that he should cut off his own ears and roast them for dinner. So Coyote tries cutting off his once-long ears, and the wind blows them away. This tale doubles as a pourquoi tale about the length of Coyote's ears. Other stories of Coyote include *Coyote and the Fire Stick* (Goldin, 1996), *Coyote in Love* (Dwyer, 1997), and Gerald McDermott's *Coyote* (1994).

Other animals are also tricksters in Native American tales. "Groundhog's Dance" in *Nursery Tales Around the World* (Sierra, 1996) depicts a little groundhog tricking his way out of being eaten by seven wolves. Many other tales feature turtles as tricksters; some feature Turtle on the losing end of a trick, resulting in the turtle's cracked pattern on its back. Gayle Ross's *How Turtle's Back Was Cracked* (1995) describes Turtle's trick to escape from his captors; he pleads not to be thrown in the river (where he wishes to be). The trick works, but first he hits a rock, cracking his back. In *The Dancing Turtle: A Folktale From Brazil* (DeSpain, 1998), a turtle dances and plays her flute to get the children to let her out of her cage; she thereby escapes her fate of becoming turtle soup. In *Jabutí the Tortoise: A Trickster Tale From the Amazon* (McDermott, 2001), the birds help patch Jabutí's shell together after he cracks it in a fall, and Jabutí rewards them by giving them bright colors.

Another famous Native American trickster is Raven. This culture hero of the northwest is known for his transformation powers. The best introduction to Raven is Gerald McDermott's *Raven* (1993). Long ago, when the world was in darkness, Raven decided to get light from the lodge of the sky chief. "Raven & Sea Gull" in *Echoes of the Elders* (Lelooska, 1997) again shows Raven as the bringer of sunlight.

African American Tricksters

The most famous trickster in African American folklore is Brer Rabbit. The standard collections of Brer Rabbit tales are those by Julius Lester in his Tales of Uncle Remus series (four volumes, 1987–1994). The story of Brer Rabbit and the tar baby is told in Gullah dialect by Virginia Hamilton in *Brer Rabbit and the Tar Baby Girl* (2003). This famous "tar baby" motif features Brer Rabbit, trapped by the farmer's sticky lure, begging not to be thrown in the briar patch (right where he wants to be). A very humorous tale about the division of crops is told in *Tops & Bottoms* (1995) by Janet Stevens. A trickster tale featuring a clever girl is San Souci's *Callie Ann and Mistah Bear* (2000a). Callie Ann's home is the target for visits by a malicious bear, disguised as "quality folk." Deep in the woods, the girl discovers the bear's cabin and tricks the bear from the inside, bringing him to his demise.

Other Tricksters

Tricksters appear in stories around the world. Celtic lore, for example, also has its mischief makers. In the Irish tale *Jamie O'Rourke and the Pooka* (dePaola, 2000), lazy Jamie is visited by a pooka, an animal spirit that sometimes appears in the shape of a goat. In "Knackers," from *Magic & Mischief: Tales From Cornwall* (Climo, 1999), miner Tom Treverrow hears the sounds of Knackers (little people who live down in the mines) and meets the creatures. *Mrs. McCool and the Giant Cuhullin* (Souhami, 2002) is the Irish tale of how Finn McCool's wife tricks the giant Cuhullin into thinking he is weaker than her husband, until the giant flees in fear.

The English folktale *Little Johnny Buttermilk* (Wahl, 1999) tells of a witch's repeated attempts to steal Johnny's bucket of buttermilk and to nab him, too, for her dinner. Every time she puts the boy in her sack, he escapes and fills the sack with something else: thorns, rocks, dishes. A clever little monkey outwits a sea full of crocodiles in the Asian tale *Counting Crocodiles* (Sierra, 1997). The monkey spies a banana tree across the vast water. Appealing to the crocodiles' vanity, she gets them to line up and be counted; they unwittingly become a bridge for the monkey to travel across to the banana island and back. Daniel San Souci's *The Rabbit and the Dragon King* (2002) is a Korean story about a clever rabbit who escapes an undersea death.

The Creole telling of "Bouki and Lapin Divide the Crops" in *How the Animals Saved the People* (Reneaux, 2001) depicts a clever trick with a French/southern U.S. flavor. Rabbit and Wolf agree to farm together, but every time they divide up the crops, Rabbit works it so that he gets the good parts and Wolf gets only the roots, vines, or stems. The Cajun telling of *Little Pierre* (San Souci, 2003) features a clever but scorned boy who outwits his older brothers. He tricks an alligator and a giant catfish and rescues a young lady from an ogre.

Although the most famous trickster characters are male (Coyote, Anansi, Brer Rabbit, etc.), there are tales emerging that feature female tricksters. In Margaret Willey's French Canadian/Michigan tale *Clever Beatrice* (2001), little Beatrice challenges a giant to three feats of strength but psychologically defeats him before he starts. *Mabela the Clever* (MacDonald, 2001b) is an African tale that depicts the classic "little guy versus the big guy" motif with a cat and mice. Another notable female trickster is in San Souci's *Callie Ann and Mistah Bear* (2000a), previously discussed.

Story collections of trickster tales abound. Seven of the stories in Mary Hoffman's *A Twist in the Tail* (1998) are trickster tales from different cultures. For example, "The Pelican and the Fish" is a Malaysian telling of a double trick. Pelican deceives and swallows some fish, but when he tries the same trick with Crab, Crab squeezes the fish out of Pelican with his pincers. In the Iroquois tale "The Fox and the Boastful Brave," Fox plays dead to get into a man's sackful of fish and then chews a hole in the sack to get out with the fish for dinner. The Nigerian story "The Tortoise Who Rode an Elephant" is a tale of Tortoise's trick played to fulfill his boast. "The Wolf Who Loved Sheep" is a West African tale of a sheep who repeatedly tricks the wolf in order to escape becoming his dinner, with humorous results.

Book cover from *Tops & Bottoms*, copyright © 1995 by Janet Stevens, used by permission of Harcourt, Inc. Jacket illustrations copyright © 1995 by Janet Stevens.

Sharon Doucet's *Lapin Plays Possum* (2002) contains three stories from the Louisiana bayou, told with Cajun flair and filled with the relentless tricks of Lapin (a wily rabbit) played on poor, dim-witted Bouki (hyena). The first tale is a great story to use when teaching about fractions. Lapin agrees to help Bouki harvest his cotton in return for one-eighth of the crop. Fearing that Lapin is getting too much, Bouki counters with "smaller" numbers: one-fourth, then one-third, then one-half.

Wendy Cooling's *Farmyard Tales From Far and Wide* (1998) includes two trickster stories. "The Right Thing to Do" features a little goat who staves off a lion and a jackal with nothing more than her clever words. In "The Water Buffalo and the Tiger," a water buffalo thinks up a way to let a tiger bite him three times without any damage. Pleasant DeSpain's *Tales of Tricksters* (2001) features nine trickster tales, including stories of a fox (France), a donkey (Switzerland), and a jackal (India). *The*

Barefoot Book of Trickster Tales (Walker, 1998) is a collection of tales about nine tricksters from around the world. Howard Norman's *Trickster and the Fainting Birds* (1999) contains seven longer tales collected among the Cree people in Canada; these stories are for older students.

Activities With Trickster Tales

Trickster tales are very successful with younger children. Although they are appropriate and enjoyable for all ages, the humor plays directly to appreciative first and second graders, who grin and guffaw as the comedy unfolds. The reading level of many picture book editions of these tales, particularly those by Eric Kimmel and Gerald McDermott, matches that of first and second graders. In addition, trickster tales are excellent stories for the practice of prediction skills—critical skills in the development of young readers.

When reading trickster tales aloud, stop briefly midstory to ask, "What do you think Anansi (Coyote, Rabbit) is going to do now?" Most likely, students will eagerly lay out their ideas for the next trick. This flurry of ideas is wonderful because children are using their creativity to extend the story. Even if their prediction is not the "right" one, students can be encouraged for their skill as storytellers, embellishing the story with new tricks. From this point, students can write their own original versions of the tale, a natural extension of language development as well as a manifestation of the folk process.

Because many trickster tales are available in easier reading levels, trickster tales can be planned as a reading unit. The sequencing of such a unit is similar to the reading unit for pourquoi tales, above. (For a detailed lesson plan, see Kraus's *Folktale Themes and Activities for Children, Vol. 2: Trickster and Transformation Tales* [1999].) Start the unit by reading aloud two or three tales with a common motif illustrative of the trickster mentality, for example, stealing food. Watch the excitement grow as children make connections to the other stories they know. Even first and second graders can contribute to lively discussions comparing two or three tales, producing excellent Venn diagram results. Here are some groupings of tales for comparison activities:

Selfishness with food: *Anansi and the Moss-Covered Rock* (Kimmel, 1988) and *Ananse's Feast* (Mollel, 1997)

Using dance to escape: *Pickin' Peas* (MacDonald, 1998) and *The Dancing Turtle* (DeSpain, 1998)

Smaller creature using words to gain the advantage: *Crocodile and Hen* (Lexau, 2001), "The Right Thing to Do" in *Farmyard Tales From Far and Wide* (Cooling, 1998), and *Clever Beatrice* (Willey, 2001)

Another strategy important to the development of young readers is the ability to retell a story, that is, to recount the basic plot and character elements in the correct sequence. Students may enjoy using simple props in the form of stick puppets. Students can draw simple shapes of the characters or objects in the story, cut them out, glue them to Popsicle sticks, lay them out at the ready, and then pick up each one at the appropriate point while telling the story.

Still another strategy to aid young readers is story mapping. Ask students to recount each plot element. Write each on the board or chart paper, drawing arrows that point to the next event or secondary plot elements. These free-form graphic organizers help students to visually "see" the map of a story.

Wrap up a unit on trickster tales with a party celebration. Students can dress up as their favorite trickster characters, with simple paper masks, ears, accordion-folded spider legs, and so on. They can vote for their favorite trickster or trick and create a classroom graph of the results. They can eat foods from trickster tales; children may not have had much experience with yams, coconut, and root crops, so this can make a good opportunity to introduce them to these foods. Children can tell trickster stories from memory or act out their favorite stories. Above all, they will come away with a strong memory of beloved trickster characters and the knowledge that cleverness is a skill we can all use.

There are many resources that list additional activities and extensive bibliographies for trickster tales. For examples, see Kraus (1999) and Young and Ferguson (1995).

Fairy Tales

Fairy tales, for many Americans, are the first and most familiar contact with folk literature. Fairy tales were not originally intended for children and were, in fact, an adult form of entertainment in Europe. It wasn't until the 19th century that these stories came into common use and were made into versions for children (Zipes, 1991). Eventually, children's versions found their way into the standard storybooks that were mass-marketed to children. Another reason for Americans' familiarity with these primarily European tales is the introduction of animated films, which have heavily influenced children's popular culture for the past 60 years. It is important, however, to stretch children's "folk literacy" past the prevalent movie versions of tales.

Scholars generally agree that the designation *fairy tale* is an unfortunate term, as very few tales actually include fairies. The narrowest interpretation of the genre is that it consists of tales of Europe and Asia (Jones, 1995), and common use often focuses primarily on the European tales. The great folklorist, Stith Thompson, notes that fairy tales are usually set in a "never-never land" with plenty of supernatural occurrences (as cited in Leach, 1972). Often the characters are rather flat (rather than a complex mixture of good and bad); they are often not named, as in "the queen" and "the youngest son," or else they have very common names. Certain expressions of language are common, such as "Once upon a time...." Motifs appear throughout the plot, such as transformations, spells, wishes, journeys, and events taking place in threes. Usually, good is rewarded and evil is punished. Beauty is usually on the "good" side. These tales come from a tradition of storytelling for entertainment and perhaps for some moral teaching, but they are not based in belief systems as are pourquoi tales and myths.

Many of Americans' most familiar fairy tales come from the German tradition, as collected by the brothers Grimm, and the French tradition, as collected by Perrault. Familiar titles (indeed, these titles help define a baseline of folk literacy) include "Little Red Riding Hood," "The Three Little Pigs," "Rumpelstiltskin," "Sleeping Beauty," "Beauty and the Beast," "Snow White," and, of course, "Cinderella." All these tales have an astonishing array of variants, none more than "Cinderella." Our fair "Cinderella" is such a universal tale, she deserves a study all her own (see chapter 14 of this book).

The body of fairy tale literature is so large that a detailed study of every tale would be lengthy indeed. Table 2.1 highlights some of the more common tales and their variants.

Other Notable Fairy Tales

Tales of enchantment are numerous and exist in many editions. Illustrations by accomplished artists serve to extend the mood of awe and wonder as these tales unfold. A quintessential collection of 12 familiar tales is Berlie Doherty's *Fairy Tales* (2000), lavishly illustrated by Jane Ray. Judy Sierra's useful collection *Can You Guess My Name?* (2002a) provides three variants each for five familiar tales: "Hansel and Gretel," "The Frog Prince," "Rumpelstiltskin," "The Three Pigs," and "The Bremen Town Musicians."

Kinuko Craft's glowing illustrations bring *Sleeping Beauty* (2002) to life. The elegant narrative describes the fairies' spells on the princess, who pricks her finger on a spindle and sleeps for a hundred years. *The Twelve Dancing Princesses* (Ray, 1996) tells the story of the princesses who wake every morning to find their shoes worn out from dancing all night, a mystery to their father the king. Finally, a young man uncovers the enchantment by which the girls escape nightly to an underground kingdom to dance with men while under a spell. A delightful modern telling of this tale is *Brothers of the Night* (Allen, 1999), set in Harlem, New York, with 12 sons of a preacher.

Table 2.1
Familiar Fairy Tale Variants

Title	Culture	Feature
SNOW WHITE AND VARIANTS		
"Snow White" in *Fairy Tales* (Doherty, 2000)	German	Traditional telling; stepmother/queen tries to kill her repeatedly; seven dwarfs and later prince save her.
"A Stepchild That Was Treated Mighty Bad" in *Stockings of Buttermilk* (Philip, 1999)	Kentucky/ Appalachian	Mountain dialect; story extends beyond wedding. Old woman helps her; mean stepmother continues to lurk.
The Seven Dwarfs (Delessert, 2001)	German	Told by one of the dwarfs, framed by the dwarfs' attendance at the wedding.
Snow White and the Seven Dwarfs (Aiken, 2002)	German	Full, detailed, traditional telling with clever rhymes for the mirror's responses. In the end, the mirror shatters and returns to its enchanter-maker. Fabric/embroidery illustrations.
Rimonah of the Flashing Sword (Kimmel, 1995)	Egyptian/ North African	Queen/witch uses bowl of water as the reflecting mirror; Rimonah is aided by 40 thieves in a cave. Her father is killed and revived as well.
Snow White and the Seven Dwarfs (Ljungkvist, 2003)	German	Brief, simple telling. Quirky, modern illustrations.
THREE LITTLE PIGS AND VARIANTS		
The Three Little Pigs (Marshall, 1989)	(Traditional)	Humorous but traditional telling. First two pigs are eaten; third outwits wolf three times.
The Three Little Pigs (Moser, 2001)	(Traditional)	Humorous illustrations. Extended version; third pig has three encounters with wolf before stewing him.
The Three Pigs (Wiesner, 2001)	(Traditional/ spinoff)	The pigs leave the story, encounter other fairy tale creatures, and reenter the brick house with new friends.
The Three Little Rabbits (Gantschev, 2001)	Balkan	Rabbits must dig a good hole. First two only build above ground and barely escape fox. Third digs hole and makes Fox promise to leave them alone.
Wait, No Paint! (Whatley, 2001)	(Humorous spinoff)	Mysterious voice interrupts story. It's the illustrator, who has run out of red paint, so the pigs can't be pink and the fire can't burn the wolf.
Three Little Pigs and the Big Bad Wolf (Rounds, 1992)	(Traditional)	Traditional, with extended ending, similar to Moser's version.
The Three Little Pigs (Kellogg, 1997)	(Humorous spinoff)	Spinoff with sophisticated word play.
The Three Little Javelinas (Lowell, 1992)	(Regional spinoff)	Southwestern U.S. flavor and setting.

(continued)

Table 2.1 (continued)
Familiar Fairy Tale Variants

Title	Culture	Feature
"The Three Geese" in *Can You Guess My Name?* (Sierra, 2002a; see also two other variants in this collection)	Italian	The third goose pours boiling water through the keyhole into the wolf's mouth. She cuts open the wolf and rescues her sisters.

RED RIDING HOOD AND VARIANTS

Title	Culture	Feature
Little Red Riding Hood (Hyman, 1983)	German	Hunter kills wolf; pulls out Grandmother and Red.
Little Red Cap (Grimm & Grimm, 1995)	German	Hunter pulls Grandmother and Red out of wolf; they sew stones into his belly.
Nekane, the Lamiña & the Bear (Araujo, 1993)	Basque	She takes food to Uncle; on the way she must outwit a bear and the lamiña, a treacherous spirit that deceives by changing shape.
Lon Po Po (Young, 1989)	Chinese	Mother leaves children at home while she goes to Grandmother's. Wolf tricks his way into the house with the children.
A Knock at the Door (Shannon, 1992)	(Various countries)	A book of 35 tales in which the children are home alone and a treacherous creature tricks the children to get in.
Petite Rouge (Artell, 2001)	Cajun	Cajun dialect and terms, told in rhyming verse. Red is a goose, stalked by a gator.
Little Red Ronnika (Jackson, 1998)	African American	Modern setting with girl and wolf. Tree trimmer opens wolf; they make wolf steaks.
Flossie & the Fox (McKissack, 1986)	African American	Told in southern U.S. dialect. Flossie must deliver eggs to Miz Viola. Fox tries to intimidate her, but she confidently rebuffs his attempts.
No Dinner! (Souhami, 1999)	Indian	Grandmother visits granddaughter; on the way she is stalked by three ferocious animals. She makes return trip rolling inside a pumpkin.
Strudwick (Kraus, 1995)	(Modern spinoff)	Male lamb dodges wolf; both are disguised as each other. Lamb visits Grandfather, who is disguised as a lion.
Ruby (Emberley, 1990)	(Modern spinoff)	Urban street setting. Ruby is a mouse, and a cat stalks her. Mastiff takes care of cat.

(continued)

Table 2.1 (continued)
Familiar Fairy Tale Variants

Title	Culture	Feature
BEAUTY AND THE BEAST AND VARIANTS		
Beauty and the Beast (Brett, 1989)	French	Basic story of prince under a spell until a beautiful woman agrees to marry the ugly beast he has been changed into.
The Dragon Prince (Yep, 1997)	Chinese	Prince, transformed as dragon, takes youngest daughter to live with him. Jealous older sister switches places with her but is discovered.
The Black Bull of Norroway (Huck, 2001)	Scottish	Bull takes girl on her life adventures; her kindness breaks the spell of an evil witch over the Duke. She confronts witch through extraordinary events to break spell forever.
The White Cat (San Souci, 1990)	French	Cat presiding over castle is really princess under spell. Prince visits her kingdom and battles dragon to release her.
RUMPELSTILTSKIN AND VARIANTS		
Rumpelstiltskin (Zelinsky, 1986)	German	Classic telling of miller's daughter who must spin straw into gold. A strange little man does the magic and demands her first child as a reward unless she guesses his name.
Tucker Pfeffercorn (Moser, 1994)	Rural southern American	Sophisticated telling with regional southern dialect. A proud young mother must spin cotton into gold. Pfeffercorn is the little man who helps her.
The Girl Who Spun Gold (Hamilton, 2000)	West Indian/ African American	Told in lilting, colloquial style. Quashiba marries King first; after a year she must spin gold. Little man helps her. No child in this story.
Whuppity Stoorie (White, 1997)	Scottish	A fairy woman cures Mum's sick pig, then demands the woman's daughter as payment, unless she can guess the fairy's name.
The Three Spinning Fairies (Ernst, 2002)	German	Cook boasts lazy daughter can spin fine flax. Queen locks her up to spin. Three unusual fairies help girl, and then she marries the prince.
"Oniroku" in *Can You Guess My Name?* (Sierra, 2002a; see also two other variants in this collection)	Japanese	An ogre builds a bridge for a master builder, then demands the builder's eyes as payment unless he guesses the ogre's name.

Leola and the Honeybears (Rosales, 1999) is an African American telling of "Goldilocks and the Three Bears." Rich paintings and text depict the young girl trying out the berry pies in the bears' house. Her reunion with her Grandmama at the end of the story is heartwarming. Beni Montresor's *Hansel and Gretel* (2001) uses brief, spare language to tell a much gentler, less scary version of the traditional tale. *The Dancing Pig* (Sierra, 1999) is a Balinese telling of the Hansel and Gretel story. Twin sisters, left home alone, are tricked by the Rangsasa, an ogress who snatches the girls and prepares to eat them. They are rescued by their pig, who enchants the ogress with dancing and music.

The intricate, glowing art of Gennady Spirin brings alive the Norwegian Tale *Boots & the Glass Mountain* (Martin, 1992). Through magic and determination, Boots acquires three magnificent horses, which he later uses to charge up a steep glass hill to rescue the princess who was placed there by the king and the Troll Chief. In Diane Wolkstein's German version of *The Glass Mountain* (1999), the princess falls down a crack deep inside the mountain, becoming the servant of Old Rinkrank, who lives there. She escapes by her wits and enjoins the help of her suitor to bring a resolution that includes birdsong and treasure.

Caldecott Award-winning Paul Zelinsky applies his talents to *Rapunzel* (1997). This compelling story of the girl imprisoned in a tower is illustrated in the style of the Italian Renaissance; copious source notes are included. The value of industriousness is taught in *Mother Holly* (Stewig, 2001). It features two sisters, one industrious and productive, the other whiny and lazy. What makes this tale different from many others is that, instead of ending with the permanent punishment of the lazy sister, she learns to lead a dutiful, industrious life.

Activities With Fairy Tales

The delightful array of variant tellings is fertile ground just begging for comparison activities. A wall-sized chart is an easy, visual method of tracking different versions of the same tale. Headings across the top of the chart should include title, reteller, country/culture, names of the main characters, pivotal or magical plot elements, and concluding outcomes.

Another charting activity is the listing of character traits. As discussed earlier, fairy tale characters are generally one-dimensional, either all good or all bad. With a few exceptions, fairy tale characters act out of motivation for higher purposes or self-serving purposes. Characterization is an important skill to be learned by young readers, and fairy tales make an easy place to start. Make a chart and have students list the main characters in a tale or a set of several tales. Challenge students to write descriptive words to illustrate a character's goodness or badness, thereby expanding students' vocabulary. Strive for refinement of description, for example, innocent,

Table 2.2
"Scrambled" Fairy Tales

The Bravest Ever Bear (Ahlberg, 1999)	Ministries and running commentary with a bear, three bears, four-and-twenty bears, Red Riding Hood, a troll and bridge, a dragon, etc.
The Jolly Postman: Or Other People's Letters (Ahlberg & Ahlberg, 1986)	Letters written from Goldilocks to the Three Bears, Jack to the Giant, Peter Piper Press to Cinderella, Red Riding Hood's attorney to the Wolf, etc.
Dear Peter Rabbit (Ada, 1994)	Letters to and from Goldilocks & Baby Bear; the Three Pigs and Peter Rabbit; Red Riding Hood and Grandmother; and the two wolves who lost in their stories.
Beware of the Storybook Wolves (Child, 2000)	Two wolves jump out of a boy's bedtime book, making threats. Wicked fairy and kind fairy godmother perform spells, with implications for Red Riding Hood and Cinderella.
Who Is It? (Grindley, 2000)	Riddle-like clues about Goldilocks, Red Riding Hood, and Jack, geared for young children.

hardworking, devoted, slovenly, tormented, thoughtless, obsessed, enraged, generous, gentle, obedient, brave.

Famous fairy tale characters have found their way into a number of original stories that pull together characters and elements from several tales. These delightful books can be used effectively either as "teasers" to introduce tales or to wrap up a study of fairy tales. These books also can be used to test one's "fairy tale literacy." And they can simply be a cheerful way for children to recognize these familiar characters interacting with one another. The letter-writing books can serve as models for students to write their own letters to fairy tale characters. See Table 2.2 for sample "scrambled" fairy tale books.

The magical quality of fairy tales serves as inspiration for artistic expression. There are many imaginative craft ideas in Kathy Ross's *Crafts From Your Favorite Fairy Tales* (1997). There are two clever sliding puppets, using a paper towel tube and string, to dramatize Rapunzel in her tower and Jack climbing the beanstalk. All in all, there are 20 projects for different fairy tales, made from materials readily found around the home. Create these projects purely as artistic enjoyment or use the finished products to help dramatize or retell the tales.

Transformation Tales

Children are turned into swans; a man changes himself into a seal; Raven transforms into a pine needle; a boy becomes a star; the downtrodden youngest son becomes an armor-clad hero. Enchantment, magic spells, spells of punishment or revenge, transformations rewarding honest hard work, transformations to play a trick, and shapeshifting—these and more are the wonder of transformation tales. Transformation tales allow us to escape from our everyday, logical, practical world into a world of enchantment. Tales of transformation and shapeshifting occur in nearly every culture (Jones, 1995).

The term *transformation tales*, as it is used here, actually covers a range of tale types and transformation types. The transformation is caused by magic or enchantment; often a transformation is performed on another being by someone such as a sorcerer (in European or Asian tales) or a god (in myths). In Native American folklore, Raven and Coyote are creator-culture-heroes that are both transformers and tricksters. In some Native American cultures, animals act as transformers of other beings. In contrast to a change caused by a transformer, shapeshifting is a voluntary act. A shapeshifter can change its own form when it wants to or when certain circumstances are present. Shapeshifters include spirit-beings, animals, ghosts, objects, and interveners. Interveners are mysterious persons or animals who appear to give advice or help, such as the fairy godmother (old man, old woman, etc.) in a Cinderella tale. Some shapeshifters achieve their changes by using some external material, such as donning the skin of an animal, as in tales of selkies, who shed their seal skin to assume human form on land.

While transformational events in European fairy tales are viewed as fantasy, transformation tales from other cultures reflect a different philosophy and ethos. Indigenous cultures that have lived very close to nature have stories that accept the phenomenon of transformation as a more natural part of living. Tales and myths of Native Americans, Maoris, Aboriginals of Australia, and many African cultures reflect this holistic view. Many of these cultures view life more transparently; there are few, if any, boundaries between everyday life, work, religion, the animal world, the spirit world, and nature. Because of this closeness with nature, it is more commonly accepted that humans can pass easily back and forth into the forms of animals, mountains, stars, and waterfalls. Often, these tales are also pourquoi tales, explaining how mountains or stars came to be. Transformation reflects a kinship with the animal world or the sky world; it reminds us that everything is connected (Kraus, 1999).

Spell-Induced Transformations

A classic European transformation tale is that of a prince or princess who has been placed under a spell by an evil sorcerer or witch and has thereby changed into an ugly creature. The spell can only be broken by a near-impossible act of love or bravery. Stories of Beauty and the Beast are prime examples (see the Fairy Tales section of this chapter). *The Frog Prince* (Grimm & Grimm, 1998) is the well-known tale of the prince under a spell that turns him into a frog. The spell is broken, in some versions, by the princess throwing the frog against the wall; in others, it is by her kissing the frog. A humorous southwestern U.S. version of this tale is *The Horned Toad Prince* (Hopkins, 2000). The Russian tale *The Frog Princess* (Harrison, & Stuart-Clark, 1998; Lewis, 1994) is a more involved tale. Three princes set out to find wives by means of following the arrow they shoot. Two men find ordinary women; the youngest finds a frog. When he discovers that his frog-wife can shed her skin and become a beautiful maiden, he burns the frog skin to keep her in human form. Unfortunately, this sets into motion a series of harrowing adventures. A similar ritual for wife selection starts the Finnish tale *The Princess Mouse* (Shepard, 2003). Mikko's wife is a mouse who eventually transforms into an enchanted princess.

The evil wizard Kostchei transforms maidens and princes into stone in the Russian story *The Firebird* in versions by Jane Yolen (2002) and Robert D. San Souci (1992). Gennady Spirin's *The Tale of the Firebird* (2002) is a different tale in which Ivan's gray wolf transforms into a horse to battle Kostchei. Other tales featuring characters placed under transformational spells by evil powers include *Snow White and Rose Red* (Grimm & Grimm, 1992) and *Tam Lin* (Yolen, 1990).

A mood of wistful longing tinges some tales of spells. "The Children of Lir" in *Irish Fairy Tales and Legends* (Leavy, 1996) tells of four children who are turned into swans by a jealous stepmother. They must remain swans for 900 years and cannot become human until they hear a holy bell. San Souci's *Nicholas Pipe* (1997a) tells of the yearning love of a woman for a merman. He can walk on land as well as swim in the sea, but the couple must face much opposition to their love. The selkie story is told in *The Seal Prince* (MacGill-Callahan, 1995). A girl loves a man who is a selkie; he can don his sealskin or take human form but is forever tied to the sea.

In some tales, the evildoer not only causes transformations but can shapeshift, too. "Little Fawn" in *Celtic Myths* (McBratney, 1997) is the story of a woman-turned-fawn who is under the spell of the Dark One. In the Russian tale *Peter and the Blue Witch Baby* (San Souci, 2000b), a horrid witch takes the shape of a lovely young woman, and also a baby, in order to gain control of the Tsar's palace.

Native American Transformation Tales

Transformational events in Native American stories are more likely to be a manifestation of closeness to nature than deeds wrought by a sorcerer. Transformations in these stories occur as a more "natural" process, as acts of interconnectedness between everyday life and the spirit world. A large number of Native American transformation tales are also pourquoi tales (see the Pourquoi Tales section of this chapter).

Stories from the people of the northwest United States and Arctic regions are especially rich in transformations. *Spirit of the Cedar People* (1998) and *Echoes of the Elders* (1997), both by Chief Lelooska, are outstanding tributes to the culture of the Kwakiutl people. In "Raven & Monster Hallibut," Raven tricks a gigantic, powerful fish into cooking himself into small pieces, which become the normal-sized fish we have today. The pourquoi tale "Puffin Rock" is the story of some children who take their canoe out too far, where a storm drives them onto a rock. The rock has supernatural power and transforms them into puffins. The origin of the loon is told in "Old Grandmother Loon." Grandmother takes her grandchildren out in her canoe; then a fog rolls in, and a canoe full of cruel warriors looms near. Grandmother sings a loud, mournful song, and she flies away as a loon, diverting attention from the children. *The Girl Who Dreamed Only Geese* (Norman, 1997) is a collection of tales from the Arctic regions. "The Man Who Married a Seagull" is the story of a seagull girl who transforms into a human being. "The Wolverine's Secret" is a story of a boy who can transform himself into a raven and back again, so he can help recover the sun and moon stolen by Wolverine.

Asian Transformation Tales

Supernatural events are common in folk tales from Asia and the Pacific Islands. The transformation of shape and health are pivotal elements in San Souci's *The Silver Charm* (2002). It is a compelling story from the Ainu people, an indigenous people from certain islands of Japan. A boy, captured by an ogre, loses his good-luck charm and falls deathly ill. A mouse transforms the boy's pets into humans who steal the charm back and restore the boy's health.

Another theme found in these tales is reward for a kind deed, such as the rescue of an animal in distress. *The Crane Wife* (Bodkin, 1998) is a well-known story from Japan. A lonely man, a sailmaker, finds a wounded crane and nurses it back to health. Some time later, a woman appears at his door in a storm. In time, she becomes his wife. Later, in a time of hunger, she agrees to weave him a magic sail, only if he agrees never to watch her work. The husband eventually breaks his promise, watching in horror as his exhausted crane-wife weaves her own feathers into the cloth. She flies away, never to return. Another tragic transformation concludes the Chinese tale *The Hunter* (Young, 2000). It tells of a man who rescues a little snake and is rewarded by the Dragon King with the power to understand the language of animals. He is charged never to tell his secret or he will be turned to stone. One day, he hears the animals talking about a coming flood that will destroy the village. Putting the villagers' lives before his own, he reveals his gift of animal language in order to warn them. Sadly, he turns to stone.

The Hawaiian tale *The Shark God* (Martin, 2001) tells the story of two children who rescue a shark entangled near the shore. Later, the children are found guilty of touching the King's drum, a forbidden act, and they face a miserable punishment. The desperate parents plead for help in the cave of the Shark God, who rescues the children. The island of Fiji is the setting for Wolfson's *Turtle Songs: A Tale for Mothers and Daughters* (1999). Invaders start to take a mother and daughter to another island. While attempting to escape, the swimming women are mercifully transformed into sea turtles, eluding their captors.

Other Transformation Tales

Although transformation tales generally refer to stories of changes in shape or physical appearance, there are a few that are notable for transformations of attitude or values. The Vietnamese tale *The Crystal Heart* (Shepard, 1998) tells of a privileged young woman who wants a man who sings a beautiful song. When he sees her, he falls in love, but when she finds out he is but a lowly fisherman, she spurns him. He dies, and his heart becomes a crystal stone. The stone finds its way to the palace. When the woman holds the stone in her hands, she hears the song and realizes her cruelty. The Armenian tale *A Weave of Words* (San Souci, 1998) tells of a young prince who cares only for hunting but who learns to value reading, writing, and weaving thanks to a courageous and independent woman. The African tales *Subira Subira* (Mollel, 2000) and *The Lion's Whiskers* (Day, 1995) tell the story of transformations in psychological acceptance. A big sister yearning for the cooperation of her younger brother (in the first tale) and a stepmother longing for acceptance by her new stepson (in the second tale) each seek the help of a holy person. In the end, the protagonists learn that the gift of patience is the "magic" that transforms their loved ones' attitudes.

San Souci's *The Secret of the Stones* (2000c) is a heartwarming African American variant of "The Elves and the Shoemakers." A hardworking childless couple returns to their home at night to discover all the chores done. A healing woman tells them that the two little stones in their house turn into two orphan children who do the housework during the day. She tells them how to break the spell. James Ransome's stunning paintings bring warmth and drama to this tale.

Flower transformations are plentiful in *Blossom Tales: Flower Stories of Many Folk* (Powell, 2002). Grapes turn into crocuses in the Sicilian tale "Crocus." Five chiefs turn into the first columbine in the Iroquois tale "Columbine." Drops of blood turn into lily of the valley blossoms in the English tale "Lily of the Valley." The Japanese tale "Peony" tells of a handsome young man who emerges from a peony garden. The princess is intrigued with him, but he eludes her and only a peony is found. She keeps the peony, which stays fresh until she marries; then it withers and dies.

For more transformation tales, consult Kraus's *Folktale Themes and Activities for Children, Volume 2: Trickster and Transformation Tales* (1999).

Activities With Transformation Tales

Transformational elements in these tales are, for the most part, a visual experience. Upon hearing a transformation tale, the listener imagines the shapechanging, the wondrous and magical alteration of appearance. Transformation tales inevitably lead to various forms of artistic expression.

A satisfying, effective, and easy art project for all ages is the accordion-fold transformation picture. On two pieces of 9" × 12" paper, have students draw or paint two pictures of the person or object before and after the transformation. For example, to illustrate *The Dragon Prince*, have students paint the prince on one page and the dragon on the other, covering both pages fully with contrasting colors (orient the paper vertically). Then, cut each picture into 1-inch strips vertically. Next, take a piece of 12" × 18" paper (orient it horizontally), and fold it back and forth, accordion-style, spacing the folds 1 inch apart. Finally, students should glue the picture strips onto the folded paper, alternating between the two pictures. To enjoy the transformation effect, hold up the paper, tilting it from side to side to change the view. Display these pictures in a hallway where the viewers can see the pictures change as they walk past them.

Book cover from *Sleeping Beauty*, illustrated by K.Y. Craft. Copyright © 2002. Used by permission of North-South Books.

Paper engineering, such as the effects seen in pop-up books, also makes effective transformation effects. A simple movable-book effect is a "flag book." Instructions for these and other pop-up effects can be found in Gwenneth Swain's *Bookworks: Making Books by Hand* (1995). Instructions for a more complicated sliding image with a window-blind effect and patterns can be found in Kraus (1999).

Transformation dolls can be easy to make and can serve as props or puppets in storytelling. The basic idea is to make a torso with a head at each end. In the middle, fasten a skirt-like piece (which could be a woman's skirt but could have the costuming for a man or animal as well). Then, flip over the skirt in one direction to show one character (a frog, for example). Flip over the skirt in the other direction and show the transformed character (a prince). Kraus (1999) provides directions for making a doll from a stuffed sock or two wooden spoons. Ross's *Crafts From Your Favorite*

Fairy Tales (1997) has directions for making a "Rags to Riches Cinderella" from poster board with a fabric skirt; the book also includes directions for a Beauty and the Beast cardboard doll body with a head that swivels around on a brass fastener.

Visual effects can be very dramatic using a multimedia program on a computer, such as KidPix, Hyperstudio, or PowerPoint. Help students draw the two pictures from before and after the transformation; these can be drawn with computer drawing tools or they can be drawn on paper and scanned in. Situate the two pictures into the slide show portion of the program. Then select a transition that provides a special effect as the slide show progresses from one picture to the next. The dissolve transition is especially effective in producing a magical illusion: The first picture slowly disappears as if in a mist and the second image slowly replaces it. Students also can use a multimedia program to tell an entire story in sequential slides. Plan the story on a storyboard first. Most multimedia programs also have a recording feature so that the student can narrate the story with each frame of the slide show. Ask for technical and creative help from your library media specialist.

Noodlehead Tales

Noodlehead stories are tales of fools, people who don't use their brains. Numskull stories, as they are sometimes called, feature characters who find or create preposterous problems and solutions through seemingly random acts of pure coincidence. The humor of the noodlehead story has a slapstick quality. These silly tales allow us to laugh at ourselves for sometimes being foolish, and they allow us to laugh to realize there are others who are even more foolish than we are. Some of the most well-known noodleheads include Jack from England and the United States, Juan Bobo from Puerto Rico, Giufa from Italy, Elsie from Germany, and Hans from Norway and Germany. In the Jewish storytelling tradition, the town of Chelm is an entire village of fools (see chapter 10 for a detailed discussion of Chelm).

Contributing to the absurdity of these tales is the fact that sometimes the noodlehead ends up the hero, or possessing new wealth or a mate. Yet the noodlehead achieves the prize with seemingly no planning or forethought. This is the critical factor that distinguishes the noodlehead from the trickster. Some noodleheads, especially Jack, seem to resemble a trickster, for example, when Jack goes back up the beanstalk to steal from the giant. But the trickster is a planner, deliberately wily and cunning. There is always a plan afoot in a trickster tale, whether the listener/reader is in on it or not. By contrast, the noodlehead performs the most illogical, outlandish acts with little or no awareness of what he is doing, and if he turns out the winner, it is a surprise to everyone, including himself. Remember, Jack traded the cow for a handful of beans, a foolish act of poor judgment, not clever forethought. Any success achieved by a noodlehead is the result of luck and circumstance.

Although many tale types teach life lessons, this is less true of the noodlehead tale. If there is a lesson to be learned, it may be that life isn't fair and that things just happen. Another possible lesson involves obeying one's parent; many noodlehead stories are about a mother's instructions to her son. The spirit of the tale is not to make fun of others but to laugh at the fool in each of us (Hamilton & Weiss, 2000).

A Sampling of Noodleheads

A good introduction to a variety of noodleheads can be found in the collection *Noodlehead Stories* (2000) by Hamilton and Weiss. In "Whose Horse Is Whose?" two men go to extraordinary lengths to distinguish one horse from the other. At the end of the story, we learn that they never noticed the horses are two different colors. "I'd Laugh, Too, If I Weren't Dead" describes a contest between two wives, each of whom sets out to prove that her husband is the bigger fool. In all, fools from 22 different countries demonstrate their inept efforts in this collection.

Jack Tales

Tales of innocent, happy-go-lucky Jack migrated from England to the Appalachian area of the United States. The standard classic collection is gathered and retold by Richard Chase in *Jack Tales* (2003). One of the newest, most distinguished collections is *The Jack Tales* (2000), told by renowned storyteller Ray Hicks. (The three tales in this collection are told by Hicks himself on the accompanying audio CD.) In "Jack and the Northwest Wind," Jack is given three magical objects by an old man; each time, he is victimized by "rowdy boys" who steal the wonders. Finally, luck turns Jack's way. In "Jack and the Bean Tree," the objects Jack steals from the giant are not magical but merely curiosities: a pocketknife, rifle, and bedspread.

Other notable tellings include *Kate and the Beanstalk* (Osborne, 2000). This feminist version casts Kate as a clever and courageous girl, rather than a simpleton. Paul Brett Johnson's *Jack Outwits the Giants* (2002) portrays Jack as a quick thinker who repeatedly escapes from the two-headed giant and his wife. *Fearless Jack* (Johnson, 2001) is a variant of "Seven at One Blow" (see the Other Noodleheads section of this chapter). Richard Walker's *Jack and the Beanstalk* (1999) features winsome illustrations. Tony Ross's *Lazy Jack* (1986) depicts a series of inept efforts that end with winning the hand of a princess. Berlie Doherty's *Famous Adventures of Jack* (2001) is a longer collection of Jack tales, all framed by the visit of Jill to Mother Greenwood. Mother Greenwood launches into one tale after another of the many Jacks she knows. Jim Harris's *Jack and the Giant* (1997) is a spinoff with a southwestern flavor.

Other Noodleheads

Several noodlehead vignettes are strung together in San Souci's *Six Foolish Fishermen* (2000d), told with Cajun flair and dialect. One fisherman tries to count all six of them to make sure they are all safe. He counts the other five, but cannot understand that he must count himself. Because he only counts five, Pierre assumes he is dead. His wife finally straightens out the mess. *Epossumondas* (2002) is Colleen Salley's new spin on the classic "Epaminondas" tale from the southern United States. A young possum takes his mother's instructions so literally that he never succeeds in bringing home cake, butter, and other items from his aunt. The Ethiopian tale *Silly Mammo* (Yohannes, 2002) is another tale of a noodlehead who always gets his mother's instructions wrong but ends up marrying the wealthy man's daughter.

The search for fools is a theme in some noodlehead stories. In the Indian story *The Foolish Men of Agra* (Singh, 1998), the emperor dispatches his minister to find the six most foolish men in Agra. The minister brings back four fools and points out that he and the emperor are indeed just as foolish for having enjoined this quest. Steven Kellogg's humorous art is the perfect medium for his *The Three Sillies* (1999). In this English tale, a young woman and her parents worry pointlessly that her future son might be killed by a mallet falling on his head, while allowing all the cider to flow onto the floor. Her suitor declares that if he can find three who are as silly as they, he will marry the girl. Judy Sierra (2002b) tells a similar version of a search for three sillies in "Silly & Sillier" in her collection by the same name. It starts when Jack's father builds a house with no windows, so he runs outside to fetch buckets full of sunlight.

The Russian tale *The Fool of the World and the Flying Ship* (Denise, 1994) starts with the acknowledged Fool of the World, who, through the magical help of the Old One and with a lot of luck, acquires a flying ship and a crew with supernatural powers. He passes the Tsar's many tests and marries his daughter. The Russian tale *At the Wish of the Fish* (Lewis, 1999) also describes a simpleton with extraordinary means of travel: Too lazy to get up from his rest, he flies through the air on the stove upon which he sleeps. Thanks to wishes granted by a magical fish, the lad marries the Tsar's daughter.

Seven at One Blow (Kimmel, 1998) and *The Brave Little Tailor* (San Souci, 1994) depict the adventures of a simple tailor who derives his ferocious reputation from the act of killing seven flies on his jelly bread. A version of this tale featuring a female heroine is Mary Pope Osborne's *The Brave Little Seamstress* (2002). She performs all sorts of feats, defeating giants and other creatures to impress the king. "Hans in Luck" in *The Barefoot Book of Mother and Son Tales* (Evetts-Secker, 1999) describes Hans's journey home after seven years' work. Starting with a burden of heavy gold, he makes a series of trades for items of decreasing value, until he has nothing and feels relieved. *Juan Bobo* (Bernier-Grand, 1994) tells four Puerto Rican tales in easy-reader format. "A Pig in Sunday Clothes" describes Juan Bobo's hilarious efforts to dress up his pig in his mama's Sunday clothes and send the pig to church. Maria Montes's *Juan Bobo Goes to Work* (2000) depicts Juan Bobo's botched attempts at bringing home a day's pay. Despite his ineptness, he ends up pleasing a rich man and earning a reward.

Activities With Noodlehead Tales

Noodlehead stories tend to be short, uncomplicated, and, of course, funny. They are the perfect kind of story with which children can practice their first storytelling experiences. Martha Hamilton and Mitch Weiss have set up their *Noodlehead Stories* (2000) for just this purpose. At the end of each story, there are some simple "tips for telling" to guide novice storytellers.

Once children have learned and practiced their stories, host a "comedy club," similar to stand-up comedy shows. Serve popcorn and create a lighthearted atmosphere.

Cumulative Tales

Cumulative stories are found among all cultures. As this type of story unfolds, plot elements or characters are added on to what went before, creating an ever-lengthening list or litany of repetition. Often, but not always, the list is recited backward. Although repetition is a feature of many folk tales, the cumulative tale is distinguished by repetition and accumulation of events as the main aspect of the telling, as a formula (Jones, 1995). These tales are rollicking fun, as much a memory game as a story. Some of the best-known cumulative tales are "The House That Jack Built" and "The Old Woman and Her Pig," in which the entire sequence is recited backward each time, with the newest item tagged onto the list. Some cumulative tales exist as songs, most notably, "The Twelve Days of Christmas" and "The Green Grass Grows All Around."

Closely related to cumulative tales are chain tales and circular tales. Cumulative tales are chain tales, but not all chain tales are cumulative (Leach, 1972). Chain tales use repetition and formulaic tellings, with one item adding and leading directly to the next, as in the song/game "The Farmer in the Dell." Chain tales may be based on numbers or days of the week as a device, as in "Solomon Grundy, Born on a Monday." Circular tales use the same sequence and pattern over and over, with the plot coming full circle to the beginning so that it can start all over again. Because of their playful nature and their repetition, cumulative and chain tales work well in the realm of younger children.

Table 2.3
Gingerbread Man Variants

Title	Culture
The Gingerbread Man (Aylesworth, 1998)	Traditional, with new refrain
The Gingerbread Boy (Egielski, 1997)	Traditional, with urban setting
The Gingerbread Man (Jones, 2002)	Traditional, with appearances by nursery tale characters
The Runaway Tortilla (Kimmel, 2000a)	Southwestern United States
The Runaway Rice Cake (Compestine, 2001)	Chinese
The Matzah Man: A Passover Story (Howland, 2002)	Jewish
"The Bun" in *Nursery Tales Around the World* (Sierra, 1996)	Russian
"The Pancake" in *Nursery Tales Around the World* (Sierra, 1996)	Norwegian
The Fine Round Cake (Esterl, 1991)	English

The Gingerbread Man

The ever-popular Gingerbread Man is getting new identities through new multicultural settings. Even in its most simple, traditional form, young children never tire of the tale. They wait, wide-eyed, and then chime in on the sudden "Snap!" right on cue with the fox. When reading cultural variations, children excitedly identify the "same" and "different" aspects of the tale. See Table 2.3 for a sampling of people's favorite runaway pastry.

Chain Tales and Circular Tales

The sequence and pattern of events in a chain tale are a compelling device. When a tale ends up right where it started, children excitedly point out, "It's a circle story!" In the Eritrean tale *Trouble* (Kurtz, 1997), a boy's father gives him a game board to help him stay out of trouble. As the boy moves through his day with his two grazing goats, people keep trading with him for his game board and all his successive possessions. His last trade is to give food to a sick family, and they give him a game board, the object he started out with. The Dahomean (African) tale *Only One Cowry* (Gershator, 2000) also centers around successive trades to accumulate dowry gifts for a future wife. *Pirican Pic and Pirican Mor* (Lupton, 2003) is a Celtic cumulative tale. Pirican Mor finds out his walnut harvest has been taken by Pirican Pic, so he goes off to find a thrashing stick. His efforts result in a lengthening list with a rhythmic chant. The chain song *The Farmer in the Dell* (O'Brien, 2000) is given a new dimension by John O'Brien's illustrations, which tell their own circle story about the farmer who falls in the dell and must be pulled out by the rest of the cast, only to fall in again.

The Turkish story "The Magpie and the Milk" in *A Twist in the Tail* (Hoffman, 1998) features both cumulative and circle story charm. A magpie spills an old woman's milk, so she angrily grabs his tail feathers away. She won't give them back until he brings her more milk, necessitating a series of deals with other characters. Finally, a cow gives milk to the magpie, and he can now give milk to the old woman, ending where the story began. A similar pattern appears in the Sufi tale *What About Me?* (Young, 2002). In this Middle Eastern teaching tale, a boy asks for knowledge from the Grand Master. The Grand Master wants a carpet first. The boy approaches the carpetmaker, who wants thread first. He asks Spinner Woman, but she wants goat hair, and so on. Finally, the clever boy offers help at a point that sets into motion all the required transactions to complete this chain/circle story. In the end, the Grand Master points out the boy already has knowledge, and the story ends with two morals. An older Caldecott Medal winner, *Why Mosquitoes Buzz in People's Ears* (Aardema, 1975), endures as an appealing combination of chain events and cumulative effect (as well as being a pourquoi tale). A mosquito's boasting puts an iguana into a grumpy mood, setting off a chain of reactions among the animals in the forest. Finally, King Lion calls upon the animals to reconstruct events. This court-like council causes recitation of the cumulative effect of the events of the forest.

Folk Songs

Cumulative folk songs add the dimension of music to the upbeat mood of these memory games. When young children learn these songs, they can begin to "read" the words as a transitional stage in reading development, part memory and part word recognition. Try a sing-along with some of these songs, which are available in picture book format in the sources listed in Table 2.4.

Other Cumulative Tales and Variants

Familiar cumulative tales are published in many editions, with both traditional retellings and variations. Representative cumulative tales and variants are shown in Table 2.5.

Table 2.4
Folk Songs

Song/Book Title	Type
Bill Grogan's Goat (Hoberman, 2002)	Chain/circular
Cat Goes Fiddle-I-Fee (Galdone, 1985)	Cumulative
Fiddle-I-Fee (Hillenbrand, 2002)	Cumulative
There Was an Old Lady Who Swallowed a Fly (Taback, 1997)	Cumulative
There's a Hole in the Bucket (Westcott, 1990)	Chain/circular
Old MacDonald (Schwartz, 1999)	Cumulative
Old MacDonald Had a Woodshop (Shulman, 2002)	Cumulative
The Farmer in the Dell (Wallner, 1998)	Chain
Hush Little Baby (Frazee, 1999)	Chain
When I First Came to This Land (Ziefert, 1998)	Cumulative

Table 2.5
Cumulative Tales and Variants

Traditional Title	Variants and Spinoffs
The Old Woman and Her Pig (Kimmel, 1992b)	*Aunt Pitty Patty's Piggy* (Aylesworth, 1999) "Anansi and the Pig" in *Nursery Tales Around the World* (Sierra, 1996)
I Know an Old Lady Who Swallowed a Fly (Karas, 1994)	*Fat Cat: A Danish Folktale* (MacDonald, 2001a) *There Was an Old Lady Who Swallowed a Trout!* (Sloat, 1998)
The Enormous Turnip (Parkinson, 1986)	*The Gigantic Turnip* (Tolstoy, 1998) *The Tale of the Turnip* (Alderson, 1999) *The Giant Carrot* (Peck, 1998)
The House That Jack Built (Winter, 2000)	*The House That Jack Built* (Stow, 1992) *This Is the House That Jack Built* (Taback, 2002) *The Do-It-Yourself House That Jack Built* (Yeoman, 1994) *This Is the Flower* (Schaefer, 2000) *This Is the Rain* (Schaefer, 2001) *The House That Drac Built* (Sierra, 1995)
Henny Penny (Butler, 1991)	*Henny-Penny* (Wattenberg, 2000) *Chicken Little* (Kellogg, 1985)

Activities With Cumulative Tales

At the heart of cumulative tales are repetition, pattern, and sequence. These three ingredients are essential elements in early language experiences for children. Because of the repetition and predictability of these stories, young children will naturally begin to recite these tales from memory. Children also may "read" these stories from books, relying mostly on memory and illustrations. This is an important prereading stage that children go through on their way to becoming independent readers. Capitalize on this opportunity by writing key words from the story on tagboard strips and arranging the words in a pocket chart or on a display board. Lead the children through the story, chanting the story and pointing at the words, to develop word recognition as a bridge to reading. Better yet, give the word strips to the children and have them bring the words over to the pocket chart or arrange and read them independently at a table. Children can build the story as they chant and can point to the words to develop sequencing and memory skills. Stories especially well suited for this activity include *The House That Jack Built* (Winter, 2000) and *Fiddle-I-Fee* (Hillenbrand, 2002).

Some stories work especially well using a flannelboard. Students can manipulate the main characters and objects of a story, placing each on the flannelboard and telling the story as they go. An easy way to put together a flannelboard storytelling set is to take a piece of heavy corrugated cardboard, cover it with fabric (felt or flannel is nice, but even an inexpensive knit fabric will work), and duct-tape the fabric to back of the board, stretching it tightly. Draw the characters and objects on plain paper, laminate them, then put a small piece of self-adhesive Velcro on the back of each story piece. Stories especially suited to use with a flannelboard are *The Enormous Turnip* (Parkinson, 1986) and *Henny Penny* (Butler, 1991).

These patterned stories also lend themselves to quickly produced stick puppet plays. Hand out simple stick puppets to children and have them act out *The Gingerbread Man* or *Henny-Penny* with a little help from you as narrator (Tables 2.3 and 2.5 include many versions of these tales).

The idea of circle stories may be extended to include other books illustrating the cycles of nature and other circular plots. See Kraus (2000) for more information on literature about nature's cycles.

Coming Full Circle

Familiarity with the types of tales in this chapter and with other folk tales is a necessary component of the educational process for all persons, young and old. Folk tales are woven into the fabric of human history. Before books and schools were widely available, folk tales were a chief vehicle for the education of the community. Folk tales contained the history of the people, knowledge of plants and animals, humor and entertainment, and belief systems. Folk tales were used as gentle teaching tools to pass along the values and customs of the culture. They gave people a method to embody their hopes, dreams, and fantastical imaginings. They provided a readily accessible art form that anyone could partake of; the only materials required were a mind, a heart, a voice, and a small gathering of participants. Folk tales also embody a teaching process. They carry the wisdom of cultures, wisdom so old that researchers cannot pinpoint the year of origin or the author of most tales.

These are not stories that one gives to children only "if there is enough time" after other more important things are accomplished. These are not stories that are "just for fun" (as much fun as they may be). These tales are a critical component of literacy—literacy as in literature and reading, as well as literacy of culture and tradition. In today's "global village," as many people now refer to our Earth, it behooves all people to have greater knowledge of and respect for the variety of perspectives held by different cultures. When we have the same stories in common, we have more common ground from which understanding and respect can grow. Indeed, the knowledge of folk tales is a fertile ground on which the seeds of understanding can take root and flourish.

The oldness and the wisdom of these tales are within us, but they need to be awakened by the reading and the telling of these stories. The tales come down through the ages, to us and through us, to succeeding generations. We need to share these stories with children any way we can, as read-alouds, as independent reading, as bedtime stories, through storytelling, in classroom reading units, and as connections to the arts: song, folk dance, visual arts, and drama.

The sense of this old wisdom was conveyed simply yet profoundly by an old man in Ethiopia, as related by Brent Ashabranner. In *The Lion's Whiskers and Other Ethiopian Tales* (1997), folklorist Ashabranner recalls the work that he and Russell Davis completed in Ethiopia in the 1950s. While preparing schoolbooks for the Ministry of Education, the two men traveled about the country and collected stories. They spent time with a very old man who

> had given us a perfect definition of a folktale: a story that has been told for so long that no one knows who told it first, a story you like to listen to, a story that sometimes makes you just a little wiser than you were before you heard it. (p. 12)

REFERENCES

Jones, S.S. (1995). *The fairy tale: The magic mirror of imagination*. New York: Twayne.

Kraus, A.M. (1998). *Folktale themes and activities for children, Vol. 1: Pourquoi tales*. Englewood, CO: Teacher Ideas Press.

Kraus, A.M. (1999). *Folktale themes and activities for children, Vol. 2: Trickster and transformation tales*. Englewood, CO: Teacher Ideas Press.

Kraus, A.M. (2000, October/November). Cycles and circles in life and literature. *Book Links, 10*(2) 16–20.

Leach, M. (1972). *Standard dictionary of folklore, mythology, and legend*. New York: Funk & Wagnalls.

Ross, K. (1997). *Crafts from your favorite fairy tales* (V. Enright, Illus.). Brookfield, CT: Millbrook.

Swain, G. (1995). *Bookworks: Making books by hand* (J. Hagerman, Illus.). Minneapolis, MN: Carolrhoda.

Young, T.A., & Ferguson, P.M. (1995). From Anansi to Zomo: Trickster tales in the classroom. *The Reading Teacher, 48,* 490–503.

Zipes, J.D. (1991). *Spells of enchantment: The wondrous fairy tales of western culture.* New York: Viking.

CHILDREN'S BOOKS CITED

Aardema, V. (1975). *Why mosquitoes buzz in people's ears* (L. Dillon & D. Dillon, Illus.). New York: Dial.

Aardema, V. (1994). *Misoso: Once upon a time tales from Africa* (R. Ruffins, Illus.). New York: Apple Soup/Knopf.

Ada, A.F. (1994). *Dear Peter Rabbit* (L. Tryon, Illus.). New York: Atheneum for Young Readers.

Ahlberg, A. (1999). *The bravest ever bear* (P. Howard, Illus.). Cambridge, MA: Candlewick.

Ahlberg, J., & Ahlberg, A. (1986). *The jolly postman: Or other people's letters.* Boston: Little, Brown.

Aiken, J. (2002). *Snow White and the seven dwarfs* (B. Downes, Illus.). New York: Dorling Kindersley.

Alderson, B. (1999). *The tale of the turnip* (F. Wegner, Illus.). Cambridge, MA: Candlewick.

Allen, D. (1999). *Brothers of the night* (M. Rowe & T. Roche, Illus.). New York: Dial.

Anderson, P. (1997). *A Grand Canyon journey: Tracing time in stone.* New York: Franklin Watts.

Araujo, F. (1993). *Nekane, the Lamiña, & the bear: A tale of the Basque Pyrenees* (H. Li, Illus.). Windsor, CA: Rayve.

Artell, M. (2001). *Petite Rouge: A Cajun Red Riding Hood* (J. Harris, Illus.). New York: Dial.

Ashabranner, B. (1997). *The lion's whiskers and other Ethiopian tales* (R.G. Davis, Illus.). North Haven, CT: Linnet/Shoe String.

Aylesworth, J. (1998). *The Gingerbread Man* (B. McClintock, Illus.). New York: Scholastic.

Aylesworth, J. (1999). *Aunt Pitty Patty's piggy* (B. McClintock, Illus.). New York: Scholastic.

Badoe, A. (2001). *The pot of wisdom: Ananse stories* (B.W. Diakité, Illus.). Toronto: Groundwood.

Bernier-Grand, C. (1994). *Juan Bobo: Four folktales from Puerto Rico* (E. Ramos Nieves, Illus.). New York: HarperCollins.

Bierhorst, J. (2001). *Is my friend at home? Pueblo fireside tales* (W. Watson, Illus.). New York: Farrar, Straus & Giroux.

Bodkin, O. (1998). *The crane wife* (G. Spirin, Illus.). New York: Gulliver/Harcourt Brace.

Brett, J. (1989). *Beauty and the beast.* New York: Clarion.

Brown, F.G. (1997). *American Indian science: A new look at old cultures.* New York: Twenty-First Century/Henry Holt.

Bruchac, J. (1991). *Native American stories* (J.K. Fadden, Illus.). Golden, CO: Fulcrum.

Bruchac, J. (2001). *How Chipmunk got his stripes: A tale of bragging and teasing* (J. Aruego & A. Dewey, Illus.). New York: Dial.

Butler, S. (1991). *Henny Penny.* New York: Tambourine.

Caduto, M.J., & Bruchac, J. (1989). *Keepers of the Earth: Native American stories and environmental activities for children* (J.K. Fadden & C. Wood, Illus.). Golden, CO: Fulcrum.

Castaldo, N. (2002). *Oceans: An activity guide for ages 6–9.* Chicago: Chicago Review.

Chase, R. (2003). *Jack tales* (B.W. Williams, Illus.). Boston: Houghton Mifflin.

Child, L. (2000). *Beware of the storybook wolves.* New York: Arthur A. Levine/Scholastic.

Climo, S. (1999). *Magic & mischief: Tales from Cornwall* (A.B. Venti, Illus.). New York: Clarion.

Compestine. Y.C. (2001). *The runaway rice cake* (T. Chau, Illus.). New York: Simon & Schuster.

Cooling, W. (1998). *Farmyard tales from far and wide* (R. Moran, Illus.). Cambridge, MA: Barefoot Books.

Craft, K.Y. (2002). *Sleeping Beauty.* New York: SeaStar/North-South.

Cummings, P. (2002). *Ananse and the lizard.* New York: Henry Holt.

Curry, J. (1999). *Turtle Island: Tales of the Algonquian nations* (J. Watts, Illus.). New York: Margaret K. McElderry/Simon & Schuster.

Day, N.R. (1995). *The lion's whiskers: An Ethiopian folktale* (A. Gilfraconi, Illus.). New York: Scholastic.

Day, N.R. (2001). *Piecing Earth & sky together: A creation story from the Mien tribe of Laos* (G. Panzarella, Illus.). Fremont, CA: Shen's Books.

Delessert, E. (2001). *The seven dwarfs.* Mankato, MN: Creative.

Denise, C. (1994). *The fool of the world and the flying ship.* New York: Philomel.

DePaola, T. (2000). *Jamie O'Rourke and the pooka.* New York: G.P. Putnam's Sons.

DeSpain, P. (1998). *The dancing turtle: A folktale from Brazil* (D. Boston, Illus.). Little Rock, AR: August House.

DeSpain, P. (2001). *Tales of tricksters* (D. Bell, Illus.). Little Rock, AR: August House.

Doherty, B. (2000). *Fairy tales* (J. Ray, Illus.). Cambridge, MA: Candlewick.

Doherty, B. (2001). *Famous adventures of Jack* (S. Lamut, Illus.). New York: Greenwillow/HarperCollins.

Doucet, S. (2002). *Lapin plays possum: Trickster tales from the Louisiana bayou* (S. Cook, Illus.). New York: Melanie Kroupa/Farrar, Straus & Giroux.

Dwyer, M. (1997). *Coyote in love.* Seattle, WA: Alaska Northwest.

Egielski, R. (1997). *The gingerbread boy.* New York: HarperCollins.

Emberley, M. (1990). *Ruby.* Boston: Little, Brown.

Ernst, L.C. (2002). *The three spinning fairies.* New York: Dutton.

Esterl, A. (1991). *The fine round cake* (A. Dugin & O. Dugina, Illus.). New York: Four Winds.

Evetts-Secker, J. (1999). *The Barefoot book of mother and son tales* (H. Cann, Illus.). Cambridge, MA: Barefoot Books.

Farley, C. (2001). *The king's secret: The legend of King Sejong* (R. Jew, Illus.). New York: HarperCollins.

Frazee, M. (1999). *Hush little baby: A folk song with pictures.* New York: Browndeer/Harcourt.

Galdone, P. (1985). *Cat goes fiddle-i-fee.* New York: Clarion/Ticknor & Fields/Houghton Mifflin.

Gantschev, I. (2001). *The three little rabbits: A Balkan folktale* (J.J. Alison, Illus.). New York: North-South.

Garland, S. (2001). *Children of the dragon: Selected tales from Vietnam* (T.S. Hyman, Illus.). New York: Harcourt.

Gershator, P. (1998). *Zzzng! Zzzng! Zzzng! A Yoruba tale* (T. Smith, Illus.). New York: Orchard.

Gershator, P. (2000). *Only one cowry* (D. Soman, Illus.). New York: Orchard.

Goble, P. (2001). *Storm Maker's tipi*. New York: Richard Jackson/Atheneum/Simon & Schuster.

Goldin, B.D. (1996). *Coyote and the fire stick: A Pacific Northwest Indian tale* (W. Hillenbrand, Illus.). New York: Gulliver/Harcourt Brace.

Grimm, J., & Grimm, W. (1992). *Snow White and Rose Red* (G. Spirin, Illus.). New York: Philomel.

Grimm, J., & Grimm, W. (1995). *Little Red Cap* (L. Zwerger, Illus.). New York: North-South.

Grimm, J., & Grimm, W. (1998). *The frog prince: Or, Iron Henry* (B. Schrader, Illus.). New York: North-South.

Grindley, S. (2000). *Who is it? Lots of fairytale fun* (R. Beardshaw, Illus.). Atlanta, GA: Peachtree.

Hamilton, M., & Weiss, M. (1999). *How and why stories: World tales kids can read and tell* (C. Lyon, Illus.). Little Rock, AR: August House.

Hamilton, M., & Weiss, M. (2000). *Noodlehead stories: World tales kids can read and retell* (A. Elsammak, Illus.). Little Rock, AR: August House.

Hamilton, V. (1996). *When birds could talk and bats could sing: The adventures of Bruh Sparrow, Sis Wren, and their friends* (B. Moser, Illus.). New York: Scholastic.

Hamilton, V. (2000). *The girl who spun gold* (L. Dillon & D. Dillon, Illus.). New York: Blue Sky/Scholastic.

Hamilton, V. (2003). *Brer Rabbit and the tar baby girl* (J. Ransome, Illus.). New York: Scholastic.

Harris, J. (1997). *Jack and the giant: A story full of beans*. Flagstaff, AZ: Rising Moon/Northland.

Harrison, M., & Stuart-Clark, C. (1998). *The Oxford treasury of world stories*. New York: Oxford University Press.

Hicks, R. (2000). *The Jack tales* (O. Smith, Illus.). New York: Callaway.

Hillenbrand, W. (2002). *Fiddle-i-fee*. New York: Gulliver.

Hoberman, M.A. (2002). *Bill Grogan's goat* (N.B. Westcott, Illus.). Boston: Little, Brown.

Hoffman, M. (1998). *A twist in the tail: Animal stories from around the world* (J. Ormerod, Illus.). New York: Henry Holt.

Hopkins, J.M. (2000). *The horned toad prince* (M. Austin, Illus.). Atlanta, GA: Peachtree.

Howland, N. (2002). *The matzah man: A Passover story*. New York: Clarion.

Huck, C. (2001). *The black bull of Norroway: A Scottish tale* (A. Lobel, Illus.). New York: Greenwillow/HarperCollins.

Huth, H. (2000). *The son of the sun and the daughter of the moon: A Saami folktale* (A. Vojtech, Illus.). New York: Atheneum/Simon & Schuster.

Hyman, T.S. (1983). *Little Red Riding Hood*. New York: Holiday House.

Jackson, B. (1998). *Little Red Ronnika* (R. Mitchell, Illus.). Akron, OH: Multicultural.

Johnson, P.B. (2001). *Fearless Jack*. New York: Margaret K. McElderry/Simon & Schuster.

Johnson, P.B. (2002). *Jack outwits the giants*. New York: Margaret K. McElderry/Simon & Schuster.

Jones, C. (2002). *The gingerbread man*. Boston: Houghton Mifflin.

Karas, G.B. (1994). *I know an old lady who swallowed a fly*. New York: Scholastic.

Keams, G. (1998). *Snail Girl brings water: A Navajo story* (R. Ziehler-Martin, Illus.). Flagstaff, AZ: Rising Moon/Northland.

Kellogg, S. (1985). *Chicken Little*. New York: Morrow.

Kellogg, S. (1997). *The three little pigs*. New York: Morrow Junior.

Kellogg, S. (1999). *The three sillies*. Cambridge, MA: Candlewick.

Kimmel, E.A. (1988). *Anansi and the moss-covered rock* (J. Stevens, Illus.). New York: Holiday House.

Kimmel, E.A. (1992a). *Anansi goes fishing* (J. Stevens, Illus.). New York: Holiday House.

Kimmel, E.A. (1992b). *The old woman and her pig* (G. Carmi, Illus.). New York: Holiday House.

Kimmel, E.A. (1994). *Anansi and the talking melon* (J. Stevens, Illus.). New York: Holiday House.

Kimmel, E.A. (1995). *Rimonah of the flashing sword: A north African tale* (O. Rayyan, Illus.). New York: Holiday House.

Kimmel, E.A. (1998). *Seven at one blow: A tale from the Brothers Grimm* (M. Lloyd, Illus.). New York: Holiday House.

Kimmel, E.A. (1999). *The birds' gift: A Ukrainian Easter story* (K. Krenina, Illus.). New York: Holiday House.

Kimmel, E.A. (2000a). *The runaway tortilla* (R. Cecil, Illus.). New York: Winslow.

Kimmel, E.A. (2000b). *The two mountains: An Aztec legend* (L.E. Fisher, Illus.). New York: Holiday House.

Kimmel, E.A. (2001). *Anansi and the magic stick* (J. Stevens, Illus.). New York: Holiday House.

Kite, P. (2001). *Insect facts and folklore*. Brookfield, CT: Millbrook.

Kraus, R. (1995). *Strudwick: A sheep in wolf's clothing*. New York: Viking/Penguin.

Kurtz, J. (1997). *Trouble* (D. Bernhard, Illus.). San Diego, CA: Gulliver/Harcourt.

Leavy, U. (1996). *Irish fairy tales and legends*. Boulder, CO: Roberts Rinehart.

Lelooska, D. (1997). *Echoes of the elders: The stories and paintings of Chief Lelooska*. New York: Dorling Kindersley.

Lelooska, D. (1998). *Spirit of the cedar people: More stories and paintings of Chief Lelooska*. New York: Dorling Kindersley.

Lester, J. (1987). *The tales of Uncle Remus: The adventures of Brer Rabbit* (J. Pinkney, Illus.). New York: Dial.

Lester, J. (1988). *More tales of Uncle Remus: Further adventures of Brer Rabbit, his friends, enemies, and others* (J. Pinkney, Illus.). New York: Dial.

Lester, J. (1990). *Further tales of Uncle Remus: The misadventures of Brer Rabbit, Brer Fox, Brer Wolf, the Doodang, and other creatures* (J. Pinkney, Illus.). New York: Dial.

Lester, J. (1994). *The last tales of Uncle Remus* (J. Pinkney, Illus.). New York: Dial.

Lewis, J.P. (1994). *The frog princess: A Russian folktale* (G. Spirin, Illus.). New York: Dial.

Lewis, J.P. (1999). *At the wish of the fish: A Russian folktale* (K. Krenina, Illus.). New York: Atheneum/Simon & Schuster.

Lexau, J. (2001). *Crocodile and hen: A Bakongo folktale* (D. Cushman, Illus.). HarperCollins.

Lind, M. (2003). *Bluebonnet girl* (K. Kiesler, Illus.). New York: Henry Holt.

Ljungkvist, L. (2003). *Snow White and the seven dwarfs*. New York: Harry N. Abrams.

London, J., & Pinola, L. (1993). *Fire race: A Karuk coyote tale about how fire came to the people* (S. Long, Illus.). San Francisco: Chronicle.

Lowell, S. (1992). *The three little javelinas* (J. Harris, Illus.). Flagstaff, AZ: Northland.

Lunge-Larsen, L., & Preus, M. (1999). *The legend of the lady slipper: An Ojibwe tale* (A. Arroyo, Illus.). Boston: Houghton Mifflin.

Lupton, H. (2003). *Pirican Pic and Pirican Mor* (Y. Heo, Illus.). New York: Barefoot.

MacDonald, M.R. (1998). *Pickin' peas* (P. Cummings, Illus.). New York: HarperCollins.

MacDonald, M.R. (2001a). *Fat cat: A Danish folktale* (J. Paschkis, Illus.). Little Rock, AR: August House.

MacDonald, M.R. (2001b). *Mabela the clever* (T. Coffey, Illus.). Morton Grove, IL: Albert Whitman.

MacGill-Callahan, S. (1995). *The seal prince* (K. Waldherr, Illus.). New York: Dial.

Marshall, J. (1989). *The three little pigs*. New York: Dial.

Martin, C. (1992). *Boots & the glass mountain* (G. Spirin, Illus.). New York: Dial.

Martin, R. (2000). *The twelve months* (V. Krykorka, Illus.). Toronto: Stoddart Kids.

Martin, R. (2001). *The Shark God* (D. Shannon, Illus.). New York: Arthur A. Levine/Scholastic.

Mayo, M. (1995). *When the world was young: Creation and pourquoi tales* (L. Brierley, Illus.). New York: Simon & Schuster.

McBratney, S. (1997). *Celtic myths* (S. Player, Illus.). New York: Peter Bedrick.

McCaughrean, G. (2000). *Starry tales* (S. Williams, Illus.). New York: Margaret K. McElderry/Simon & Schuster.

McDermott, G. (1993). *Raven: A trickster tale from the Pacific northwest*. New York: Harcourt Brace Jovanovich.

McDermott, G. (1994). *Coyote: A trickster tale from the American southwest*. New York: Harcourt Brace.

McDermott, G. (2001). *Jabutí the tortoise: A trickster tale from the Amazon*. New York: Harcourt.

McKissack, P.C. (1986). *Flossie & the fox* (R. Isadora, Illus.). New York: Dial.

Mollel, T.M. (1997). *Ananse's feast: An Ashanti tale* (A. Glass, Illus.). New York: Clarion.

Mollel, T. (2000). *Subira subira* (L. Saport, Illus.). New York: Clarion.

Montes, M. (2000). *Juan Bobo goes to work: A Puerto Rican folktale* (J. Cepeda, Illus.). HarperCollins.

Montresor, B. (2001). *Hansel and Gretel*. New York: Atheneum/Simon & Schuster.

Moser, B. (1994). *Tucker Pfeffercorn: An old story retold*. Boston: Little, Brown.

Moser, B. (2001). *The three little pigs*. Boston: Little, Brown.

Musgrove, M. (2001). *The spider weaver: A legend of kente cloth* (J. Cairns, Illus.). New York: Blue Sky/Scholastic.

Nordenstrom, M. (2002). *Pele and the rivers of fire*. Honolulu, HI: Bess Press.

Norman, H. (1997). *The girl who dreamed only geese: And other tales of the far north* (L. Dillon & D. Dillon, Illus.). New York: Gulliver/Harcourt Brace.

Norman, H. (1999). *Trickster and the fainting birds* (T. Pohrt, Illus.). New York: Gulliver/Harcourt Brace.

O'Brien, J. (2000). *The farmer in the dell*. Honesdale, PA: Boyds Mills Press.

Osborne, M.P. (2000). *Kate and the beanstalk* (G. Potter, Illus.). New York: Atheneum/Simon & Schuster.

Osborne, M.P. (2002). *The brave little seamstress* (G. Potter, Illus.). New York: Atheneum/Simon & Schuster.

Parkinson, K. (1986). *The enormous turnip*. Niles, IL: Albert Whitman.

Peck, J. (1998). *The giant carrot* (B. Root, Illus.). New York: Dial.

Philip, N. (1999). *Stockings of buttermilk: American folktales* (J. Mair, Illus.). New York: Clarion.

Powell, P.H. (2002). *Blossom tales: Flower stories of many folk*. North Kingstown, RI: Moon Mountain.

Ray, J. (1996). *The twelve dancing princesses*. New York: Dutton.

Reneaux, J.J. (2001). *How animals saved the people: Animal tales from the south* (J. Ransome, Illus.). New York: HarperCollins.

Riordan, J. (1999). *The coming of night: A Yoruba tale from West Africa* (J. Stow, Illus.). Brookfield, CT: Millbrook.

Rockwell, A. (2000). *The boy who wouldn't obey: A Mayan legend*. New York: Greenwillow/HarperCollins.

Rosales, M. (1999). *Leola and the honeybears*. New York: Scholastic.

Ross, G. (1995). *How Turtle's back was cracked: A traditional Cherokee tale* (M. Jacob, Illus.). New York: Dial.

Ross, T. (1986). *Lazy Jack* (R. Ayto, Illus.). New York: Dial.

Rounds, G. (1992). *Three little pigs and the big bad wolf*. New York: Holiday House.

Salley, C. (2002). *Epossumondas* (J. Stevens, Illus.). New York: Harcourt.

San Souci, D. (2002). *The rabbit and the dragon king: Based on a Korean folk tale* (E.K. Neilan, Illus.). Honesdale, PA: Boyds Mills Press.

San Souci, R.D. (1990). *The white cat: An old French fairy tale* (A. Gennadii, Illus.). New York: Orchard.

San Souci, R.D. (1992). *The firebird* (K. Waldherr, Illus.). New York: Dial.

San Souci, R.D. (1994). *The brave little tailor* (D. San Souci, Illus.). Garden City, NY: Bantam Doubleday Dell.

San Souci, R.D. (1997a). *Nicholas Pipe* (D. Shannon, Illus.). New York: Dial.

San Souci, R.D. (1997b). *Two bear cubs: A Miwok legend from California's Yosemite Valley* (D. San Souci, Illus.). Yosemite National Park, CA: Yosemite Association.

San Souci, R.D. (1998). *A weave of words* (R. Colón, Illus.). New York: Orchard.

San Souci, R.D. (2000a). *Callie Ann and Mistah Bear* (D. Daily, Illus.). New York: Dial.

San Souci, R.D. (2000b). *Peter and the blue witch baby* (A. Natchev, Illus.). New York: Doubleday/Random House.

San Souci, R.D. (2000c). *The secret of the stones: A folktale* (J. Ransome, Illus.). New York: Phyllis Fogelman/Penguin Putnam.

San Souci, R.D. (2000d). *Six foolish fishermen* (D. Kennedy, Illus.). New York: Hyperion.

San Souci, R.D. (2002). *The silver charm: A folktale from Japan* (Y. Ito, Illus.). Garden City, NY: Doubleday.

San Souci, R.D. (2003). *Little Pierre: A Cajun story from Louisiana* (D. Catrow, Illus.). New York: Harcourt.

Schaefer, L.M. (2000). *This is the flower* (L.B. George, Illus.). New York: Greenwillow/HarperCollins.

Schaefer, L.M. (2001). *This is the rain* (J. Wattenberg, Illus.). New York: Greenwillow/HarperCollins.

Schwartz, A. (1999). *Old MacDonald*. New York: Scholastic.

Shannon, G. (1992). *A knock at the door* (J. Caroselli, Illus.). Phoenix, AZ: Oryx.

Shepard, A. (1998). *The crystal heart: A Vietnamese legend* (J.D. Fiedler, Illus.). New York: Atheneum.

Shepard, A. (2000). *Master man: A tall tale of Nigeria* (D. Wisniewski, Illus.). New York: HarperCollins.

Shepard, A. (2003). *The princess mouse: A tale of Finland* (L. Gore, Illus.). New York: Atheneum.

Shulman, L. (2002). *Old MacDonald had a woodshop* (A. Wolff, Illus.). New York: G.P. Putnam's Sons.

Sierra, J. (1995). *The house that Drac built* (W. Hillenbrand, Illus.). New York: Gulliver/Harcourt Brace.

Sierra, J. (1996). *Nursery tales around the world* (S. Vitale, Illus.). New York: Clarion.

Sierra, J. (1997). *Counting crocodiles* (W. Hillenbrand, Illus.). New York: Gulliver/Harcourt Brace.

Sierra, J. (1999). *The dancing pig* (J. Sweetwater, Illus.). New York: Gulliver/Harcourt Brace.

Sierra, J. (2002a). *Can you guess my name? Traditional tales around the world* (S. Vitale, Illus.). New York: Clarion.

Sierra, J. (2002b). *Silly & sillier* (V. Gorbachev, Illus.). New York: Knopf.

Singh, R. (1998). *The foolish men of Agra: And other tales of Mogul India* (F. Zaman, Illus.). Toronto: Key Porter Kids/Firefly.

Singh, R. (1999). *Moon tales* (D. Lush, Illus.). London: Bloomsbury.

Sloat, T. (1998). *There was an old lady who swallowed a trout!* (R. Ruffins, Illus.). New York: Henry Holt.

Souhami, J. (1999). *No dinner! The story of the old woman and the pumpkin*. New York: Marshall Cavendish.

Souhami, J. (2002). *Mrs. McCool and the giant Cuhullin*. New York: Henry Holt.

Spirin, G. (2002). *The tale of the firebird*. New York: Philomel.

Stevens, J. (1995). *Tops & bottoms*. New York: Harcourt Brace.

Stewig, J.W. (2001). *Mother Holly* (J. Westerman, Illus.). New York: North-South.

Stow, J. (1992). *The house that Jack built*. New York: Dial.

Swanson, D. (1992). *Why seals blow their noses: North American wildlife in fact and fiction* (D. Penhale, Illus.). Stillwater, MN: Voyageur.

Taback, S. (1997). *There was an old lady who swallowed a fly*. New York: Viking/Penguin.

Taback, S. (2002). *This is the house that Jack built*. New York: Putnam.

Tolstoy, A. (1998). *The gigantic turnip* (N. Sharkey, Illus.). Cambridge, MA: Barefoot Books.

Vogel, C.G. (1999). *Legends of landforms: Native America lore and the geology of the land*. Brookfield, CT: Millbrook.

Vogel, C.G. (2001). *Weather legends: Native American lore and the science of weather*. Brookfield, CT: Millbrook.

Wahl, J. (1999). *Little Johnny Buttermilk: After an old English folktale* (J. Mazzucco, Illus.). Little Rock, AR: August House.

Walker, R. (1998). *The Barefoot book of trickster tales* (C. Munoz, Illus.). Cambridge, MA: Barefoot Books.

Walker, R. (1999). *Jack and the beanstalk* (N. Sharkey, Illus.). Cambridge, MA: Barefoot Books.

Wallner, A. (1998). *The farmer in the dell*. New York: Holiday House.

Wargin, K. (1998). *The legend of Sleeping Bear* (G. van Frankenhuyzen, Illus.). Chelsea, MI: Sleeping Bear.

Wargin, K. (1999). *The legend of Mackinac Island* (G. van Frankenhuyzen, Illus.). Chelsea, MI: Sleeping Bear.

Wattenberg, J. (2000). *Henny-Penny*. New York: Scholastic.

Westcott, N.B. (1990). *There's a hole in the bucket*. New York: Harper & Row.

Whatley, B. (2001). *Wait, no paint!* New York: HarperCollins.

White, C. (1997). *Whuppity Stoorie: A Scottish folktale* (S.D. Schindler, Illus.). New York: G.P. Putnam's Sons.

Wiesner, D. (2001). *The three pigs*. New York: Clarion/Houghton Mifflin.

Willey, M. (2001). *Clever Beatrice: An upper peninsula conte* (H. Solomon, Illus.). New York: Atheneum.

Winter, J. (2000). *The house that Jack built*. New York: Dial.

Wolfson, M.O. (1999). *Turtle songs: A tale for mothers and daughters* (K. Sachi, Illus.). Hillsboro, OR: Beyond Words.

Wolkstein, D. (1999). *The glass mountain* (L. Bauer, Illus.). New York: Morrow Junior.

Wolkstein, D. (2001). *The day ocean came to visit* (S. Johnson & L. Fancher, Illus.). San Diego, CA: Gulliver/Harcourt.

Yeoman, J. (1994). *The do-it-yourself house that Jack built* (Q. Blake, Illus.). New York: Atheneum/Simon & Schuster.

Yep, L. (1997). *The dragon prince: A Chinese Beauty & the Beast tale* (K. Mak, Illus.). New York: HarperCollins.

Yohannes, G. (2002). *Silly Mammo: An Ethiopian tale* (B. Belachew, Illus.). Grand Forks, ND: EBCEF/African Sun.

Yolen, J. (1986). *Favorite folktales from around the world*. New York: Pantheon.

Yolen, J. (1990). *Tam Lin* (C. Mikolaycak, Illus.). New York: Harcourt Brace Jovanovich.

Yolen, J. (2002). *The firebird* (V. Vagin, Illus.). HarperCollins.

Young, E. (1989). *Lon Po Po: A Red-Riding Hood story from China*. New York: Philomel.

Young, E. (2000). *The hunter: A Chinese folktale*. New York: Atheneum.

Young, E. (2002). *What about me?* New York: Philomel.

Zelinsky, P.O. (1986). *Rumpelstiltskin*. New York: Dutton.

Zelinsky, P.O. (1997). *Rapunzel*. New York: Dutton.

Ziefert, H. (1998). *When I first came to this land* (S. Taback, Illus.). New York: G.P. Putnam's Sons.

CHAPTER 3

The Moral of the Story: Learning About Fables

Nancy J. Johnson and Angela Sorgatz Vroom

One of the most common connections across cultures, generations, and ages is moral stories, translated into life lessons. Although many of the lessons appear specific to a time period ("Always carry a dime in case troubles beset you and you need to call home"), the certainty is this: Every child has heard myriad lessons meant to guide him or her toward a more successful life, and every adult has found himself or herself in the position of telling children stories with explicit morals to encourage certain behaviors for good living. If any literary genre speaks to everyone, then it must certainly be the fable, because fables address problems faced in everyday life and introduce either a solution or a lesson to solve the problem.

Most frequently credited with the origination of fables is Aesop, a now-legendary Greek slave born in Phrygia around the year 620 B.C., who later lived on the island of Samos off the coast of Asia Minor. The specifics of his early life cannot be confirmed and are widely disputed. What is known is Aesop's knack for using fables to make a point, win an argument, or decide an issue. Credited as a teller of stories, Aesop eventually became famous for his logoi (Greek for legend) and the idea that he became a free man because of his storytelling abilities. Although it is difficult to ascertain much about the actual Aesop, his legacy rests in how he demonstrated that wisdom could be found in spare texts often cleverly disguised as entertaining stories. It is widely believed that Aesop never wrote down any of his fables and that when he died the remnants of his stories existed only in what others remembered of them. Over the next several generations, the tales passed from teller to teller, eventually being put into script as "recalled" interpretations. One can only imagine how many of his fables were lost.

But Aesop is not the only, or the original, teller of short tales with pithy messages. Until the mid-1950s, scholars traced Greek fables to a dual source in both Greek folklore and Indian literary fables known as the Fables of Bidpai. In the introduction to Barbara Bader's *Aesop & Company: With Scenes From His Legendary*

Life (1991), mention is made of the discovery of cuneiform tablets from 1800 B.C. tracing the origins of fables to ancient Sumeria, more than 10 centuries before the time Aesop supposedly lived. The Sumerian fables, similar to Aesop's, are brief stories, illustrative of truths, which makes sense given that ancient Sumerians were educated and maintained laws and a clear concept of justice. Somewhere along the line, these tales traveled through the ancient Near East through Asia Minor to mainland Greece, and they have since been credited to Aesop. They were first recorded in prose by Demetrious, Greek statesman and governor of Athens, in the fourth century B.C. in a handbook for writers and speakers. Later they appeared as poetry in ancient Greek collections and were eventually translated from Latin to French and then into English by William Caxton, England's first printer.

The pleasure of fables, then and now, is that they belong to no one time period, one country, or one social class or faction. It is said that fables were told by kings to instruct their sons in lessons of wise ruling (Bader, 1991). In addition, fables were also translated along with biblical psalms and stories by Martin Luther. They became the staple of 19th-century readers in the early United States and were told widely on the frontier. History notes that a young Abraham Lincoln recited them aloud in the evenings, wove them into courtroom statements as a lawyer, and referred to them directly throughout his presidential years, including reference to Aesop's fable of the bundle of sticks when he appealed for party unity during the 1853 election (Bader, 1991).

Both orally and in print, fables made their way around the world years before the American colonies were founded and are still retold today. Evidence exists that some were translated from Spanish into Nahuatl, the Aztec language, including fables told by the Ojibwa of what is now northern Minnesota. Spanish and Portuguese missionaries brought fables with them to Japan. African fables include tales of native animals in contests of the smart against the stupid, and Philippine fables appear with the familiar animal characters of the fox, crow, squirrel, and hawk.

What Are Fables and Why Do They Still Exist Today?

Although variants exist across the ages, the common elements of most fables are what make them easily told and accessible to today's readers. They are concise, told in a narrative form, include few characters (often talking animals exhibiting human behaviors), and seek to convey a hidden lesson, usually intended to improve human conduct. They have been written in voluminous collections, retold through text and illustration in single editions, and recast with voice, sound, and image for film and television. Every publication season, newly told and illustrated variants appear, keeping alive age-old lessons and the genre of the fable.

Perhaps the most natural reason fables exist today is because of their universal appeal and easy adaptability. Many everyday expressions have been taken from these stories. Not only do fables echo life lessons but they also tell universal truths and present themes prevalent in life and in all genres of literature. In addition, the human belief that actions result in consequences can be taught and reinforced clearly through the medium of the fable.

Some Recommended Fables

Most library shelves house both illustrated single fables and collections, with Aesop's tales dominating what is available. Although many of these collections will be older editions, a surprising wealth of fables illustrated by fine artists, featuring lively and beautifully illustrated variants, are published annually. In recent years, fable accessibility has been enhanced by publishers' attention to retellings, specifically featuring fables told and retold in diverse cultures and through the telling of original, often modernized, versions.

The fables featured in this chapter are presented by format (collections or single fable books) and categorized as either retold or original fables. The challenges in creating such distinctions include determining whether an author is actually retelling or presenting a true variant of a known fable or whether the fable is original, even though it includes familiar characters or situations. Where they exist, author and illustrator notes or source notes have guided these determinations, but not all books include this information. When this information was unavailable, we relied on our best judgment as to how to categorize the book.

Retold Collected Fables

Aesop & Company features 19 of Aesop's familiar fables retold by Barbara Bader from recent translations. Each of the spare, crisply told narratives concludes with the explicit moral set off in bold italicized font. Bader includes a lengthy introduction that provides a thoughtful history of Aesop's fables and concludes the collection with further information on Aesop's legendary life. The fables are illuminated by Arthur Geisert's black-lined etchings on sepia-toned backgrounds and convey distinct personalities and detailed settings.

In his compilation titled *Aesop's Fables* (2000), Jerry Pinkney has collected "some of the best well-known and lesser-known" Aesop's fables, inspired by the effect these fables had on his own life. Each of the 61 retellings is accompanied by its one-line moral set off at the bottom of the page, as well as by a stunning illustration created by Pinkney for the book. It is the art that gives this book such great appeal. The realistic illustrations, done in pencil, colored pencil, and watercolors, are richly detailed and capture the essence of each fable.

Aesop's fables meet Aztec interpretation in John Bierhorst's *Doctor Coyote: A Native American Aesop's Fables* (1987). Translated from a 16th-century adaptation of Aesop's fables, these tales give Coyote, a well-known trickster, a prominent role. The tales follow Coyote as he lives and grows, made wiser by his adventures. He never stops using tricks, but in the end, his tricks are centered less on personal gain and more on what is right or good. Wendy Watson's pen-and-ink with watercolor illustrations are inspired by "on location" scenes from New Mexico, adding to the authentic feel of these Coyote fables.

With its simple, pointed tales reflective in design, *Demi's Reflective Fables* (Demi, 1988) is as much a work of art as it is a retelling of traditional Chinese fables. Not only do the stories themselves promote reflection with their corresponding morals, but Demi also has included a Mylar mirror on the front jacket flap which can be used to literally reflect the art that accompanies each fable. Meant to inspire deeper thinking, the mirror covers the story and leaves only the art open to view— two views, as it is reflected in the mirror. The art is detailed and insightful; it adds to the meanings of the fables and helps portray the reflective nature of the morals.

Original Collected Fables

With its alliterative, lyrical prose, Julius Lester's *Ackamarackus: Julius Lester's Sumptuously Silly Fantastically Funny Fables* (2001) begs to be read aloud. Each of these six original fables is accompanied by two morals that are sometimes serious, sometimes silly, but always right in line with the story. After all, what other moral would fit with the fable of "How Bernard the Bee Lost His Buzz" than "Why buzz when you can balalaika?" or the punny "Always be all that you can bee"? Emilie Chollat's acrylic and collage illustrations add zest to the fables and show the animal characters in all their idiosyncratic glory.

Arnold Lobel has crafted 20 original stories in his book *Fables* (1980), which offers such morals as "Without a doubt, there is such a thing as too much order" and "Even the taking of small risks will add excitement to life." More modern in their wording than most fables, these fables and morals seem to delve into specific aspects of life, such as "A child's conduct will reflect the ways of his parents." Each fable is one page in length, with the moral offset in italics at the bottom and an accompanying illustration on the facing page. Lobel's watercolor and pen-and-ink illustrations complement the fables and show a key scene from each, giving the reader a strong visual and humorous interpretation of the text.

Many young children have been delighted with Leo Lionni's classic animal picture books. These include tales about Frederick the field mouse whose wisdom helped his family endure the dark days of winter, Alexander the house mouse who learned the magic of friendship, Swimmy the minnow whose imagination proved how being small can be used in big ways, and a fish who realizes his small pond isn't such a bad place to live. While the morals in each of these stories are not explicitly stated, their wise lessons come through clearly in Lionni's collage-rich tellings. *Frederick and His Friends: Four Favorite Fables by Leo Lionni* (2002) compiles these four original fables into one collection, accompanied by a companion CD featuring a lively recording of each story.

Any book by Jon Scieszka and Lane Smith is guaranteed to be fun to read and view. In *Squids Will Be Squids: Fresh Morals, Beastly Fables* (1998), Scieszka and Smith have taken the familiar world of the fable and brought it to life with modern morals and quirky characters. Readers will love such tales as "Elephant and Mosquito," which ends with the sensible moral "Don't ever listen to a talking bug." That's just good advice, and similar words of wisdom abound in this book. Even the "serious historical foreword" and "very serious historical afterword" have morals to them. Smith's illustrations lend themselves to the humor of the writing, and his unique perspective adds to the personality of the characters.

Retold Single Fables

Janet Stevens brings new life to the familiar fable *The Tortoise and the Hare* (1984) by creating two very distinct personalities for these well-known characters. The story takes place in a quiet animal neighborhood where Hare—rude, loud, and obnoxious—browbeats Tortoise into racing him. Tortoise, meek and mild, needs the encouragement of his friends to reluctantly accept Hare's challenge. What follows, of course, is that Hare, cocky and self-assured, ends up losing the race to Tortoise, who is slow and steady. Stevens's watercolor and colored pencil illustrations show Hare at his brassy best and Tortoise as a shy figure, encouraging readers to cheer on Tortoise and rejoice in Hare's expected downfall.

Caroline Repchuk's *The Race* (2002) is another lively retelling of the familiar tortoise and hare fable. Written in rhyming couplets, the fable follows Tortoise and Hare as they race around the world from England to New York, taking the long route. This story is great fun to read aloud, as the rhythm lends itself well to voice, yet looking at the illustrations also adds to the story. Alison Jay uses alkyd paint with crackle-glaze varnish to produce humorous, detailed pictures that flow with the story and keep the reader turning the page. Even the picture postcards sent by Hare to Pig and Goose back home tell part of the tale. The endpapers also are designed cleverly to illustrate before and after shots of Hare's and Tortoise's suitcases.

Pat Mora's fable *The Race of Toad and Deer* (2001) is a retelling of a Mayan fable that mirrors the tortoise and the hare theme. Mora's text, however, focuses on how teamwork (a positive attribute) wins the race, rather than how pride and vanity (negative attributes) lead to losing. Although the deer is vain, this is not what makes him lose; rather, the tricky teamwork and steady hopping of the toads lead to the deer's losing. Mora also has intermingled key Spanish words within the text, adding to the atmosphere of the story. Domi's vibrant watercolors, appearing as double-page spreads, reflect the culture of the telling and enliven the text as the reader follows the race between toad and deer.

Book cover from *The Race* copyright © 2002 by Caroline Repchuk, illustrated by Alison Jay. Used by permission of Chronicle Books LLC, San Francisco.

What happened to Hare after his fateful race with Tortoise? In *Tops & Bottoms* (1995), Janet Stevens provides an answer. Fast-talking, sly Hare has new troubles—he lost his land to Tortoise and now has no income or food for his family. Meanwhile, their neighbor, wealthy, lazy Bear, spends all his time sleeping while his land lies fallow. So Hare and Mrs. Hare come up with a plan—they will plant, water, and weed Bear's land and split the profits with him. They even let Bear choose whether he wants to plant tops or bottoms. As Hare tricks, tricks, and tricks again, Bear becomes increasingly angry and awake. In the end, both Bear and Hare have learned their lessons. Stevens's delightful illustrations appear as double-page spreads from top to bottom. The art is watercolor, colored pencil, and gesso on handmade paper; the drawings illuminate Hare's energy and exaggerate Bear's laziness, showcasing a number of ways it is possible for Bear to drape himself across the porch chair.

Jim Aylesworth retells the fable of Tricky Fox, a sly fellow who bets his brother that he can fool a human into giving him a pig in a sack, in this newer version of *The Tale of Tricky Fox* (2001). Brother Fox claims no one can pull off such a trick and says he'll eat his hat if Tricky Fox can do it. Tricky Fox sets his sights on the first victim, a kindly older lady who takes him in for the night. Playing the part of a tired, feeble fox, he promises no tricks; he just wants to sleep. His only concern is his sack—he "don't like for anyone to look in it." That well-placed line leads to a chain of events, wherein Tricky Fox works his way up to getting that pig. Yet not all his victims are as easy to fool, and, though the end of the story isn't such a surprise, the moral is funny and fresh. Barbara McClintock's illustrations, rendered in watercolor, black ink, and gouache, capture the tone of old nursery rhyme books with muted colors and a lot of lines.

Three Samurai Cats: A Story From Japan (Kimmel, 2003) is a retold fable featuring a daimyo (a powerful lord) whose castle is no longer his own. Instead it has been inhabited by a nasty rat, oblivious to traps, poison, and guard dogs. Seeking outside wisdom to vanquish the rodent, the daimyo travels to a famous shrine renowned for its skilled fighters, all samurai cats. The first samurai is quickly defeated. The second slinks away after his amazing swordsmanship is outmatched by the rat's lightning kick. The third samurai cat eventually arrives at the castle, but his decrepit appearance leaves the daimyo concerned. Weeks pass and the samurai does little but eat and sleep while the bold rat becomes a bigger pest. Then one day, the rat's greed entraps him. Borrowing from the stories of Zen masters, the lesson to "Draw strength from stillness and learn to act without acting" concludes this fable accompanied by Mordicai Gerstein's expressive and colorful illustrations, rendered using pen and ink with oil paint.

Amy Lowry Poole takes the fable of *The Ant and the Grasshopper* (2000) and places it in the summer palace of the Imperial Chinese Emperor. Grasshopper, fun-loving and carefree, entertains the Emperor, Empress, and their guests throughout the summer with his music. The ants, of course, work steadily all summer long, ignoring the grasshopper's calls to play. The grasshopper and the ants each keep to their routines, with the expected results. While the weather is warm and the food abundant, Grasshopper enjoys his life. Yet when the weather turns cool and the Emperor and his household leave, Grasshopper has ample time to wish he had heeded the advice of the ants. The story ends on a different note than usual. Instead of being taken in by the ants, Grasshopper's future is uncertain as the last page leaves him huddled alone in the empty palace courtyard. Lowry's illustrations, applied with ink and gouache on rice paper, add a distinct style to the tale.

Elizabeth Dahlie's *Bernelly & Harriet: The Country Mouse and the City Mouse* (2002) updates the classic fable by telling the story of two mouse cousins: Bernelly, a country mouse who loves spending time outdoors teaching fly fishing and tying flies, and Harriet, a famous artist who paints in her cozy apartment in the city. When Bernelly's boots spring a leak, she travels to the city to visit her cousin and go shopping. Certain that city life is the best, Harriet overwhelms her cousin with visits to the museum, the ballet, and fancy stores. Reciprocating as hostess, Bernelly invites her cousin to a relaxing visit in the country. While each mouse tries to appreciate the other's life, they find happiness in their very own homes. Dahlie's lively and affectionate gouache pastel paintings capture the best of both mouse worlds.

Based on the fable poem "The Blind Men and the Elephant" by John Godfrey Saxe (see Felleman, 1936), Ed Young creates a picture book that speaks about the nature of wisdom in *Seven Blind Mice* (1992). The mice in question, living together near a pond, are startled one day to find "a strange Something" there. Each takes a turn to investigate this Something, and each returns with a different idea of what it is.

Red Mouse is certain it is a pillar, but Green Mouse insists it is a snake. As the week nears its end and six of the mice have each declared a different idea about the Something, they argue about the nature of the beast. It takes the careful exploration of White Mouse to finally settle the debate. Young's colorful cut-paper collage and watercolor illustrations are made all the more vibrant by their placement on black backgrounds. The simplicity of design allows the reader to experience what the mice experience—glimpses of parts of the Something—and not until the end, in a double-page spread, is the entire picture shown.

Young brings to life another fable about knowledge in *What About Me?* (2002), a retelling of a Sufi teaching tale. This Middle Eastern tale centers on a young boy who wants knowledge but does not know how to get it. He seeks out a Grand Master and asks the question, "How may I gain a little bit of your knowledge?" The Grand Master requests that the boy bring him a small carpet. Unquestioning, the boy sets off immediately. The carpet maker, however, will not give the boy a carpet for nothing; he tells him to first find some thread. The boy's search takes him to a chain of people, each asking, "What about me?" and placing a new demand on him in order to complete his quest and gain the carpet. The boy's unceasing devotion to his task pays off in the end; he gains his knowledge, yet not in the manner he thought he would. Young's collage and watercolor illustrations, set against a textured background, vividly show the boy's journey toward knowledge.

With a strong message that all must work together in order to succeed in life, young readers will enjoy Won-Ldy Paye and Margaret H. Lippert's *Head, Body, Legs: A Story From Liberia* (2002). This retold tale begins, "Long ago, Head was all by himself," and suggests how he rolls from place to place, eating only what can be reached on the ground but hungering for sweet cherries beyond his reach. When he meets two Arms, he convinces them to form a partnership in order to pick and eat the cherries. So they eat until they're satisfied and then spy a luscious mango tree across the river. Head and Arms then meet and attach to Body and finally team up with Legs in order to negotiate on tiptoe to pick the delicious mangoes. Julie Paschkis's bright-colored backgrounds, decorative borders, and stylized black body shapes perfectly echo this silly and strange fable of cooperation from Liberia's Dan people.

Original Single Fables

Original fables, like the literary folk tales in which known authors use traditional conventions to create new stories, have become increasingly common. Teachers and students delight in comparing these new fables with more traditional ones. Reading original fables also has inspired many students to create their own.

Walter Dean Myers offers the original fable *The Story of the Three Kingdoms* (1995). The kingdoms of the forest, the sea, and the air are ruled by the Elephant, the Shark, and the Hawk, respectively. Each believes his kingdom to be the greatest and challenges the other two to enter his kingdom and test his power, so he might prove that his kingdom is best. But none of the three will venture into each other's kingdoms. The issue might never be resolved but for the advent of the People. Laughed at by the three rulers at first, the People do not seem made for greatness. Yet by sharing their stories and the resulting wisdom, the People find a way to live within the three kingdoms alongside the ruling animals. Ashley Bryan's illustrations add intense color and beautiful designs to this fable.

Several of Aesop's fables feature the fox, sometimes crafty, sometimes silly. Aki Sogabe has woven all the fox fables into one story—a day in the fox's life—in her beautifully redesigned *Aesop's Fox* (1999). The story begins with Fox searching for breakfast on a summer morning, a search that will bring him many adventures throughout the day, ending only at nightfall. The morals of the fables are woven into the story as Fox's thoughts or dialogue or, alternatively, as the dialogue of his animal compatriots, which include Rooster, Boar, Crow, Leopard, Old Lion, Deer, Donkey, and Raccoon. Some of these friends dispense advice to Fox, and some are the recipients of advice from him. Sogabe's cut paper, airbrush, and watercolor illustrations shine throughout the story as they set the scene and add details to the narrative.

Another original fable, Jeff Brumbeau's *The Quiltmaker's Gift* (2000), speaks of the true nature of happiness. A woman, living on a mountaintop for longer than anyone can recall, crafts the most beautiful quilts ever seen. But these quilts cannot be bought. Instead they are given away to those in need. A greedy king, enraged to learn the woman has never given him one of her beautiful quilts, journeys to the mountaintop to demand one. She agrees to give him one on the condition that he first gives away everything he owns. A battle of wills follows, culminating with the king's reluctant generosity. As he travels his world, making gifts of his treasures, the king also takes a journey of self-discovery, leading him to understand what makes him truly happy. Gail de Marcken's watercolor illustrations lend rich vitality to this original fable as she captures the scenes from both the quiltmaker's and the king's perspectives.

Classroom Activities

- Read aloud and discuss paired fables (e.g., pair an Aesop's fable with a retelling), focusing on features of the fables that are the same and features that differ. Using a Venn diagram, create a class chart demonstrating similarities/differences. Then invite students to work individually or in teams to pair another Aesop's fable with a retelling and to create a Venn diagram of their own.

- Examine the worldwide influence of fables by placing a large world map on the classroom wall. Then, as each fable is read, create a notecard recording the title of the fable, the name of its author/illustrator, and its country of origin or retelling. Tape each notecard to the wall outside the map, and use colored yarn and thumbtacks to connect the card to the corresponding country.

- Compare three or more variants of a fable, such as "The Tortoise and the Hare," on a motif chart (see Figure 3.1).

- After reading a variety of fables with the class, develop a list of common elements reflected by most fables (short narratives, few main characters [may include talking animals], concludes with a lesson or moral). Then, create a class list of life lessons students have heard on a regular basis (e.g., be kind to your friends *and* enemies; treat other people as you would like them to treat you; do not always wish you lived someone else's life; do not whine when you don't get your way). Ask students to write original fables to teach these lessons, working independently or in pairs. Suggest that they begin by choosing a moral or lesson, either from the class list or

Figure 3.1
Motif Chart for "The Tortoise and the Hare" Variants

Title	Author/Reteller	Main Characters	Problem	Lesson Learned
The Tortoise and the Hare	Janet Stevens	Tortoise Hare	Cocky Hare browbeats Tortoise into a race he doesn't think he can win.	Slow and steady wins the race.
The Race of Toad and Deer	Pat Mora	Toad Deer	How can Toad win a race against a much faster Deer?	Teamwork and persistence win the race.

by borrowing a moral they have read about in fables. Have students outline the plot and include characters that will move the plot toward an effective conclusion. Encourage the writing of a rough draft, reading aloud to guide revision, editing, and writing a final manuscript. Suggest that students illustrate their fables, and then bind all fables in a class-published book. (See Figure 3.2 for a fifth-grade example.)

- Invite students to retell an age-old fable in their own words. These can be prepared for oral storytelling or written down and illustrated to make into class books.

- Compare the illustrations of three (or more) variants of the same fable. Discuss what media the illustrators used, how the illustrations interpreted and extended ideas in the text, what dominant colors were used and for what effect, how different illustrators depicted the same character, and even how artists from various time periods interpret the same fable differently.

- Dramatize fables for younger audiences, either by writing and acting out short scripts or by writing and producing puppet plays.

Figure 3.2
Fifth-Grade Student Fable

BLACK COW AND WHITE COW

Once in a pasture two cows were a'wandering. Well one cow was black and one was shite so their mothers wouldn't let the two cows talk. But while the white cow's mother was shopping the little white cow went up to the little black cow and said, "I'm white and white is a better color than black." So again the quarrel was started. The next day the little black cow said, "Yesterday, you said you were better but I KNOW I'm better." They both thought they were best. And they both really were.

Moral: The color shouldn't interfer with your friends.

Figure 3.3
Quilt Square

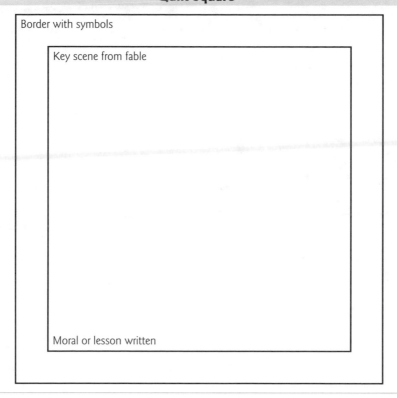

Border with symbols

Key scene from fable

Moral or lesson written

- Create a fables story quilt, with each student designing a quilt square to represent a favorite fable. Using 9" × 9" paper squares with 1-inch borders, encourage students to select a dominant color for the border background and a significant symbol (or symbols) to replicate throughout their borders. Have them select one scene from the fable to represent in the middle of the quilt square and write out the moral or lesson of the fable at the bottom of the square. (Figure 3.3 provides a quilt square template.)

Conclusion

Often enjoyable as read-alouds, fables can inspire original writing, prompt comparison and analysis, and invite examination of stories across cultures. Learning about fables creates opportunities to experience wise or clever solutions to common problems. Whether they appear in collections or as individual stories, whether they are retold or original versions, fables offer readers simple truths and good advice. Their morals are easily understood and apply to all lives, making them timeless.

CHILDREN'S BOOKS CITED

Aylesworth, J. (2001). *The tale of tricky fox* (B. McClintock, Illus.). New York: Scholastic.

Bader, B. (1991). *Aesop & company: With scenes from his legendary life* (A. Geisert, Illus.). Boston: Houghton Mifflin.

Bierhorst, J. (1987). *Doctor coyote: A Native American Aesop's fables* (W. Watson, Illus.). New York: Macmillan.

Brumbeau, J. (2000). *The quiltmaker's gift* (G. de Marcken, Illus.). New York: Scholastic.

Dahlie, E. (2002). *Bernelly & Harriet: The country mouse and the city mouse*. Boston: Little, Brown.

Demi. (1988). *Demi's reflective fables*. New York: Grosset and Dunlap.

Felleman, H. (Ed.). (1936). *The best loved poems of the American people*. New York: Doubleday.

Kimmel, E.A. (2003). *Three samurai cats: A story from Japan* (M. Gerstein, Illus.). New York: Holiday House.

Lester, J. (2001). *Ackamarackus: Julius Lester's sumptuously silly fantastically funny fables* (E. Chollat, Illus.). New York: Scholastic.

Lionni, L. (2002). *Frederick and his friends: Four favorite fables by Leo Lionni*. New York: Knopf.

Lobel, A. (1980). *Fables*. New York: Harper & Row.

Mora, P. (2001). *The race of toad and deer* (Domi, Illus.). Toronto: Groundwood.

Myers, W.D. (1995). *The story of the three kingdoms* (A. Bryan, Illus.). New York: HarperCollins.

Paye, W., & Lippert, M.H. (2002). *Head, body, legs: A story from Liberia* (J. Paschkis, Illus.). New York: Henry Holt.

Pinkney, J. (2000). *Aesop's fables*. New York: SeaStar.

Poole, A.L. (2000). *The ant and the grasshopper*. New York: Holiday House.

Repchuk, C. (2002). *The race* (A. Jay, Illus.). San Francisco: Chronicle.

Scieszka, J. (1998). *Squids will be squids: Fresh morals, beastly fables* (L. Smith, Illus.). New York: Viking.

Sogabe, A. (1999). *Aesop's fox*. San Diego: Browndeer/ Harcourt.

Stevens, J. (1984). *The tortoise and the hare*. New York: Scholastic.

Stevens, J. (1995). *Tops & bottoms*. San Diego: Harcourt Brace.

Young, E. (1992). *Seven blind mice*. New York: Philomel.

Young, E. (2002). *What about me?* New York: Philomel.

CHAPTER 4

Mythology: A Cosmic Theater

Sam L. Sebesta and Dianne L. Monson

yths are the oldest stories. Oldest of all are myths of creation. These stories tell of the forming of Earth and sky, the birth of gods and goddesses, and the beginnings of humankind. Then come other myths of gods, heroes and gods, and ordinary people who encountered gods and monsters and tricksters.

To early "people who are without writing" (Levi-Strauss, 1999, p. 19), these stories were real; they were believed. They were so numerous and connected that they formed a powerful network of belief akin to telepathy among members of a community (Moffett, 1991). As time went by, myth mixed with history. Stories that are today called legends sprouted from distantly remembered incidents, but they still had the aura of myth. (See chapter 5 for a detailed discussion of legends.)

Even with "the waning of the gods and the fading of the voices" (Moffett, 1991, p. 831), mythology persisted. It continued to inspire painting, sculpture, architecture, dance, and poetry. Borrowings from mythology permeate the English language, including words such as *chaos*, *cosmos*, *fury*, and derivatives of *geo-*; dinosaur names; names of planets; and names attached to products such as *Ajax*, *atlas*, *Mercury*, and *Saturn*. In fact, Isaac Asimov (1961) filled a book with terms borrowed from Greek and Roman mythology; a second thick volume also could be created to cite language derived from the mythologies of other cultures. And mythology has found a growing audience through the medium of literature for the young.

In the next section of this chapter, we define and distinguish between the terms *myth* and *legend*.

Defining Mythology

What is myth, and what is not? Sometimes the term is applied loosely, as in "the myth of living happily ever after." Sometimes, narrowly, it denotes only the stories about ancient gods and goddesses, especially those with a "message" to guide human behavior. Hence "the message sets myths apart from ordinary stories" (Bellingham,

2001, p. 7). Likewise, Paul Goble (1999), after noting that "myth has come to mean a fairy tale created to entertain children," insists on myth "in its true sense of 'sacred story.'"

One attribute assigned to myth is that it explains origins, especially those stories telling how gods and goddesses created Earth, parts of Earth, and Earth's creatures. But when does a pourquoi (origin story) cease being a myth and become a folk tale, a story from "the folk"? The delineation is vague, especially in modern collections. The anthology *Cats of Myth* (Hausman & Hausman, 2000) commences, in fact, with an East Indian selection labeled "folk tale." In *The Crystal Pool* (1999), renowned collector Geraldine McCaughrean labels as myth the battle between Porcupine and Beaver ("A Prickly Situation") and an earthly Japanese tale titled "Dear Dog," although neither story seems to contain the superbeings or exalted settings often associated with myth. And in the Introduction to her classic collection *Greek Myths*, Olivia Coolidge (2001) apparently uses the terms *myth*, *legend*, and *tale* interchangeably.

So the term *myth* seems nebulous, its "correct" application depending on the particular characteristics in the eye of the beholder or compiler. Yet there does seem to be a distinctive tone of myth. Edith Hamilton (1942) asserts, "The myths as we have them are the creation of great poets" (p. 14). Others point to the literary evolution of myths, whether through the manuscripts of epics or through generations of expert tellers. Perhaps in cosmic scale and exalted tone, myth maintains its distinction.

Why Mythology Now?

Fifty years ago, myths for children generally came from Greek, Roman, and Norse sources. Critic Lillian Smith (1953) expressed the prevalent opinion held by myth-givers: "Those of the Greeks have been found to exceed all others in beauty of imagination, in poetic conception, and in grace of expression" (p. 65). Furthermore, the appropriate age for appreciating myths was deemed to be the intermediate years and above.

In contrast, today's offerings of mythology for children and young adults cover six continents and the spaces between. (So far, no myths have been collected from Antarctica, but perhaps this is only a matter of time.) In the current *Subject Guide to Children's Books in Print* (2002), 243 volumes of mythology are listed: 122 of these are *not* exclusively Greek, Roman, or Norse. Clearly, to mythographers and children's literature transmitters, the myth world is well-rounded and fully represented.

As a result, today's collections of myths for children encourage comparison and contrast. Northrop Frye (1964) refers to "the shape of mythology" following "the rhythm of the sun and the seasons," where "the same literary patterns turn up within different cultures" (p. 112). For example, *The Illustrated Book of Myths* (Philip,

1995) presents creation myths from Egypt, Serbia, Scandinavia, China, Japan, Australia, Iran, the Americas, and Sumeria, all grouped together so that a reader or listener may comprehend the common purpose yet appreciate the inventive diversity of these far-flung cultural representations. As this reteller observes, "When you begin to compare all these stories, a fascinating pattern begins to emerge" (p. 9).

Nor are myths today limited to older readers. Look at *The Star-Bearer: A Creation Myth From Ancient Egypt* (Hofmeyr, 2001) or *The Shark God* (Martin, 2001), a monster-turned-beneficent myth from Hawaii. The first presents small, simplified figures like hieroglyphs; the second shows forms immense and real. There is no doubt that both of these single-myth picture books must be labeled "all ages." Ancient, honest, and nondidactic, myths testify to the "oneness" of humanity, simultaneously proving the wonder of diversity. Modern editions make them accessible to all ages.

At this writing, myths are on Broadway and are having a successful run, especially due to Mary Zimmerman's (2002) dramatization of Ovid's *Metamorphoses* (Greek-Roman myths collected by Ovid in the time of the Emperor Augustus). What has astonished critics and theatergoers is the power of myth today to open the theater of the imagination.

In this production, an actor playing Poseidon, god of the sea, stands at one side of the stage pouring water from a bucket onto a toy ship. At stage center, an actor playing the captain of the ship writhes in a pool of water. He struggles against imagined breakers— and drowns.

The audience gasps at the action, then at itself, realizing how fully these seemingly disconnected bits of business have awakened imagination. For a moment, the credibility of myth is palpable, as it must have been in an early age, all hanging on a suggested incident while, as one critic puts it, "the spectator's wish to believe does the rest" (Gurewitsch, 2001, p. 6).

In a similar manner, those who read or listen to myths may call on imagination to build cosmic

Book cover from *The Crystal Pool: Myths and Legends of the World* by Geraldine McCaughrean, illustrated by Bee Willey. Jacket illustration copyright © 1999 Bee Willey. Used with the permission of Margaret K. McElderry Books, an imprint of Simon & Schuster Children's Publishing Division.

scenery, view cosmic action, and consider cosmic order and harmony. Pangu, in China, stretches up to separate sky from Earth, his body forming mountains and the moon. Danu, in Ireland, sends her subjects underground to become the Faery people in a Land of Youth. Or some new myth emerges from Guatemala, from newly discovered cave paintings of the Maya (Wilford, 2002).

Even young readers (or, perhaps, especially young readers) distinguish between this exercise of the literary imagination and what they learn to accept as reality. In fact, the ability to project the imagination lies at the heart of the humanities and of a rich life of understanding and empathy. Mythology awakens and exercises the literary imagination on a cosmic scale.

Sources of Myths

Creation Stories

Creation stories are found in the mythology of virtually every culture. *Misoso: Once Upon a Time Tales From Africa* (Aardema, 1994) is an excellent source of myths from that continent. A full-color map in the book shows the origins of these tales, from Sierra Leone on Africa's west coast to the Niger and Ghana, Gabon, Namibia, and on down to South Africa. The first tale, from the Temne people of Sierra Leone, tells of a time when the Earth was begun but not finished and describes how crying came into the world. A number of the other tales in this collection are pourquoi explanations for natural events.

In the Beginning (Hamilton, 1988) is a book of creation myths from a variety of cultures, illustrated with striking paintings by Barry Moser. The collection includes creation myths from North America, Melanesia, Guinea, Russia, Africa, Australian Aborigines, Babylon, Central America, Polynesia, Micronesia, Egypt, India, the Old Testament of the Bible, Greece, and the Icelandic Edda. Included are stories of the Egyptian god Ra; the Greek personages Zeus and Pandora; the Frost Giant from the Norse (Icelandic) Edda; Nejambi the Creator, from Zambia; Karora the Creator, from the Australian Aborigines; and Earth Starter the Creator, from the Maidu Indians of California.

Following are other sources you might want to examine:

The Spring Equinox: Celebrating the Greening of the Earth (Jackson, 2002)—tales from plains Cree, Maya, Romans, Indians, Iranians, Jews, and modern-day Europeans

The Wonderful Sky Boat and Other Native American Tales of the Southeast (Curry, 2001)

The Great Canoe: A Karina Legend (Maggi, 2001)—a Venezuelan tale

Spirit of the Cedar People: More Stories and Paintings of Chief Lelooska (Lelooska, 1998)—northwest coast Indian tales

The Fire Children: A West African Creation Tale (Maddern, 1993)

Tibetan Folk Tales (Hyde-Chambers & Hyde-Chambers, 1981)

The Star-Bearer: A Creation Myth From Ancient Egypt (Hofmeyr & Daly, 2001)

Dreamtime: Aboriginal Stories (Oodgeroo, 1993)

Humor is an important element in many pourquoi tales. Good examples of this are found in *How the Guinea Fowl Got Her Spots: A Swahili Tale of Friendship* (Knutson, 1996), *How Many Spots Does a Leopard Have? And Other Tales* (Lester, 1989), and *Head, Body, Legs: A Story From Liberia* (Paye & Lippert, 2002).

Gods and Goddesses

If stories about creation are the backbone of mythology, the gods, goddesses, and other amazing creatures are necessary to carry the action forward into new realms. *Gods, Goddesses, and Monsters: An Encyclopedia of World Mythology* (Keenan, 2000) is a well-written compilation of myths. It is organized by regions of the world and includes Far Eastern, African, Egyptian, Australian, and Celtic mythology. In this volume, the characters are categorized as divine beings, fearless herocs and tricksters, ferocious monsters, and magical animals.

Ingri and Edgar Parin D'Aulaire have written and illustrated two classic collections: *D'Aulaires' Book of Greek Myths* (1962) and *D'Aulaires' Norse Gods and Giants* (1986). The fine illustrations underscore the tone of each volume. Their treatment of Greek myths includes a family tree showing the primary gods, beginning with Gaea (Earth) and Uranus (sky), who are the parents of the six Titans and their wives and of the three Cyclopes. The stone etchings shown in the book give a strong visual effect. They introduce the Norse myths with a double-page spread at the beginning of the book showing the nine Norse worlds. Midgard, the Earth, lies between the higher worlds of the gods and Hel and Niflheim of the underworld. In their introduction, the D'Aulaires credit the Icelandic Prose Edda (tales from Viking mythology) and Poetic Edda (poems of the Vikings) as the major sources.

Gods and Goddesses of the Ancient Norse (Fisher, 2001) stands out as an eminently readable and strikingly illustrated introduction to Norse mythology. The endpapers show a map of the Scandinavian lands, a family tree for the Norse gods and goddesses, a pronunciation guide, and a short bibliography of other resources to visit to learn more about the topic. Fisher introduces each member of this family, beginning with Hela, goddess of death. The final pages describe the final battle to take place between the gods and their enemies, the giants of Jotunheim—the battle called Ragnarok, which would result in the death of all the gods by the hand of the last two giants, who would then devour the sun, moon, and stars, bringing an end to the universe. The Norse believed, however, that this would lead to a new universe where gods and goddesses would rule a world free from evil, an interesting conclusion to an otherwise devastating tale.

Stories From the Silk Road (Gilchrist, 1999) is a collection from quite another part of the world. The Silk Road was a main thoroughfare since ancient times for travelers from Xi'an to Tehran. The book includes a map of the ancient trade route where West meets East and explores the movement of stories from Europe to Damascus to Samarkand, to Kashgar and to Xi'an, through Persia, Afghanistan, and Tibet, to China. It reflects the lives of people living in these mountain and desert kingdoms and the mythologies that sprang from their tales. This compilation includes mythical beings such as dragons as well as powerful gods such as the Dragon King, the Thunder God, and the Sand God. It is an excellent read-aloud book.

In *The Mystery of the Maya: Uncovering the Lost City of Palenque* (Lourie, 2001), maps and photos help to trace the history of Mayan civilization in the remote jungles of Mexico and Central America. The Mayan mythological civilization was made up of three layers: the Underworld, the Middleworld where the Maya lived, and the Heavens, home of powerful gods. The gods of the Maya were many, including the god of corn and the god of rain. This is an informational book rather than a story collection.

Wings (Myers, 2000) is a fantastic retelling of the Icarus myth. It casts the main character as Ikarus Jackson, whose large wings set him apart from other children, who think him strange. In the hands of this storyteller, we know that he is amazing and wonderful, not odd.

Following are other interesting accounts of the deities:

The Book of Goddesses (Waldherr, 1995)—represents 19 cultures and includes African, Javanese, Welsh, Hawaiian, Sumerian, Tibetan, Indian, Aborigine, Cuban, and Slavic myths

Marriage of the Rain Goddess: A South African Myth (Wolfson, 1996)—a Zulu tale

The Shark God (Martin, 2001)—a Hawaiian tale

Atalanta's Race: A Greek Myth (Climo, 1995)

Odin's Family: Myths of the Vikings (Philip, 1996)

Tricksters

Few can resist the humor and sheer fun of trickster tales. *A Ring of Tricksters* (Hamilton, 1997) is one not to miss because it is a terrific read-aloud. The author gives readers 11 trickster tales from North America, the West Indies, and Africa, along with an interesting section that includes regional descriptions and explanations about the development of each tale.

Jabuti the Tortoise: A Trickster Tale From the Amazon (McDermott, 2001) is good storytelling enhanced by stunning illustrations. In this story of how colorful birds were created, Jabutí the trickster is a victim, tricked by Vulture, who offers to carry the tortoise on his back to a festival of heaven for all the birds of the air. When Jabutí falls from Vulture's back, his shell is broken on a rock. As Jabutí plays a song for them, the birds mend his broken shell. Each bird that touches him gets a new color, and that is why Toucan has a red and yellow beak, Macaw has bright orange feathers, and Hummingbird has green underneath.

A discussion of tricksters would not be complete without mention of Raven. *How Raven Stole the Sun* (Williams, 2001) is a Tlingit myth, part of a series titled Tales of the People. The series is by Native American artists and writers and is a fine celebration of Native American culture. The tale is very simply told and well illustrated.

(See chapters 2 and 7 for more trickster tales to consider.)

Collections

This section will discuss some of the good collections of myths that are appropriate for the elementary grades and middle school. *The Kingfisher Book of Mythology* (Bellingham, 2001) is organized by regions: northern lands, Africa, Mediterranean lands, eastern Asia, Central and South America, and South Pacific lands. Each region is introduced by a specialist of that area and includes archaeological information. A detailed glossary of mythological characters from each region also is included.

The Barefoot Book of Tropical Tales (Mans, 2000) includes stories from the Democratic Republic of Congo (formerly Zaire), Cape Verde, Haiti, Antigua, Puerto Rico, Malaysia, and Sri Lanka, as well as Benin in West Africa, the home of this storyteller. Some of these tales explain the influence of gods on people; others tell of heroes and magical events.

Geraldine McCaughrean has emerged as a major reteller of myths. Her book *The Crystal Pool: Myths and Legends of the World* (1999) is a stylish compilation of myths from India, Iceland, China, Egypt, Japan, and Greece as well as from Native Americans, Sumerians, Maori, and other aboriginal peoples. There are, in addition, legends from a number of cultures.

The dialogue in McCaughrean's retellings truly brings the stories to life. *Greek Myths* (1993) is an example of this. The tales are perfectly written for expressive read-alouds and also for readers to create theater arrangements in which each character's part is read by a different person. *Roman Myths* (2001) is a good companion to her volumes *Greek Gods and Goddesses* (1998) and *Greek Myths*. Here is a great retelling of the story of Romulus and Remus, who were left in a basket on the banks of the Tiber River, were raised by a wolf, and grew up to become the builders of the city of Rome.

The Illustrated Book of Myths (Philip, 1995) is a thematic grouping of stories, beginning with creation myths from Egyptian, Serbian, Norse, Chinese, Japanese, Australian, Iranian, Native American, and Sumerian cultures. Other sections include Beginnings, Gods and People, Gods and Animals, and Visions of the End. A pic-tomap of the world shows main sources of and characters from the myths.

I Am Arachne: Fifteen Greek and Roman Myths (Spires, 2001) offers unique retellings that feature first-person narratives. Pandora, Arachne, King Midas, Narcissus and Echo, and others tell their own stories, often with humorous effect. The pen-and-ink drawings reinforce the amusing outcomes of many tales.

Here are some other collections with myths from a wide variety of cultures:

A First Book of Myths (Hoffman, 1999)—14 tales from the Australian, Norse, Indian (The Ramayana), Egyptian, Japanese, Greek, Roman, Native American, and African cultures

Sun, Moon, and Stars (Hoffman, 1998)—Norse, Egyptian, Navajo, Latvian, Korean, Chinese, Mayan, Japanese, Australian, and Pawnee stories

Moon Tales: Myths of the Moon From Around the World (Singh & Lash, 1999)—myths from Chinese, Jewish, West African, Polynesian, Siberian, Canadian, Indian, Australian Aboriginal, Japanese, and English cultures

Golden Tales: Myths, Legends, and Folktales From Latin America (Delacre, 1996)—myths from Inca, Zapotec, Chatino, and Taino cultures, along with a pronunciation guide

Tales From Africa (Medlocott, 2000)—myths from Ghana, Malawi, Zimbabwe, Yoruba (West Africa), Egypt, Angola, and Botswana

The Names Upon the Harp: Irish Myth and Legend (Heaney, 2000)

A Gift From Zeus: Sixteen Favorite Myths (Steig, 2001)

One-Hundred-and-One Asian Read-Aloud Myths and Legends (Verniero, 2001)—stories from China, Japan, Korea, Vietnam, Tibet, and Mongolia

Myth Study in the Classroom

An easy way to begin sharing mythology with your students is by using modern books with mythological allusions. In *Hour of the Olympics* (Osborne, 1998), two modern children are transported by a time warp back to ancient Greece. They mingle with the athletes there and discover just how powerful Zeus and the victory goddess Nike can be to a people who believe in them. It takes Pegasus the winged horse to rescue the children and get them home, where the reader leaves them as they gaze at the Pegasus constellation in the sky. Students can read this short (70 pages) paperback in groups or on their own (its reading level is marked 2.3) and help themselves to other mythology selections displayed by teacher or librarian.

Likewise, middle graders can discover mythological notables as teens in the Young Hero series by Jane Yolen and Robert J. Harris. Imagine young Odysseus and his friend Penelope hiding on an island with only a satyr to help them escape pirates (*Odysseus in the Serpent Maze*, 2001), or the squeak-through adventures in *Hippolyta and the Curse of the Amazons* (2002). And, of course, there's Harry Potter. Students don't have to know that Professor McGonagall's first name is Minerva—which happens to be the Roman name for Athena the goddess of wisdom—nor do they have to know that Fluffy the three-headed monster dog in *Harry Potter and the Sorcerer's Stone* (Rowling, 1997) is a replica of Cerberus, the three-headed guard dog of the Underworld in Greek mythology. But someone is likely to know or find out and to share such tidbits. Modern books with ancient allusions can light the way to mythology.

Reading Aloud

Many authors cited in this chapter imbue mythology with a flowing, cadenced style that needs reading aloud to be shared and enjoyed. Geraldine McCaughrean's far-reaching myth tellings capture the essence of oral language. Read aloud also the title myth in Laurence Yep's *The Rainbow People* (1989), a wistful story written in a wistful style.

One oral reading concern is what to do about names. Some myth versions are packed with difficult-to-say names—Quetzalcoatl, Heimdall, Atrahasis, Tuathe De Danaan, Nephthys—that make readers stumble and listeners lose credence. Fortunately, many editions give pronunciation help within the text or in a glossary. Sometimes, you can make a chart of the names the oral readers will encounter. Rehearse the list with the audience before the reading.

Storytelling

A common mistake is to confuse storytelling with retelling. Retell is a researcher's tool to measure recall. But storytelling is much more: the attempt to arouse an audience to "live through" the story, building the scenery and observing the action in their minds as the story is rendered. That, after all, is how myth began.

To tell a myth, find one that you want to tell. Good candidates are those so complex that they would confuse listeners if read aloud (you can simplify them in the telling) or those in summary form that need elaboration. Robert Hull's *Pre-Columbian Stories* (1994), one in the Tales From Around the World series, has stories with both characteristics.

Read the myth with your full attention several times. Then—and this is the most important step—close the book, lay it aside, and hide it. Only in this way can you become independent of print and make the story your own.

Practice telling the myth to a chair or a dog (both are patient and noncritical), and then you are ready to tell it to a human audience, preferably a small, patient, noncritical group of children.

Once you've modeled the preparation and the telling, invite students to also storytell myths. But don't begin by placing a student in front of a whole class. Instead, organize groups of three or four students to share myths through storytelling. Teach them that positive audience response is a necessary part of this enterprise.

Visuals

Gilgamesh, the Sumerian half-god half-man, leaves his city, Uruk, to pass through the Mashu Mountains and the garden of the Sun God, to cross the Waters of Death to find, at last, immortal Utnapishtim and the secret of living forever (Zeman, 1995). That journey, and the journey back with its surprising finish, inspires a memorable pictomap to be sketched as you read or tell the story and to be finished later with small drawings depicting main incidents. Come to think of it, many myths describe journeys, from the underwater wanderings of the Inuit Sedna to the Greeks' Phaethon, who, in his father's chariot, plunges from the top of the sky into the hidden river of Mother Earth. Devising a pictomap, large or small, with brief, well-placed illustrations, will help young readers discover the unity and "wholeness" of such tales.

To extend the pictomap idea, suppose that you want to show students the diversity of myth. Spread a world map on the wall (or use a globe); surround it with careful but quick sketches, each from a different myth from a different culture; connect each sketch to its place on the map with yarn or string. A good source for this project is *The Kingfisher Book of Mythology* (Bellingham, 2001).

Before embarking on a visual project to extend students' response to myth, think of a myth's purpose. For instance, Shirley Climo's *Stolen Thunder: A Norse Myth* (1994) is a comedy. A giant steals Thor's hammer and demands the goddess Freya as ransom, causing the gods to do some fancy cross-dressing to foil the plot. Maybe a cartoon strip is appropriate here, as it would be with many trickster myths.

As far as materials for visual exercises, clay can be most satisfying. Roll it, soften it, and slowly it may come to embody the myth you (or a student) are thinking of. Imagine that you are creating a sculpture to be placed in a revered place in the homes of people who will thus be reminded of their ancestors. What, for instance, would such sculptures be to symbolize the Native American myths in *Paul Goble Gallery* (Goble, 1999), which includes "Her Seven Brothers" and "The Girl Who Loved Wild Horses"?

Drama

What of a Greek myth symbolized in clay by a lone feather floating in the sea? The feather on the sea is, of course, from "Icarus and Daedalus." There are many modern versions, but find, if you can, the old one by Josephine Preston Peabody (1935) because it is like watching a drama, scene by scene. In the beginning, Daedalus and his son Icarus are imprisoned at the top of a tower on the island of Crete. Daedalus constructs wings from seagull feathers and wax. After a few experimental flights, the two fellows begin their escape across the sea—but Daedalus warns his son to stay close.

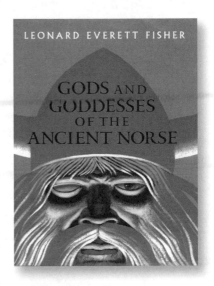

"At first, there was terror in the joy," continues the account (p. 276). Too soon, Icarus "stretched his arms to the sky and made toward the highest heavens" (p. 276). Too near the sun, the wax securing the wings melted, and Icarus "fell like a leaf tossed by the wind" into the sea (p. 276). Daedalus in his sorrow offered his wings to the gods and never attempted to fly again.

A cautionary tale? A story of heroes who test the limits? Myths, like the oracle at Delphi, are not inclined to do your thinking for you, but they do invite you to explore their labyrinth of values.

Book cover from *Gods and Goddesses of the Ancient Norse* by Leonard Everett Fisher. Copyright © 2001. Used by permission of Holiday House.

Picture Daedalus and Icarus in the tower. Better yet, have students play the roles of Icarus and Daedalus in that prison. Is Icarus an angry teen or a loving one? (One modern version pictures him as a very young child. Is that what you'd prefer him to be?) What do the father and son say to each other? You can divide a whole classroom into pairs to extemporize the conversation and action in the scene. It is the essence of play making (Ward, 1957).

Now *do* the sea. Is that difficult? Yes, but drama is a series of problem-solving steps. In one classroom in which students reenacted this story, a blue bedspread manipulated near the floor by four students made a satisfactory sea, while three students moved back and forth across the sea—the halcyon birds that (the ancient Greeks believed) flew in the hollows of the waves to calm them. Far away, across the room, the sun (a student dressed in red) beamed down.

It became a matter of making a routine for the action: three turns of the halcyons, the exact slow motion of the waves, Daedalus miming his steady flight ahead, and Icarus's sudden jubilation and rise toward the sun. Yes, it all required practice, side coaching by the teacher, and self-evaluation along the lines of "what was good about the way we played it this time."

In the end, the whole drama, less than 10 minutes in length, was put to music (segments from Prokofiev piano concertos). The result, to the surprise of students and teacher alike, was a drama in dance form.

Not every classroom will want to take on a drama project such as this. Drama, however, may be done in pieces, starting with the smallest warm-ups and evolving gradually, as described by Nellie McCaslin in *Creative Drama in the Classroom* (1990).

A quite different form of drama is Readers Theatre, radio-like dialogue with minimal movement or props but with plenty of sound effects, build-ups, and expression. Some myths are written in dialogue, so the transition to Readers Theatre is easy. There are at least two published script sources you can use: *Greek Myths: 8 Short Plays for the Classroom (Grades 4–8)* by John Rearick (1997) and *From Atalanta to Zeus: Readers Theatre From Greek Mythology* by Suzanne I. Barchers (2001).

Reading researchers tend to like Readers Theatre because it develops expression and fluency. Those who love mythology and who wish to keep it fresh in the hearts of children have additional reasons to love Readers Theatre.

Conclusion

Myths are the bedrock of civilization, older and deeper than folk tales and other lore. We can introduce children to the motifs of modern literature through these myths as they come alive through storytelling and drama.

REFERENCES

Frye, N. (1964). *The educated imagination*. Bloomington, IN: Indiana University Press.

Gurewitsch, M. (2001, December 2). Theater's quicksilver truth: All is change. *The New York Times*, section 2, pp. 1, 6.

Hamilton, E. (1942). *Mythology*. Boston: Little, Brown.

Levi-Strauss, C. (1999). *Myth and meaning: Cracking the code of culture*. New York: Schocken Books.

McCaslin, N. (1990). *Creative drama in the classroom* (5th ed.). White Plains, NY: Longman.

Moffett, J. (1991). Current issues and future directions. In J. Flood, J.M. Jensen, D. Lapp, & J.R. Squire (Eds.), *Handbook of research on teaching the English language arts* (pp. 827–838). New York: Macmillan.

Smith, L. (1953). *The unreluctant years*. Chicago: American Library Association.

Subject Guide to Children's Books in Print. (2002). New Providence, NJ: Bowker.

Ward, W. (1957). *Playmaking with children*. New York: Appleton-Century-Crofts.

Wilford, J.N. (2002, March 14). Archaeologists find Mayan masterpiece in Guatemala. *The New York Times*, p. A10.

CHILDREN'S BOOKS CITED

Aardema, V. (1994). *Misoso: Once upon a time tales from Africa* (R. Ruffins, Illus.). New York: Knopf.

Asimov, I. (1961). *Words from the myths* (W. Barss, Illus.). Boston: Houghton Mifflin.

Barchers, S.I. (2001). *From Atalanta to Zeus: Readers Theatre from Greek mythology*. Englewood, CO: Teacher Ideas Press.

Bellingham, D. (2001). *The Kingfisher book of mythology*. New York: Kingfisher.

Climo, S. (1994). *Stolen thunder: A Norse myth* (A. Koshkin, Illus.). New York: Clarion.

Climo, S. (1995). *Atalanta's race: A Greek myth* (A. Koshkin, Illus.). New York: Clarion.

Coolidge, O. (2001). *Greek myths*. Boston: Houghton Mifflin.

Curry, J. (2001). *The wonderful sky boat and other Native American tales of the southeast* (J. Watts, Illus.). New York: Margaret K. McElderry.

D'Aulaire, I., & D'Aulaire, E.P. (1962). *D'Aulaires' book of Greek myths*. New York: Bantam Doubleday Dell.

D'Aulaire, I., & D'Aulaire, E.P. (1986). *D'Aulaires' Norse gods and giants*. New York: Doubleday.

Delacie, L. (1996). *Golden tales: Myths, legends, and folktales from Latin America*. New York: Scholastic.

Fisher, L.E. (2001). *Gods and goddesses of the ancient Norse*. New York: Holiday House.

Gilchrist, C. (1999). *Stories from the silk road* (N. Mistry, Illus.). Cambridge, MA: Barefoot Books.

Goble, P. (1999). *Paul Goble gallery: Three Native American stories*. New York: Simon & Schuster.

Hamilton, V. (1988). *In the beginning* (B. Moser, Illus.). San Diego: Harcourt.

Hamilton, V. (1997). *A ring of tricksters* (B. Moser, Illus.). New York: Blue Sky/Scholastic.

Hausman, G., & Hausman, L. (2000). *Cats of myth: Tales from around the world* (L. Baker, Illus.). New York: Simon & Schuster.

Heaney, M. (2000). *The names upon the harp: Irish myth and legend* (P.J. Lynch, Illus.). New York: Levine/Scholastic.

Hoffman, M. (1998). *Sun, moon, and stars* (J. Ray, Illus.). New York: Dutton.

Hoffman, M. (1999). *A first book of myths* (R. Langton & K. Kimber, Illus.). New York: Dorling Kindersley.

Hofmeyr, D., & Daly, J. (2001). *The star-bearer: A creation myth from ancient Egypt*. New York: Farrar, Straus & Giroux.

Hull, R. (1994). *Pre-Columbian stories* (V. Cleall & C. Robinson, Illus.). New York: Thomson.

Hyde-Chambers, F., & Hyde-Chambers, A. (1981). *Tibetan folk tales*. Boulder, CO: Shambhala.

Jackson, E. (2002). *The spring equinox: Celebrating the greening of the Earth* (J.D. Ellis, Illus.). Brookfield, CT: Millbrook.

Keenan, S. (2000). *Gods, goddesses, and monsters: An encyclopedia of world mythology*. New York: Scholastic.

Knutson, B. (1996). *How the guinea fowl got her spots: A Swahili tale of friendship*. Minneapolis, MN: Carolrhoda.

Lelooska, D. (1998). *Spirit of the cedar people: More stories and paintings of Chief Lelooska*. New York: Dorling Kindersley.

Lester, J. (1989). *How many spots does a leopard have? And other tales* (D. Shannon, Illus.). New York: Scholastic.

Lourie, P. (2001). *The mystery of the Maya: Uncovering the lost city of Palenque*. Honesdale, PA: Boyds Mills Press.

Maddern, E. (1993). *The fire children: A West African creation tale* (F. Lessac, Illus.). New York: Dial.

Maggi, M.E. (2001). *The great canoe: A Kariña legend*. Toronto: Groundwood.

Mans, R. (2000). *The Barefoot book of tropical tales* (D. Hyde, Illus.). Cambridge, MA: Barefoot Books.

Martin, R. (2001). *The shark god* (D. Shannon, Illus.). New York: Levine/Scholastic.

McCaughrean, G. (1993). *Greek myths* (E.C. Clark, Illus.). New York: Margaret K. McElderry.

McCaughrean, G. (1998). *Greek gods and goddesses* (E.C. Clark, Illus.). New York: Margaret K. McElderry.

McCaughrean, G. (1999). *The crystal pool: Myths and legends of the world* (B. Willey, Illus.). New York: Margaret K. McElderry.

McCaughrean, G. (2001). *Roman myths* (E.C. Clark, Illus.). New York: Margaret K. McElderry.

McDermott, G. (2001). *Jabutí the tortoise: A trickster tale from the Amazon*. New York: Harcourt.

Medlocott, M. (2000). *Tales from Africa* (A. Akintola, Illus.). New York: Kingfisher.

Myers, C. (2000). *Wings*. New York: Scholastic.

Oodgeroo. (1993). *Dreamtime: Aboriginal stories* (B. Bancroft, Illus.). New York: Morrow.

Osborne, M.P. (1998). *Hour of the Olympics* (S. Murdocca, Illus.). New York: Random House.

Paye, W., & Lippert, M.H. (2002). *Head, body, legs: A story from Liberia* (J. Paschkis, Illus.). New York: Henry Holt.

Peabody, J.P. (1935). "Icarus and Daedalus." In E. Johnson, C.E. Scott, & E.R. Sickels (Eds.), *Anthology of children's literature* (pp. 276–277). Cambridge, MA: Houghton Mifflin.

Philip, N. (1995). *The illustrated book of myths* (N. Mistry, Illus.). New York: Dorling Kindersley.

Philip, N. (1996). *Odin's family: Myths of the Vikings* (M. Foa, Illus.). New York: Orchard.

Rearick, J. (1997). *Greek myths: Eight short plays for the classroom (grades 4–8)*. New York: Scholastic.

Rowling, J.K. (1997). *Harry Potter and the sorcerer's stone* (M. Grandpre, Illus.). New York: Levine/Scholastic.

Singh, R., & Lash, D. (1999). *Moon tales: Myths of the moon from around the world*. London: Bloomsbury.

Spires, E. (2001). *I am Arachne: Fifteen Greek and Roman myths* (M. Gerstein, Illus.). New York: Farrar, Straus & Giroux.

Steig, J. (2001). *A gift from Zeus: Sixteen favorite myths* (W. Steig, Illus.). New York: HarperCollins/Cotler.

Verniero, J.C. (2001). *One-hundred-and-one Asian read-aloud myths and legends*. New York: Black Dob & Leventhal.

Waldherr, K. (1995). *The book of goddesses*. Hillsboro, OR: Beyond Words.

Williams, M. (2001). *How Raven stole the sun* (F. Vigil, Illus.). New York: Abbeville.

Wolfson, M.O. (1996). *Marriage of the rain goddess: A South African myth* (C.A. Porms, Illus.). New York: Barefoot.

Yep, L. (1989). *The rainbow people* (D. Wiesner, Illus.). New York: HarperCollins.

Yolen, J., & Harris, R.J. (2001). *Odysseus in the serpent maze*. New York: HarperCollins.

Yolen, J., & Harris, R.J. (2002). *Hippolyta and the curse of the Amazons*. New York: HarperCollins.

Zeman, L. (1995). *The last quest of Gilgamesh*. Toronto: Tundra.

Zimmerman, M. (2002). *Metamorphoses: A play based on D.R. Slavitt's Metamorphoses of Ovid*. Evanston, IL: Northwestern University Press.

CHAPTER 5

Legend Has It: What Legends Bring to Classroom Learning

Darcy H. Bradley

When I was invited to write this chapter, I thought it would be a straightforward and relatively easy task. After all, I reflected, I'm an avid and lifelong student of children's and adolescents' literature. Little did I know how difficult it would be to find a satisfactory definition for the word *legend* so that I could guide teachers to the most worthwhile stories. My lengthy search led me to consider how and why this complex genre is situated in traditional tales and to consider the relationship of the legend to other genres such as epics, myths, tall tales, biographies, historical fiction, and even fantasy.

In writing this chapter, I have chosen not to include stories from Native American peoples that might be construed as legends. Issues around what can or should be appropriated from oral tradition to writing are complex and not easily resolved. According to Beverly Slapin, executive director and cofounder of Oyate (an organization devoted to preserving the integrity of Native American stories) and coeditor with Doris Seale of *Through Indian Eyes: The Native American Experience in Books for Children* (1998),

> The word "legend" itself is not a Native construct. "Traditional literatures" or "stories" are more fitting. Since for millennia the oral tradition has been the primary method of teaching for Native peoples, many people say that once a traditional story is put down in writing, it's no longer a traditional story. (B. Slapin, 2002, personal communication)

Native American storyteller and writer Joseph Bruchac, who has written or audiorecorded more than 60 texts, says that he does not "really use the words *myth* or *legend* to talk about Native American stories. I prefer to talk about traditions and stories" (2002, personal communication). The Bruchac family devotes a press to multicultural books and recordings. For selections of quality texts or audiotapes and for help in understanding issues around Native American literature, explore the excellent list of fiction and nonfiction resources available at www.oyate.com. Other useful published resources for adults and children can be found through the Bruchace' Greenfield Review Press in New York and Pemmican Press in British Columbia, Canada. (See also chapter 13 in this book.)

Definitions and Characteristics of Legends

This book is focused on traditional tales or stories, which all have a genesis in oral retellings. And because legends are stories about real people who have been or are admired, people's own retellings are likely to change, much like the old whisper game of "Telephone," and variations will be found in written legends as well. So it is not surprising that different definitions of the term *legend* exist.

For the purposes of this chapter, a legend is defined as a story or collection of stories about a person researchers are fairly sure existed (Stoodt-Hill & Anspaugh-Corson, 2001; Temple, Martinez, Yokota, & Naylor, 2001) and in which the story is strongly influenced by the time period or setting (Anderson, 2001; Mooney, 2001; Rosenberg, 1997; Tunnell, Darigan, & Jacobs, 2002).

Exemplary legends have three main characteristics: (1) The main character is an enduring symbol for something important during a dramatically changing historic period, or for some cultures the legend is a "teaching story" built around a person well known to that culture; (2) the theme is presented without didacticism in order to show readers how and why people develop or use certain qualities; and (3) source notes are used by the author and/or illustrator of a written story to validate the story, person, time period, and setting.

As to the first characteristic of exemplary legends, enduring symbols for a culture or ideal are people "we love to hear and to read about...who have accomplished great tasks" (Rosenberg, 1997, p. xxviii). As an example of a lasting figure from a historic period of great change, William Tell is a symbol for freedom from tyranny and commitment to the rights of the individual in the feudal times of the 13th century. Hátim of Tyyi' is noted by Arabs for his generosity. He continually gave away all he had to the needy.

Next, all legends are to some extent "stories that teach," depending on what the reader, listener, or culture values. Robin Hood was a champion for the poor and oppressed during the conflict between the Saxons and Normans; Gilgamesh, a Mesopotamian king who lived more than 5,000 years ago, represents the conflicts inherent in the human condition and the cautious use of power. Legends definitely have theme and plot but are less didactic than fables and wonder tales. The value of this characteristic for child and adolescent readers is to help them understand how setting and history influence how writers write and what tone, language, and style are used to influence readers' interpretations. Legends explain and explore the most complex aspects of human nature, which is why they are generally most suitable for fourth-grade students and higher. The intricate aspects of character motivation, political conflicts of the time, personal beliefs that run afoul of cultural values, and real or embellished deeds offer much material for thought and discussion. Legends offer exciting stories about memorable, action-oriented people, so they can become cultural cornerstones of time periods or events that students will build on as they read biographies, history, social studies, and even fantasies.

The third characteristic of quality legends is that they contain source notes. Without source notes, often necessary to authenticate the text and illustrations, books or stories do not survive critical scrutiny (Hearne, 1993a, 1993b). One example of a well-sourced book is Lulu Delacre's *Golden Tales: Myths, Legends, and Folktales From Latin America* (1996). Who retells or rewrites the legends can be a matter of concern for each culture, so it is important to know the backgrounds of the authors or illustrators and what attempts have been made to verify the retellings. In this case, Delacre lets the reader know that she grew up in Puerto Rico, and she demonstrates her careful research through detailed notes about each story and its accompanying artwork in a section at the end of her book titled "Notes and Sources" (pp. 69–74). On the dedication page, she also credits the authorities she consulted to validate her work.

What's in a Word?

Considering the linguistic, etymological, and cultural aspects of the term *legend* is a worthwhile journey for teachers and their students. Linguistically, since the 15th century the term *legend* has been used broadly to refer to someone whose fame or achievement is likely to endure. Today, use of the terms *legend* and *legendary* permeates U.S. culture; it is not uncommon to hear a celebrity figure in music, sports, or television introduced as "a legend in her own time" or labeled, for example, as Michael Jordan is, "the legendary basketball superstar...." When people accomplish remarkable feats today, often one hears, "that's the stuff that legends are made of."

Legends, similar to other types of traditional stories, usually feature the language style of the storyteller. For example, the first words in *The Ballad of Mulan* (Zhang, 1998) read, "Long ago, in a village in northern China, there lived a girl named Mulan. One day she sat at her loom weaving cloth. *Click-clack! Click-clack!*" (n.p.). In a retelling of an Arthurian story, Rosemary Sutcliff (1980) writes,

> And in the Great Hall of Arthur's palace stood the Round Table, which could seat a hundred and fifty knights, each with his name written in fairest gold on the high back of his chair behind him: the Knights of the Fellowship of the Round Table, which had been formed long ago when Arthur was new and young to his kingship, for the spreading of justice and mercy and chivalry and the upholding of right against might throughout the land. (p. 7)

Exposure to and discussion about the rich vocabulary and language structure typically found in legends can develop readers and writers who understand and use the complexities and beauty of language in their own lives and stories. Readers (or listeners) who link this "long ago" type of language to their prior experiences with wonder tales, fables, and tall tales are ready to learn about the more complex and serious life lessons the legend offers.

The word *legend* comes from the Latin *legenda*, meaning "for reading or to be read" (*American Heritage Dictionary of the English Language*, 2000). From the 14th century comes the Middle English *legende*, which refers to a collection of saints' lives. The Medieval Latin *legenda* means "appointed to be read on respective saints' days" and is a Latin derivative of *legere*, literally "to read" (Stein, 1967). Legends often were written about saints, although some texts chosen for this chapter are classified as biographies. A saint is a Christian construct "formally recognized by the Christian Church as having attained an exalted position in heaven and as being entitled to veneration on Earth" (Stein, 1967, p. 1261). In the helpful, handsome, and matter-of-fact picture book *Lives and Legends of the Saints*, Armstrong (1995) focuses on 20 male and female saints. The author has selected famous paintings from prominent museums and painters around the world to complement each short, one-page story. Listed by the Library of Congress as both biography and legend, this text helps explain the relationship between saints and the legends that grew up around them.

Culturally, legends usually represent and highlight an exemplary character trait for the people of that culture at that time. However, what is exemplary for one culture or from one culture's history may not always be what is exemplary for another culture, and the way desirable character traits manifest themselves—even among similar groups or cultures—can vary. For some cultures, saints embody desirable characteristics such as kindness, sacrifice, and religious vision. For example, in his passion to bring the printed word to others, Columba started a war in Ireland for the right to keep and share a book he had secretly copied (Brown, 2002). Horrified at the number of deaths on both sides of this short war, he exiled himself for his deed, only later to be invited to return to Ireland to settle disputes in less dramatic ways. Yet Francis of Assisi is said to have never hurt another living creature and to have been gentle all his life (Mayo, 2000).

For other cultures, royalty or leaders are remembered as models for courage, power, and bravery. Some believe, for instance, that from 1000 B.C. to 600 B.C., a race of women called Amazons ruled a country bordering the Black Sea. It is said that the Amazonian "Scathach: The Warriors' Teacher" (Mayer, 1999) trained many of the Celtic warriors and instructed them "in weaponry, courage, and compassion" (p. 31). In addition to being well-versed in fighting, Scathach was said to be a poet and prophet.

Some leaders are recognized for their wisdom and common sense. For example, the collection of stories about the renowned judge Ooka Tadasuke of 18th-century Japan are examplars for fairness and integrity (Edmonds, 1994).

Legends tend to focus on the positive character traits of people historians are sure existed in olden times. What tends to separate a legend from a biography is that the stories in legends are difficult to authenticate, and although there is a core of truth, the stories might have been recast a bit to push the boundaries of truth or believability. For example, legend has it that Columba, a man who was later canonized by the Catholic church, could read and write because he ate a cake that contained all the letters of the alphabet. The truth here could be that a literate adult in Columba's life formed letters with dough while baking bread or that Columba was a precocious learner who quickly and at a very early age picked up the basics of how to read and write.

Differentiating Legends From Other Genres

Experts struggle to clarify the blurry lines between tall tales, myths, legends, and epics. And because legends are based on historical figures, the line bleeds further into biography, historical fiction, and even to high fantasy. So, what distinguishes a legend from these other genres?

Tall tales and legends often are confused with each other, especially in the United States. Although many cultures have a form of the tall tale, this story style is often thought to be a construction from American pioneer times and is generally associated with a fictitious character such as Pecos Bill, Paul Bunyan, or Sally Ann Thunder Ann Whirlwind Crockett (the invented wife of Davy Crockett). A legendary person can become a tall tale when something about him or her is so exaggerated that it becomes humorous and unbelievable, such as with the stories in Ariane Dewey's *The Narrow Escapes of Davy Crockett* (1990) and Rosalyn Schanzer's *Davy Crockett Saves the World* (2001). Although the real Crockett was a Tennessee frontiersman who was known as an extraordinary soldier, scout, and politician but was killed at the Alamo, it is doubtful that "By the time he was 8 years old he weighed 200 pounds with his shoes off, his feet clean, and his stomach empty" (Dewey, 1990, p. 5) or, as the popular 1950s Disney series theme song says, that he "kilt him a b'ar when he was only 3." Tall tales generally find an appreciative audience in older primary and intermediate students and are excellent vehicles for building prior knowledge for understanding the usually more serious and lengthy legend form. Once students have a background in folk tale or wonder tale structure, the tall tale seems like a natural next step for them, as it is usually short, it is structurally similar to a folk tale or wonder tale, and the problem or challenge in the story is resolved with good humor (Mooney, 2001).

Legends also are frequently confused with myths, but mythical characters usually didn't exist "in the flesh" as legendary figures did. Legends portray a human hero or heroine such as Robin Hood or Boadicea, rather than a deity such as Zeus (Anderson, 2001). Myths are thought to explain aspects of culture or to explain how something came to be in the natural world, and they often involve deities or personified elements of nature (Mooney, 2001).

Although legends and epics are typically based on real people, epics are typically long and complex narratives constructed around the actions of a single cultural or national hero, such as in Homer's *Iliad* and *Odyssey* (Huck, Kiefer, Hepler, & Hickman, 2004). Epics are challenging to read because they often are told in verse, are much longer than legends, and sometimes are grounded in mythology (Lynch-Brown & Tomlinson, 2001). Because of their complex narrative construction and length, epics tend to be more suitable for middle school or high school students. A few epics have been simplified for younger readers, though, such as Zeman's series of three picture books about Mesopotamian King Gilgamesh (Zeman, 1992, 1993, 1995) and Williams's *The Horn of Roland* (1968).

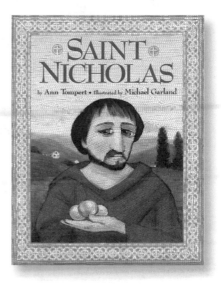

Book cover from *Saint Nicholas*, written by Ann Tompert, illustrated by Michael Garland. Copyright © 2000. Published by Caroline House, Boyds Mills Press, Inc. Reprinted by permission.

Biographies differ from legends because they are based strictly on facts that can be verified. Sources for legends are difficult to authenticate because there are frequently many contradictory pieces of information and because accurate written recording practices are a modern development. Also, in a legendary treatment of a historical figure, there may be an aspect of the supernatural, the mystical, or the reverential.

Historical fiction offers a realistic view of the past, often using verifiable historical figures, settings, and themes. Although good writing lets us believe that King Arthur was given the sword Excalibur from a hand that appeared out of a lake, it isn't realistic in the way the rules of historical fiction writing dictate.

Fantasy often draws from or echoes the content found in the oldest legends. It is background knowledge from legendary figures such as Robin Hood, King Arthur, Cuchulainn, Gilgamesh, and others that allows readers to enter and better understand the monumental battles between the good and evil forces found in J.K. Rowling's Harry Potter series, Lloyd Alexander's Prydain Chronicles, Susan Cooper's Dark Is Rising series, and J.R.R. Tolkien's The Lord of the Rings trilogy, to name but a few enduring fantasies. Many fantasies have protagonists who go on a quest to find something or someone, quests that are likely modeled on the quests and journeys Celts or medieval knights took in old stories to "find" or "defend" something. Fantasy writers rarely source their writing, and they create or imagine settings, worlds, and events that, while believable, generally have no basis in fact.

Legends for the Classroom

The legends discussed in this section are organized alphabetically by country or region and then dated in order from oldest to youngest. They are followed by classroom activities and a closing section on urban legends. Some of the titles included are not always identified as legends by the Library of Congress or even by the authors themselves; nor is the list exhaustive. The titles chosen are based on the definitions presented earlier in this chapter. When experts can't agree on what specifically defines a legend, this disagreement gives some leeway, within reason, to include texts that might cross genres and subgenres.

Africa

AGASSU (DATE UNKNOWN, WEST AFRICA). According to Dupre (1993), stories in West Africa are either *heho* (stories about people who never existed) or *hwenoho* (stories based on people who actually lived). Agassu's story is said to be the latter type. Agassu was a slave, captured from the Adja tribe as a boy by another African tribe. As an adult, he escaped from his captors with help and encouragement from the voices he heard during a sea storm about his heritage as a king. He returned to his people and was accepted as a rightful ruler. From Agassu comes the notion of forgiveness, as his first act as leader was to free those who had brought misery and torment to others. The fascinating collages in Dupre's book, composed of images from African art and civil rights history, enhanced with acrylics and oils, add a dimension of beauty to this well-constructed legend. Dupre has added an author's endnote that links Agassu to others who have fought for civil rights, such as W.E.B. Dubois, Ida P. Wells, and Rosa Parks.

MELLA (DATE UNKNOWN, ZIMBABWE). Mayer (1999) retells the story of this character in "Mella: Young Friend of the Python." When others of her tribe were too frightened to do anything, Mella is said to have visited the fearsome Python Healer in order to save her ailing father's life. Mella's actions allow her father, the tribal leader, to live a long and happy life. When her father dies later of old age, Mella becomes the ruler of her people. From Mella comes the notion that courage has its own rewards.

SUNDIATA KIETA (C. 1217–1255, MALI). It is said that when Sundiata was born to a rich Malian ruler, he neither spoke nor walked for the first seven years of his life. Although he was to become the heir of Mali, conspirators contrived to exile Sundiata for another seven years. After he became stronger and demonstrated courage and leadership to those he met during his exile travels, Sundiata returned to save Mali from an invasion and resumed his leadership role. As explained in the picture book *Sundiata: Lion King of Mali* (Wisniewski, 1992), legend has it that while Sundiata ruled Mali, no one was allowed to "interfere with another's destiny. You, your children, and your children's children shall find their appointed place within this land forever" (n.p.). Wisniewski details in an endnote where the necessary artistic license was taken and what was authenticated about this king. Color photographs of two-dimensional cut paper constructions capture the story in the bright, vivid colors and geometric patterns often associated with West Africa.

British Isles

CELTIC MEN AND WOMEN (FIRST CENTURY B.C.). Celtic stories about Finn MacCool, the Champion of Ulster (one of the four old kingdoms that are now known as Ireland and Northern Ireland) who protected the old high kings of those times, were thought to have been recorded by his poet and warrior son, Ossian. Although these histories, called *cycles*, are complex and often violent, one of the most popular tales of Finn MacCool tells how he tricked and defeated the hero Cuchulainn (despite the several-century difference in time period). Tomie dePaola's book *Fin M'Coul: The Giant of Knockmany Hill* (1981) shows how Finn's wife is perhaps the cleverer of the couple. Robert Byrd's florid pictures and simple, humorous retelling *Finn MacCoul and His Fearless Wife: A Giant of a Tale From Ireland* (1999) tells more about Finn's early life. In an entertaining 30-minute animated video titled *Finn McCoul* (1991), based on Brian Gleeson's book, children will be enchanted by the Irish brogue of the narrator, Catherine O'Hara, who is accompanied by traditional Irish music from The Boys of the Lough. All of these versions are humorous and will appeal to young children. Although these retellings are more like tall tales, they certainly provide some of the background knowledge for students to be ready to meet these folk heroes in more complex treatments.

Adolescents will appreciate the intricate and detailed retellings of Cuchulainn and Finn MacCool found in Marie Heaney's *The Names Upon the Harp: Irish Myth and Legend* (2000). These stories explain the Ulster cycle, which is about Cuchulainn (also spelled Cucullin or Cuhullin), and the Finn cycle for Finn MacCool. These fierce, short tales explain, for example, how Cuchulainn came be called the Hound of Ulster and how Finn became wise from inadvertently tasting the Salmon of

Knowledge. Those students who are familiar with the stories of Finn written for younger children will understand why Finn can suddenly solve a problem after he sucks on his thumb.

There are many variants of a story from Irish legend titled "Bricriu's Feast" (Heaney, 2000) found in the later Arthurian legends around "Sir Gawain and the Green Knight" (see, for example, Hastings, 1981, and Sutcliff, 1981). Whether by the name of Bricriu or Sir Gawain, the hero proves his bravery by facing a foe that never dies, no matter how many times he is beheaded. When he shows up for a payback beheading, Bricriu/Sir Gawain is spared for his brave and chivalrous behavior.

Celtic women were known for courage, too. Mariana Mayer's *Women Warriors: Myths and Legends of Heroic Women* (1999) compiles short legends on brave women from many cultures, which will be appreciated by older children. "Morrigan: Fierce Goddess of War" is said to have lived in Cuchulainn's time and been a fierce adversary of his, who accurately prophesied his death. "Gwendolen: First Warrior Queen

Book cover from *Excalibur* by Hudson Talbott. Copyright © 1996. Used by permission of HarperCollins Publishers.

of Britain" ruled Britain with Locrin (allegedly the Roman Brutus's son) in 1065 B.C., but when her husband betrayed her for another woman, Gwendolen cut off his head and then ruled Britain by herself. During the Roman Empire of the first century when Nero was Emperor, Boadicea ("Boadicea: Woman With the Sword") was said to have raised an army of 230,000 in an attempt to defeat the Roman legions. When she lost the battles, rather than admit failure, Boadicea poisoned herself as a gesture of disdain for her enemies. Her daughters took up the fight, and conditions later became better for all Britain while it was under Roman rule. Rosemary Sutcliff's fictionalized account of Boadicea in *Song for a Dark Queen* (1979) is difficult to put down. In Milton Meltzer's *Ten Queens: Portraits of Women of Power* (1998), a more biographical account of this woman, here named *Boudicca*, is illustrated with maps and several fiery portraits of Boudicca and her daughters by Bethanne Anderson.

Advanced books, two about Cuchulainn and the other about Finn MacCool, will be appreciated by those readers who can't read enough Celtic history and legend. Bob Stewart's well-researched *Cuchulainn: Hound of Ulster* (1988) combines informational text about weapons and warrior training with detailed pen-and-ink drawings and photographs of artifacts. Included, too, are retold stories that trace the birth and death of Cuchulainn, with handsome color drawings of rugged and believable-looking men and women of the times (e.g., some of the men are tattooed, wear kilts, and drive chariots pulled by piebald horses; some of the women have long, red hair and wear plain dresses). Rosemary Sutcliff retells *The Hound of Ulster* (1963) and *The High Deeds of Finn MacCool* (1967) for adolescents and adults. Although some of her books are out of print, many have been reissued in paperback. Sutcliff's vivid and well-told legends are worth the search.

From this Celtic lore came the idea that a culture is worth protecting, no matter the cost. The seed of chivalry was planted and took root here. Courtesy, generosity to those less fortunate, valor, and excellence with weapon handling are the cultural traits that were deemed worthy of preserving by this culture.

ST. PATRICK (380–461, IRELAND). Although it is generally considered an informational book because it cites the customs and history for St. Patrick's Day, Gibbons (1994) ends her book, suitable for younger children, with a section on legends about Patrick. For example, it is said that Patrick rid Ireland of snakes, turned poison meant for him into ice, and had a cloak that was fireproof; when he died the sun shone in the sky for 12 days and nights. Also known as Maewyn, Patrick became the patron saint of Ireland. Although he had been captured from another part of Britain and enslaved by the Irish as a boy, after he escaped to France and grew up to become a Christian bishop, he returned to Ireland to convert the people from Druidism to Christianity. In *Saint Patrick and the Peddler* (Hodges, 1993b) a legend is told about how Patrick appears in the dreams of a poor Irish peddler to help him find the gold hidden beneath an old cottage hearth, possibly the one Patrick had inhabited himself as a shepherd. Acrylic paintings by Paul Brett Johnson give this picture book an appealing modern flavor. Patrick is said to represent the notion of help and service, even when all appears hopeless.

ARTHUR AND GUINEVERE (FIFTH CENTURY, BRITAIN). Some of the most enduring stories are those written and told about King Arthur, who is claimed as a historical figure in most parts of the British Isles. Hudson Talbott's Tales of King Arthur series will appeal to intermediate-grade readers and above. This picture book series, well-written and handsomely illustrated, includes *King Arthur: The Sword and the Stone* (1991), *King Arthur and the Round Table* (1995), *Excalibur* (1996), and *Lancelot* (1999). Because of the large picture book format, quality writing in moderate density, and illustrations to linger over, these books are compelling read-alouds that will likely entice even reluctant readers to reread the series.

Equally pleasing and well written is another Arthurian quartet by Robert D. San Souci. *Young Merlin* (1990) begins, "There are many stories of Merlin the Magician's birth, childhood, and youth. This is one..." and brings intermediate and higher readers just to the point before Arthur's birth. Drawn from the author's study of other folk tales, ballads, poems, history, and literature about Arthurian times, *Young*

Guinevere (1993), *Young Lancelot* (1996), and *Young Arthur* (1997) foreshadow the drama to come in the characters' adult lives. Jamichael Henterly's paintings capture many Celtic and medieval nuances (e.g., Stonehenge, Celtic jewelry, tartans) and the imagined beauty of the young characters. Selina Hastings's retellings *Sir Gawain and the Green Knight* (1981) and *Sir Gawain and the Loathly Lady* (1985) are illustrated richly with jewel-toned color plates of castles, crones, "damosels," horses with exquisitely decorated bridles and saddles, and knights. These two sophisticated retellings are appropriate for older readers because of the more complex language and the sorts of temptations the knights overcome (e.g., a woman is set upon seducing Sir Gawain). The theme of self-acceptance prevalent in William Steig's *Shrek!* (1993) and the film version of the story (which is far different from Steig's book) will be appreciated on a much deeper level by those who are familiar with the trials and tribulations of Gawain.

The picture books mentioned here can serve as background for and introduction to the more complex legends found in Jane Yolen's The Young Merlin Trilogy (*Passager*, 1996b; *Hobby*, 1996a; and *Merlin*, 1997) and the books of Rosemary Sutcliff (*The Light Beyond the Forest*, 1980; *The Sword and the Circle*, 1994; *The Road to Camlann*, 1982). Yolen's slight paperbacks with their rich writing explore Merlin's boyhood and foreshadow his destiny as advisor to Arthur. Sutcliff's series addresses the rise and fall of Arthur, Guinevere, and the Knights of the Round Table. With this background knowledge, students are likely to bring deeper understandings to the fascinating and challenging fantasy treatments of Lloyd Alexander's Prydain Chronicles, Susan Cooper's Dark Is Rising series, and J.R.R. Tolkien's Lord of the Rings trilogy.

COLUMBA (ALSO KNOWN AS COLUMCILLE, 521–527, IRELAND). Columba is known for his devotion to the idea that "words and ideas matter and cherishing them is a labor of the ages" (Brown, 2002, author's endnote). Long before the printing press made its debut, books had to be copied by hand, which is what Columba spent a good portion of his life doing. A war was even fought over Columba's right to copy, and keep the copy of, a particular book.

Although cataloged as biographies, the fascinating story of Columba is retold in Don Brown's *Across a Wide Dark Sea* (2002) and Jean Fritz's *The Man Who Loved Books* (1981). Brown's book has aspects of what is referred to as "fuzzy" (Pappas, Kiefer, & Levstik, 1999) or "hybrid" genre (Pappas, 2002, personal communications); that is, it has aspects of informational text, historical fiction, legend, and biography. For example, there are wonderful illustrations of the scribes' tools, a page of hand lettering from the time of Columba, and a cutaway drawing of a coracle (the leather boat Columba used to exile himself when his passion for books caused a war). Brown's book says, "legend has it that as one hand wrote, the other one glowed and made light for Columcille to see" (n.p.) Fritz notes that her story of Columba is "drawn from an old legend, much of which is certainly true" (author's endnote). In Fritz's book, Trina Schart Hyman's handsome brown, black, and white stylized illustrations and intricate medieval borders capture the time period and Columba's passion for books. The story of Columba offers readers an example of unswaying commitment to a cause.

ROBIN HOOD (13TH CENTURY, BRITAIN). "There is no justice for us Saxon English under these dogs of Normans!" (Edens, 2002). So says a freezing man in a harsh British winter, poaching the king's deer. As Robin of Locksley comes upon this scene, he helps the man and his son by sheltering them at his farm. In the next chapter, Robin's land is taken from him when he is accused of poaching. This large-format version of the Robin Hood tale is faithfully compiled by Cooper Edens and reprinted from a classic illustrated edition of 1906, based on 21 stories from E. Charles Vivian's texts. The 36 illustrations and images chosen by the author come from a variety of artistic traditions (e.g., engravings, paintings, and tapestries) and from artists such as N.C. and Andrew Wyeth, Howard Pyle, and even unknown illustrators from 1508. Older children and adolescents are more likely than younger children to understand the formal language, appreciate why the illustrations do not match in style, and value what some would consider the traditional retellings of Robin Hood. Robin was sympathetic to the suffering of others and made it his business to help the poor and oppressed. It is said that he was "the most fearless champion of freedom the land had ever known" and that "his name lives on in our ballads, our history, and our hearts—so long as the English tongue is known" (p. 171).

Younger children might appreciate the formal gilt-edged paintings and one-page stories of Margaret Early's 1996 picture book *Robin Hood*. In "How Robin Hood Becomes an Outlaw," this version explains that when Robin could not satisfactorily avenge his father's death (his father died while defending his property from seizure for not paying the high taxes demanded by the Sheriff of Nottingham), he was compelled to become a clever outlaw. Early's versions are simplified and more accessible to younger children compared to Cooper's compilation but are equally riveting and well told. Michael Morpurgo's *Robin of Sherwood* (1996), illustrated in action-packed watercolor sketches by Michael Foreman, is retold through the dream of a modern-day 12-year-old boy. When the boy finds an ancient arrowhead after a storm uproots his favorite tree, it starts a dream sequence in which the boy becomes Robin Hood and lives his adventures.

Unusual treatments of the Robin Hood stories are found in *Robin's Country* (Furlong, 1997) and in Theresa Tomlinson's *The Forestwife* (1995) and sequel *Child of the May* (2000). *Robin's Country* is told from the perspective of a runaway mute slave, called Dummy, who accidentally discovers Robin Hood's hideaway. How

Dummy finds his voice and himself is a classic tale of self-realization through the use of the Robin Hood legend. Although predictable, the book fleshes out the times by showing the violence and dishonesty among the ruling clergy and royalty, and it has a satisfying ending. Tomlinson's duo of books uses the Robin Hood stories as a springboard for a more feminist perspective, focusing on a Maid Marian who never does care all that much for Robin Hood. Here, Marian is portrayed as a feisty and independent young woman who doesn't end up with Robin after all. The book is action-packed, vibrant, and populated with many female characters, and the author relates in the afterword how various Robin Hood stories were woven into these books.

Most of the versions mentioned here take Robin Hood from young manhood through his death and are illustrated in a variety of styles that capture the mood and times of the Norman and Saxon adversaries. A search of the internet uncovers many fascinating websites and links devoted to the enduring lore surrounding Robin Hood.

China

MULAN (960–1279). Originating from the Soong Dynasty, the story of Mulan (also called Fa Mulan and Hua Mu Lan) "continues to inspire Chinese girls and women with the belief that women—if given the opportunity—are capable of accomplishing all the same feats as men" (Zhang, 1998, endnote). Mulan's virtue is filial piety and strength of character. She dresses up as a man to take the place of her elderly father in war. After she learns the art of war and becomes a famous general, she reveals herself as a woman and marries. San Souci's (1998) retelling is illustrated handsomely in a Chinese scroll-style tradition by Jean and Mou-Sien Tseng. *The Ballad of Mulan* (Zhang, 1998) is told in fewer words than San Souci's version, uses endpapers illustrated with dynasty maps, and shows Mulan's journey as a warrior and general. Both authors (and their illustrators) have written careful notes about their research to authenticate the history, character, illustration style, and format of their books, and the elements of the tradition of retelling. Further information about nontraditional heroines of Chinese folklore can be found in Suzanne Li's helpful article "Mulan and More: Heroines of Chinese Folklore in Picture Books" (2000).

Czech Republic

JUDAH LOEW BEN BEZALEL (1513–1609). According to an author's note in David Wisniewski's Caldecott Medal-winning book, *Golem* (1996), Rabbi Loew was a renowned Cabalist and a powerful leader in 16th-century Prague. A Cabalist is well versed in the "mystical body of knowledge aimed at understanding the hidden nature of God and putting this understanding to practical use, to heal the sick and combat evil" (n.p.). During the 16th century, Prague was a city where there were violent clashes: "Czech against German, Protestant against Catholic, Christian against Jew" (n.p.). *Golem* tells the story of a clay giant created by Rabbi Loew to defend the Jews from persecution. Rabbi Loew created this giant and named him Joseph, and his only job was to protect the Jews. The life given to the golem, however, proved problematic; he was too powerful and yet loved the beauty that life had to offer. The rabbi had to destroy Joseph.

A more bitter version of this tale is retold by McCaughrean (1997b) in "The Golem." In this adaptation, Golem is portrayed as an angry monster and the Rabbi as forgetful. Nevertheless, these cautionary tales about the possible costs of loosing power beyond human control is thought to have influenced the writing of Mary Shelley's *Frankenstein* (1998) and may even be prophetic in terms of today's dabblings in robotics, artificial intelligence, and cloning. (See also chapter 10 for information about Golem stories.)

France

JOAN D'ARC (1412–1431). Some legendary figures were of humble origin. For instance, Joan of Arc was "an ordinary peasant child, sunburned and strong, used to hard work" (Stanley, 1998, n.p.), one of five children who grew up in a small French village. Two of the best books for adolescents about Joan are Diane Stanley's *Joan of Arc* (1998) and Margaret Hodges's *Joan of Arc: The Lily Maid* (1999). Although both are classified as biographies, Stanley asks what sense we are to make of Joan's "miraculous visions and voices." Were they divine revelations, hallucinations of deprivation or illness, or a suggestive prophecy? Despite the transcript of the judicial proceedings of Joan's trial and other written accounts, historians can only "spin the occasional theory...in studying history, we have to accept what we know, and let the rest remain a mystery" (endnote, n.p.). Stanley's rich, formal, gilded paintings and matter-of-fact writing style offer an in-depth, accessible view of Joan's leadership and inspiration to unite the French people against Britain. Hodges's version is less text-dense, with sketchbook-style dry point and etched colored illustrations. Worth finding for older readers is *Joan of Arc* by Maurice Boutet de Monvel (1980). Reprinted from the 1886 French version translated in 1887, the full-color illustrations convey a pageantry and drama not found in the more modern versions of today. From Joan's story comes the notion that help sometimes comes from unexpected places and that one person's fervor and belief can make a difference.

Germany

HANS COBBLER (C. 900S). In *The Hero of Bremen* (Hodges, 1993a), Hans Cobbler walks "on knuckles and knees, dragging his legs behind him" (n.p.) because his legs are crippled. Hans loves retelling the stories of Roland, the famous alleged nephew of Charlemagne who helped make Bremen a free city. In this legend, when the town of Bremen outgrows itself, the people try to buy land from a countess and her greedy nephew. The nephew suggests that he and his aunt will sell the amount of land to the city that a man can walk around in a day, but the nephew demands to choose the man. Selected is Hans, who can only drag himself slowly and painfully along. With the help of the townspeople and the spirit of Roland, Hans secures a large tract for a market-place, which still stands there today. Charles Mikolaycak's realistic watercolors capture the flavor of the first century and show that Hans was just as important a hero to Bremen as Roland was. In fact, a statue of Roland erected in the 1400s to "The Hero of Bremen" is said also to feature the form of Hans Cobbler at Roland's feet. Hans's perseverance and belief in the best side of people are rewarded in the end.

Italy

ST. FRANCIS (1182–1226). Francis gave up a life of wealth and luxury to embrace poverty and help those who were impoverished. Tomie dePaola has written many books about saints, one of which is *Francis: The Poor Man of Assisi* (1982), suitable for older children. This particular version of Francis's life includes the story of Clare, who renounced her life of luxury as well to become a nun. Some believe that Francis is responsible for helping people recreate the *créche* (Nativity) scenes used at Christmases today, and that a cross spoke to him. An interesting companion book to this one is the legend of *The Clown of God* (dePaola, 1978), in which a Sorrento juggler named Giovanni, in his final days, meets some of the monks of Francis's order and makes a statue of Jesus smile. The contribution from the juggler is the idea of using the life gifts each of us have or develop to honor our lives and the lives of others.

In Margaret Hodges's *Brother Francis and the Friendly Beasts* (1991), Ted Lewin's trademark luminous, realistic paintings show how what is known about Francis comes from "legends that simply show how he loved all living things; they have a truth of their own" (n.p.). Author Margaret Mayo and illustrator Peter Malone have added to the legacy of Francis a small volume of stories titled *Brother Sun, Sister Moon* (2000). Most of the books on Francis include a spiritual poem of the same name he was said to have written at the end of his life. Of special note in this version are some "little tales" that relate to Francis's special relationships with animals, such as "The Friendly Falcon" and "The Playful Fish." Many stories are told about the kindnesses of Francis, later called the patron saint of "animals, birds, zoologists, and merchants" (Armstrong, 1995, p. 24).

Japan

OOKA TADASUKE (1677–1751). Ooka Tadasuke was a famous Japanese judge. In *Ooka the Wise: Tales of Old Japan* (Edmonds, 1994), the themes that run through these 17 well-retold stories are that goodness and honesty are rewarded, evil and lying are punished, the punishment needs to fit the crime, and the ability to help people save face is a useful quality. One example of making the punishment fit the crime comes from "Ooka and the Stolen Smell." When a tempura shop owner tries to make a student who can only afford to eat plain rice pay for the smells that enhance the food, Ooka declares that the student must pay the shop owner with the sound of coins clinking. The stories range from three to five pages and would make suitable read-aloud choices for older children. They also would be good models for retelling aloud or for writing or rewriting a "social justice"-type story.

Latin America

GUANINA AND SOTOMAYER (16TH CENTURY). Organized around the Tainos (the native people of what is now called Puerto Rico, Hispaniola, Cuba, Jamaica, and the Bahamas), Zapotecs (Mexico), Muisca (Columbia), and Incas (Bolivia), Delacre's *Golden Tales: Myths, Legends, and Folktales From Latin America* (1996) offers an accessible and rare view of stories from this part of the world. One legend tells of Guanina, the niece of a Taino leader. She and Spaniard Don Cristobal de Sotomayer fell in love in 1511. Although the Spanish thought they had "conquered" the Tainos, the Tainos attacked and killed Sotomayer and his men. Guanina had warned Sotomayer of the impending attack, but he was too arrogant to believe her. It is said that Guanina lay beside Sotomayer after he was killed and died of a broken heart. Other legends, as well as folk tales, are told and illustrated with authenticity in this wonderful collection of stories for older elementary students or adolescents.

MARTIN DE PORRES (1579–1639, PERU). Martin had a special gift for healing animals and people. In *The Pied Piper of Peru*, Ann Tompert (2002) tells a story of Martin from the point of view of a female mouse named Juana. Suitable for younger children, this charming and gentle story recounts how Martin rid the priory of destructive mice but in a way that provided for their safety and welfare. Realistic watercolors capture the many humorous moments in the story, for example, when the monks discover holes in their cheeses and bedding and when the mouse family moves into a barn. It is said that Martin "was credited with many of what were considered miraculous cures. Numerous people from Lima, rich and poor, flocked to the priory seeking his help" (author's note, n.p.). Martin was able to solve problems without violence and with a compassionate understanding of others, human or animal, much like St. Francis of Assisi.

Middle East

GILGAMESH (C. 2700 B.C., MESOPOTAMIA; WHAT IS NOW IRAQ). From Mesopotamia almost 5,000 years ago comes what is thought to be one of the oldest written stories. The story of Gilgamesh the King of Sumeria wasn't written down until the seventh century B.C., when it was written on clay tablets in cuneiform. These tablets were discovered and unearthed by archaeologists in the 1800s. Over time, many scholars have transcribed this complex story, which often is treated as an epic, into many languages. Ludmila Zeman has carefully researched and retold the story in three fascinating picture books (*Gilgamesh the King*, 1992; *The Revenge of Ishtar*, 1993; and *The Last Quest of Gilgamesh*, 1995). Gilgamesh's story is compelling because it characterizes the journeys humans take on the way to becoming fully developed. He starts as a selfish and cruel but powerful king who uses his subjects to build a great wall around the city, forsaking all else. Through various experiences, Gilgamesh learns the value of friendship, courage, loss, frailty, and the legacy he leaves to his people. The illustrations are almost cartoon-like and are detailed and colorful. The author obviously has taken care to preserve authenticity (e.g., endpapers in one book are in cuneiform, and another's show a Sumerian board game).

Older readers fascinated by this ancient story might tackle Bernarda Bryson's *Gilgamesh* (1967) or Irving Finkel's *The Hero King Gilgamesh* (1998). Both texts are carefully researched, well written, and lavishly illustrated with drawings or photographs of Sumerian relics and artifacts. Geraldine McCaughrean's *Gilgamesh the Hero* (2003) updates the story with more modern and humorous language. Karen Foster's *The City of Rainbows* (1999) brings to life King Mer-Kar, a royal ancestor of Gilgamesh.

From *Fabled Cities, Princes, & Jinn From Arab Myths and Legends* (Al-Saleh, 1985) comes a fascinating mix of history and legend. For example, when Hātim's people were starving in the story "Hātim of Tayyí," he killed his own beloved horse to feed them. It is said, the "qualities of nobility and heroism were not the monopoly of men. There were many Arabian women whose sense of honor, eloquence and courage, generosity of spirit, passionate loyalty, and gracious manners were celebrated in verse and legend" (p. 78). Legends around Hātim and others in these stories foster the notion of putting others above self.

ST. GEORGE (245–314, LYCIA; WHAT IS NOW TURKEY). George represents courage in the face of fear and is now known as the patron saint of Boy Scouts, knights, and soldiers, among others. Known for slaying a dragon while he was a soldier for the Roman Empire in northern Africa, George "represents the triumph of good over evil and is often shown with a red cross on his armor or on his flag" (Armstrong, 1995, p. 23). The 1985 Caldecott Medal winner *Saint George and the Dragon* (Hodges, 1984) is based on a segment of Spenser's *The Faerie Queen* (1988) and is lushly illustrated with the trademark idealized princesses and princes, horses, dwarfs, dragons, and embellished borders of Trina Schart Hyman. Careful research by the illustrator on the herbs and flowers of the times makes the borders and illustrations on every page highly symbolic. For example, on a page that shows St. George fighting the dragon, the illustrations feature agrimony, a plant said to be a charm to ward off serpents. Synge's (1978) chapter on St. George is a more political retelling, suitable for older students studying or interested in medieval times.

ST. NICHOLAS (275–343, LYCIA; WHAT IS NOW TURKEY). Unpredictable and dire circumstances often are linked to legendary figures. St. Nicholas, the believed antecedent for Santa Claus, was the only child of wealthy and kindly parents who died of the plague when Nicholas was only 13 years old. Despite (or perhaps because of) this tragedy, Nicholas was later canonized by the Catholic church for his consistently kind and giving ways over his long life. Cataloged as a picture book biography, Tompert's *Saint Nicholas* (2000) tells the story of Nicholas bringing children back to life, calming angry seas, and providing food for the needy in remarkable ways. Michael Garland's mosaic-style illustrations bring a pleasing beauty and simplicity to the story. Marianna Mayer's *The Real Santa Claus* (2001) starts with Clement Moore's classic poem "A Visit From St. Nicholas," then takes a more matter-of-fact turn to document Nicholas's life and miracles. The illustrations are selected from Renaissance paintings, which are presented elegantly within many gold borders. The narrative paintings are well matched to the text describing Nicholas's alleged deeds. This book sheds light on what Christmas means to many and helps readers understand how the transformation occurred from ordinary man to patron saint of maidens, travelers, and children, to today's Santa Claus.

Spain

RODRIGO DÍAZ DE VIVAR "EL CID" (1043–1099). El Cid was a Spaniard who drove many Moors out of parts of northern Spain in the late 11th century and took the city of Valencia, one of their last strongholds, for Spain. The story "The Death of El Cid: A Spanish Legend" (McCaughrean, 1995) tells how his dead body and spirit were used in one last battle to encourage his fighters, who were well outnumbered by the Moors, to hold Valencia. Although the assassin sent by the Moors to kill him had been successful, the body of El Cid was tied to his horse by his wife Jimena and his friend Alvar Fanez and sent out to lead the last battle. After that it was said that "the soul of El Cid was at rest, and that his spirit was ranging free, untethered and invisible, high above the heads of his victorious army" (p. 99).

A book-length version, *El Cid* (McCaughrean, 1997a), tells in exciting detail how El Cid became exiled and what he did to regain the Spanish king's favor, and it further explores the treachery that resulted in El Cid's untimely death. In an endnote, the author says, "To Spanish children today, the whole story of El Cid, from his banishment to his last legendary ride, is an accepted and well-loved part of their nation's history."

Switzerland

WILLIAM TELL (LATE 1200S–EARLY 1300S). Traditional stories say that William (Wilhelm) Tell is the man responsible for creating what is today called Switzerland. After refusing to obey the command to kneel to the Austrian Mayor Gessler, Tell was ordered to shoot an apple off his son's head or be killed. When Tell accomplished this feat, Gessler arrested him anyway. After (or during) a daring escape, Tell killed Gessler, which started a series of events that politically united three small countries against Austrian rule. Nina Bawden's version of the story, *William Tell* (1981), is filled with rich vocabulary suitable for young children to hear. For example, Bawden says that under the alleged cruelty of the Austrian rulers, "soldiers and bailiffs grew fat and lazy and arrogant, and the people, thin, sullen and frightened" (n.p.). Leonard Everett Fisher's 1996 version of *William Tell* uses suspense in writing and illustration, as when Tell is taking aim at his son and the apple:

> William Tell took his time. He squinted down the path his arrow would take. He looked hard at the apple on Jemmy's head. He held the crossbow straight and steady in front of him and lined up the arrow with the center of the apple. William Tell let the arrow fly. (n.p.)

On the matching double-page illustration, the focal point is an arrow flying straight and true toward an unseen mark.

Australian author and artist Margaret Early's *William Tell* (1991) is a complex version suitable for older listeners and readers. While viewing gold and elaborately patterned borders used to frame the text and detailed scenes of what we might imagine medieval life was like, readers can ponder the not-so-clear rights and wrongs of this fascinating story. Tell represents the belief that people have a right to intellectual and political freedom.

United States

JOHN CHAPMAN (1774–1845). Chapman, also known as Johnny Appleseed, was born in Massachusetts but is remembered as a "first naturalist" for his travels around many parts of the United States, giving people apple seeds and seedlings for planting. The versatile apple was a valuable contribution to society because it could be stored for long periods, made into butter or cider, cooked into pies or fruit leathers, and more. Chapman is said to have loved nature and people and to have gotten along well with everyone and everything. Although cataloged by the Library of Congress as biographies, Will Moses's *Johnny Appleseed: The Story of a Legend* (2001) and Steven Kellogg's *Johnny Appleseed: A Tall Tale* (1988) also could be called legends. Although both authors document their stories of Johnny in their author's notes, exaggerations of his life are alluded to and mentioned or shown in both books. Moses uses story-telling devices such as "they say..." and "others say...," and in a story about Johnny putting his canoe on an ice cake to keep from getting crushed in the river, he mentions, "folks loved the one about Johnny riding the ice floe" (n.p.). Kellogg uses some of the same devices, and on a two-page spread with no text and his lively painting style, he shows seven Johnny Appleseed vignettes, including Johnny making friends with a bear and catching a huge rainbow trout. In an appealing version for older children, "Johnny Appleseed: Rainbow Walker," Stoutenburg (1966) writes, "Judging by all the apple trees there are, east and west, north and south, it seems someone must have carried on the planting Johnny Appleseed began" (p. 85). Younger children will enjoy listening to the enthralling baritone of Garrison Keillor reading James Kunstler's *Johnny Appleseed* (1995), and adults may enjoy discovering the history of the American apple and John Chapman's frontier legacy in Michael Pollan's nonfiction *The Botany of Desire: A Plant's-Eye View of the World* (2001).

JOHN HENRY (C. 1840–1870). John Henry stories were first told in ballads and songs and were based on a 6-foot-tall, 200-pound ex-slave who was hired by the Chesapeake and Ohio Railroad as a "steel man," a position also known as hammer driver. Hammer drivers "drilled" into rock so dynamite could be inserted to blow away enough rock for train tunnels. One day, when a man shows up with a steam drill, a contest results between John Henry and the machine. Julius Lester's Caldecott Honor-winning book selection *John Henry* (1994), illustrated in Jerry Pinkney's trademark detailed realism using pencil, colored pencil, and watercolors, offers a beautifully retold version, faithful to an old ballad Lester himself sang at one time. Film actor Samuel L. Jackson (1998) brings this story to life in an 18-minute video. Some versions say that Henry died after winning the contest with the steam drill—whether of exhaustion or a stroke, no one is sure. It is said that then, "whether it was a whisper or a thought, everyone had the same knowing at the same moment: 'Dying ain't important. Everybody does that. What matters is how you do your living'" (Lester, 1994). This theme is revisited many times in other genres and in many cultures.

Older versions of the John Henry story stand the test of time. Adrien Stoutenburg's (1966) pictureless version is retold for older children in "John Henry: Hammerman." This version shows how John met Li'l Willie, his lifelong spike man, and paints a vivid picture of the contest between John and the steam drill. In Ezra Jack Keats's *John Henry: An American Legend* (1987), John extinguishes a lit fuse with his hammer after a cave-in in addition to beating the steam-powered machine for speed in clearing rock for the tunnel. In Lester's more modern version, "Some say [John Henry] was buried on the White House lawn late one night while the President and the Mrs. President was asleep" (afterword, n.p.).

MOSE HUMPHREYS (EARLY TO MID-1800S). Mose Humphreys, a legendary 19th-century New York city firefighter with superhuman qualities, is thought by some to be the first American urban folk hero. In Mary Pope Osborne's (2002) picture book treatment, artists Steve Johnson and Lou Fancher paint Mose in larger-than-life perspectives that show that "When others ran away from danger, Mose ran toward it" (n.p.). Mose is said to have disappeared after saving many people's lives in a terrible hotel fire. He represents the courage and tenacity of firefighters throughout history and the human need to believe that heroes live on in some way and that their spirits do not die.

"PIE-BITER" (MID-1800S–EARLY 1900S). *Pie-Biter* (1983) was carefully researched by the author-illustrator team of Ruthanne Lum McCunn and You-shan Tang, who neatly blend facts and styles from both Western and Chinese culture. When Hoi came to the United States from China as a boy, he grew up working on the railroad. It is said that his fondness for all kinds of pie—"peach, pumpkin, vinegar, carrot, or gooseberry...Dutch apple, huckleberry, and lemon" (n.p.)—earned him the name Pie-Biter from his colleagues and made him extra strong and in demand for the hard work of laying rail. What was really remarkable about Pie-Biter, however, was his entrepreneurial spirit. After completing the railroad, he started his own successful packing business, earned a fortune, and decided to return to China and stay there permanently.

CASEY JONES (1863–1900) AND SIM WEBB (1874–1957). Casey was the engineer on a train named the Cannonball, and Sim was the fireman who shoveled coal into the engine. *Casey Jones' Fireman: The Story of Sim Webb* (Farmer, 1999) tells the story in picture book form about Casey's refusal to let go of the engine brake, which saves the lives of Sim and the train passengers on the Cannonball but not Casey's. Farmer tells the story from Sim's point of view and has used Sim's autobiography to authenticate parts of the story. In this version of the story, against Sim's advice, Casey borrows a suspicious golden train whistle from a devilish character. Using this mysterious whistle in what became Casey's last run almost causes the end of the world. James Bernardin's paintings detail the setting and crash event in richly colored dark paintings. Allan Drummond's *Casey Jones* (2001) captures the story of Casey and Sim in train-chuffing rhythms for the younger set: "But nobody told Casey/there was trouble ahead,/so he hung on with the throttle out,/and on they sped." Drummond's book begs for dramatic interpretation. Farmer's book is perfect for further analysis of human strengths and flaws. Casey is considered heroic for trying to stop his passenger train from hitting a freight train and insisting that Sim jump off the train before the crash. Sim is celebrated for his exemplary work habits.

Teaching Legends in the Classroom

Legends are rich sources of information to enliven discussions in history and social studies classes. Legends can be used to examine religious perspectives, persecution, and the "truths" of history with your students. For example, it is thought by some that Arthurian legends were designed around a Christian king to tell more appealing stories to overcome the Druid worship of the times but that the stories were loosely based on the Celtic people's own heroes. It is also fascinating to explore why people from one culture might adapt another culture's stories for their own. What are the multifaceted reasons this kind of thing might have happened? Was this action conscious or unconscious, conscionable or unconscionable, or some or all of the above?

What compels Robin Hood to take from the rich and give to the poor? One version of how Robin Hood became an outlaw tells of his encounter with some wealthy farmers on the way to an archery tournament. When the men taunted Robin about his youth and lack of skill and tried to prevent him from continuing his journey, he shot all of them dead. Yet another version says a wealthy magistrate robbed the child Robin of his lands when his parents died and left Robin a helpless orphan. As Robin grew to manhood, he sought to avenge that wrong by stealing food and money from the nobles and distributing it to the weak and poor. Although Robin and his Merry Men were said to be kind to the needy and oppressed, those actions were seemingly driven by revenge. Does that make him an admirable or despicable character, or something in between?

What drives Fa Mulan to dress like a man and take her father's place in a war? Does this action make her tragic, heroic, or both? The Maiden of Yueh, who, some say, trained Chinese men in fencing hundreds of years ago during the Tang Dynasty, is a model for the many versions of Fa Mulan legends. Fa Mulan dressed as a man to take the place of her unfairly conscripted elderly and frail father to fight the Tartars. Does this make Fa Mulan an early feminist, or is she a figure of filial duty, a trait important to many Chinese people even today?

Although legendary figures sometimes do wrong to do right, their stories prepare readers to analyze and understand the consequences of decisions people make and the uncertainty of life that adults know comes with age and experience. Role models such as Robin Hood, St. Nicholas, and Fa Mulan demonstrate that despite the dire life circumstances most people face at some point in their lives, difficulties can be overcome with grace and fortitude.

Legends also extend students' knowledge of Western-style story structures. As with fables and tall tales, there is usually a beginning, middle, and end to the plot of the story. Comparable to many traditional stories of any culture, legends have a moral, or something to teach. Unlike in a fable, though, the moral usually must be inferred from a legend. Although some experienced readers assume that the moral or teaching in legends is obvious, that is not true for many students who lack experience with these structures or need explicit help in linking one related genre to the next.

Following are classroom ideas to use when teaching with legends.

Assessing What Students Know About Legends

Key to any aspect of teaching about genre is knowing (a) what the students understand, (b) what the students understand to some extent, and (c) what the students do not understand at all. I've found it useful to read aloud a short legend for the age group I'm working with, such as a version of an Arthur or Robin Hood legend. I tell the students that I am going to read a legend and ask them to think about what they can add to their knowledge of legends. Either a discussion can follow in which a chart of alleged characteristics is constructed by the whole group, or small groups can gather to chart their understandings, then share them with the large group. The charts can be used for comparison purposes, to mark what might have come from the group's prior knowledge instead of the read-aloud (or vice versa), or to hold up to further readings of legends in order to confirm, clarify, or disconfirm the contents of the original lists.

Sheila Muldaur has constructed a series of genre assessments titled *The Proficient Reader Record* (2004) to determine starting points for instruction around genre. Although the construct of legend is not yet included in these assessments, a chapter on how teachers can create their own assessments is a valuable tool. Helpful questions to determine what to teach students include the following:

What genre is (name of text)? (If the students do not know, tell them the genre before asking the next questions.)

How can you tell it is a legend?

Where do legends come from?

Tell (or write) the beginning, middle, and end of this legend in four or five thoughts (or lines) and share it with another student.

Who are the characters in this story? What makes (him, her, them) legendary?

Why do you think the author wrote this legend? What did the author want the reader to think about while listening to (or reading) this legend?

If what we just read was a good example of a legend, what would you need to include if you wrote a legend about someone?

What qualities do all legends seem to have in common?

Are legends true or not true? How does a reader or writer of legends find that out?

Helping Students Know the Legend Genre

If teaching the legend genre is part of your curriculum, students can be grouped and regrouped for reading and writing instruction in that genre based on the strengths and needs they exhibit. Teacher think-alouds, in which teachers model their thought processes as they read aloud, can be used to model how legends work, as the teacher reads aloud or models writing a legend in front of the class daily and over time. If legends are linked to a history or social studies unit, students can be responsible for exploring a legendary figure independently or with a small group. They can report their findings and demonstrate their understanding to the class through the construction and performance of a play or a Readers Theatre presentation.

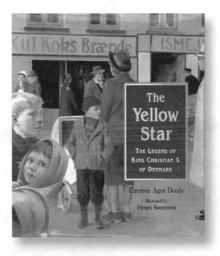

Many of the picture books mentioned in this chapter can be used during social studies units, especially in middle school settings. For example, classes studying the Nazi occupation of Europe and Scandinavia during World War II would benefit from hearing Deedy's version of *The Yellow Star: The Legend of King Christian X of Denmark* (2000), which explores how the king and his Danish subjects resisted the Nazis and showed solidarity with the Jewish people. This legend shows that even during modern times, courageous acts of people who are revered often are embellished. After a decree was released that stated, "All Jews must sew onto their clothing a yellow star"

Book cover from *The Yellow Star: The Legend of King Christian X of Denmark*, written by Carmen Agra Deedy, illustrated by Henri Sorensen. Copyright © 2000. Used by permission of Peachtree Publishers.

(n.p.), it is said that when the respected King Christian rode out among his people with a yellow star sewn on his own clothes, all the Danish citizens did the same. Although this story cannot be corroborated, Deedy asks a remarkable question for readers to consider in the afterword: "What if we could follow that example today against violators of human rights?" (n.p.). The realistic double-page color paintings by Danish citizen Henri Sorenson dramatize the conflict between the king and a Nazi officer and portray the indomitable spirit of the Danes.

With enough experience reading and listening to legends, students can learn to retell a favorite legend in writing or orally. I construct a legend in writing in front of students, even older students, to share my thinking about how to do this task and to show how I overcome my own writing or speaking challenges. Writing demonstrations that show how to plan, draft, and publish a legend are worthwhile models for intermediate and adolescent students to observe as they begin to construct a legend. Learning to retell a legend is another purposeful activity, as it requires reading and rereading, internalizing the story, and applying skills that also can be used for effective public speaking. Help for analyzing the constructs of a legend can be found in *Text Forms and Features: A Resource for Intentional Teaching* (Mooney, 2001). Teachers who want to learn more about the art of storytelling might want to consult *Children Tell Stories* (Hamilton & Weiss, 1990) or *The Storyteller's Start-Up Book: Finding, Learning, Performing, and Using Folktales* (MacDonald, 1993).

What's Next for the Legend?

As history is being created every minute—and even as this chapter is being written— some legends may continue to endure or become obsolete. As the demographics of countries change, will the stories listed in this chapter stay the same, change, or disappear? No one knows for sure because societies change continuously, people move and take their stories with them to other places, and instantaneous access via the Internet to distant locations and people we might never meet offers us a wider view of history and legends in the making than this chapter begins to present.

An interesting new construct is the "urban legend," which Horning (1997) identifies as a tale that "recounts bizarre or supernatural occurrences, sworn to be true as the teller generally claims the event happened to a friend of a friend" (p. 50). These "urban" constructs sometimes seem more like antilegends, as they do not exactly fit the characteristics explored earlier in this chapter. Because many of these tales are grisly, scary, risqué, or generally unsavory stories of the human condition, they are more suitable for (and popular with) teens and adults. Although it is hard to know how urban legends will affect the definition of, or what we regard as, quality tellings and retellings, they are a common finding in an Internet search and have even found their way into trade books. Perhaps the most authoritative collector and reteller of urban legends is Jan Harold Brunvand, who has made a career of studying urban legends, compiling them, and explaining how they came to be. *Too Good to Be True:*

The Colossal Book of Urban Legends (Brunvand, 2001) might be a good starting place for those who wish to explore this unique genre.

Conclusion

Considering why legends about the people mentioned in this chapter have endured begins to build the background knowledge young readers and writers need to make sense of the ambiguities about people, places, and history. Legends are useful for developing students' understanding about desirable character traits in themselves and others, the kind of people they want to become, and the costs and rewards attendant to living a life composed of thoughtful deeds, kind or courageous acts, and soul-searching self-awareness. Who among us now will be tomorrow's legends, and what actions will genuinely earn them that status?

REFERENCES

American heritage dictionary of the English language (4th ed.). (2002). Boston: Houghton Mifflin. Available: http://www.bartleby.com

Anderson, N.A. (2001). *Elementary children's literature: The basics for teachers and parents*. New York: Allyn & Bacon.

Brunvand, J.H. (2001). *Too good to be true: The colossal book of urban legends*. New York: W.W. Norton.

Hamilton, M., & Weiss, M. (1990). *Children tell stories: A teaching guide*. Katonah, NY: Richard C. Owen.

Hearne, B. (1993a). Cite the source: Reducing cultural chaos in picture books, part one. *School Library Journal, 39*(7), 22–27.

Hearne, B. (1993b). Respect the source: Reducing cultural chaos in picture books, part two. *School Library Journal, 39*(8), 33–37

Horning, K.T. (1997). *From cover to cover: Evaluating and reviewing children's books*. New York: HarperCollins.

Huck, C.S., Kiefer, B.Z., Hepler, S., & Hickman, J. (2004). *Children's literature in the elementary school* (8th ed.). New York: McGraw-Hill.

Li, S. (2000). Mulan and more: Heroines of Chinese folklore in picture books. *Book Links, 9*(5), 15.

Lynch-Brown, C., & Tomlinson, C.A. (2001). *Essentials of children's literature* (4th ed.). Upper Saddle River, NJ: Pearson.

MacDonald, M.R. (1993). *The storyteller's start-up book: Finding, learning, performing, and using folktales*. Little Rock, AR: August House.

Mooney, M. (2001). *Text forms and features: A resource for intentional teaching*. Katonah, NY: Richard C. Owen.

Muldaur, S. (2004). *The proficient reader record*. Katonah, NY: Richard C. Owen.

Pappas, C., Kiefer, B., & Levstik, L. (1999). *An integrated language perspective in the elementary school: An action approach* (3rd ed.). New York: Longman.

Pollan, M. (2001). *The botany of desire: A plant's-eye view of the world*. New York: Random House.

Rosenberg, D. (1997). *Folklore, myths, and legends: A world perspective*. Lincolnwood, IL: NTC Publishing Group.

Slapin, B., & Seale, D. (Eds.). (1998). *Through Indian eyes: The Native American experience in books for children* (4th ed.). Los Angeles: American Indian Studies Center.

Stein, J. (Ed.). (1967). *The Random House dictionary of the English language: The unabridged edition*. New York: Random House.

Stoodt-Hill, B.D., & Anspaugh-Corson, L.B. (2001). *Children's literature: Discovery for a lifetime* (2nd ed.). Upper Saddle River, NJ: Merrill Prentice-Hall.

Temple, C., Martinez, M., Yokota, J., & Naylor, A. (2001). *Children's books in children's hands: An introduction to their literature* (2nd ed.). Boston: Allyn & Bacon.

Tunnell, M.O., Darigan, D.L., & Jacobs, J.S. (2002). *Children's literature: Engaging teachers and children in good books*. Upper Saddle River, NJ: Pearson.

CHILDREN'S BOOKS CITED

Alexander, L. (1999). *The chronicles of Prydain* (5 vols.). New York: Henry Holt.

Al-Saleh, K. (1985). *Fabled cities, princes, & jinn from Arab myths and legends*. New York: Shocken.

Armstrong, C. (1995). *Lives and legends of the saints: With paintings from the great art museums of the world*. New York: Simon & Shuster.

Bawden, N. (1981). *William Tell* (R. Allamand, Illus.). New York: Lothrop, Lee & Shepard.

Boutet de Monvel, M. (1980). *Joan of Arc*. New York: Viking.

Brown, D. (2002). *Across a wide dark sea*. Brookfield, CT: Roaring Book.

Bryson, B. (1967). *Gilgamesh*. New York: Holt, Rinehart and Winston.

Byrd, R. (1999). *Finn MacCoul and his fearless wife: A giant of a tale from Ireland*. New York: Dutton.

Cooper, S. (1987). *Dark is rising* (5 vols.). New York: Simon & Schuster.

Deedy, C.A. (2000). *The yellow star: The legend of King Christian X of Denmark* (H. Sorensen, Illus.). Atlanta, GA: Peachtree.

Delacre, L. (1996). *Golden tales: Myths, legends, and folktales from Latin America*. New York: Scholastic.

dePaola, T. (1978). *The clown of God*. New York: Harcourt Brace Jovanovich.

dePaola, T. (1981). *Fin M'Coul: The giant of Knockmany Hill*. New York: Holiday House.

dePaola, T. (1982). *Francis: The poor man of Assisi*. New York: Holiday House.

Dewey, A. (1990). *The narrow escapes of Davy Crockett*. New York: Morrow.

Drummond, A. (2001). *Casey Jones*. New York: Farrar, Straus & Giroux.

Dupre, R. (1993). *Agassu: Legend of the leopard king*. Minneapolis, MN: Carolrhoda.

Early, M. (1991). *William Tell*. New York: Harry Abrams.

Early, M. (1996). *Robin Hood*. New York: Harry Abrams.

Edens, C. (Ed.). (2002). *Robin Hood*. San Francisco: Chronicle.

Edmonds, I.G. (1994). *Ooka the wise: Tales of old Japan* (S. Yamazaki, Illus.). Hamden, CT: Shoestring.

Farmer, N. (1999). *Casey Jones' fireman: The story of Sim Webb* (I. Bernardin, Illus.). New York: Dial.

Finkel, I. (1998). *The hero king Gilgamesh*. Lincolnwood, IL: NTC Publishing Group.

Fisher, L.E. (1996). *William Tell*. New York: Farrar, Straus & Giroux.

Foster, K. (1999). *The city of rainbows: A tale from ancient Sumar*. Philadelphia: University of Pennsylvania Press.

Fritz, J. (1981). *The man who loved books* (T.S. Hyman, Illus.). New York: G.P. Putnam's Sons.

Furlong. M. (1997). *Robin's country*. New York: Knopf.

Gibbons, G. (1994). *St. Patrick's Day*. New York: Holiday House.

Hastings, S. (1981). *Sir Gawain and the green knight* (J. Wijngaard, Illus.). New York: Lothrop, Lee & Shepard.

Hastings, S. (1985). *Sir Gawain and the loathly lady* (J. Wijngaard, Illus.). New York: Mulberry.

Heaney, M. (2000). *The names upon the harp: Irish myth and legend*. New York: Scholastic.

Hodges, M. (1984). *Saint George and the dragon* (T.S. Hyman, Illus.). Boston: Little, Brown.

Hodges, M. (1991). *Brother Francis and the friendly beasts* (T. Lewin, Illus.). New York: Charles Scribner's Sons.

Hodges, M. (1993a). *The hero of Bremen* (C. Mikolaycak, Illus.). New York: Holiday House.

Hodges, M. (1993b). *Saint Patrick and the peddler* (P.B. Johnson, Illus.). New York: Orchard.

Hodges, M. (1999). *Joan of Arc: The lily maid*. New York: Holiday House.

Jackson, S.L. (1998). (Narrator). *John Henry* [Video]. Weston, CT: Weston Woods.

Keats, E.J. (1987). *John Henry: An American legend*. New York: Knopf.

Keillor, G. (Reader). (1995). *Johnny Appleseed*, by J.H. Kunstler [Audiotape and Book]. New York: Simon & Schuster.

Kellogg, S. (1988). *Johnny Appleseed: A tall tale*. New York: Morrow.

Lester, J. (1994). *John Henry* (J. Pinkney, Illus.). New York: Dial.

Mayer, M. (1999). *Women warriors: Myths and legends of heroic women*. New York: HarperCollins.

Mayer, M. (2001). *The real Santa Claus*. New York: Penguin Putnam.

Mayo, M. (2000). *Brother Sun, Sister Moon: The life and stories of St. Francis* (P. Malone, Illus.). Boston: Little, Brown.

McCaughrean, G. (1995). *The golden hoard: Myths and legends of the world* (B. Willey, Illus.). New York: Simon & Schuster.

McCaughrean, G. (1997a). *El Cid* (V. Ambrus, Illus.). Oxford, UK: Oxford University Press.

McCaughrean, G. (1997b). *The bronze cauldron: Myths and legends of the world* (B. Willey, Illus.). New York: Simon & Schuster.

McCaughrean, G. (2003). *Gilgamesh the hero* (D. Parkins, Illus.). Grand Rapids, MI: Eerdmans.

McCunn, R.L. (1983). *Pie-Biter* (Y. Tang, Illus.). San Francisco: Design Enterprises.

Meltzer, M. (1998). *Ten queens: Portraits of women of power* (B. Andersen, Illus.). New York: Dutton.

Morpurgo, M. (1996). *Robin of Sherwood* (M. Foreman, Illus.). New York: Harcourt Brace.

Moses, W. (2001). *Johnny Appleseed: The story of a legend*. New York: Philomel.

O'Hara, C. (Narrator). *Finn McCoul* [Audiocassette]. Rowatan, CT: Rabbit Ears Productions.

Osborne, M.P. (2002). *New York's bravest* (S. Johnson & L. Fancher, Illus.). New York: Knopf.

Rowling, J.K. (1998–2003). Harry Potter series (5 vols.). New York: Scholastic.

San Souci, R.D. (1990). *Young Merlin* (D. Horne, Illus.). New York: Bantam Doubleday Dell.

San Souci, R.D. (1993). *Young Guinevere* (J. Henterly, Illus.). New York: Bantam Doubleday Dell.

San Souci, R.D. (1996). *Young Lancelot* (J. Henterly, Illus.). New York: Bantam Doubleday Dell.

San Souci, R.D. (1997). *Young Arthur* (J. Henterly, Illus.). New York: Bantam Doubleday Dell.

San Souci, R.D. (1998). *Fa Mulan* (J. Tseng & M. Tseng, Illus.). New York: Hyperion.

Schanzer, R. (2001). *Davy Crockett saves the world*. New York: HarperCollins.

Shelley, M. (1998). *Frankenstein: Or, the modern Prometheus*. Oxford: Oxford University Press.

Spenser, E. (1988). *The Faerie Queen*. New York: Penguin Classics.

Stanley, D. (1998). *Joan of Arc*. New York: HarperCollins.

Steig, W. (1993). *Shrek!* New York: Farrar, Straus & Giroux.

Stewart, B. (1988). *Cuchulainn: Hound of Ulster*. New York: Sterling.

Stoutenburg, A. (1966). *American tall tales*. New York: Viking.

Sutcliff, R. (1963). *The hound of Ulster*. New York: Dutton.

Sutcliff, R. (1967). *The high deeds of Finn MacCool*. New York: Dutton.

Sutcliff, R. (1979). *Song for a Dark Queen*. New York: HarperCollins.

Sutcliff, R. (1980). *The light beyond the forest: The quest for the Holy Grail*. New York: Dutton.

Sutcliff. R. (1981). *The sword and the circle: King Arthur and the knights of the round table*. New York: Dutton.

Sutcliff, R. (1982). *The road to Camlann: The death of King Arthur*. New York: Penguin Putnam.

Synge, U. (1978). *The giant at the ford and other legends of the saints*. New York: Atheneum.

Talbott, H. (1991). *King Arthur: The sword and the stone*. New York: Morrow.

Talbott, H. (1995). *King Arthur and the round table*. New York: Morrow.

Talbott, H. (1996). *Excalibur*. New York: Morrow.

Talbott, H. (1999). *Lancelot*. New York: Morrow.

Tolkien, J.R.R. (1981). The Lord of the Rings (3 vols.). New York: Ballantine

Tomlinson, T. (1995). *The Forestwife*. New York: Yearling.

Tomlinson, T. (2000). *Child of the May*. New York: Yearling.

Tompert, A. (2000). *Saint Nicholas* (M. Garland, Illus.). Honesdale, PA: Boyds Mills Press.

Tompert, A. (2002). *The pied piper of Peru* (K. Kasparavicius, Illus.). Honesdale, PA: Boyds Mills Press.

Williams, J. (1968). *The horn of Roland* (S. Morrison, Illus.). New York: Thomas Y. Crowell.

Wisniewski, D. (1992). *Sundiata: Lion king of Mali*. New York: Clarion.

Wisniewski, D. (1996). *Golem*. New York: Clarion.

Yolen, J. (1996a). *Hobby*. New York: Scholastic.

Yolen, J. (1996b). *Passager*. New York: Scholastic.

Yolen, J. (1997). *Merlin*. New York: Scholastic.

Zeman, L. (1992). *Gilgamesh the king*. Plattsburgh, NY: Tundra.

Zeman, L. (1993). *The revenge of Ishtar*. Plattsburgh, NY: Tundra.

Zeman, L. (1995). *The last quest of Gilgamesh*. Plattsburgh, NY: Tundra.

Zhang, S.N. (1998). *The ballad of Mulan*. Union City, CA: Pan Asian.

CHAPTER 6

Tall Tales: An American Folk Invention

Linda M. Pavonetti

Tall tales are as varied as their tellers, ranging from one-liners—"What gives him his strength is rock juice. He breaks boulders in half by spitting on them, then squeezes a glass of rock juice from the pieces, then drinks it" (Schwartz, 1975, p. 19)—to animals such as the luferland, whose "legs are triple jointed—so that it can run equally fast in any direction" (Simon, 1958, p. 50)—to the fully developed exploits of familiar characters such as Paul Bunyan, John Henry, and Sally Ann Thunder Ann Whirlwind Crockett. Such far-fetched stories are commonly known as tall tales, lying tales, "windies," "whoppers," or "gallyfloppers" (Schwartz, 1975).

Tall tales are like other traditional literature in that collectors frequently have discovered comparable stories in distant locales. These narratives usually have similar themes and motifs and have been adapted to fit the idiomatic language, social mores, and geographic landmarks of their most recent local storyteller. Variations of the "it was sooooooooo cold" story originated long before television late shows, stand-up comedians, and comic strips.

> You wanta know the coldest morning I ever knew? Well, our hired man went out to the barn with the milk pails, whistlin' like he allus did. You know, it was so cold, them notes froze right in the air. When he came back to the house, there they was, hangin' right in front of him, so he snapped 'em off and brought 'em back into the house and set 'em in the back o' the stove. You know, we had the sweetest music you ever heard for about an hour. (Glimm, 1983, p. 39)

Glimm notes that tales about frozen words and frozen music are common in northern Pennsylvania and Canada and across the colder areas of the United States. Alvin Schwartz (1975) provides three variants of the same story. In one, a man was "strong enough to break the air with his fists, which enabled him to speak" (p. 90). The second "it was so cold" story involves women: One called her son to come home, but her words froze in the air. He never heard her until the spring thaw—so he was two months late coming home. Another version, which Schwartz claims as an original "lie," has two girls quarreling, but it was so cold their words came out as ice cubes, one for each word. "But they were so angry, they collected the ice cubes in sacks and took them home. Then they melted them and listened to their words and enjoyed a good fight" (p. 91).

Defining the Tall Tale

In order to define the tall tale, it is necessary to place it within the context of folk literature. Some children's literature authorities consider tall tales to be a type of legend (Cullinan, 1989), albeit "one or two steps removed" (Temple, Martinez, Yokota, & Naylor, 2002, p. 444). Others writers list tall tales as a subgenre of folk literature (e.g., Goforth, 1998; Huck, 1997). May Hill Arbuthnot began by classifying the tall tale under the general heading "Folk Tales in the United States" (1964, p. 265), then expanded it, using the appellation "Tall Tales and Other Native Inventions" (Arbuthnot, 1964, p. 268; Sutherland, 1997).

Egoff (1967) differentiates between folk tales—an extensive genre of traditional oral stories anonymously originating in the past—and tall tales. The latter she defines as a specific subgenre of traditional literature, also anonymous but with a particular emphasis on national or regional characteristics.

Most experts agree that "tall tales are exaggerated, humorous tales about historical or imaginary humans and animals, who accomplish the 'impossible' in rugged environments" (Goforth, 1998, p. 83). However, true folklorists, such as Richard Dorson, care little for this family of tales because there is insufficient evidence that they come from the oral tradition. Indeed, Dorson coined the term *fakelore* to describe his view of the commercialization of the "raw data of folklore by invention, selection, fabrication, and similar refining processes" (Dorson, 1959, p. 4).

The History of the Tall Tale

Many people believe that tall tales are an American invention, but that, in itself, is a tall tale. A more accurate portrayal is that tall tales are an American *perfection*. Tall tales seem to have existed long before Columbus discovered America, before Conestoga wagons or trail drives.

The actual historical heritage of the tall tale is as elusive as the origins of any oral literature. Is the *Odyssey* a tall tale? It is assumed that its origins are in the oral tradition, but who really knows the accuracy with which it was related? Literary history seldom associates tall tales with the ancient Greeks, but Plutarch (c. 46–120) is reputed to have been the first to record a version of the frozen words story:

> Antiphanes said humorously that in a certain city words congealed with the cold the moment they were spoken, and later, as they thawed out, people heard in the summer what they had said to one another in the winter. (Brown, 1987, p. 11)

Brown relates other versions including one that was published in 1528 in Castiglione's *Book of the Courtier* (1976).

Among the indications that tales of lying did not originate in the United States are the stories of Baron Münchausen, progenitor of the *Münchausen*, a term frequently used in conjunction with information about tall tales. Dorson (1959) explains that the "most redoubtable truth-twister [was] Baron Münchausen (Rudolph Eric Raspe, 1720–1797), whose solemn-faced narratives of *His Marvelous Travels and Campaigns in Russia* made his name a synonym for gorgeous fabrications" (p. 227). Just as the "fish story" immediately invokes a vision of a small fish transformed into a giant catch, so the term *Münchausen* has become associated with fabricated or exaggerated versions of real adventures.

It is likely that the age of American folklore arrived with the expulsion of British rule during the Revolutionary War. During the earliest days of the United States' colonization, folk tales, like tea, were British imports. Religion was the primary concern of the original immigrants, who rejoiced in their newfound freedom to openly practice their religion. As with everything else, even oral storytelling was overshadowed by the omnipresence of "somber, God-fearing, anxiety-laden supernatural tales" (Dorson, 1973, p. 57). However, as the governance and unification of the previously independent colonies replaced the primacy of religious matters, a unique American folklore began to develop.

The early tales of lying often followed a set formula, with characteristics similar to other forms of oral tales: quick hook, rapid pace, expressive first-person voice, and a focus on "virtuoso accumulation of absurdities rather than the content" (Dorson, 1972, p. 71). Dorson suggested that the Münchausen-like tales of lying developed into an American mutation—the tall tale: "The Tall Tale, as this subvariant is known, flourished in America and still continues to bear new fruits...American pioneers developed new Münchausen-like heroes, and the unexplored land offered sufficiently remarkable natural phenomena to boast about" (Dorson, 1972, p. 71). Examples of these new Münchausen-like American heroes are Jim Bridger and Gib Morgan, who elaborated their real-life adventures as mountain man and wildcat oil driller. In turn, these tall tales made their way into print versions that continue to enjoy popularity within the pages of illustrated children's books and adult anthologies.

The first examples of written tall tales appeared in newspapers shortly after the War of 1812. These amusing and generally exaggerated stories fit into one of three categories: scenes the author had observed, remarkably good tales the writer repeated, and totally fictitious stories invented for the paper. Often, newspapers carried hybrids of all three types. Copyright laws, in their infancy at the time and not always respected, did not deter newspapers from reprinting entertaining and amusing accounts from their competitors (Dorson, 1973).

The tall tales that arose between 1820 and the Civil War featured actual, living characters such as Johnny Appleseed, Davy Crockett, and Mike Fink, who are still commemorated in modern picture storybook adaptations. Extraordinary animals, storms, and invented or composite figures succeeded these protagonists.

Some tall tales have been traced, in large part, to advertising campaigns and newspaper stories. Although Maine folklorists would debate this claim, Paul Bunyan appears to have his origins in the stories told in the logging camps of Michigan. A young night reporter, James McGillivray, is credited with the first print version of Paul Bunyan's exploits. His story "The Round River Drive" appeared in the August 10, 1906, edition of the Oscoda-Au Sable, Michigan, *Press* (as cited in Rogers, 1999). He credits stories he heard when he was a 13-year-old boy, scaling logs on the Au Sable River near Grayling, Michigan.

Popularity of the Tall Tale

These spoken and written narratives accented the humorous. They drew their fun from character quirks and eccentricities, clever tricks and...a humor of democracy, portraying common folk in their pursuits and pastimes, catching their local idioms. (Dorson, 1973, p. 58)

Tall tales emphasized characteristics of the American frontier, especially humor, in the form of preposterous exaggerations. Their setting was the westward-moving edges of the new nation where bears replaced dragons; anecdotes involved 'gators, cattle drives, 'coon hunts, gambling, fighting, and shooting; and far-fetched fabrications elevated to heroic stature the men and women who dared cross the Appalachian Mountains. Possibly the vast, overwhelming expanse of an unexplored wilderness gave rise to the excessive nature of the stories themselves. Michael Cart (1995) posits that the early settlers coped by balancing the "natural extravagance with the contrived extravagance of the oral yarns the pioneers began telling around lonely campfires" (p. 106).

Arbuthnot (1964) contends that tall tales were reflective of American optimism and bravado. A can-do spirit of overcoming insurmountable obstacles permeates the tales. "These stories appeal to Americans because they are success epics with a sense of humor" (Arbuthnot, 1964, p. 268). The humorous core in America's maturing folk literature masked an underlying heroic tendency. "All mythical heroes have been exaggerations but they have been serious ones. America came too late for that.... That is the natively American thing—not that her primitive humor is exaggerative, but that her primitive exaggerations were humorous" (Eastman, as cited in Botkin, 1944, p. 175)

Because of sociocultural conditions, the late 19th and early 20th centuries nudged tall tales in a slightly different direction. Invented heroic composites rather than glorified historical persons became the central characters. During this period, local pride expanded into a fierce nationalism spurred on by improved transportation and communications. Consequently, those characters who formerly had been mere regional figures became national folk heroes. Furthermore, the industrialization of the United States caused a shift in the types of occupations these characters pursued. Paul Bunyan, John Henry, Casey Jones, Joe Magarac, and Febold Feboldson emerged as new-fashioned American heroes. It is worthy of note that early American storytellers chose hunters and boatmen, explorers, and farmers for their folk heroes instead of presidents and war heroes (Pavonetti & Combs, 1999).

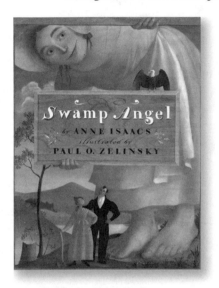

Book cover from *Swamp Angel* by Anne Isaacs, illustrated by Paul O. Zelinsky, copyright © 1994 by Paul O. Zelinsky, illustrations. Used by permission of Dutton, A Division of Penguin Young Readers Group, A Member of Penguin Group (USA) Inc., 345 Hudson Street, New York, NY 10014. All rights reserved.

When children's books began emerging as a legitimate literary province, authors and illustrators adapted the tall tale to the emerging format of the 32-page picture storybook. During the early 20th century, James Daugherty created the artwork for several tall tales, including a retelling of the story of John Henry (Shapiro, 1945). He earned the 1939 Newbery Medal for his book *Daniel Boone* (1938), written about another larger-than-life figure, and extended his involvement by transforming the Aesop's fable about Androcles and the lion into a rustic, homespun tall tale he titled *Andy and the Lion* (1939). The characters in these books, both through the text and illustrations, surpassed the confines of realism and history, becoming larger than life. "These tough, swaggering big-talk giants stood for the American working man" (Hearn, Clark, & Clark, 1996, p. 36).

The trend toward isolation that followed World War I and the Great Depression may have been the impetus for a shift in the focus of children's literature from European to American themes, narratives, and heroes. Louise Seaman Bechtel, head of Macmillan's juvenile book division (the first such division established by a major U.S. publishing company), called the emergence of tall tales "a refreshing new note in children's books...[that] accomplished much for American children" (as cited in Hearn et al., 1996, p. 35).

The evolution of the tall tale for children, with its hyperbole and outrageous adventures, paralleled the appearance of another U.S. phenomenon, the comic book. Contrary to the disdain and contempt with which they viewed Popeye and Superman, however, librarians and publishers enlarged their catalog of tall tales and other chronicles of the American frontier. Bechtel explained this trend: "They [tall tales] fitted both the comic-book aspects of heroism and a changing concept of the fairy tale. They loosened up our use of a truly American prose" (as cited in Hearn et al., 1996, p. 36).

Richard Dorson, one of the United States' most respected folklorists, deplored the commercialization of tall tales by children's authors, publishers, advertising agencies, and corporate giants. His principal concern was that the stories were not true folklore in that they were "devoid of any field sources and derivative from previous writings" (1959, p. 216). He contended that Americans treasured their new heritage, rooted in the oral tradition and overflowing with heroes who "reflected American power, efficiency, and indestructibility" (p. 216). Dorson's scathing rant focused on several issues:

1. The tall tale protagonists derive little, if any, of their feats from the oral tradition. Instead, the feats are the invention of "money-writers."

2. Unlike legendary figures such as Daniel Boone and Johnny Appleseed, the heroes of tall tales are not folk heroes at all and are seldom based on historical prototypes.

3. The mood of "gargantuan whimsy oozing through" (Dorson, 1959, p. 214) tall tales is not indicative of the way authentic lumberjacks, cowboys, or steelworkers felt about their occupations.

4. These fake folk heroes have replaced traditional folk heroes, such as the Greek and Roman gods of mythology, in the minds of American children.

Dorson and other purists may have disdained the popularization and consequent degradation of the tall tale from a scholarly, philological, or anthropological discipline to what they considered to be an insipid populist derivative, but purists and populists agree that this subgenre of traditional literature has secured its place in children's books. A quick perusal of the *Children's Catalog*, which from its inception in 1909 has recommended titles for well-rounded library collections, confirms the ascendant stature of tall tales. Up through the ninth edition of the *Children's Catalog* (McConnell & West, 1956), tall tales are subsumed within the Dewey Decimal System classification number 398.2, legends and folk tales:

> Sagas, romances, legends, ballads in prose form, and hero stories are classified 398.2
> instead of with the literature of the country of origin, in order to keep the traditional

material together and make it more readily available to children. The *Aeneid*, the *Iliad*, and the *Odyssey* are exceptions to this rule, being classified 873 and 883. (McConnell & West, 1956, p. 51).

Within five years, when the 10th edition of the *Children's Catalog* (West & Shor, 1961) became available, the Dewey classification 398.2 had been changed to specifically include tall tales: "Sagas, romances, legends, ballads, and fables in prose form and fairy tales, folk tales, and *tall tales* [emphasis added] are included here.... Myths are classified 291–293. Modern fairy tales are classified with Fiction or Story collections" (p. 50).

The trend from 1956 to the present has been to increase library holdings in folk literature but to decrease the percentage of recommended tall tales (see Table 6.1). The difference between the earlier catalogs and current ones is that "modern fairy tales are classified with Fiction, Story collections (SC), or Easy books (E)" (Price & Yaakov, 2000, p. 10). Because the sixth edition of *A to Zoo* (Lima & Lima, 2001) lists 44 picture storybook titles (anthologies and chapter books are not treated in this resource) under the heading of tall tales, it seems reasonable to conclude that fewer "real" tall tales and more literary tall tales (i.e., parodies, original tales, modernized versions, point of view, and other fictionalized versions that do not come from the oral tradition) are being published at the present time. The trend is to read, enjoy, and use more tall tales in U.S. classrooms, regardless of whether those tales are authentic oral tradition tall tales or original literary tall tales.

Tall Tale Characters in Children's Books

Because of the popularity of folk literature in general and tall tales in particular, parents, teachers, and students seldom run out of new reading materials in this category. Whether new retellings of the old favorites such as Paul Bunyan, or original

Table 6.1
Children's Catalog Classification (398.2): Percentage of Tall Tales

Year	Total Entries	Tall Tales	Percentage
1956	108	22	20.3%
1961	184	22	12.0%
1971	367	24	6.5%
1996–2000	468	13	2.7%

literary tales that extend those much-loved stories—*The Morning the Sun Refused to Rise: An Original Paul Bunyan Story* (Rounds, 1984)—tall tales occupy considerable shelf space in schools, homes, classrooms, and public libraries, as well as bookstores. Recently, tall tales have begun including people of color and women, a widely applauded trend. Characters such as Annie Christmas, a brave African American woman, and Big Jabe (Nolen, 2000), whose marvelous feats helped slaves on the plantation, provide characters for all children to admire. Many collections of tall tales focus on a theme, be it an industry such as logging, or a region such as the southwestern United States, with Pecos Bill or *The Gullywasher* (Rossi, 1995), which includes Spanish words and Mexican American characters. These regional tales often are printed by university or local presses and are distributed to limited markets. There is a large amount written about Paul Bunyan in Michigan logging books, for example, but few students outside the state would be as interested as local children in these narrowly focused tales.

Tall Tale Collections and Anthologies

Tall tales, just like other folk tales, are available in assorted formats. Audio and video renditions are popular. Picture books, poems, biographies, chapter books, early readers, and anthologies exist for both adult and child audiences. One of the best ways to begin enjoying tall tales is to delve into several anthologies.

Both for the quality of its art and its language, *American Tall Tales* (Osborne, 1991) is one of the best compilations for any library. The nine stories, although comprehensive, are so well written that they leave readers wishing for more. Osborne's language is easily read, yet conveys the idiomatic humor that characterizes oral retellings: "Davy [Crockett] brought his knuckles together like two thunderclouds. But the sparks froze before he could even begin to collect them.... His hat froze to his head and twenty icicles formed under his nose" (p. 13). Michael McCurdy's wood engravings, tinted with watercolors, impart a sense of boldness and magnitude. An introductory map provides scaffolding for readers to contextualize heroes, and the extensive bibliography affords adults and students the opportunity for further reading or research.

Robert D. San Souci and Andrew Glass have teamed up as author and illustrator, respectively, to produce *Larger Than Life: The Adventures of American Legendary Heroes* (San Souci, 1991). Containing only five stories, San Souci's book chronicles one tale from the lives of four men—John Henry, Old Stormalong, Strap Buckner, and Paul Bunyan—and a yarn pitting Slue-Foot Sue against Pecos Bill.

Paul Robert Walker has assembled an illustrated collection of tall tale figures in *Big Men, Big Country* (1993) that supplements the typical cast of characters with lesser known figures Big Mose Humphreys (the New York City fireman), Jim

Bridger, and John Darling. Big Mose Humphreys, formerly a minor tall tale character, has taken on increased notoriety since the destruction of the World Trade Center. Mary Pope Osborne released a picture storybook *New York's Bravest* (2002), illustrated by the husband and wife team of Steve Johnson and Lou Fancher, that tells of Humphreys's legendary deeds.

Alvin Schwartz is one of many students' favorite authors, primarily known for his urban legends *Scary Stories to Tell in the Dark* (1981). He is, however, also a serious folklorist. One of his more interesting traditional collections features tall tales and the kinds of critters that seem to complement them so perfectly. *Whoppers: Tall Tales and Other Lies Collected From American Folklore* (Schwartz, 1975) includes 145 "outlandish tale[s] about something that never happened and never could" (p. 11).

An "oldie but goodie" that has been a staple in classroom and school libraries since the mid-1960s is Adrien Stoutenburg's *American Tall Tales* (1966). This collection includes some of the best-known folk legends—Paul Bunyan, Pecos Bill, Davy Crockett, John Henry, and Johnny Appleseed. Because it is targeted to a school audience, this book contains no traces of the drinking, gambling, cursing, or other such aspects of the freewheeling frontier life that embellished the original tales told 'round the fire.

Vaughn Ward edited a volume—written for an adult audience—that can nevertheless be shared with students: *I Always Tell The Truth (Even If I Have to Lie to Do It!): Stories From the Adirondack Liars' Club* (1990). Included in this book is a story from Joseph Bruchac—an Abenaki author, poet, storyteller, and musician—already a well-respected classroom favorite. Bruchac tells a tall tale about his grandfather that ranks alongside some of the exploits of Paul Bunyan. Some of the stories in this compilation are quite brief, but others, such as Bruchac's, stretch on for several pages.

Walter Blair's *Tall Tale America: A Legendary History of Our Humorous Heroes* (Blair, 1987) is a fine anthology, suitable for children but on a challenging reading level. The original edition was illustrated by Glen Rounds. Peter Poulakis published *American Folklore* (1969) as part of the Scribner Student Paperback series. It provides a version of "Casey Jones" followed by "Sim Webb's Account of the Wreck." These stories can be used in conjunction with Nancy Farmer's picture storybook, *Casey Jones's Fireman: The Story of Sim Webb* (1998).

Another Alvin Schwartz collection, *Chin Music: Tall Talk and Other Talk* (1979), is an outstanding dictionary of words that will transform an ordinary statement into a colorful tall tale expression. Schwartz collected these synonyms, idioms, portmanteau, and made-up words from American folklore: "People just made them up when they needed a good way of saying what was on their minds.... That's how they made up 'whoopity-scoot,' 'argufy,' 'gollybuster'...and other words and sayings" (1979, p. 11). Alphabetically arranged, this is a great resource for adults and students who love words and word play. The final section provides three ways to make up words:

Add a new ending to a familiar word, combine two words, or make a word from pleasing sounds. As he does in all his books, Schwartz provides thorough notes and sources and an extensive bibliography.

Many other anthologies of traditional folk literature, such as Joanna Cole's *Best-Loved Folktales of the World* (1983), include one or more tall tales. When determining which version to share with students, look for rich, idiomatic language that will allow children to engage not only with the heroes but also the storytellers of days gone by.

Book cover from *Cut From the Same Cloth: American Women of Myth, Legend, and Tall Tale* by Robert D. San Souci, illustrated by Brian Pinkney, copyright © 1993 by Brian Pinkney, illustrations. Published by Philomel, A Division of Penguin Young Readers Group, A Member of Penguin Group (USA) Inc., 345 Hudson Street, New York, NY 10014. All rights reserved.

There are several American folklorists who rise above the rest. They actively collected tales—using strict ethnographic data-gathering standards—from the Great Depression into the middle of the 20th century. Several of these collectors were academics; some revisited the work done during the 1930s as part of the Folklore Project, a branch of the Federal Writers' Project that was funded through President F.D. Roosevelt's Works Projects Administration (WPA) from 1936 to 1940. Some, such as Benjamin A. Botkin, were instrumental in organizing and administering the Folklore Project. His seminal work, *A Treasury of American Folklore: Stories, Ballads, and Traditions of the People* (1944), continues to be one of the finest collections of American folklore. He catalogs tall tales throughout the book: There are six sections of "Heroes and Boasters" in Part 1; those are followed by Part 2, "Boosters and Knockers," which includes "Tall Talk"; and Part 4, "Liars," with a section titled "Yarns and Tall Tales" followed by "From the Liars' Bench." Botkin deserves credit for preserving the American tall tale and its ancillary anecdotes. His book is probably the most important collection step in building a library of American folklore. For more information on the Folklore Project, visit the Library of Congress website at www.memory.loc.gov/ammem/wpaintro/wpahome.html.

Similarly, Richard M. Dorson and Richard Chase also are responsible for preserving much of American folklore. Dorson was a professor at the Indiana University Folklore Institute. He provided not only academic insight into American folklore but also went into the field and actively studied and recorded folklore in northern Michigan, especially the Upper Peninsula. This is the area that, according to many collectors, gave birth to the Paul Bunyan tales. Chase collected Jack Tales and Grandfather Tales from the southern Appalachians, publishing them during the 1940s (Chase, 1948). He also collected a number of songs that he published in several volumes, including *American Folk Tales and Songs* (Chase, 1971).

Vance Randolph compiled tales from the Ozarks during the 1920s. He reported that when he first began collecting folklore, he "was accompanied by a young woman who wrote down every word in shorthand...[later] we used the Library's [of Congress] recording machine...and transcribed them from aluminum discs" (Randolph, 1993, p. xii). Other regional tall tale collections include stories collected in Pennsylvania, Michigan, Kentucky, and especially the Appalachian Mountains. *The Monster Stick & Other Appalachian Tall Tales* (Lepp & Lepp, 1999) comes from winners of the West Virginia State Liars Contest. Original tall tales are still being fabricated at storytellers' competitions across the United States.

A Word of Caution

Some of the best tall tales appear in anthologies that are meant for adult readers. In his introduction to *Stiff as a Poker: A Collection of Ozark Folk Tales* (1993), Vance Randolph notes,

> I blue-penciled a lot of cusswords.... Many of our finest Ozark yarns are full of obscenities, but I have done no bowdlerizing. My feeling is that these bawdy items cannot be cleaned up without eviscerating them. If a story contains "unprintable" words I omit the whole thing instead of trying to expurgate it. (p. xii)

Consequently, it is important to recognize these two types of resources: those appropriate for children's reading and listening and those that are suitable for adults as storytelling, reading, retelling, or resource material for teaching tall tales and other types of American traditional literature.

Individual Tall Tale Heroes

Paul Bunyan

Paul Bunyan is the granddaddy of all tall tales. Ask any American—man, woman, or child—to tell you a tall tale, and it will likely involve Paul Bunyan and Babe the Blue Ox. *Paul Bunyan Swings His Axe* (McCormick, 1977a), an early children's version of this larger-than-life logger's saga, has been in print continuously since the 1930s. The book's 17 chapters chronicle Bunyan's escapades from his birth until the day that he "disappeared from the woods. Some say he is still roaming the forest of the West...the woodsmen say the low rumbling thunder in the mountains on a summer night is Paul Bunyan calling his faithful ox" (p. 111). This is a great read-aloud for younger age groups because of the relatively short chapter length, but its actual target audience is upper elementary and middle school readers. McCormick wrote a companion book, *Tall Timber Tales* (McCormick, 1977b), which offers more stories about Bunyan.

Generations of readers have admired *Ol' Paul the Mighty Logger* (Rounds, 1976) because of Glen Rounds's wonderfully droll illustrations. However, the stories included in this volume, whether traditional or original literary tales, are uproarious fun. "The Bedcats" is a perennial favorite with students, but the stories of the "Whirling Whimpus," the Bear-Behind, and the Flu-Flu Bird are little-known chapters in Bunyan's biography that will leave readers smiling. *The Morning the Sun Refused to Rise* is an original Paul Bunyan tale, also written by Glen Rounds (1984).

Louis Untermeyer provides young people with a multichapter volume of Paul Bunyan's exploits. *The Wonderful Adventures of Paul Bunyan* (1945) begins when he outgrows his cradle during his first week of life and continues through his more familiar logging experiences. Untermeyer adds a chapter "Paul and Pecos Bill" as well as a chapter on "Paul's Courtship." This literary fabrication provides a marvelous entré into *The Bunyans* (Wood, 1996), in which Paul and his wife retire (after many years of hard work) to perfect their golf game. Their children, Little Jean and Teeny, follow in their parents' prodigious footsteps, producing their own amazing achievements. David Shannon's updated illustrations underscore the impressive size of the Bunyan babies, while placing the entire family in a more contemporary context. Although Wood's version of how Bunyan and his wife met varies from more traditional retellings, it does not detract from the enjoyment of visualizing Paul Bunyan and his children.

The Story of Paul Bunyan (Emberley, 1963) is notable more for Ed Emberley's woodcut illustrations than for the quantity or quality of Barbara Emberley's story. The best known of the Bunyan stories is Steven Kellogg's retelling *Paul Bunyan: A Tall Tale* (1984). This intricately illustrated book provides imaginative visual story prompts, especially in its almost-wordless full-page images.

Even Shel Silverstein, in his own irreverent and inimitable style, immortalized Paul Bunyan in *Where the Sidewalk Ends* (1974):

> He shook the dirt from off of his clothes,
> He scratched his butt and he wiped his nose.
> "Y'know, bein' dead wasn't no fun at all"...says Paul...
> ...So he jumps on his ox with a fare-thee-well,
> He says, "I'll find out if they's trees in hell."
> And he rode away, and that was all...we ever seen...of Paul. (pp. 124–125)

Pecos Bill

James Cloyd Bowman, who wrote one of the most definitive histories of Pecos Bill (1961), alleged that Pecos Bill and Paul Bunyan were blood-brothers.

> When the great armies of lumberjacks swung singing into the virgin forests, they found an outlet for their suddenly released imagination in Paul Bunyan; and when, about the

same time, other great armies of singing cowboys galloped into the Range Country of the Southwest, they created Pecos Bill. ("Concerning the Tall Tales of Pecos Bill," n.p.)

Bowman's book, most suitable as an adult reference, details Pecos Bill's life with the coyotes, his horse, Widow Maker, all the natural wonders of the southwestern United States created by Bill, as well as his courting and winning of Slue-Foot Sue. Steven Kellogg's version, *Pecos Bill* (1986), is widely read by children who love his colorful, humorous illustrations.

John Henry

In the introduction to *John Henry and His Hammer* (Felton, 1950), John Henry is acclaimed, not as a great national leader, but as a representative of the working class. "He has no position, no wealth, no external trappings...he was only a man with a hammer" (n.p.). Henry was one of a new breed of heroes; he fought industrialization—and won. This book's illustrations are somewhat stereotypical in their representations of African Americans, so it may be better to keep this as a teacher reference or a read-aloud.

Book cover from *John Henry* by Julius Lester, illustrated by Jerry Pinkney, copyright © 1994 by Jerry Pinkney, illustrations. Used by permission of Dial Books for Young Readers, A Division of Penguin Young Readers Group, A Member of Penguin Group (USA) Inc., 345 Hudson Street, New York, NY 10014. All rights reserved.

Ezra Jack Keats's book *John Henry: An American Legend* (1965) draws its strength from the power of the illustrations. Both books relate the battle between man and machine as the Chesapeake and Ohio Railroad pushed westward through the mountains of West Virginia. John Henry became the archetype of resistance to industrialization as progress inevitably overtook the old ways. Keats, renowned for his collage illustrations, masterfully uses color and line to produce depth, motion, vibration, and strength. Julius Lester's 1994 edition of *John Henry* merges an eloquent voice with expressive illustrations. Jerry Pinkney's watercolor paintings flawlessly complement and enhance Julius Lester's unique storytelling style. This is one of the most exciting tall tale retellings available for children today.

Johnny Appleseed

Perhaps because they find it improbable that anyone could walk from Massachusetts to Indiana planting apple trees along the way, contemporary young people regard Johnny Appleseed as a tall tale character. Many are amazed to learn that John

Chapman, the source of the Johnny Appleseed tall tales, actually lived during the late 1700s and early 1800s. In his author's note at the conclusion of *Johnny Appleseed: A Tall Tale* (1988), Steven Kellogg comments on the stature of Johnny Appleseed in modern society:

> When a folktale attains the status of a myth and embodies a cherished ideal of the people, then its true worth no longer lies merely in the dead facts that may have inspired it, but in the new, living, and creating force that it has become in the present. (Price, 1954, as cited in Kellogg, 1988, n.p.)

Old and new versions chronicling the saga of Johnny Appleseed abound, from Reeve Lindbergh's book-length poem (1990), to Margaret Hodges's *The True Tale of Johnny Appleseed* (1997), which presents known facts with little hyperbole. Rosemary and Stephen Vincent Benét's poem (2001), taken from *A Book of Americans* (Benét & Benét, 1933), has been issued as a picture storybook with illustrations by S.D. Shindler. Two recent additions to the Johnny Appleseed legend include an interesting fictionalization told from the point of view of Johnny's half-brother, Nathaniel. *Folks Call Me Appleseed John* (Glass, 1995) offers a distinctive view of this real-life tall tale hero. Author/illustrator Andrew Glass's oil paintings endow this version with a homespun warmth and strength. Will Moses, great-grandson of "Grandma" Moses, recently contributed a charming supplement to the John Chapman folklore. *Johnny Appleseed, the Story of a Legend* (Moses, 2001) is striking because of Moses's folk art paintings. Additionally, the story itself is well written and enjoyable.

Mike Fink

Mike Fink is memorialized in several anthologies, but he seldom appears alone. Steven Kellogg's *Mike Fink: A Tall Tale* (1992) is the only book that is entirely devoted to Fink's exploits. He makes an appearance as River Roarer Mike Fink in *American Tall Tales* (Stoutenburg, 1966). Fink lives up to his name as he stalks and attempts to frighten Davy Crockett's wife in Caron Lee Cohen's *Sally Ann Thunder Ann Whirlwind Crockett* (1985).

Lesser Known Tall Tale Characters

In addition to the outrageous personalities we readily identify from familiar tall tales—Paul Bunyan, Pecos Bill, Johnny Appleseed, and Mike Fink—there are numerous regional or ethnic characters whose colorful exploits are unfamiliar but worth investigating.

Sid Fleischman, one of the most recognized names in humorous children's literature, narrates the tale *Jim Bridger's Alarm Clock and Other Tall Tales* (1978). "Jim Bridger was a long-haired mountain man.... He wandered through the wilderness of the Old West before almost anyone else...and first discovered the Great Salt Lake" (p. 4). Other genuine tall tales, rooted in the oral tradition, include *Febold Feboldson* (Dewey, 1984), the story of a Nebraska wheat farmer; *Gib Morgan, Oilman* (Dewey, 1987), about a Pennsylvania oil-field worker; and a Daniel Boone variant, *Bewildered for Three Days: As to Why Daniel Boone Never Wore His Coonskin Cap* (Glass, 2000). *The Legend of Strap Buckner: A Texas Tale* (Wooldridge, 2001) and *Old Dry Frye: A Deliciously Funny Tall Tale* (Johnson, 1999) purport to be based in fact, but they read more like original literary tales.

Modern Literary Tall Tales

Traditional tales have no author; they have been promulgated by word of mouth, frequently passed down through numerous generations. Conversely, a literary tale can be credited to a specific author, be it Hans Christian Andersen or Glen Rounds. Andersen is considered the father of modern fantasy because he used a format he noticed in his mother's folk tales to create original stories. Many modern tales arise in just such a fashion. Most of the recent U.S. publications calling themselves tall tales are actually original literary tales borrowing their structure—and frequently their characters—from traditional tall tales. These stories are fun to read and allow students to explore the commonalities and distinctions between folklore and "fakelore." This is one of the fastest-growing segments of folk literature, so only a minuscule sampling of available original tales has been included in Figure 6.1.

The Strong Female in Tall Tales

Robert D. San Souci, in the preface to his book *Cut From the Same Cloth: American Women of Myth, Legend, and Tall Tale* (1993), discusses the difficulty he had collecting stories of larger-than-life American women. He knew there had to be some included in the traditional literature, but he could find only one or two. He asks, "Why did these [female] characters fail to achieve the fame of their male counterparts?" (p. xii), then suggests several reasons for their lack of notoriety:

1. Women were supposed to stay at home and take care of the family.

2. Women were not supposed to be "explorers, hunters, warriors, or rulers" (p. xii), even though they often were.

3. The stories were told by men who, even when weaving a yarn about Paul Bunyan's wife or other superhuman females, relegated them to the realm of the home and children.

Figure 6.1
Representative Literary Tall Tales

Sid Fleischman. (1992). *McBroom's Wonderful One-Acre Farm: Three Tall Tales* (Greenwillow). Fleischman is responsible for this series of literary tall tales (11 in all) about a farmer, McBroom, whose soil is so fertile that crops are ready for harvest the same day they are planted.

Helen Ketteman. (1991). *The Year of No More Corn* (Orchard). Gramps tells Beany about the corn crop catastrophe of 1928.

———(1995). *The Christmas Blizzard* (Scholastic). This Christmas tall tale is narrated by Maynard Jenkins, who tells how Santa Claus moved to Lizzard, Indiana.

———(1995). *Luck With Potatoes* (Orchard). Who would expect that Cow Hollow, Tennessee, would change farmer Clemmon Hardigree's bad luck to good when he plants potatoes in a cow pasture?

———(1998). *Heat Wave* (Walker). A passing heat wave gets stuck on the weathervane, and it takes a feisty young female to free it.

———(1999). *Shoeshine Whittaker* (Walker). Shoeshine manages to make a living in the Wild West town of Mudville.

Joan Lowery Nixon. (1986). *Beats Me, Claude* (Viking). Nixon's Texas roots show through in her hilarious series about Claude and his wife.

Jerdine Nolen. (1994). *Harvey Potter's Balloon Farm* (Lothrop, Lee & Shepard). A young African American girl harvests a bumper crop of balloons.

———(1998). *Raising Dragons* (Harcourt Brace). An unusual egg hatches into a dragon.

David Rounds. (1992). *Cannonball River Tales* (Sierra Club). Febold Feboldson makes an appearance in these stories about a talking rabbit and a flying silver dragon who live near the Cannonball River.

Aaron Shepard. (1993). *The Legend of Slappy Hooper: An American Tall Tale* (Charles Scribner's Sons). Slappy gets in trouble because his signs are so realistic.

———(1993). *The Legend of Lightning Larry* (Charles Scribner's Sons). Instead of bullets, Lightning Larry shoots lightning bolts and changes Brimstone and its residents.

"It was unusual to have a woman pictured as a huntress...not merely someone who cleaned her husband's kill...or a hero who rescued men from monsters. Tales of such women went against popular thinking and made people uncomfortable" (San Souci, 1993, p. xii).

Jane Yolen echoes San Souci's cry for more stories of strong women. She contends, "these women's wonder tales...[show that] women as well as men can be intelligent, inventive, brave. Heroism is not a gender-driven activity. And because to keep silent in the face of such heroism is to deny it ever existed" (as cited in San Souci, 1993, p. xv).

The collection is interesting in its composition—five sections derived from U.S. geographic locations: northeast, south, midwest, southwest, and west. Each section includes tales of three women, and the majority are tales of indigenous peoples—

Native American, Eskimo, Hawaiian, and Mexican American women. Four are tales of African American women, and only three are of Anglo-American women. Whereas Anglo-American culture is male dominated, other cultures honor the stories of strong women, which is evidenced in the inclusion of strong women in their traditional oral histories.

Brian Pinkney's black-and-white scratchboard illustrations supplement San Souci's text by illustrating the muscular power of these women without diminishing their femininity. Annie Christmas wears a dress, flowered hat, fancy shoes, and her signature pearls, while sporting muscles that would make Hercules whimper. The beauty and composure of her face are clearly evident as she poles her keelboat down the Mississippi River in a race against the Natchez Belle. This African American demigoddess "always wore a string of freshwater pearls to which she added one pearl every time she whipped a man in a fight. By the time she died, stories say, that necklace measured thirty feet" (San Souci, 1993, p. 36).

Each of the tales is preceded by a brief context-setting description of the time, place, and the culture that gave rise to the heroine and her history. San Souci also provides notes regarding his sources, as well as a five-page bibliography. Now available in paperback, this anthology of strong American females provides a voice for women, as well as for some cultural groups that are underrepresented in American traditional literature.

Perhaps the best-known female protagonist in tall tale literature is Sally Ann Thunder Ann Whirlwind Crockett (Cohen, 1985; Kellogg, 1995). As an infant, she could "out-talk, out-grin, out-scream, out-swim, and out-run any baby in Kentucky" (Kellogg, 1995, n.p.). She skins a grizzly bear, marries Davy Crockett, and protects her family from a horde of alligators. Cohen's slightly longer text has Sally Ann besting Mike Fink, much to his chagrin.

Other strong female tall tale protagonists include *Clever Beatrice* (Willey, 2001), *Swamp Angel* (Isaacs, 1994), *Steamboat Annie and the Thousand-Pound Catfish* (Wright, 2001), and the young African American girls in Jerdine Nolen's *Harvey Potter's Balloon Farm* (1994) and *Raising Dragons* (1998).

Tall Tales in the Classroom

A Tall Tales Genre Study

School districts throughout the United States recognize the value of diversifying students' understanding of—and ability to read and write within—a variety of genres. Tall tales are a perfect introduction to the more complex subgenre of traditional literature. Although younger children usually learn about fairy tales and older students study the myths of ancient Rome and Greece, intermediate-grade students have the sense of humor, the ability to lie with impunity (knowing that they are lying for a good cause), the vocabulary, and the reading skills to enjoy listening, reading, writing, and responding to tall tales. Furthermore, it is possible to integrate a tall tales unit across the curriculum, incorporating local, state, or national history and geography, art, and music. Tall tales studies also can be extended with research projects, providing reinforcement for important expository text-reading skills.

During a classroom study of Davy Crockett, whose Münchausen-like exaggerations of his own escapades have been recounted in several volumes of the Davy Crockett Almanacs (e.g., see Chemerka, 2000), there is ample potential for integrated curricular applications. For example, while reading excerpts from his writings, students learn that Crockett used the nickname *Wolverine* to refer to Michigan residents. "The chaps from the Wolverine state are the all-greediest, ugliest, an sourest characters on all Uncle Sam's twenty-six farms, they are, in thar nature, like their wolfish name-sakes..." (May, 1987, p. 65). A bit of historical research discloses that this was a derisive term probably introduced by Ohioans during the 1830s because of a boundary dispute between themselves and Michiganians. In reading about Davy Crockett, students have the opportunity to consider his ascent from backwoodsman to the U.S. Congress, to explore the fur-trading industry, to determine the meaning of and estimate the time period Crockett referred to with the phrase "Uncle Sam's twenty-six farms," and to investigate some of the interstate boundary disputes that occurred during the early years of the United States.

Maps and geography figure prominently in many tall tales, especially the Paul Bunyan saga. McCormick's endpapers (1977a) provide students with concrete locations for contextualizing the various Bunyan stories. Students can generate individual or group maps based on McCormick's and create an illustrative legend for the sites of Paul's escapades. Steven Kellogg's map (1984) is quite different from McCormick's, but it is a great vehicle for comparing different illustrators' concepts. Osborne (1991) also features a map locating many of the more popular tall tales in her anthology.

Functioning as both author and illustrator of an informational resource for students, Andrew Glass researched some of the actual historical characters that provided the gist for tall tales from the early 19th century. *Mountain Men: True Grit and Tall Tales* (Glass, 2001) contributes numerous informational elements that supply a starting point for combining language arts and social studies. *Giants in the Land* (Appelbaum, 1993) offers nonfiction insights into the logging industry.

A language arts block is a natural place for tall tales, as they can form a basis for listening, reading, writing, speaking, or performing. Because of the variety and availability of tall tale heroes and variants, it is easy to create compare-and-contrast assignments such as "How does Mike Fink compare to Pecos Bill?" Reports can be written or oral, and the potential for creative reporting is virtually limitless: talk show interviews, Readers Theatre, dioramas, murals, poetry or musical interpretations, etc. Reading a book such as *I Was Born About 10,000 Years Ago* (Kellogg, 1996), in which a modern child narrates his own tall tale memoir, can provide students with a starting point for writing personal narratives.

The following tall tales genre study ideas are purposely sketchy so that details relevant to specific situations can be individualized, but the overall essence may spark ideas.

DAY ONE

1. Share several stories with the students.

   - Read "Paul Bunyan's Cornstalk" in Joanna Cole's *Best-Loved Folktales of the World* (1983, p. 668).

   - Web the characteristics of the tale to discover what the students know about tall tales.

   - Create a chart of tall tale characteristics. This will remain in the classroom so that you and the students may add characteristics during the course of the unit.

2. Brainstorm: What is the purpose of these tales?

3. Read pp. 1–15 of *Sally Ann Thunder Ann Whirlwind Crockett* (Cohen, 1985) as a Directed Listening–Thinking Activity (DLTA).* Students should have typed copies of the text for group activities after the read-aloud is complete. Color transparencies of the illustrations can be displayed as you read aloud to the students.

   *There is little difference between a DLTA and a DRTA (Directed Reading–Thinking Activity): One is constructed around a story that will be read aloud by the teacher; the other is for a story the students will read silently. Each incorporates preplanned stopping points where students respond to questions or predict outcomes that encourage metacognition.

4. In small groups, have students highlight/mark the characteristics or elements of a tall tale on their typed copies of the text.

5. As a class, have students report the characteristics they have discovered. If there are any new characteristics, they should add them to the chart created in step 1.

Example of State/District Standards
(Add applicable standards each day for your district)

Listening #1: Students will summarize information from an oral presentation.

Reading #1: Students will construct a graphic organizer for identifying major concepts.

DAY TWO

1. Do a DLTA or DRTA with the book *Mike Fink* (Kellogg, 1992).

2. Either in small groups or as a class, have students discuss the similarities and differences between Paul Bunyan and Mike Fink.

3. Create a Venn diagram of the similarities and differences between Paul and Mike.

4. Add any newly discovered tall tale characteristics to the class chart.

DAY THREE

1. Have students read "The Tall Cornstalk" in Richard Chase's *Grandfather Tales* (1948, p. 186) in pairs or in small collaborative groups.

2. Ask students to take notes by highlighting or marking tall tale characteristics/ elements on their copies of the story. Follow up by having the whole group report on and discuss their findings.

3. As a whole group, compare this version of the cornstalk story to the version that was read aloud on day one (Cole, 1983). Have the Cole version available for reference if the students' memories need to be refreshed.

DAY FOUR

1. Do a DRTA (Nessel, Jones, & Dixon, 1989) with "The Bedcats" in Glen Rounds's *Ol' Paul the Mighty Logger* (1976, p. 27). (See Figure 6.2.)

2. Provide students with copies of "The Splinter Cat" and "The Billdad" from Botkin's *A Treasury of American Folklore* (1944, p. 649). Read these two tales in small groups.

3. Reassemble and discuss the tales as a whole group.

DAY FIVE

1. Following the example of tall tale creatures in the previous day's readings, students will draw, name, and write a caption for their own tall tale creature. Give students the following directions: "Be sure to describe how your animal behaves and any unusual characteristics that may not be apparent from your illustrations."

2. Other books (in addition to those already read) to have available that may help students formulate an original tall tale creature are the following:
    - Gorham, M. (1952). *The Real Book of American Tall Tales*. Chapter 15 is titled "Snolligosters, Etc." and details a number of bigger than life animals.
    - Schwartz, A. (1976). *Kickle Snifters and Other Fearsome Critters*.
    - Stoutenburg, A. (1968). *American Tall-Tale Animals*.

To prepare for this activity, locate a copy of Glen Rounds's "The Bedcats" (1976, p. 27). Type or copy the story in three sections: (1) paragraphs 1–4, (2) paragraphs 5 and 6, (3) paragraphs 7–10. At the beginning of each section, add the statement "Read until you come to the end of this section." At the end of each section, add "Please stop reading here." You may add your post-reading questions (see below) at the end of each section.

Before beginning the story, elicit your students' understanding of the genre, content, vocabulary, and this specific tale with your own prereading questions or the ones provided here:

- What do you know about Paul Bunyan? What kind of a person was he? Do you think that he would be afraid of any normal kinds of animals?

- The name of the story we're going to read is "The Bedcats" by Glen Rounds. It's a Paul Bunyan story. What do you think is going to happen in this story? What sorts of things do you expect to find in this story?

- Have you ever heard the expression "Sleep tight; don't let the bedbugs bite"? Do you know what it means? What is a bedbug?

Next, either read aloud or direct the students to read silently. If you are reading the story to your students, stop at the end of each section and ask the comprehension questions you have prepared or the sample questions that follow. If this is a DRTA and the students are reading silently, you may include the questions at the end of each section. If it is a DLTA, the questions might be on a transparency so students can refer back to the questions. Have the students discuss the questions in small groups, with a partner or as a whole class, or have them write individual responses on their handouts or in their reading logs. Try to vary your approach.

Postreading Questions

Section 1 (paragraphs 1–4)

- You made predictions about what was going to happen in this Paul Bunyan story. What has happened to those predictions? Which predictions are consistent with the story? Which ones have you changed? What happened in the story that made you change your predictions?

- What kind of trouble do you think will be waiting for Paul Bunyan in this old camp?

- What do you think is going to happen in the rest of this story?

Section 2 (paragraphs 5 and 6)

- Did your predictions work out? If not, how have you changed them?

- What do you think is going to be in the bag?

- What do you think is going to happen in the rest of this story?

Section 3 (paragraphs 7–10)

- How did the story turn out? Was it consistent with your predictions? What did you have to change, and what made you change your predictions?

- Do you think this is a good example of a tall tale? Why?

Day Six

1. Read aloud the tall tale *John Henry* (Lester, 1994).

2. Show the video *John Henry* (Lester & Pinkney, 1998).

3. Discuss the book and video. Add characteristics to the chart.

4. Have additional versions of John Henry and Casey Jones stories available for independent reading.

Day Seven

1. Discuss the class chart of tall tale characteristics.

2. Elicit ideas from students about why people started telling these types of stories. What is an author's purpose for telling these tales?

3. Read aloud a literary tall tale: *Here Comes McBroom!* (Fleischman, 1992a) or other McBroom tall tales (see Fleischman, 1992b), *Beats Me, Claude* (Nixon, 1986) or other Claude tales (see Nixon, 1987, 1989), or *Swamp Angel* (Isaacs, 1994).

4. Work with students as a whole group to write an original tall tale.

Day Eight

1. Read aloud a variation of "Split Dog" (e.g., Chase, 1971, pp. 97–98) and "One Bullet Left" (Young & Young, 1989, pp. 66–67).

2. As a group, discuss the concept of liars' tales.

3. In groups of four or five, have students write an original tall tale. This may take several days.

4. Reassemble, and have all the groups share their stories.
    - If any groups are not finished, have them give progress reports.
    - Have each group accept feedback from other students for needed clarifications of or improvements to the stories.

Concluding Assignment: An Original Tall Tale

1. Review the purposes, elements, and characteristics of tall tales.

2. Have each student conference with you after writing an outline of the original tall tale characters they created on day five. This outline should include the character's name, birth circumstances, physical description, childhood feats, environment, occupation, adult accomplishments, companions, and death (if applicable).

3. Using their original character as protagonist, students will create an individual tall tale that demonstrates their understanding of the genre. This assignment should involve the reiterative writing process steps of writing, revising, conferencing with peers and/or the teacher, and editing.

After each student's tall tale is in its final form, students should trace their body shapes on butcher paper and then decorate them to reflect their character's stature and occupations. The "published" tale can be incorporated as part of the figure. Create a display (possibly in the library or main hall) for other students and visitors to enjoy.

Analyzing Tall Tale Characteristics

One of the more important functions of any tall tale unit includes an analysis of why a specific story—whether from traditional literature or an author's imagination (i.e., a literary tale)—should be called a tall tale. One group of fourth-grade students developed a word wall to describe the characteristics of the various heroes they met during their study. Their teachers had determined beforehand which characteristics they felt were necessary to an understanding of tall tales and, through the stories they chose, led the students to note those benchmarks.

The five major characteristics that the teachers stressed loosely correlated to character, plot, setting, theme, and style:

1. The theme revolves around issues of ordinary folk.
2. The plot involves exaggerated situations and incidents.
3. Characters are larger-than-life common folk. They frequently champion the underdog and resist developments that supplanted traditional occupations of the late 19th century.
4. The settings are frontier and untamed areas of the United States.
5. These tales rely on humor, hyperbole, and dialect (style).

As new tales and heroes were introduced, students noted their characteristics in their journals, then compared them with the ones previously listed on the word wall. This afforded the students an opportunity to develop listening, note-taking, skimming, and critical thinking skills.

At the end of the unit when students evaluated their experience with tall tales, the teachers discovered how valuable the word wall activity was in their own assessment of the students' growth. In virtually every essay, students observed several of the key characteristics:

"Tall tales aren't true...." (plot, style)

"Tall tales are storys [sic] that get exaggerated." (plot, style)

"I learned about Mike Fink and how he bragged thinking he was all big and bad and then we have Sally Ann Thunder Ann Whirlwind Crocket [sic] who fears almost nothing!" (characterization)

"[The characters] were mainly outside workers in the United States." (characterization, setting)

"Most tall tales start from the persons [sic] birth." (setting, context)

"You can make them [the characters] do things they really can't." (plot)

"Tall tales are suppose [sic] to be funny..." (style)

Conclusion

The best of the stories we can give our children, whether they are stories that have been kept alive through the centuries by...oral transmission, or the tales that were made up only yesterday—the best of these stories touch that larger dream, that greater vision, that infinite unknowing. They are the most potent kind of magic...for they catch a glimpse of the soul beneath the skin.

Touch magic. Pass it on. (Yolen, 2000, p. 50)

Tall tales touch that magic inside each of us, child or adult. They are a bit naughty even if they have been "cleaned up." They allow us to lie—just a little—without hurting anyone. They feed our imaginations, which are often starved by too much testing and too little tomfoolery. For just a short while, they allow us to suspend our disbelief and participate in a world-class joke—on us!

When children create their own tall tales, learning becomes play: the hyperbole, the exaggeration, the feats of derring-do expand young minds and imaginations. Each child accepts the cape, or the lasso, or the ax, and suddenly becomes braver, stronger, and more handsome than ever before.

Grade level should not matter: Tall tales deserve a place in everyone's curriculum. Find one that speaks to you. Read it aloud the first day of classes. Touch the magic that tall tales generate. Then pass it on to your students.

REFERENCES

Arbuthnot, M.H. (1964). *Children and books* (3rd ed.). Chicago: Scott Foresman.

Blair, W. (1987). *Tall tale America: A legendary history of our humorous heroes*. Chicago: University of Chicago Press.

Botkin, B.A. (1944). *A treasury of American folklore: Stories, ballads, and traditions of the people*. New York: Crown.

Bowman, J.C. (1961). *Pecos Bill: The greatest cowboy of all*. Chicago: Albert Whitman.

Brown, C.S. (1987). *The tall tale in American folklore and literature*. Knoxville: University of Tennessee Press.

Cart, M. (1995). *What's so funny? Wit and humor in American children's literature*. New York: HarperCollins.

Castiglione, B. (1976). *Book of the Courtier*. New York: Penguin. (Original work published 1528)

Chase, R. (Ed.). (1948). *Grandfather tales: American-English folk tales*. Boston: Houghton Mifflin.

Chase, R. (Ed.). (1971). *American folk tales and songs*. New York: Dover.

Chemerka, W.R. (2000). *The Davy Crockett almanac and book of lists*. Austin, TX: Eakin.

Cullinan, B.E. (1989). *Literature and the child* (2nd ed.). San Diego: Harcourt Brace Jovanovich.

Dorson, R.M. (1959). *American folklore*. Chicago: University of Chicago Press.

Dorson, R.M. (1972). *Folklore and folklife: An introduction*. Chicago: University of Chicago Press.

Dorson, R.M. (1973). *America in legend: Folklore from the colonial period to the present*. New York: Pantheon.

Egoff, S.A. (1967). *The republic of childhood: A critical guide to Canadian children's literature in English*. Oxford, UK: Oxford University Press.

Glimm, J.Y. (1983). *Flatlanders and ridgerunners: Folktales from the mountains of northern Pennsylvania*. Pittsburgh, PA: University of Pittsburgh Press.

Goforth, F.S. (1998). *Literature & the learner*. Belmont, CA: Wadsworth.

Hearn, M.P., Clark, T., & Clark, H.N.B. (1996). *Myth, magic, and mystery: One hundred years of American children's book illustration*. Boulder, CO: Roberts Rinehart, in co-operation with the Chrysler Museum of Art.

Huck, C.S. (1997). *Children's literature in the elementary school* (6th ed.). Madison, WI: Brown & Benchmark.

Lepp, P., & Lepp, B. (1999). *The monster stick & other Appalachian tall tales*. Little Rock, AR: August House.

Lima, C.W., & Lima, J.A. (2001). *A to zoo: Subject access to children's picture books* (6th ed.). Westport, CT: Bowker-Greenwood.

May, G.S. (1987). *Michigan: An illustrated history of the Great Lakes State*. Northridge, CA: Windsor.

McConnell, M.L., & West, D.H. (Eds.). (1956). *Children's catalog: A classified catalog of 3,204 children's books recommended for public and school libraries with an author, title, and subject index* (9th ed.). New York: H.W. Wilson.

Nessel, D.D., Jones, M.B., & Dixon, C.N. (1989). *Thinking through the language arts*. New York: Macmillan.

Pavonetti, L.M., & Combs, C.M. (1999). American hyperbole: The tall tale. *Journal of Youth Services in Libraries*, *12*(2), 37–42.

Price, A., & Yaakov, J. (Eds.). (2000). *Children's catalog: 2000 supplement to the 17th edition*. New York: H.W. Wilson.

Randolph, V. (1993). *Stiff as a poker: A collection of Ozark folk tales*. New York: Barnes & Noble.

Rogers, D.L. (1999). *Paul Bunyan: How a terrible timber feller became a legend*. Bay City, MI: Historical Press.

Sutherland, Z. (1997). *Children and books* (9th ed.). New York: Longman.

Temple, C.A., Martinez, M., Yokota, J., & Naylor, A. (2002). *Children's books in children's hands: An introduction to their literature* (2nd ed.). Boston: Allyn & Bacon.

Ward, V. (Ed.). (1990). *I always tell the truth (even if I have to lie to do it!): Stories from the Adirondack Liars' Club*. Greenfield, NY: Greenfield Review.

West, D.H., & Shor, R. (Eds.). (1961). *Children's catalog* (10th ed.). New York: H.W. Wilson.

Young, R., & Young, J.D. (Eds.). (1989). *Ozark tall tales: Collected from the oral tradition*. Little Rock, AR: August House.

Yolen, J. (2000). *Touch magic: Fantasy, faerie, & folklore in the literature of childhood* (Expanded ed.). Little Rock, AR: August House.

CHILDREN'S BOOKS CITED

Appelbaum, D.K. (1993). *Giants in the land* (M. McCurdy, Illus.). Boston: Houghton Mifflin.

Benét, R., & Benét, S.V. (1933). *A book of Americans*. New York: Farrar and Rinehart.

Benét, R., & Benét, S.V. (2001). *Johnny Appleseed* (S.D. Schindler, Illus.). New York: Margaret K. McElderry.

Cohen, C.L. (1985). *Sally Ann Thunder Ann Whirlwind Crockett* (A. Dewey, Illus.). New York: Greenwillow.

Cole, J. (Ed.). (1983). *Best-loved folktales of the world* (J.K. Schwarz, Illus.). New York: Anchor/Doubleday.

Daugherty, J. (1938). *Daniel Boone*. New York: Viking.

Daugherty, J. (1939). *Andy and the lion*. New York: Viking.

Dewey, A. (1984). *Febold Feboldson*. New York: Greenwillow.

Dewey, A. (1987). *Gib Morgan, oilman*. New York: Greenwillow.

Emberley, B. (1963). *The story of Paul Bunyan* (E. Emberly, Illus.). New York: Simon & Schuster.

Farmer, N. (1998). *Casey Jones's fireman: The story of Sim Webb* (J. Bernardin, Illus.). New York: Phyllis Fogelman.

Felton, H.W. (1950). *John Henry and his hammer* (A.A. Watson, Illus.). New York: Knopf.

Fleischman, S. (1978). *Jim Bridger's alarm clock and other tall tales* (E. Von Schmidt, Illus.). New York: E.P. Dutton.

Fleischman, S. (1992a). *Here comes McBroom! Three more tall tales* (Q. Blake, Illus.). New York: Greenwillow.

Fleischman, S. (1992b). *McBroom's wonderful one-acre farm: Three tall tales* (Q. Blake, Illus.). New York: Greenwillow.

Glass, A. (1995). *Folks call me Appleseed John*. New York: Bantam Doubleday Dell.

Glass, A. (2000). *Bewildered for three days: As to why Daniel Boone never wore his coonskin cap*. New York: Holiday House.

Glass, A. (2001). *Mountain men: True grit and tall tales*. New York: Doubleday.

Gorham, M. (1952). *The real book of American tall tales* (D. Herbert, Illus.). Garden City, NY: Watts.

Hodges, M. (1997). *The true tale of Johnny Appleseed* (K. Bulcken Root, Illus.). New York: Holiday House.

Isaacs, A. (1994). *Swamp Angel* (P.O. Zelinsky, Illus.). New York: Dutton.

Johnson, P.B. (1999). *Old Dry Frye: A deliciously funny tall tale*. New York: Scholastic.

Keats, E.J. (1965). *John Henry: An American legend*. New York: Pantheon.

Kellogg, S. (1984). *Paul Bunyan: A tall tale*. New York: Morrow.

Kellogg, S. (1986). *Pecos Bill: A tall tale*. New York: Morrow.

Kellogg, S. (1988). *Johnny Appleseed: A tall tale*. New York: Morrow Junior.

Kellogg, S. (1992). *Mike Fink: A tall tale*. New York: Morrow Junior.

Kellogg, S. (1995). *Sally Ann Thunder Ann Whirlwind Crockett*. New York: Morrow Junior.

Kellogg, S. (1996). *I was born about 10,000 years ago: A tall tale*. New York: Morrow Junior.

Ketteman, H. (1991). *The year of no more corn* (R.A. Parker, Illus.). New York: Orchard.

Ketteman, H. (1995a). *The Christmas blizzard* (J. Warhola, Illus.). New York: Scholastic.

Ketteman, H. (1995b). *Luck with potatoes* (B. Floca, Illus.). New York: Orchard.

Ketteman, H. (1998). *Heat wave* (S. Goto, Illus.). New York: Walker and Co.

Ketteman, H. (1999). *Shoeshine Whittaker* (S. Goto, Illus.). New York: Walker & Co.

Lester, J. (1994). *John Henry* (J. Pinkney, Illus.). New York: Dial.

Lester, J., & Pinkney, J. (1998). *John Henry* [Video recording]. Westport, CT: Scholastic/Weston Woods Studios.

Lindbergh, R. (1990). *Johnny Appleseed: A poem* (K. Jakobsen, Illus.). Boston: Little, Brown.

McCormick, D.J. (1977a). *Paul Bunyan swings his axe*. Caldwell, ID: Caxton.

McCormick, D.J. (1977b). *Tall timber tales: More Paul Bunyan stories*. Caldwell, ID: Caxton.

Moses, W. (2001). *Johnny Appleseed: The story of a legend*. New York: Philomel.

Nixon, J.L. (1986). *Beats me, Claude* (T.C. Pearson, Illus.). New York: Viking.

Nixon, J.L. (1987). *Fat chance, Claude* (T.C. Pearson, Illus.). New York: Viking.

Nixon, J.L. (1989). *You bet your britches, Claude* (T.C. Pearson, Illus.). New York: Puffin.

Nolen, J. (1994). *Harvey Potter's balloon farm* (M. Buehner, Illus.). New York: Lothrop, Lee & Shepard.

Nolen, J. (1998). *Raising dragons* (E. Primavera, Illus.). San Diego: Harcourt Brace.

Nolen, J. (2000). *Big Jabe* (K. Nelson, Illus.). New York: Lothrop, Lee & Shepard.

Osborne, M.P. (1991). *American tall tales* (M. McCurdy, Illus.). New York: Scholastic.

Osborne, M.P. (2002). *New York's bravest* (S. Johnson & L. Fancher, Illus.). New York: Knopf.

Poulakis, P. (1969). *American folklore* (M. Ebert, Illus.). New York: Charles Scribner's Sons.

Rossi, J. (1995). *The gullywasher*. Flagstaff, AZ: Northland.

Rounds, D. (1992). *Cannonball River tales* (A. Berenzy, Illus.). San Francisco, CA: Sierra Club.

Rounds, G. (1976). *Ol' Paul the mighty logger*. New York: Holiday House.

Rounds, G. (1984). *The morning the sun refused to rise: An original Paul Bunyan story*. New York: Holiday House.

San Souci, R.D. (1991). *Larger than life: The adventures of American legendary heroes* (A. Glass, Illus.). New York: Doubleday.

San Souci, R.D. (1993). *Cut from the same cloth: American women of myth, legend, and tall tale* (B. Pinkney, Illus.). New York: Philomel.

Schwartz, A. (1975). *Whoppers: Tall tales and other lies collected from American folklore* (G. Rounds, Illus.). New York: HarperCollins.

Schwartz, A. (1976). *Kickle snifters and other fearsome critters* (G. Rounds, Illus.). Philadelphia: Lippincott.

Schwartz, A. (1979). *Chin music: Tall talk and other talk* (J. O'Brien, Illus.). New York: Lippincott.

Schwartz, A. (1981). *Scary stories to tell in the dark* (S. Gammell, Illus.). New York: Harper & Row.

Shapiro, I. (1945). *John Henry and the double jointed steamdrill* (J.H. Daugherty, Illus.). New York: J. Messner.

Shepard, A. (1993a). *The legend of Lightning Larry* (T. Goffe, Illus.). New York: Charles Scribner's Sons.

Shepard, A. (1993b). *The legend of Slappy Hooper: An American tall tale* (T. Goffe, Illus.). New York: Scribner's.

Silverstein, S. (1974). *Where the sidewalk ends*. New York: Harper.

Simon, T. (1958). *Far out tales*. New York: Scholastic. [Scholastic also released this in 1970 as *Ripsnorters and ribticklers*.]

Stoutenburg, A. (1966). *American tall tales* (R.M. Powers, Illus.). New York: Viking.

Stoutenburg, A. (1968). *American tall-tale animals* (G. Rounds, Illus.). New York: Viking.

Untermeyer, L. (1945). *The wonderful adventures of Paul Bunyan* (E.G. Jackson, Illus.). New York: Heritage.

Walker, P.R. (1993). *Big men, big country: A collection of American tall tales* (J. Bernardin, Illus.). San Diego: Harcourt Brace Jovanovich.

Willey, M. (2001). *Clever Beatrice* (H. Solomon, Illus.). New York: Atheneum.

Wood, A. (1996). *The Bunyans* (D. Shannon, Illus.). New York: Scholastic.

Wooldridge, C.N. (2001). *The legend of Strap Buckner: A Texas tale* (A. Glass, Illus.). New York: Holiday House.

Wright, C. (2001). *Steamboat Annie and the thousand-pound catfish* (H. Fine, Illus.). New York: Philomel.

Sampling Folk Literature Across Cultures

CHAPTER 7

Folk Tales From the African Diaspora: The Power of the Oral Tradition

Deborah L. Thompson

uring Middle Passage (the middle leg of the Transatlantic Slave Trade that brought captured Africans to the Americas and the Caribbean) and their subsequent enslavement, captured Africans had many things taken from them—their names, their native languages, their ways of life, their cultural foundations, and their families. Voice and memory were the only things left to them. With those two very powerful gifts, Africans created a treasure trove of wonderful stories, from those of tricky Anansi to those of clever Brer Rabbit. Courlander (1996) notes that the range of oral literary forms brought to the New World from Africa were wide ranging and seemingly endless. These forms included, but were not limited to, creation myths, tales that explain natural phenomenon (etiological tales or pourquoi tales), proverbs, spirituals, moral tales, riddles, dilemma tales, adventure tales, and—the most prevalent and well known—the trickster tales.

As diverse as their backgrounds and memories, Africans brought to the New World folklore from every part of the continent, from Kenya in the east to South Africa and Botswana in the south to Ghana and Nigeria in the west. Once in the New World, Africans developed a literary canon rooted in oral tradition and tempered by that peculiar institution, slavery. Today, people are connected to those distant storytellers through the folk tales that came from Africa and evolved in the American south, the Caribbean, and South America, specifically Brazil.

African Folk Tales

African folk tales cover a variety of literary forms, their richness in character and rhythm transported to the New World during the Diaspora (the dispersion and settlement of African peoples beyond the continent of Africa). The animal trickster tale is the best documented of the African folk narratives (Berry, 1991; Gates & McKay, 1997; Hill, 1998). Most of these tricksters had to use cunning to outwit larger and more powerful animals in order to survive. The animal tricksters in these tales represented the fauna of the countries from which they evolved; therefore, tales of Hare (or Rabbit) came from east Africa, parts of Nigeria, and Angola. Tortoise tales were native to the Yoruba, Ibo, and Edo peoples of Nigeria. Anansi (Spider) tales came from throughout West Africa, including Ghana, Liberia, and Sierra Leone (Levine, 1977). Of these tricksters, one in particular was likely to cause as much trouble for himself as for the others around him—Anansi the Spider.

Colorful, imaginative characters are only one aspect of the African folk tale. The possibilities for audience participation abound, because telling an Anansi, Tortoise, or any other tale would never be a solo event for the griot, or village storyteller. This person had every expectation that the audience would become involved in the storytelling, as the following examples reveal (see Berry, 1991; Offodile, 2001):

Griot: Shall I tell you or shall I not? **Audience:** Yes, tell us!

Griot: Now this story, I didn't make it up. **Audience:** Who did, then?

Griot: I have a story to tell you. **Audience:** Tell us a funny one.

In addition to the opportunities for communal participation, the tales would include the patterns of call and response (i.e., the audience verbally responding to a particularly exciting segment of the story). The griot or the audience also might assist the storytelling by playing the story drum (often constructed from gourds and used during storytelling), rattles, clappers, and other instruments, plus the original instrument—the human voice. In the modern retellings we enjoy reading, today's authors have added accompanying sound effects. One can see how Ashley Bryan and Verna Aardema have attempted to capture the "sounds" of these participatory tales in the following two passages:

Beat the story-drum, pum! pum! Tell us a big story, brum! brum! The one about Elephant and Bush Cow, thrum-thrum! And of Monkey the messenger, pittipong-pittipong! (Bryan, 1998, p. 54)

Jackal looked at the little house. "Who's in Rabbit's house?" he asked. The bad voice replied, "I'm the Long One. I eat trees and trample on elephants..." "I'm going!" cried Jackal. And off he went—kpidu, kpidu, kpidu. (Aardema, 1977, n.p.).

Bryan and Aardema are not the only modern authors who have found the tales of tricksters too delightful to resist retelling. Readers of all ages have a wealth of retold tales from which to choose, such as Joyce Arkhurst's *The Adventures of Spider* (1964), Gail Haley's *A Story, A Story* (1970), Gerald McDermott's *Anansi the Spider*

(1972) and *Zomo the Rabbit* (1992), the Eric Kimmel/Janet Stevens collaborations beginning with *Anansi and the Moss-Covered Rock* (Kimmel, 1988, 1992, 1994, 2001), Pat Cummings's *Ananse and the Lizard* (2002), Aardema's *Anansi Does the Impossible* (1997), and Tololwa Mollel's *Ananse's Feast* (1997) and *The Flying Tortoise* (1994).

Trickster tales are not the only literary import from Africa; the moral tale has become a part of our modern storytelling repertoire as well. Moral tales are cautionary and instructive in value and help teach readers to avoid succumbing to such human foibles as greed, arrogance, envy, or dishonesty. Moral tales differ from fables in types of characters, complexity, and clarity of lesson: Moral tales can have either human or animal characters, whereas fables feature animal characters with human characteristics; moral tales can have multiple episodes, while fables have single episodes; and moral tales are more didactic than fables.

Moral tales can be absurd like *Traveling to Tondo* (Aardema, 1991), in which Bowane the Civet sets out to meet his bride accompanied by his friends pigeon, python, and tortoise. The agreeable friends wait and wait for one another throughout the trip—they wait for Bowane to return to his village to get his water dish so they can

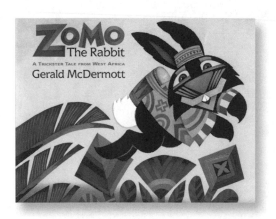

Book cover from *Zomo The Rabbit: A Trickster Tale From West Africa*, copyright © 1992 by Gerald McDermott, used by permission of Harcourt, Inc.

all drink from a watering hole, wait two weeks under a palm tree so pigeon can eat ripened palm nuts, wait an indeterminate amount of time for python to digest a small antelope he caught, and wait years for a log to rot before tortoise can continue down to the road. By the time they reach their destination, Bowane's betrothed has tired of waiting for him and has married another civet. As Bowane and his friends are being chased away by his lost bride's husband, he realizes that sometimes there can be too much consenting among friends.

Sebgugugu the Glutton (Aardema, 1993) is a humorous but bittersweet tale with some similarity to Grimm's *The Fisherman and His Wife* (Jarrell, 1980). The protagonist, Sebgugugu, listens neither to his wife nor to Imana, the Lord of Rwanda. Each time Imana gives the family help (e.g., a vine that never quits bearing fruit or a herd of cows that provides endless gallons of milk), Sebgugugu becomes greedy and thinks he can do Imana one better. Alas, his greed angers Imana, so the ruler's last act is to take everything away from Sebgugugu, including his family. The consequence of breaking a promise is the moral of McDermott's *The Magic Tree* (1973). In Rosa Guy's retelling of *Mother Crocodile* (1981), a Senegalese moral tale, the young crocodiles' failure to listen to the stories of the older and wiser mother crocodile almost ends tragically. Had not one of them remembered the escape route along the riverbed, they may have ended up becoming handbags.

Julius Lester's *The Man Who Knew Too Much* (1994b) serves as both a tragic moral tale and an etiological tale (a tale of explanation) that explains the consequences of a man's immense arrogance. The man's failure to listen to his wife leads to a tragic event—he accidentally kills his own son—an event the Baila People of Zambia use to explain how murder came into the world. Other etiological tales explain how the leopard got its spots (Lester, 1989); why the sun seems to wink before it sets and why bats fly only at night (Mollel, 1992); how thunder and lightning came to be (Bryan, 1993); or why the sky is far away (Gerson, 1992). All these tales and others invite us all to share the word and the world of African griots. Table 7.1 lists examples of types of tales and selected touchstone titles.

African American Folk Tales

African American folk tales come from parts of the New World where black communities were established during and after slavery (Abrahams, 1985). Industrialization and the nature of slavery in different regions of the United States dictated the types of

Table 7.1
African Folk Tale Types and Touchstone Texts

Type	Examples With Country of Origin
Trickster	• *Anansi Does the Impossible: An Ashanti Tale* (Ghana) (Aardema, 1997) • *Ananse's Feast: An Ashanti Tale* (Ghana) (Mollel, 1997) • *Ananse and the Lizard* (Ghana) (Cummings, 2002) • *The Flying Tortoise: An Igbo Tale* (Nigeria) (Mollel, 1994)
Moral	• *The Man Who Knew Too Much* (Zambia) (Lester, 1994b) • *The Magic Tree* (Nigeria) (Echewa, 1999) • *Mother Crocodile* (Senegal) (Guy, 1981) • *Traveling to Tondo* (Zaire/Congo) (Aardema, 1991)
Etiological (Pourquoi)	• *The Orphan Boy* (Masai/Kenya) (Mollel, 1990) • *The Man Who Knew Too Much* (Zambia) (Lester, 1994b) • *Why the Sky Is Far Away* (Nigeria) (Gerson, 1992) • *The Story of Lightning and Thunder* (Nigeria) (Bryan, 1993)
Dilemma	• *The Cow-Tail Switch* (Liberia) (Courlander & Herzog, 1987)

folk tales that evolved in each community. In the industrialized north, there was a need for blacks to become literate; therefore, they adopted a variety of literary/ written conventions making it possible for Phillis Wheatley to write poetry, Jupiter Hammon to write essays, and Olaudah Equiano to write autobiography. Due to this early black literary tradition, there are few African American folk tales that can be traced to the northern states (Hill, 1998).

On the other hand, in the agricultural south where it was illegal and sometimes fatal for slaves to become literate, the spoken word was the one tool at the slaves' disposal over which they had some control. African folklore merged with the harsh realities of slavery provides readers today with a world of reading pleasure. In addition to the animal trickster tales that were the most frequently recited, there were other tales in the slaves' oral literary repertoire. There were slave/human trickster tales, conjure tales, supernatural tales, spirituals, tales of black flight, and tales in which "there is one darn thing happening after another" (Gates & McKay, 1997).

The trickster tale, the most prevalent African story form handed down from enslaved storytellers, clearly can be traced to Africa. (For a more general discussion of trickster tales, refer to chapter 2 of this book.) In most parts of the south, Anansi the Spider morphed into the trickster Brer Rabbit (Hare). The Brer Rabbit tales came to us in written form from a collection of 184 African folk tales compiled by Joel Chandler Harris (2002). These were stories he had heard as a child. First published in 1881, the stories were written as if Harris were the old slave, Uncle Remus, telling the tales of Brer Rabbit, Brer Bear, and their friends to an attentive young white child (Jacobs, n.d.; Marshall, 1998). Today's readers can enjoy these tales in a four-volume collection by Julius Lester (1987, 1988, 1990, 1994a), illustrated by Jerry Pinkney, or in an adaptation in three volumes by Van Dyke Parks (1986 [with Malcolm Jones], 1987, 1989), illustrated by Barry Moser.

Book cover from *Jump! The Adventures of Brer Rabbit* by Joel Chandler Harris, illustrated by Barry Moser, copyright © 1986 by Van Dyke Parks and Malcolm Jones, used by permission of Harcourt, Inc.

Very few spider tales can be traced to enslaved blacks. The one geographic area in the United States where Anansi stories can be found is the Sea Islands off the coast of South Carolina, home of the Gullah people. To the Gullah, wily, cunning Anansi the Spider was a perfect story character. However, the majority of Gullah stories do not focus on Anansi the Spider; instead, most Gullah trickster tales have Aunt Nancy as their trickster character (Blumenfeld, n.d.). Although mentioned in numerous articles on the Web and in books on folklore, Aunt Nancy stories that have been published in book form are almost impossible to find. Phyllis Root calls her feisty, tricky Appalachian granny an original character (*Aunt Nancy and Old Man Trouble*, 1996), but she admits to having "found" her heroine after reading that Anansi stories evolved into Aunt Nancy stories in the Caribbean (Ingram Book Group, 2000).

Human tricksters also hold a favored place in African American folklore. The best-known human trickster was a slave named John (also called High John the Conqueror or just High John), who constantly outwitted his master. John and Old Marster (Old Master) tales did exist during slavery, but the tales were rarely recited openly, because for a slave to recite such tales would reveal to the master ways in which his slaves constantly subverted his orders (Gates & McKay, 1997). We know of many of these High John stories through Zora Neale Hurston, who compiled the first collection of John and Old Marster tales in her book *Mules and Men* (1990). Readers can enjoy many of the High John tales in Steve Sanfield's *The Adventures of High John the Conqueror* (1989). A popular picture book version of one of the High John tales, with a rabbit as High John and a bear as the master, is *Tops & Bottoms* (Stevens, 1995). An actual human trickster, a slave named Jim, is the protagonist in Angela Medearis's *The Freedom Riddle* (1995). The author's note states that the book was based on a true story that had been told to William Faulkner.

Conjure (magic) tales were used by the slaves to equalize the balance of power between slave and master (Hill, 1998). In *The Ballad of Belle Dorcas* (Hooks, 1990), Belle asks Granny Lizard, a free-issue "cunger" (conjure) woman famed for her spells and root workings, to cast a powerful spell on her true love, Joshua, to keep him from being sold by the cruel master. In Robert D. San Souci's *The Secret of the Stones* (1999), an old magician has cast a spell on two children that turns them into stones. In *Freedom's Fruit* (Hooks, 1996), Mama Marina, a conjure woman, casts a spell on Master Alston's grapes as a way to buy the freedom of two young slaves. Also of note is the master's request for Mama Marina to conjure the grapes to keep the slaves from eating his fruit. Hill (1998) reveals that masters publicly scoffed at spells and conjures, but privately they were afraid to punish or interfere with slaves considered to be conjurers. Although not a conjure tale per se, San Souci's *The Talking Eggs* (1989) does include a witch woman.

Tales of flight revealed the enslaved Africans' continued belief that they would escape slavery and return to their homelands in Africa (Gates & McKay, 1997; Hill, 1998). Virginia Hamilton's "The People Could Fly" in the book of the same name (1985) revealed this wish of the people to fly to escape the burdens of slavery. The flying theme also is seen in tales such as Faith Ringgold's *Tar Beach* (1991) and *The Invisible Princess* (1999).

Supernatural tales—tales of ghosts, "haints" (ghouls, goblins, and other things that go bump in the night), spirits, etc.—came to the New World from Africa with the captives. Some ghosts were considered benevolent; others, not so. As with other forms of folklore, African American supernatural tales had their uses. Some were cautionary tales, such as "Bloody Bones" (Lyons, 1991), which reveals the fate of one who talks too much. Some supernatural tales were forms of simple amusement, such as *Tailypo!* (Wahl, 1991), and still others were stories in which the slaves could create a world in which no master could enter or control (Malvasi, 1999).

Examples of folk tale types and titles are listed in Table 7.2.

Table 7.2
African American Folk Tale Types and Touchstone Texts

Type	Examples
Trickster	• *The Tales of Uncle Remus: The Adventures of Brer Rabbit* (Lester, 1987) • *A Ring of Tricksters* (Hamilton, 1997) • *Lapin Plays Possum: Trickster Tales From the Louisiana Bayou* (Doucet, 2002) • *Callie Ann and Mistah Bear* (San Souci, 2000) • *Tops & Bottoms* (Stevens, 1995)
Conjure	• *The Ballad of Belle Dorcas* (Hooks, 1990) • *Freedom's Fruit* (Hooks, 1996) • *The Secret of the Stones* (San Souci, 1999)
Flight	• *The People Could Fly* (Hamilton, 1985)
Human Tricksters	• *The Adventures of High John the Conqueror* (Sanfield, 1989) • *The Freedom Riddle* (Medearis, 1995) • *Little Eight John* (Wahl, 1992)
Moral	• *When Birds Could Talk and Bats Could Sing* (Hamilton, 1996)
Pourquoi	• *Why Heaven Is Far Away* (Lester, 2002) • *Imani's Music* (Williams, 2002) • *Her Stories* (Hamilton, 1995)
Supernatural	• *Raw Head, Bloody Bones* (Lyons, 1991) • *The Dark Thirty* (McKissack, 1992) • *The Headless Haunt and Other African American Ghost Stories* (Haskins, 1994) • *Moaning Bones* (Haskins, 1998)

African Caribbean and South American Folk Tales

Despite common assumptions about the slave trade, the United States did not receive the majority of captured Africans during the Middle Passage. The United States only received about 10% of Africans brought to the New World; the remaining 90% were enslaved either in the Caribbean or in South America. These enslaved peoples took their gift of story to the Caribbean and South America, specifically Brazil. As with the enslaved Africans in the United States, the stories most frequently told were the animal trickster tales.

There are literally hundreds of Anansi (Anancy and also Aunt Nancy) tales that have originated from the Caribbean, for example, James Berry's *First Palm Trees* (1997), an original tale, and his Anancy stories collection *Spiderman Anancy* (1989). In some of these stories, Anancy is a spider, and in others, a man. Amy MacDonald introduces us to a human trickster from Haiti in *Please, Malese* (2002). According to MacDonald, the name *Malese* comes from the French word that means *malice*. This is appropriate, because for sheer boldness and audacity, Malese's antics rival Anansi's.

Although Anansi tales are prevalent in the Caribbean, they are practically nonexistent in South America. Levine (1977) believes that because spiders are not as ubiquitous in South America as they are in other parts of the New World, Anansi stories would not be very common among the folk stories that evolved from South America. Although there have been very few Anansi tales found in South America, the absence of Anansi leaves room for the Brazilian trickster, Jabutí the Tortoise (McDermott, 1995).

Many of the tales that have emerged from South America and are available for children have not been influenced by African oral traditions; instead, the Spanish settlers and the indigenous peoples of the region have influenced these tales. Also, slaves in the Caribbean (and the United States) included in their stories elements of the European tales they heard from their masters. These gifted enslaved storytellers would then merge what they heard from their masters and integrate that information into the tales they brought with them from their homes in Africa. San Souci has retold several cross-cultural tales from Martinique: *The Faithful Friend* (1995) is a variant of Grimm's "Faithful John" (Zipes, 1992), and *Cendrillon* (1998) is a variant of Perrault's version of *Cinderella, or the Little Glass Slipper* (Brown, 1954). Virginia Hamilton's *The Girl Who Spun Gold* (2000) is a Rumpelstiltskin tale featuring the very colorful character Lit'mahn Bittyun and an easy-to-read West Indian patois that make it a wonderful read-aloud.

Supernatural and etiological tales also come to us from the Caribbean and Brazil. Mary Joan Gerson (1994) retells an etiological tale from Brazil—*How Night Came From the Sea*—based on a Nigerian folk tale. Lynn Joseph, a native of Trinidad and Tobago, has retold a series of family stories replete with a wealth of colorful characters such as jumbies, Ligahoo, a powerful shapechanger, and papa Bois in *A*

Wave in Her Pocket (1991). Joseph also has written a companion book, *The Mermaid's Twin Sister* (1994), which introduces readers to new supernatural characters and a variant of the European tale "Stone Soup."

Trickster and Other African Diaspora Tales in the Classroom

McDermott (n.d.) notes that tricksters have special appeal for children because of their ability to triumph over larger foes, not by physical strength but by wit and cunning. He adds that tricksters are wise but lovable rogues who have dual personalities. They are often triumphant but are just as often outwitted by cunning rivals or an excess of their own cleverness. They always survive to live another day. The rhythms of the stories, the survival skills of the characters, and the colorful vocabulary and settings make trickster tales excellent instructional springboards. Trickster and other African and African American folk tales are especially enjoyable for reading aloud, storytelling, Readers Theatre, comparing and contrasting, dramatizing, illustrating, and a myriad of other classroom projects. Following are ways in which African folk tales and their variants can be used in the classroom.

Compare trickster tales: Compare trickster tales to see the connections across and among the tales and the cultures from which they emerged. Select a variety of trickster tales and construct a table with attributes for comparison (e.g., origin of story, trickster, trickster's virtue, trickster's flaw, who was tricked, result of trick). A variation on this activity would be to compare all the trickster tales of one author (e.g., Verna Aardema) to see how his or her tales are alike and different.

Create a new story based on a trickster tale: Use an existing trickster tale as a model for creating a new trickster tale. Table 7.3 offers a framework for this activity.

Table 7.3
Creating a New Story Based on a Trickster Tale

Model	New Tale
Character:	Character:
Problem:	Problem:
Setting:	Setting:
Tasks:	Tasks:
Others:	Others:

Make cultural connections: Research the cultures/countries from which the tales come. For this activity, a Peters Projection world map is recommended instead of the standard Mercador Projection map. (The Peterson map shows the continents and their countries in their proper proportions; for example, the United States on this map is no longer shown as being larger than the entire African continent.) In addition to the basic research, examine how the influences of these cultures emerge from a tale such as *Sukey and the Mermaid* (San Souci, 1992).

Create literary passports: Literary passports (Johnson & Louis, 1987) are ways in which students can do in-depth character analyses. Use Johnson and Louis's basic passport format with a few additional areas of identification to create a complex character analysis like the one in Figure 7.1.

Compare diaspora folk tale variants to other cultural variants: Trickster tales are not the only tales that can be compared. There are many tales that have other cultural variants: *Mufaro's Beautiful Daughters* (Steptoe, 1988) is a "Cinderella" variant; so too is *Cendrillon* (San Souci, 1998). Your students could construct a comparison table like the one in Table 7.4.

Figure 7.1
Literary Passport

Name		Hair Color	
Height		Eye Color(s)	
Species		Weight	
Place of Birth		Home	
Occupation			
Visas		Passport Photograph	
Issued by			

Table 7.4
Comparisons of Folk Tale Variants

Tale	Variant(s)	Similarities	Differences
The Faithful Friend (San Souci, 1995)			
The Talking Eggs (San Souci, 1989)			
Sebgugugu the Glutton (Aardema, 1993)			
The Orphan Boy (Mollel, 1990)			
Flossie and the Fox (McKissack, 1986)			
The Girl Who Spun Gold (Hamilton, 2000)			
Rimonah of the Flashing Sword: A North African Tale (Kimmel, 1995)			
Cendrillon (San Souci, 1998)			

Study Anansi and spiders: Explore the world of spiders in fact and fiction. What is the most common type of spider illustrators use to draw Anansi? If he were not going about tricking his fellow animal friends, what would a real-world Anansi be doing? Surviving? Hunting and gathering?

Create the *Folk Tale Times*: Create a news magazine, newspaper, or news show about the antics of tricksters in the United States and abroad. Their story antics will provide fodder for each column.

Construct African storytelling instruments: Construct instruments to accompany classroom storytelling sessions. Story drums, rattles, gongs, and other rhythmic instruments are fun to make and to use during story hour.

Compare Brer Rabbit then and now: How have modern storytellers such as Julius Lester and Van Dyke Parks adapted the Uncle Remus tales for modern listeners and readers? Check out any edition of Harris's original Uncle Remus tales—Richard Chase's 1955 compilation is a good choice—and compare them to the modern versions retold by Lester or Parks. How has the language changed since the late 19th century? Is there anything in the modern stories to suggest that the status of African Americans has changed since Harris recorded the tales? If so, what examples show this change?

Conclusion

African, African American, Caribbean, and South American folk tales are wondrous and rhythmic gifts to modern readers and storytellers the world over. African folk tales, the foundation for all other Diaspora tales, have given readers a glimpse into the customs and traditions of peoples who told stories for a myriad of a reasons, from communication to entertainment to teaching moral lessons. African American folk tales reveal the power of the enslaved Africans' imagination despite the extreme conditions under which they had to live and work (Patton, n.d.). The life experiences of these African and African American storytellers have provided us with stories of tricksters, conjurers, princesses, mermaids, and other characters that connect all peoples of the Diaspora with their world neighbors. These experiences are rooted in the deep memories of loved ones lost in a strange new land and loved ones left in Africa. The stories in which the weak and small triumph over the rich and powerful (e.g., the tales of Anansi, Brer Rabbit, or High John) are the triumphs of incredible genius. We are richer because we can share in these characters' triumphs through reading and sharing those stories.

REFERENCES

Abrahams, R.D. (1985). *Afro-American folktales: Stories from the black traditions*. New York: Random House.

Berry, J. (1991). *West African folktales*. Evanston, IL: Northwestern University Press.

Blumenfeld, L. (n.d.). *Gullah people of the Sea Islands*. Retrieved April 7, 2003, from http://www.chatham.edu/PTI/African%20American%20History%2002/Blumenfeld_02.htm.

Courlander, H. (1996). *A treasury of African folklore*. New York: Marlowe.

Gates, H.L., & McKay, N.Y. (1997). *The Norton anthology of African American literature*. New York: W.W. Norton.

Hill, P.L. (Ed.). (1998). *Call and response: The Riverside anthology of the African American literary tradition*. Boston: Houghton Mifflin.

Hurston, Z.N. (1990). *Mules and men*. New York: Harper Perennial.

Ingram Book Group. (2000). *Getting to the root of Aunt Nancy*. Retrieved June 16, 2003, from http://www.ingrambookgroup.com/Company_info/ibchtml/Resource_Center/Whats_New/bb_aunt_nancy.asp.

Jacobs, H. (n.d.). *Remembering Joel Chandler Harris*. Retrieved April 16, 2003, from http://www.gsu.edu/~dsihhj/harris.htm

Johnson, T.D., & Louis, D. (1987). *Literacy through literature*. Portsmouth, NH: Heinemann.

Levine, L.W. (1977). *Black culture and black consciousness: Afro American folk thought from slavery to freedom*. New York: Oxford University Press.

Malvasi, M.G. (1999). *Raw heads and bloody bones*. Retrieved on March 23, 2003, from http://www.suite101.com/article.cfm/3679/22801

Marshall, H. (1998). *Folklore in America*. Retrieved March 1, 2003, from http://www.lclark.edu/%7Eria/FOLKTA%7E1.HTM.

McDermott, G. (n.d.). *Trickster tales*. Retrieved March 14, 2003, from http://www.friend.ly.net/scoop/biographies/mcdermottgerald

Offodile, B. (2001). *The orphan girl and other stories: West African folktales*. New York: Interlink.

Patton, J. (n.d.). *African-American folktales and their use in an integrated curriculum*. Retrieved March 18, 2003, from http://www.yale.edu/ynhti/curriculum/units/1993/2/93.02.08.x.html

CHILDREN'S BOOKS CITED

Aardema, V. (1977). *Who's in Rabbit's house? A Masai tale* (L. Dillon & D. Dillon, Illus.). New York: Dial.

Aardema, V. (1991). *Traveling to Tondo: A Tale of the Nkundo of Zaire* (W. Hillenbrand, Illus.). New York: Knopf.

Aardema, V. (1993). *Sebgugugu the Glutton: A Bantu tale from Rwanda* (N.L. Clouse, Illus.). Trenton, NJ: Africa World.

Aardema, V. (1997). *Anansi does the impossible: An Ashanti tale* (L. Disimini, Illus.). New York: Atheneum.

Arkhurst, J.C. (1964). *The adventures of Spider: West African folktales* (J. Pinkney, Illus.). Boston: Little, Brown.

Berry, J. (1989). *Spiderman Anancy* (G. Couch, Illus.). New York: Henry Holt.

Berry, J. (1997). *First palm trees: An Anancy Spiderman story* (G. Couch, Illus.). New York: Simon & Schuster.

Brown, M. (1954). *Cinderella, or the little glass slipper*. New York: Scribner's.

Bryan, A. (1993). *The story of lightning & thunder*. New York: Atheneum.

Bryan, A. (1998). *African tales, uh-huh*. New York: Atheneum.

Chase, R. (Compiler.). (1955). *The complete tales of Uncle Remus (Joel Chandler Harris)*. Boston: Houghton Mifflin.

Courlander, H., & Herzog, G. (1987). *The cow-tail switch and other West African stories*. New York: Henry Holt.

Cummings, P. (2002). *Ananse and the lizard*. New York: Henry Holt.

Doucet, S. (2002). *Lapin plays possum: Trickster tales from the Louisiana bayou* (S. Cook, Illus.). New York: Farrar, Straus & Giroux.

Echewa, T.O. (1999). *The magic tree: A folktale from Nigeria* (E.B. Lewis, Illus.). New York: Morrow.

Gerson, M. (1992). *Why the sky is far away: A Nigerian folktale* (C. Golembe, Illus.). Boston: Joy Street/Little, Brown.

Gerson, M. (1994). *How night came from the sea: A story from Brazil* (C. Golembe, Illus.). Boston: Joy Street/ Little, Brown.

Guy, R. (1981). *Mother Crocodile* (J. Steptoe & B. Diop, Illus.). New York: Doubleday.

Haley, G.E. (1970). *A story, a story*. New York: Atheneum.

Hamilton, V. (1985). *The people could fly: American black folktales* (L. Dillon & D. Dillon). New York: Knopf.

Hamilton, V. (1995). *Her stories: African American folktales, fairy tales, and true tales* (B. Moser, Illus.). New York: Scholastic.

Hamilton, V. (1996). *When birds could talk and bats could sing: The adventures of Bruh Sparrow, Sis Wren, and their friends* (B. Moser, Illus.). New York: Scholastic.

Hamilton, V. (1997). *A ring of tricksters: Animal tales from America, the West Indies, and Africa* (B. Moser, Illus.). New York: Scholastic.

Hamilton, V. (2000). *The girl who spun gold* (L. Dillon & D. Dillon, Illus.). New York: Blue Sky/Scholastic.

Harris, J.C. (2002). *The complete tales of Uncle Remus*. Boston: Houghton Mifflin.

Haskins, J. (1994). *The headless haunt and other African American ghost stories* (B. Otero, Illus.). New York: HarperCollins.

Haskins, J. (1998). *Moaning bones: African American ghost stories* (F. Marshall, Illus.). New York: Lothrop.

Hooks, W.H. (1990). *The ballad of Belle Dorcas* (J.B. Pinkney, Illus.). New York: Knopf.

Hooks, W.H. (1996). *Freedom's fruit* (J. Ransome, Illus.). New York: Knopf.

Jarrell, R. (Trans.). (1980). *The fisherman and his wife* (M. Zemach, Illus.). New York: Farrar, Straus & Giroux.

Joseph, L. (1991). *A wave in her pocket: Stories from Trinidad* (J.B. Pinkney, Illus.). New York: Clarion.

Joseph, L. (1994). *The mermaid's twin sister: More stories from Trinidad* (D. Perrone, Illus.). New York: Clarion.

Kimmel, E.A. (1988). *Anansi and the moss-covered rock* (J. Stevens, Illus.). New York: Holiday House.

Kimmel, E.A. (1992). *Anansi goes fishing* (J. Stevens, Illus.). New York: Holiday House.

Kimmel, E.A. (1994). *Anansi and the talking melon* (J. Stevens, Illus.). New York: Holiday House.

Kimmel, E.A. (1995). *Rimonah of the flashing sword: A North African tale* (O. Rayyan, Illus.). New York: Holiday House.

Kimmel, E.A. (2001). *Anansi and the magic stick* (J. Stevens, Illus.). New York: Holiday House.

Lester, J. (1987). *The tales of Uncle Remus: The adventures of Brer Rabbit* (J. Pinkney, Illus.). New York: Dial.

Lester, J. (1988). *More tales of Uncle Remus: Further adventures of Brer Rabbit, his friends, enemies, and others* (J. Pinkney, Illus.). New York: Dial.

Lester, J. (1989). *How many spots does a leopard have? And other tales* (D. Shannon, Illus.). New York: Scholastic.

Lester, J. (1990). *Further tales of Uncle Remus: The misadventures of Brer Rabbit, Brer Fox, Brer Wolf, the Doodang, and other creatures* (J. Pinkney, Illus.). New York: Dial.

Lester, J. (1994a). *The last tales of Uncle Remus* (J. Pinkney, Illus.). New York: Dial.

Lester, J. (1994b). *The man who knew too much: A moral tale from the Baila of Zambia* (L. Jenkins, Illus.). New York: Clarion.

Lester, J. (2002). *Why heaven is far away* (J. Cepeda, Illus.). New York: Scholastic.

Lyons, M.E. (1991). *Raw head, bloody bones: African American tales of the supernatural*. New York: Atheneum.

MacDonald, A. (2002). *Please, Malese: A trickster tale from Haiti* (E. Lisker, Illus.). New York: Farrar, Straus & Giroux.

McDermott, G. (1972). *Anansi the Spider*. New York: Henry Holt.

McDermott, G. (1973). *The magic tree: A tale from the Congo*. New York: Henry Holt.

McDermott, G. (1992). *Zomo, the Rabbit: A trickster tale from West Africa*. San Diego: Harcourt.

McDermott, G. (1995). *Jabutí the Tortoise: A trickster tale from the Amazon*. San Diego: Harcourt.

McKissack, P.C. (1986). *Flossie & the fox* (R. Isadora, Illus.). New York: Dial.

McKissack, P.C. (1992). *The dark thirty: Southern tales of the supernatural* (J.B. Pinkney, Illus.). New York: Knopf.

Medearis, A.S. (1995). *The freedom riddle* (J. Ward, Illus.). New York: Lodestar.

Mollel, T.M. (1990). *The orphan boy: A Masai story* (P. Morin, Illus.). New York: Clarion.

Mollel, T.M. (1992). *A promise to the sun: An African story* (B. Vidal, Illus.). Boston: Joy Street/Little Brown.

Mollel, T.M (1994). *The flying tortoise: An Igbo tale* (B. Spurl, Illus.). New York: Clarion.

Mollel, T.M. (1997). *Ananse's feast: An Ashanti tale* (A. Glass, Illus.). New York: Clarion.

Parks, V.D. (1987). *Jump again! More adventures of Brer Rabbit* (B. Moser, Illus.). San Diego: Harcourt.

Parks, V.D. (1989). *Jump on over! The adventures of Brer Rabbit and his family* (B. Moser, Illus.). San Diego: Harcourt.

Parks, V.D., & Jones, M. (1986). *Jump! The adventures of Brer Rabbit* (B. Moser, Illus.). San Diego: Harcourt.

Ringgold, F. (1991). *Tar Beach*. New York: Crown.

Ringgold, F. (1999). *The invisible princess*. New York: Crown.

Root, P. (1996). *Aunt Nancy and Old Man Trouble*. Cambridge, MA: Candlewick.

Sanfield, S. (1989). *The adventures of High John the Conqueror* (J. Ward, Illus.). New York: Orchard.

San Souci, R.D. (1989). *The talking eggs* (J. Pinkney, Illus.). New York: Dial.

San Souci, R.D. (1992). *Sukey and the mermaid* (J.B. Pinkney, Illus.). New York: Four Winds.

San Souci, R.D. (1995). *The faithful friend* (J.B. Pinkney, Illus.). New York: Simon & Schuster.

San Souci, R.D. (1998). *Cendrillon: A Caribbean Cinderella* (J.B. Pinkney, Illus.). New York: HarperCollins.

San Souci, R.D. (1999). *The secret of the stones: A folktale* (J. Ransome, Illus.). New York: Phyllis Fogelman.

San Souci, R.D. (2000). *Callie Ann and Mistah Bear* (D. Daily, Illus.). New York: Dial.

Steptoe, J. (1988). *Mufaro's beautiful daughters*. New York: Lothrop.

Stevens, J. (1995). *Tops & bottoms*. San Diego: Harcourt Brace.

Wahl, J. (1991). *Tailypo!* (W. Clay, Illus.). New York: Henry Holt.

Wahl, J. (1992). *Little Eight John* (W. Clay, Illus.). New York: Lodestar.

Williams, S. (2002). *Imani's music* (J. Daly, Illus.). New York: Atheneum.

Zipes, J. (Trans.). (1992). *The complete fairy tales of the Brothers Grimm* (J. Gruelle, Illus.). New York: Bantam.

ADDITIONAL RECOMMENDED AFRICAN AND AFRICAN AMERICAN FOLK TALES

Aardema, V. (1975). *Why mosquitoes buzz in people's ears* (L. Dillon, Illus.). New York: Dial.

Aardema, V. (1990). *Bringing the rain to Kapiti Plain* (B. Vidal, Illus.). New York: Dial.

Aardema, V. (1994). *Misoso: Once upon a time tales from Africa* (R. Ruffins, Illus.). New York: Apple Soup/Knopf.

Aardema, V. (1996). *The lonely lioness and the ostrich chicks* (Y. Heo, Illus.). New York: Knopf.

Aardema, V. (1997). *This for that: A Tonga tale* (V. Chess, Illus.). New York: Dial.

Aardema, V. (1999). *Koi and the kola nuts: A tale from Liberia* (J. Cepeda, Illus.). New York: Atheneum.

Bryan, A. (1977). *The dancing granny*. New York: Simon & Schuster.

Bryan, A. (1980). *Beat the story-drum, pum-pum*. New York: Atheneum.

Bryan, A. (1986). *Lion and the ostrich chicks*. New York: Aladdin.

Bryan, A. (2003). *Beautiful blackbird*. New York: Atheneum.

Chocolate, D.N. (2001). *Spider and the Sky God: An Akan legend* (D. Albers, Illus.). Bridgewater, NJ: Troll.

Dee, R. (1988). *Two ways to count to ten: A Liberian folktale* (S. Meddaugh, Illus.). New York: Henry Holt.

Hamilton, V. (1988). *In the beginning: Creation stories from around the world* (B. Moser, Illus.). San Diego: Harcourt.

Hamilton, V. (1990). *Dark way: Stories from the spirit world* (L. Davis, Illus.). San Diego: Harcourt.

Hausman, G. (1998). *Doctor Bird: Three lookin' up tales from Jamaica* (A. Wolff, Illus.). New York: Philomel.

Kurtz, J. (1997). *Trouble* (D. Bernhard, Illus.). San Diego: Gulliver/Harcourt.

Lester, J. (1991). *Black folktales* (T. Feelings, Illus.). New York: Grove.

Lilly, M. (1998). *Kwian and the lazy sun: A San legend* (C. Reasoner, Illus.). Bridgewater, NJ: Troll.

Medearis, A.S. (1994). *The singing man: Adapted from a West African folktale* (T.D. Shaffer, Illus.). New York: Holiday House.

Medlicott, M. (1996). *The river that went to the sky: Twelve tales by African storytellers* (A. Akintola, Illus.). New York: Kingfisher.

Mollel, T.M. (1993). *The king and the tortoise* (K. Blankley, Illus.). New York: Clarion.

Mollel, T.M. (1993). *The princess who lost her hair: An Akamba legend* (C. Reasoner, Illus.). Bridgewater, NJ: Troll.

Sierra, J. (1992). *The elephant's wrestling match* (J.B. Pinkney, Illus.). New York: Lodestar.

Tchana, K. (2002). *Sense Pass King: A story from the Cameroon* (T.S. Hyjman, Illus.). New York: Holiday House.

Temple, F. (1998). *Tiger soup: An Anansi story from Jamaica*. New York: Richard Jackson.

CHAPTER 8

When Tigers Smoked Pipes: Asian Folk Literature

Belinda Y. Louie

Years ago, Asian storytellers captured their audiences with tales that took place when tigers smoked pipes, or long ago in the kingdom of a million elephants. People young and old enjoyed the stories about how common folks used their wits to overcome rich and powerful officials. They were enchanted by stories about how spirits and ghosts crossed the paths of earthlings. Children learned how kindness and self-sacrifice would be rewarded, whereas wicked scheming would be punished. Women treasured the stories about how wives and daughters saved the day with their resourcefulness, courage, intelligence, and determination. Everyone had a good laugh on hearing a humorous tale.

Today, many of these stories are retold or translated into English, allowing readers across the world to enjoy the pleasure of Asian folk tales. Many authors include background materials or original sources for the tales. Some provide descriptions of the ancient versions and cultural beliefs associated with each story. This supporting information helps readers to check the authenticity of the folk tales. Some authors present original folk tales that are new creations based on the country's customs, values, and beliefs. Readers can compare an original tale with other known authentic folk tales of the same culture to see whether the new story is consistent with the traditional tales. This chapter will present tales that take place in Cambodia, China, Japan, Korea, Laos, the Philippines, Thailand, and Vietnam under five themes: wit overcomes power, spirits and humans, kindness and wickedness, women with strength, and humor and folly. Although Asian countries are diverse in their traditions and heritage, they share many common beliefs because of mutual influences after being close neighbors for centuries. These tales, which record the pulses of people in the East, have entertained their tellers and listeners for 5,000 years. Perhaps the stories will also bring inspiration and enjoyment to young readers in the West.

Wit Overcomes Power

One of the major themes in Asian folk tales is that of a small but quick-witted animal or person getting the better of someone stronger and meaner than himself or herself. A smart rabbit finds a way to escape from the grasp of the dragon king, a gentle scholar lures a thief to return his money, and a poor lad finds a way to weigh an elephant and saves his favorite animal from the greedy king. In ancient societies, peasants saw themselves as weak and powerless compared with the government officials, rich landlords, and kings who ruled over them. Thus, common villagers often amused themselves by telling stories in which they had the upper hand in their struggles against bullies. Even though they were oppressed in reality, they released their tensions and gained satisfaction by overpowering their oppressors in the story world.

Cambodian people have endured a long history of war and catastrophe. The small rabbit in *Brother Rabbit: A Cambodian Tale* (Ho & Ros, 1997) reflects the strong will of the Cambodians in their struggles against strong and ruthless authorities. The rabbit outsmarts a crocodile and an elephant, animals much bigger than he, to serve his needs. In *The Rabbit's Judgment* (Han, 1994), a Korean folk tale, a rabbit calmly tricks an ungrateful tiger to jump back into the deep pit from which he was rescued by a kind person. The tiger, who tries to repay kindness with evil, can then no longer threaten the safety of the man and the rabbit. In Virginia Pilegard's *The Warlord's Puzzle* (2000), a simple farm lad puts back the broken pieces of a beautiful square tile; scholars and wise men had been unable to solve the tangram, a Chinese geometric puzzle, despite the warlord's wrath. This story speaks to the truth that intelligence is not exclusively owned by men with rank or learning. Young children, just like small animals, sometimes can solve a problem better than learned adults.

Spirits and Humans

Folk tales often reflect beliefs and superstitions that have guided ordinary people's lives from generation to generation. However, this world is not the only one that affects people's lives here and now. In parallel worlds, inhabitants such as ancestors' souls, heavenly beings, animal spirits, household spirits, demons, and monsters interact with humans on Earth or in their own residing places. A ghost who harms travelers can become a young woodcutter's wife. A god who lives in the dusty attic can make sandals to help out the poor family with whom he stays. Palaces under the ocean, kingdoms above the clouds, and remote regions in the mountains are places that human beings can visit when accompanied by a spirit guide. Thus, in older days (and still to some people today), spirits and humans sometimes cross each other's paths. Whether the encounter is a blessing or a curse depends on the nature of the spirit and the character of the human.

Mysterious Tales of Japan (Martin, 1996) consists of 10 haunting tales in which humans' lives are tangled with those from the spirit world. A woman falls in love with a pine tree. A man is whisked away to marry a princess when 300 years have gone by without his knowledge. Two of the tales, *The Snow Wife* (San Souci, 1993) and *The Boy Who Drew Cats* (Hodges, 2002), have their own picture book versions. In *Monkey King* by Ed Young (2001), *The Making of the Monkey King* by Robert Kraus and Debby Chen (1998), and *The Magical Monkey King* by Ji-li Jiang (2002), the authors present a much-beloved Chinese legend. From his birth to his later adventures accompanying his master to obtain the sutras, Buddhist sacred texts, the monkey king travels freely and acts mischievously in human villages, heavenly courts, and spirit hideouts. He moves seamlessly between human and spirit dwellings as though those dwellings exist side by side.

Many Asians believe that their ancestral spirits often protect them and even communicate with them. Yasuyo, in Laura Williams's *The Long Silk Strand* (1995), climbs up a silk strand to talk to her diseased grandmother. Although Yasuyo misses her grandmother's company, she is much encouraged by her grandmother's words. Choon-Yi, in Paul Yee's *Ghost Train* (1996), comes to the United States to look for her father, not knowing that he died while building the railroads. Her father's spirit reveals to her what has happened and asks her to transport his spirit home by drawing and burning a picture of him on a train. In *Jouanah* (Coburn, 1996), a young Hmong girl finds happiness and love with the aid of her dead mother's spirit.

Kindness and Wickedness

Because stories always have been such a treasured part of people's lives, people rely on them to pass along their customs and beliefs from the old to the young. Many Asian folk tales are influenced by Confucianism and Buddhism. Confucianism shapes the social structure and maintains that the young have to respect the old, that the people should be loyal to their rulers, that friends should respect one another, and that women must subject themselves to their fathers and husbands. In a Confucian society, order and harmony can be achieved when each person stays within his or her role and is content. Buddhism emphasizes the necessity not to be selfish and to be kind to all living things. This philosophy holds that enlightenment will only come when one is totally empty of selfish desires. By achieving freedom from desire and recognizing that this mortal life is but an illusion, a person can escape the cycles of reincarnation. Many folk tales remind people to be kind to animals because they may have been one's family members or friends in previous lives. Most Asian folk tales emphasize that kindness will be rewarded and wicked schemers will eventually be punished. Cambodians consider telling and retelling of these stories to be almost like a "speech-teach" (Carrison, 1987, p. 12). Being kind to helpless animals, needy neighbors, and even a downtrodden bully brings fortune and prosperity to the people who render the good deeds.

Kimiko Kajikawa (2000) tells a hilarious story in which two neighbors learn to live in harmony. In *Yoshi's Feast*, fan maker Yoshi loves the smell of the eels broiled by his fishmonger neighbor, Sabu. Being a miser himself, Yoshi never buys the eels, but satisfies his yearning by taking in the aroma of broiled eels for breakfast, lunch, and dinner. When challenged by Sabu to pay for the aroma, Yoshi rattles his coins, "chin chin jara jara...chin jara jara,"

making the payment with the sound of his money. As the story ends, the feuding neighbors become amiable friends, helping each other to become prosperous and enjoying each other's company. In *Older Brother, Younger Brother* by Nina Jaffe (1995), Hungbu respects and submits to his older brother's decisions even though he and his family suffer. He even takes the blame for his older brother's mistakes so that no dishonor will be brought on his father and older brother. Hungbu is later rewarded with much fortune after nursing a swallow with a broken wing, whereas his older brother suffers from his own

Book cover from *Yoshi's Feast*, written by Kimiko Kajikawa, illustrated by Yumi Heo. Copyright © 2000. Used by permission of Dorling Kindersley.

greed. Seeing his older brother distraught, Hungbu helps him to rebuild his life. At the end of the story, the two brothers promise to help each other always and to honor their father's memory.

Buddhism prevails in the book *Cambodian Folk Stories From the Gatiloke* (Carrison, 1987), which consists of 15 folk stories with origins in the teaching of Buddhist monks. In these stories, kindhearted but foolish people still suffer ill consequences if they allow themselves to be preyed on by wicked folks. Retribution may not come within one's life but in the life cycles yet to come. *A Tale of Two Rice Birds: A Folk Tale From Thailand* by Clare Meeker (1994) is a tale of reincarnation and enduring love. After the rice bird wife flies into the forest fire bearing grudges against her mate, the rice bird husband dives into the fire also, praying that they will resume their relationship in their next lives. Many people believe in fate, which is a Buddhist belief. In *Red Thread*, a Chinese folk tale by Ed Young (1993), marriage between a man and a wife is determined by fate, the two being connected by an invisible red thread. In *The Two Brothers*, a Cambodian story by Minfong Ho and Saphan Ros (1995), the fortunes of two brothers are also controlled by their very different fates, even though they shared a similar life in childhood.

Folk tales celebrate many humble and naive heroes who are rewarded for their gentle nature and kind acts. The words "when you see a bee fly from someone's nose, good fortune will be yours" open a delightful tale in Jan Long's *The Bee and the Dream* (1996). Shin, an honorable and honest person, finds shining treasure after he purchases the dream from his friend. A rich and greedy man who envies Shin's good fortune ends up digging up a swarm of bees instead. In Rosalind Wang's *The Fourth Question: A Chinese Tale* (1991), hardworking Yee-Lee wonders why he is so poor. During his journey of looking for the wise man who can answer this question, Yee-Lee agrees to take along three questions—from the mother whose daughter is mute, from a tree owner whose tree is barren, and from a dragon who wants to return to heaven. Finding that the wise man will only answer three questions, Yee-Lee puts the others' questions before his own. In the end, as others resolve their problems, their solutions also bring wealth and happiness to Yee-Lee.

Women With Strength

May they be shrewd bargainers or beautiful warriors, human princesses or animal spirits, women in Asian folk tales use their strength in their traditional roles of wives and daughters. They do not seek positions of power and control; they simply employ their talents to help their husbands and fathers. The women may engage in *oni* (monster) fighting or feather weaving, protect their husbands from harm or petition for their fathers, sacrifice their lives for the villagers or trap orange ants to get money for their families. An insightful magistrate wisely comments, "The spirits of sorrow would not dare to pass over your threshold, for then they would have *you* to deal with!" (Wyndham, 1971, p. 36). Common folks like to tell tales about gentle and caring women who are also strong and determined to protect their households. By providing numerous role models in their folk tales, storytellers want to remind people that women, from the king's princess to the fox's maiden, should be in a supporting role, as defined by the Asian societal structure, which honors male leadership.

In "Little Finger of the Watermelon Patch" from Lynette Dyer Vuong's *The Brocaded Slipper and Other Vietnamese Tales* (1982), the main character proves her worth when she helps her prince husband-to-be in three contests to secure him the position of king. The prince does not mean to marry her at the beginning because of her short fingers, but because Little Finger behaves as an honorable wife would, the prince marries her at the end of the story. In *Beautiful Warrior*, Emily McCully (1998) tells a story about Wu Mei, a nun who is a master of Chinese martial arts. Mingyi, a scatterbrained young girl, seeks out Wu Mei to learn martial arts to save herself from a forced marriage to a bandit. After Mingyi overpowers the bully to the amazement of all, she decides to follow Wu Mei to perfect her skills and to lead an independent life. Although Wu Mei and Mingyi are strong women, they have no alternative but to take on the role of nuns if they want to pursue free and self-directed lives.

Humor and Folly

Imagine that a grouchy landlord could fall head-over-heels and sink into the pool in the top of his head; that a ferocious tiger could be scared away by a father's talk of dried persimmons as he tries to soothe his crying baby; and that a beautiful puppet could lure away a nasty, hungry monster. Asian folk tales have two invaluable functions—entertaining the adult listeners and educating the young ones in the audience. One of the common characteristics of folk tales is that they are also amusing to the people who create and preserve them. By making fun of the strong and the powerful, the tales help the storytellers and the listeners to feel less frightened of some common fears: people with wealth or in high position, fierce animals, and demons. After all, these powerful beings are all capable of succumbing to weaknesses and committing follies. Interesting to children, these tales capture children's attention so that they will stay to learn the tales' lessons and values.

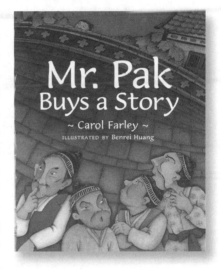

Book cover from *Mr. Pak Buys a Story* by Carol Farley, illustrated by Benrei Huang. Text copyright © 1997 by Carol Farley. Illustrations copyright © 1997 by Benrei Huang. Used by permission of Albert Whitman & Company.

Flying turtles and tiger-eating toads pique the listeners' interest in finding out what happens to the animals. Steve Epstein includes many humorous Laotian stories in *Tales of Turtles, Tigers, and Toads* (1996a) and *Xieng Mieng: The Cleverest Man in the Kingdom* (1996b). Two swans use a stick to transport a turtle to a new pond. Everything goes smoothly until the turtle opens his mouth and lets go of the stick, trying to tell the world below that it is he, the turtle, that carries the swans. Ironically, vanity costs the turtle his life. A frightened tiger running away from a toad presents another hilarious tale. How foolish is the tiger who believes in the toad who claims to live on a regular diet of tigers? It is also satisfying to find out how trickster Xieng Mieng wins over the proud and clever (but not quite clever enough) king.

Some stories are just for sheer enjoyment. *The Two Bullies* by Junko Morimoto (1997) and *Three Strong Women* by Claus Stamm (1990) make fun of men who are giants. They may be strong outside, but they are shown to be gentle and fearful inside like men much smaller in size. In Laurence Yep's *The Khan's Daughter* (1997), a simple shepherd stumbles through numerous challenges to win the hand of the

Khan's daughter. A foolish servant uses his master's gold coins to buy a silly story in Carol Farley's *Mr. Pak Buys a Story* (1997), not realizing that the rambling lines of the story will save his life later. Unexpected follies of common folks appeal to listeners young and old, reminding them not to take life too seriously.

Teaching Ideas

Making Masks and Puppets

Children in elementary classrooms will enjoy making masks or puppets for the characters in folk tales. They can use the masks or puppets to act out different stories. Because folk tales are ideal for reading aloud, teachers should consider using Readers Theatre, in which a narrator reads the story while other people act it out.

Students in the upper elementary grades can read a collection of Asian folk tales to identify the characters and animals who think well on their feet. They then can choose their favorite character or animal and write his or her next encounter with a powerful yet foolish person or animal. When students choose the country for their story, they should include at least three cultural characteristics from that country to increase the authenticity of their tales. For example, in Japanese folk tales, the characters could wear kimonos, which are a traditional style of dress; sit on tatami, which are sitting mats; and sleep on futons, which are foldable beds. Books such as *In Search of the Spirit: The Living National Treasures of Japan* (Hamanaka & Ohmi, 1999) and *D Is for Doufu: An Alphabet Book of Chinese Culture* (Krach, 1997) are good resource books for the students. Teachers can present other information books (see the list provided at the end of this chapter) to help students understand the land, the people, and the culture of their Asian folk tales of interest. These books also include pictures and information that can help students to make culturally authentic puppets. (More information about using folk tales and creating classroom drama can be found in chapter 16 of this book.)

Spirit, Spirit, What Are You?

Students at a wide range of grade levels can make charts to describe different spirits (ancestral spirits, heavenly beings, animal spirits, household spirits, demons, and monsters) that they encounter in the stories. Younger students can draw pictures in their charts, and older students can use text to describe the spirits. In folk tales that involve spirits, some sort of transformation usually takes place. Students can discuss why the spirits transform and how the transformations affect the lives of human beings with whom the spirits are in contact. You may want to remind students that many people in Asia believe in the existence of spirits. (Note: To study the Asian belief in spirits does not mean that the teacher or school endorses this belief.)

Creating Books of Values

Folk tales are filled with characters portraying values that are highly treasured and values that are strongly abhorred. Students can create two books: a book of virtue and a book of vice. In each book, students can describe the "positive" or "negative" values and identify the behaviors that are associated with them. Young students can focus on one or two virtues or vices, and older students can work on more items. *Voices of the Heart* (Young, 1997), *Confucius: The Golden Rule* (Freedman, 2002), *To Swim in Our Own Pond* (Tran, 1998), and *Tigers, Frogs, and Rice Cakes* (Holt, 1999) are good resources for students to learn more about the cultural values of various Asian countries.

You can guide students to discuss in what ways and to what extent they share the values of the Asian folk tale characters. Ask students, Even if you share the same values, how will the values be reflected in your own lives? Who is right and who is wrong if students and story characters do not share the same values? For example, students may not agree that they should take the blame for their siblings' mistakes. Help students to understand that people share many universal values but that we all also have our own unique sets of values, which are often specific to our cultural groups. Remind students that when we encounter differences in values, we just need to understand and respect the differences without passing judgment.

Character Portraits

The strong women portrayed in many folk tales are also role models for wives and daughters. Students need to realize that these women use their strength and intelligence to serve the common good of the family and the community. Younger students can make life-size character portraits for women of strength in Asian folk tales. On the backs of the portraits, students can write down the strengths of each female character and how she helps people around her. Older students can compare a strong woman in an Asian folk tale with another one that students know from stories of other cultures. These women can be compared in areas of their intelligence and skills, the motivation behind their actions, why they earn respect from others, and what the women might consider to be personal success.

Women with strength can be found across cultures, yet how they use their strength is shaped by the social expectations and gender roles of their cultures. You also can select information books (see list at the end of this chapter) for students to examine the roles of contemporary Asian women. Do Asian women's roles differ in the modern world compared with those in the folk tales? Although today's Asian women have different tasks and jobs, do they still work to serve their families and communities?

Storytelling

What can be more entertaining than telling a good and funny story to friends? Students should select a folk tale that they really like and prepare it for retelling. Point out that retelling is not merely reciting a story; the student storytellers do not need to be word perfect, but they do need to capture the attention of the audience by delivering a lively story. They should first identify the funniest element of the story and then work on building the suspense, using the right tone, and controlling their pacing to accomplish the utmost effect of bringing laughter (or whatever the desired response is) to all that are involved. Students also can retell their stories from the perspective of a character: that of a small animal, a foolish king, or an old tree who observes the events unfolding around it.

Conclusion

Asian folk tales are as diverse and rich as the people they portray. The stories educate the young and entertain all those who love listening to stories. True to this spirit, when you introduce Asian folk tales into the classroom, you should engage students in learning about the values and traditions of the corresponding Asian countries. At the same time, both teachers and students can enjoy the stories when they read them aloud or when they act them out. This chapter simply offers "a taste of Asia." I invite you to read more and to dig deeper. The further you go into the reading experience, the more mysteries you will discover and the more excitement you will find.

CHILDREN'S BOOKS CITED

Carrison, M.P. (1987). *Cambodian folk stories from the Gatiloke* (C. Kong, Illus.). Rutland, VT: Charles E. Tuttle.

Coburn, J.R. (1996). *Jouanah: A Hmong Cinderella* (T. Lee & A. O'Brien, Illus.). Fremont, CA: Shen's Books.

Epstein, S. (1996a.) *Tales of turtles, tigers, and toads*. Laos: Vientiane Times.

Epstein, S. (1996b.) *Xieng Mieng: The cleverest man in the kingdom*. Laos: Vientiane Times.

Farley, C.C. (1997). *Mr. Pak buys a story* (B. Huang, Illus.). Morton Grove, IL: Albert Whitman.

Freedman, R. (2002). *Confucius: The golden rule*. New York: Arthur A. Levine.

Hamanaka, S., & Ohmi, A. (1999). *In search of the spirit: The living national treasures of Japan*. New York: Morrow.

Han, S.C. (1994). *The rabbit's judgment* (Y. Heo, Illus.). New York: Henry Holt.

Ho, M., & Ros, S. (1995). *The two brothers* (J. Tseng & M. Tseng, Illus.). New York: Lothrop, Lee & Shepard.

Ho, M., & Ros, S. (1997). *Brother rabbit: A Cambodian tale* (J. Hewitson, Illus.). New York: Lothrop, Lee & Shepard.

Hodges, M. (2002). *The boy who drew cats* (A. Sogabe & L. Hearn, Illus.). New York: Holiday House.

Holt, K.D. (1999). *Tigers, frogs, and rice cakes: A book of Korean proverbs* (S.H. Sticker, Illus.). Fremont, CA: Shen's Books.

Jaffe, N. (1995). *Older brother, younger brother* (W. Ma, Illus.). New York: Viking.

Jiang, J.L. (2002). *The magical monkey king: Mischief in heaven* (H. Su-Kennedy, Illus.). New York: HarperCollins.

Kajikawa, K. (2000). *Yoshi's feast* (Y. Heo, Illus.). New York: Dorling Kindersley.

Krach, M.S. (1997). *D is for doufu: An alphabet book of Chinese culture* (H. Zhang, Illus.). Fremont, CA: Shen's Books.

Kraus, R., & Chen, D. (1998). *The making of the monkey king* (W. Ma, Illus.). Union City, CA: Pan Asian.

Long, J.F. (1996). *The bee and the dream: A Japanese tale* (K. Ono, Illus.). New York: Dutton.

Martin, R. (1996). *Mysterious tales of Japan* (T. Kiuchi, Illus.). New York: G.P. Putnam's Sons.

McCully, E.A. (1998). *Beautiful warrior: The legend of the nun's kung fu*. New York: Scholastic.

Meeker, C.H. (1994). *A tale of the two rice birds: A folktale from Thailand* (C. Lamb, Illus.). Seattle, WA: Sasquatch.

Morimoto, J. (1997). *The two bullies* (I. Morimoto, Illus.). New York: Crown.

Pilegard, V.W. (2000). *The warlord's puzzle* (N. Debon, Illus.). Gretna, LA: Pelican.

San Souci, R.D. (1993). *The snow wife* (S. Johnson, Illus.). New York: Dial.

Stamm, C. (1990). *Three strong women: A tall tale from Japan* (J. Tseng & M. Tseng, Illus.). New York: Viking.

Tran, N.D. (1998). *To swim in our own pond: A book of Vietnamese proverbs* (X-Q. Dang, Illus.). Fremont, CA: Shen's Books.

Vuong, L.D. (1982). *The brocaded slipper and other Vietnamese tales* (V.D. Mai, Illus.). Reading, MA: Addison-Wesley.

Wang, R.C. (1991). *The fourth question: A Chinese tale* (J. Chen, Illus.). New York: Holiday House.

Williams, L.E. (1995). *The long silk strand: A grandmother's legacy to her granddaughter* (G. Bochak, Illus.). Honesdale, PA: Boyds Mills Press.

Wyndham, R. (1971). *Tales the people tell in China* (J. Yang, Illus.). New York: Julian Messner.

Yee, P. (1996). *Ghost train* (H. Chan, Illus.). Toronto: Groundwood.

Yep, L. (1997). *The khan's daughter: A Mongolian folktale* (J. Tseng & M. Tseng, Illus.). New York: Scholastic.

Young, E. (1993). *Red thread*. New York: Philomel.

Young, E. (1997). *Voices of the heart*. New York: Scholastic.

Young, E. (2001). *Monkey king*. New York: HarperCollins.

FURTHER RECOMMENDED READING

Adams, E.B. (1981). *Herdboy and weaver*. Seoul, Korea: Seoul International.

Adams, E.B. (1981). *Hungbu Nolbu: Two brothers and their magic gourds* (C. Dong-Ho, Illus.). Seoul, Korea: Seoul International.

Adams, E.B. (1982). *Korean Cinderella* (R. Heller, Illus.). Seoul, Korea: Seoul International.

Adams, E.B. (1982). *Woodcutter and nymph*. Seoul, Korea: Seoul International.

Bodkin, O. (1998). *The crane wife* (G. Spirin, Illus.). San Diego: Gulliver.

Brittan, D. (1997). *The Hmong*. New York: PowerKids.

Brittan, D. (1997). *The people of Cambodia*. New York: PowerKids.

Brittan, D. (1997). *The people of Laos*. New York: PowerKids.

Brittan, D. (1997). *The people of Thailand*. New York: PowerKids.

Chang, C. (1994). *The seventh sister: A Chinese legend* (C. Reasoner, Illus.). Mahwah, NJ: Troll.

Chang, M., & Chang, R. (1994). *The cricket warrior: A Chinese tale* (W. Hutton, Illus.). New York: Margaret K. McElderry.

Chen, K. (2000). *Lord of the cranes: A Chinese tale* (J. James, Illus.). New York: North-South.

Choi, Y. (1997). *The sun girl and the moon boy*. New York: Knopf.

Climo, S. (1993). *The Korean Cinderella* (R. Heller, Illus.). New York: HarperCollins.

Compestine, Y.C. (2001). *The runaway rice cake* (T. Chau, Illus.). New York: Simon & Schuster.

Compestine, Y.C. (2001). *The story of chopsticks* (Y. Xuan, Illus.). New York: Holiday House.

Czernecki, S. (1997). *The cricket's cage: A Chinese folktale* (C. Ching, Illus.). New York: Hyperion.

Day, N.R. (2001). *Piecing Earth and sky together: A creation story from the Mien tribe of Laos* (G. Panzarella, Illus.). Fremont, CA: Shen's Books.

Demi. (1996). *The dragon's tale and other animal fables of the Chinese zodiac*. New York: Henry Holt.

Demi. (1998). *The greatest treasure*. New York: Scholastic.

Demi. (1999). *The donkey and the rock*. New York: Henry Holt.

Diamond, J. (1989). *Laos*. Chicago: Children's Press.

Esterl, A. (1994). *Okino and the whales* (M. Zawazki, Illus.). San Diego: Harcourt Brace.

Fang, L. (1994). *The chi-lin purse: A collection of ancient Chinese stories* (J. Lee, Illus.). New York: Farrar, Straus & Giroux.

Fritsch, D.M. (1997). *A part of the ribbon: A time travel adventure through the history of Korea*. Wethersfield, CT: Turtle.

Fu, S. (2001). *Ho Yi the archer: And other classic Chinese tales* (J. Abboreno, Illus.). North Haven, CT: Linnet.

Gilchrist, C. (1999). *Stories from the silk road* (N. Mistry, Illus.). Cambridge, MA: Barefoot Books.

Gill, J. (1999). *Basket weaver and catches many mice* (Y. Choi, Illus.). New York: Knopf.

Goodman, J. (1991). *Thailand*. New York: Marshall Cavendish.

Gollub, M. (2000). *Ten oni drummers* (K. Stone, Illus.). New York: Lee & Low.

Greene, E. (1996). *Ling-Li and the phoenix fairy: A Chinese folktale* (Z. Wang, Illus.). New York: Clarion.

Han, C. (1993). *Why snails have shells: Minority and Han folktales of China* (J. Li, Illus.). Honolulu, HI: University of Hawaii Press.

Han, C. (1997). *Tales from within the clouds: Nakhi stories of China* (J. Li, Illus.). Honolulu, HI: University of Hawaii Press.

Han, O.S., & Plunkett, S.H. (1993). *Sir Whong and the golden pig*. New York: Dial.

Han, O.S., & Plunkett, S.H. (1996). *Kongi and Potgi: A Cinderella story from Korea*. New York: Dial.

Han, S.C. (1991). *Korean folk and fairy tales* (W. Chong, Illus.). Elizabeth, NJ: Hollym.

Han, S.C. (1995). *The rabbit's escape* (Y. Heo, Illus.). New York: Henry Holt.

Han, S.C. (1999). *The rabbit's tail: A story from Korea* (R. Wehrman, Illus.). New York: Henry Holt.

Hanh, T.N. (1993). *A taste of Earth and other legends of Vietnam*. Berkeley, CA: Parallex.

He, L.Y. (1985). *The spring of butterflies and other folktales of China's minority peoples* (D. Aiging, Illus.). New York: Lothrop, Lee & Shepard.

Heo, Y. (1996). *The green frogs*. Boston: Houghton Mifflin.

Hong, C.J. (1997). *The legend of the kite*. Norwalk, CT: Soundprints.

Huynh, Q.N. (1986). *The land I lost: Adventures of a boy in Vietnam*. New York: HarperTrophy.

Huynh, Q.N. (1999). *Water buffalo days: Growing up in Vietnam*. New York: HarperTrophy.

Ishii, M. (1982). *The tongue-cut sparrow* (S. Akaba, Illus.). New York: Lodestar.

Johnston, T. (1990). *The badger and the magic fan* (T. dePaola, Illus.). New York: Scholastic.

Kalman, B. (2000). *China: The culture*. New York: Crabtree.

Kalman, B. (2000). *China: The land*. New York: Crabtree.

Kalman, B. (2000). *China: The people*. New York: Crabtree.

Kalman, B. (2000). *Japan: The culture*. New York: Crabtree.

Kalman, B. (2000). *Japan: The land*. New York: Crabtree.

Kalman, B. (2000). *Japan: The people*. New York: Crabtree.

Kendall, C. (1988). *The wedding of the rat family* (J. Watts, Illus.). New York: Margaret K. McElderry.

Kimmel, E.A. (1998). *Ten suns: A Chinese legend* (Y. Xuan, Illus.). New York: Holiday House.

Kimmel, E.A. (1999). *The rooster's antlers: A story of the Chinese zodiac* (Y. Xuan, Illus.). New York: Holiday House.

Kirollos, S. (1989). *The wind children and other tales from Japan* (Y. Yaura, Illus.). London: Andre Deutsch.

Krudop, W.L. (2000). *The man who caught a fish*. New York: Farrar, Straus & Giroux.

Kwan, M.D. (2002). *The Chinese storyteller's book: Supernatural tales*. North Clarendon, VT: Tuttle.

Kwon, H.H. (1993). *The moles and the mireuk* (W. Hubbard, Illus.). Boston: Houghton Mifflin.

Langston, L. (1995). *The magic ear* (V. Bosson, Illus.). Custer, WA: Orca.

Lee, J.M. (1989). *Toad is the uncle of heaven: A Vietnamese folk tale*. New York: Henry Holt.

Lee, J.M. (2002). *Bitter dumplings*. New York: Farrar, Straus & Giroux.

Lerner Publications. (1996). *Laos in pictures*. Minneapolis, MN: Author.

Livo, Norma J., & Cha, D. (1991). *Folk stories of the Hmong: Peoples of Laos, Thailand, and Vietnam*. Englewood, CO: Libraries Unlimited.

Lorbiecki, M. (1997). *Children of Vietnam*. Minneapolis, MN: Carolrhoda.

Louie, A. (1982). *Yeh-Shen: A Cinderella story from China* (E. Young, Illus.). New York: Philomel.

Lum, D. (1994). *The golden slipper* (M. Nagano, Illus.). New York: Troll.

MacDonald, M.M. (1998). *The girl who wore too much: A folktale from Thailand* (Y. Davis, Illus.). Little Rock, AR: August House.

Mamdami, S. (1999). *Traditions from China*. Austin, TX: Steck-Vaughn.

Marston, E. (1996). *The fox maiden* (T. Kiuchi, Illus.). New York: Simon & Schuster.

Marton, F. (1997). *Lady Kaguya's secret: A Japanese folktale*. New York: Annick.

McMahon, P. (1993). *Chi-hoon: A Korean girl*. Honesdale, PA: Boyds Mills Press.

Milne, A.R. (1972). *Mr. Basket knife and other Khmer folk-tales*. London: George Allen & Unwin.

Morimoto, J. (1986). *The inch boy*. New York: Viking Kestrel.

Myers, T. (2000). *Basho and the fox* (O. Han, Illus.). New York: Marshall Cavendish.

Namioka, L. (1995). *The loyal cat* (A. Sogabe, Illus.). San Diego: Harcourt Brace.

Namioka, L. (2001). *The hungriest boy in the world* (A. Sogabe, Illus.). New York: Holiday House.

Namioka, N. (1998). *The laziest boy in the world* (Y. Xuan, Illus.). New York: Holiday House.

Nhuan, N.T. (1995) *Tam Cam: A Vietnamese Cinderella story*. Fremont, CA: Shen's Books.

Nickles, G. (2002). *Philippines: The culture*. New York: Crabtree.

Nickles, G. (2002). *Philippines: The land*. New York: Crabtree.

Nickles, G. (2002). *Philippines: The people*. New York: Crabtree.

O'Brien, A.S. (1993). *The princess and the beggar*. New York: Scholastic.

Ozaki, Y.T. (1967). *The Japanese fairy book*. New York: Dover.

Paterson, K. (1990). *The tale of the mandarin ducks* (L. Dillon & D. Dillon, Illus.). New York: Lodestar.

Poole, A.L. (1999). *How the rooster got his crown*. New York: Holiday House.

Porte, B.A. (2000). *Ma Jiang and the orange ants* (A. Cannon, Illus.). New York: Orchard.

Pray, R. (2001). *Jingu: The hidden princess* (X. Li, Illus.). Fremont, CA: Shen's Books.

Provensen, A. (2001). *The master swordsman & the magic doorway*. New York: Simon & Schuster.

Quayle, E. (1989). *The shining princess: And other Japanese legends* (M. Foreman, Illus.). New York: Arcade.

Rappaport, D. (1991). *The journey of Meng* (M. Yang, Illus.). New York: Dial.

Reasoner, C. (1994). *The magic amber*. Mahwah, NJ: Troll.

Rhee, N. (1993). *Magic spring*. New York: G.P. Putnam's Sons.

Riordan, J. (1994). *Korean folk tales*. Oxford, UK: Oxford University Press.

Romulo, L. (2000). *Filipino children's favorite stories* (J. De Leon, Illus.). Hong Kong: Periplus Editions.

Sakade, F. (1958). *Kintaro's adventures and other Japanese children's stories* (Y. Hayashi, Illus.). Rutland, VT: Charles E. Tuttle.

Sakade, F. (1958). *Peach boy and other Japanese children's favorite stories*. Rutland, VT: Charles E. Tuttle.

San Souci, D. (1999). *In the moonlight mist* (E.K. Neilan, Illus.). Honesdale, PA: Boyds Mills Press.

San Souci, R.D. (1992). *The samurai's daughter* (S. Johnson, Illus.). New York: Dial.

San Souci, R.D. (1996). *Pedro and the monkey* (M. Hays, Illus.). New York: Morrow.

San Souci, R.D. (2002). *The silver charm: A folktale from Japan* (Y. Ito, Illus.). New York: Doubleday.

Say, A. (1974). *Under the cherry blossom tree: An old Japanese tale*. New York: Houghton Mifflin.

Schecter, C. (1993). *Sim Chung and the river dragon* (J. Otani, Illus.). New York: Bantam.

Schroeder, A. (1994). *Lily and the wooden bowl: A Japanese folktale* (I. Yoriko, Illus.). New York: Bantam Doubleday Dell.

Shepard, A. (1998). *The crystal heart: A Vietnamese legend* (J. Fiedler, Illus.). New York: Atheneum.

Sierra, J. (1999). *Tasty baby belly buttons: A Japanese folktale* (M. So, Illus.). New York: Knopf.

Snyder, D. (1993). *The boy of the three-year nap* (A. Say, Illus.). Boston: Houghton Mifflin.

Spagnoli, C. (1991). *Judge rabbit and the tree spirit: A folktale from Cambodia* (L. Wall & N. Hom, Illus.). San Francisco: Children's Press.

Spivak, D. (1997). *Grass sandals: The travels of Basho* (D. Hitz, Illus.). New York: Atheneum.

Takabayashi, M. (2001). *I live in Japan*. Boston: Houghton Mifflin.

Tompert, A. (1996). *The jade horse, the cricket, and the peach stone* (W. Trang, Illus.). Honesdale, PA: Boyds Mills Press.

Torre, B.L. (1990). *The luminous pearl: A Chinese folktale* (C. Inouye, Illus.). New York: Orchard.

Uchida, Y. (1949). *The dancing kettle and other Japanese folk tales* (R. Jones, Illus.). New York: Harcourt Brace.

Va, L. (1987). *A letter to the king*. New York: HarperCollins.

Vathanaprida, S. (1994). *Thai tales: Folktales of Thailand* (B. Rohitasuke, Illus.). Englewood, CO: Libraries Unlimited.

Wang, R.C. (1995). *The treasure chest: A Chinese tale* (W. Hillenbrand, Illus.). New York: Holiday House.

Waters, F., & Birkbeck, P. (1999). *The emperor and the nightingale* (H. Andersen, Illus.). London: Bloomsbury.

Wells, R. (1996). *The farmer and the poor god*. New York: Simon & Schuster.

Wisniewski, D. (1989). *The warrior and the wise man*. New York: Lothrop, Lee & Shepard.

Xiong, B. (1989). *Nine-in-one, grr! Grr!* (N. Hom & C. Spagnoli, Illus.). San Francisco: Children's Press.

Xuan, Y.S. (1999). *The dragon lover: And other Chinese proverbs*. Fremont, CA: Shen's Books.

Ye, T.X. (1997). *Three monks, no water* (H. Chan, Illus.). Buffalo, NY: Annick.

Ye, T.X. (1998). *Weighing the elephant* (S. Langlois, Illus.). Buffalo, NY: Annick.

Yee, P. (1989). *Tales from gold mountain: Stories of the Chinese in the New World* (S. Ng, Illus.). New York: Macmillan.

Yeh, C.C., & Baillie, A. (1991). *Bawshou rescues the sun* (M. Powell, Illus.). New York: Scholastic.

Yep, L. (1989). *The rainbow people* (D. Wiesner, Illus.). New York: Harper & Row.

Yep, L. (1991). *Tongues of jade* (D. Wiesner, Illus.). New York: HarperCollins.

Yep, L. (1993). *The man who tricked a ghost* (I. Seltzer, Illus.). Mahwah, NJ: BridgeWater.

Yep, L. (1993). *The shell woman & the king* (M. Yang, Illus.). New York: Dial.

Yep, L. (1994). *The boy who swallowed snakes* (J. Tseng & M. Tseng, Illus.). New York: Scholastic.

Yep, L. (1994). *The junior thunder lord* (R. Van Nutt, Illus.). Mahwah, NJ: BridgeWater.

Yep, L. (1995). *The city of dragons* (J. Tseng & M. Tseng, Illus.). New York: Scholastic.

Yep, L. (1995). *Tiger woman* (R. Roth, Illus.). Mahwah, NJ: BridgeWater.

Yep, L. (1997). *The dragon prince: A Chinese beauty & the beast tale* (K. Mak, Illus.). New York: HarperCollins.

Young, E. (1989). *Lon Po Po*. New York: Philomel.

Young, E. (1997). *Mouse match*. San Diego: Harcourt Brace.

Young, E. (1998). *The lost horse*. San Diego: Harcourt Brace.

Zhang, S.N. (1994). *Five heavenly emperors: Chinese myths of creation*. Plattsburgh, NY: Tundra.

Zhang, S.N. (1998). *The ballad of Mulan*. Union City, CA: Pan Asian.

Zhang, S.N., & Zhang, H.Y. (2000). *A time of golden dragons*. Plattsburgh, NY: Tundra.

CHAPTER 9

European Folk Tales and Their Value Today

Ellen A. Greever and John Warren Stewig

This chapter begins with a discussion of the origins of the written folk tale in Europe and the study of folklore. It continues with background on European tales in the United States and then discusses detailed uses of folk and fairy tales with children. (Because the most commonly known European folk tales today are fairy tales, the terms are used interchangeably in this chapter.)

Development of European Folk Tales

European folk and fairy tales have a long and involved history. Like all folk tales, they existed in a variety of forms for centuries before they began to be written down in the Middle Ages and then systematically collected in the 19th century. Recent research suggests that the classical Greeks and Romans were familiar with versions of many tales that are still well known today, including "Cinderella," "Snow White," and "Little Red Riding Hood" (Anderson, 2000). The best-known classical example of a fairy tale is "Cupid and Psyche," a precursor to "Beauty and the Beast," incorporated by the Roman writer Apuleius into his novel *The Golden Ass* in the 2nd century (Hearne, 1989). The earliest written collection was probably the *Gesta Romanorum*, a collection of 181 tales written in Latin during the late 13th century. The collection was widely translated and available throughout Europe (Zipes, 2000).

One of the earliest collections of vernacular folk and fairy tales was Basile's *The Tale of Tales, or Entertainment for Little Ones*, commonly known as the *Pentamerone*, written in Neapolitan Italian, 1634–1636. The *Pentamerone* contains the earliest known European versions of many of the best-known fairy tales, including "Cinderella," "Sleeping Beauty," and "Puss in Boots" (Zipes, 2000).

Fairy tales became stylish at the French court of Louis XIV in the late 17th century. Charles Perrault and Madame Marie-Catherine d'Aulnoy are the best known of the many who retold and reshaped tales (ones we now consider classics) for the entertainment of the court. Mme. d'Aulnoy coined the term *fairy tale* with the publication of her collection *Tales of the Fairies* in 1697–1698. Perrault published his collection *Stories or Tales From Past Times or Mother Goose Tales* in 1697. Perrault's collection contains the origins of what have become the best-known versions of "Cinderella," "Sleeping Beauty," and "Little Red Riding Hood," among others. It was Perrault who had Cinderella's slipper made of glass (apparently through mishearing the French word for fur) and who introduced the fairy godmother and the pumpkin coach to the story. Both d'Aulnoy and Perrault felt free to alter the stories they retold to suit their audiences, and although they both used stories from folklore for the basis of much of what they wrote, their stories clearly show the influence of literary traditions of the time (Zipes, 2000).

The French tradition of the literary fairy tale continued through the 18th century. Mme. Leprince de Beaumont published "Beauty and the Beast," based on an old folk tale, in her *Young Misses' Magazine* in 1757. De Beaumont's version of the story is the basis for all the contemporary variations of the story (Hearne, 1989). She was also one of the first writers to present her fairy tales as being explicitly for children. All her stories were intended to provide moral guidance and to educate readers. The French fairy tales and folk tales continued to be published in the early 19th century, particularly Perrault's *Mother Goose Tales*, but there was no attempt to seek out the folklore roots of France and French culture in the 19th century, as became popular in Germany and elsewhere in Europe (Zipes, 2000).

The interest in folklore that began in Germany in the late 18th and early 19th centuries eventually spread throughout Europe and formed the basis of the study of folklore as it exists today. The popularity of literary fairy tales, both German originals and ones translated from the French, sparked an interest in the origins of the material. Johann Gottfried Herder developed a theory that attempted to distinguish orally transmitted folk tales from the printed French tales that were widely available. Herder's ideas laid the groundwork for later theories about folk culture and a national folk memory that brothers Jacob and Wilhelm Grimm and many others used both in the collection of folk tales and in developing ideas of German nationalism. Recent research, however, suggests that many of the stories available in Germany in the late 18th and early 19th centuries were heavily influenced by the French tales (Zipes, 2000). Some researchers go so far as to say that any hope for authenticity and oral purity in European folklore is pointless, because "oral literature [in Europe] has not existed in isolation since Homeric times" (Warner, 1994).

The Brothers Grimm were aware of the influence that French stories were having on German culture, and in their first edition of *Kinder-und Hausmarchen (Children's and Household Tales)* in 1812, they discussed the need for authentic German material, although this edition contains several stories from Perrault (replaced in later editions by German variants). The Grimms were strongly interested in

German nationalism and in the idea that the many small German principalities should be united under one government. Although the Brothers Grimm are the most famous early collectors of folk tales and fairy tales, they did not collect "pure" folk tales from the peasantry. They invited storytellers to come to them, and they listened to the stories several times before writing them down. The tellers were primarily educated young women from the middle class and the aristocracy, who were familiar with both folk tales and literary fairy tales, which they mixed freely. The Grimms were also quite free in their editing of the stories. They changed them for dramatic flow and made a variety of alterations in keeping with their priorities. It was

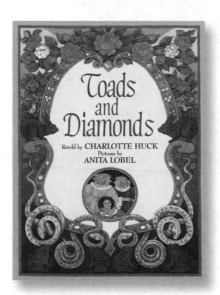

Book cover from *Toads and Diamonds*, written by Charlotte Huck, illustrated by Anita Lobel. Copyright © 1996. Used by permission of HarperCollins Publishers.

the Grimms who changed the mothers in "Hansel and Gretel" and "Snow White" into stepmothers, for instance. They also did not limit themselves to storytellers for their sources; they took tales from a variety of printed texts as well (Warner, 1994; Zipes, 1992).

Nevertheless, the impact the Brothers Grimm had on the development of folklore and the development of the literary fairy tale was significant. They published seven large editions of *Children's and Household Tales* between 1812 and 1857 as well as 10 smaller 50-story editions in the same period. Their complete works remains one of the most influential tale collections in the Western world (Zipes, 2000).

Others quickly followed the Grimms' example. In Norway, P.C. Asbjornsen and Jorgen Moe met as students, and when they realized they shared an interest in folklore, they decided that they would try to do for Norway what the Brothers Grimm had done for Germany. As folklorists, they were far superior to the Grimms, for they tried to keep their written versions as close as possible to the language of their informants and they collected from more authentic sources. Although they did eventually begin to mix and fuse variants, they retained the plots of the traditional stories, and the writing kept a sense that the reader was hearing the stories being told. Their first collection, *Norwegian Folktales*, appeared in 1841 and was followed by multiple editions through the 1840s and 1850s (Zipes, 2000).

In Russia, Aleksandr Afanasyev began collecting folklore and published his eight-volume collection *Russian Fairy Tales* between 1855 and 1863, followed by *Russian Folk Legends* and *Russian Fairy Tales for Children*. Afanasyev's collections are particularly significant because of his systematic collection, description, and classification of the material (Zipes, 2000).

Early 19th-century British folk tale collections were largely translated from other languages, with Perrault's stories being especially popular. The works of the

Brothers Grimm were first translated into English by Edgar Taylor in 1823 as *German Popular Stories*. Sir Walter Scott collected Scottish ballads in his *Minstrelsy of the Scottish Borders* (1801–1802) and used folklore elements in much of his writing. The Irishman Thomas Crofton Croker published *Fairy Legends and Traditions in the South of Ireland* (1825–1828). Thomas Keightley's *Fairy Mythology* (1828) covered a wide range of European legends (Zipes, 2000).

One of the first collections of English folk tales, Benjamin Tabert's *Popular Fairy Tales* (1818), is remembered as much for his editing of the tales to improve their moral tone as it is for the stories themselves. Joseph Jacobs's classic *English Fairy Tales* was not published until 1890 (Avery & Bull, 1965). Jacobs was a major collector/reteller of a wide range of folklore. In 1888, he published an edition of the fables of Bidpai, from India. After *English Fairy Tales*, he published several other volumes of tales from different cultures. He also published a six-volume edition of *The Arabian Nights* in 1896. Because Jacobs's editions were meant explicitly for children, he edited them to clarify dialect and modified material to make it more suitable. Jacobs also included source notes for all his collections, and if the notes were not sufficiently detailed to suit modern researchers, they were still more informative than those usually provided (Zipes, 2000).

The other noteworthy 19th-century British folklorist was Andrew Lang, a Scottish scholar and poet. Although a prolific scholar on a wide range of subjects including anthropology and comparative mythology, he is best remembered for his 12 collections of fairy tales, beginning with *The Blue Fairy Book* in 1889 and continuing through the color spectrum to *The Lilac Fairy Book* in 1910. The collections were not limited to British tales, and the first book included stories by Mme. d'Aulnoy, Perrault, and the Grimms, as well as Norse, Scottish, and English folk tales. Lang himself selected the material, but the retelling was usually handled by others, principally his wife, Leonora Blanche Alleyne Lang. He also included literary tales, although the series focused primarily on folklore. Somewhere in the middle of the series, he moved beyond the boundaries of Europe and began including tales from Africa, American Indians, Brazil, India, Japan, Persia, and Turkey (Silvey, 1995; Zipes, 2000).

Discussion of the 19th-century collectors and retellers of folk tales would not be complete without mentioning Hans Christian Andersen of Denmark. Although Andersen's stories were literary fairy tales rather than folk retellings, he used a wide range of folklore for source material, and his impact on the genre of the fairy tale was significant. He is regarded by many as the father of modern fairy tales. He published multiple collections, beginning with *Fairy Tales, Told for Children* (1835–1842), *New Fairy Tales* (1844–1848), *Stories* (1852–1855), and *New Fairy Tales and Stories* (1858–1872). His work was almost immediately translated into many languages, with the first English edition appearing in 1846. Andersen's stories are noteworthy for his colloquial style, his use of irony, and the decidedly unhappy endings in some of his most famous stories. Many of his early stories have their origins in Danish folk tales and are close to straight retellings, such as "The Princess and the Pea," "The Swineherd," and "The Wild Swans." Medieval European literature provided the basis for "The Emperor's New Clothes," and elements of "The Little Mermaid" came from such diverse sources as the Celtic selkie stories and *The Arabian Nights* (Silvey, 1995; Warner, 1994; Zipes, 2000). In examining Andersen's work, it becomes obvious that the dividing line between the retold folk tale and the literary fairy tale is not very clear.

Folklore Scholarship

Early studies of folklore focused first on collecting the stories and then on questions about the origins of the tales. The Brothers Grimm studied the stories they collected using comparative linguistics and mythology. They (and most other 19th-century researchers) believed that folk tales were the inheritance of a common Indo-European past and that if they could find old enough versions from all possible cultures, they would eventually be able to reconstruct the "original" form of the stories. These scholars studied others' collections (particularly those with detailed source information) and collected stories themselves from as many sources as they could find, and they attempted to map the various versions. Partly because of the difficulty in finding true oral sources, this approach did not have widespread success.

The method did, however, produce an important early work on the comparison of similar folk tales—Antti Aarne's *The Types of the Folktale*, first translated and expanded by Stith Thompson in 1928, with a revised edition in 1961 (Aarne & Thompson, 1971). *The Types of the Folktale* pulled together similar stories from all over Europe (and to some extent from the rest of the world) and reduced them to the barest list of common elements. Thompson also produced the six-volume *Motif-Index of Folk-Literature*, which organized the smallest distinguishable elements from a wide range of stories into categories for easy comparison. For example, there are whole categories of magic objects, nonhuman creatures, and events from stories, such as Cinderella's attendance at the ball and losing her slipper (Thompson, 1955–1958). Together, these two works are still the primary resources for comparison of European folklore and, to some extent, folk tales from other parts of the world (Zipes, 2000).

In the 1920s, Vladimir Propp used a formalist approach to analyze Afanasyev's Russian fairy tales, and he arrived at a classification of functions, defined as the actions of characters as they relate to the development of the plot. Propp decided that there could be no more than 31 functions in a given tale. Propp's work is more standardized than Thompson's motif approach, but he made no claims about its usefulness beyond the Russian stories he used to develop it (Propp, 1968). Other approaches include that of Max Luthi, who considered the folk tale as literature and discussed the characteristic elements of the stories in literary terms (Luthi, 1970).

Two principal schools of psychoanalytic approaches were quite common and provided important insights into the symbolism of folk tales. The Jungians, such as Maria Luise von Franz, viewed folk tales and fairy tales as representing archetypes of psychological phenomena. They explained the similarity of stories from so many different parts of the world as springing from a "collective unconscious." The Freudians, typified by Bruno Bettelheim's classic *The Uses of Enchantment* (1976), examined folk and fairy tales for their role in individual psychological development. Although Bettelheim's work has been questioned since his death due to charges of plagiarism, it still remains the most concise exposition of the Freudian analysis of folk tales.

Sociological and ideological critics, such as Jack Zipes (1979, 1983a, 1983b, 1988, 1997), examine the stories in the context of the cultures from which they come. Zipes has adapted Marxist and cultural historicist ideas to study folk tales and literary fairy tales and presents persuasive arguments about the place of the stories over time. Feminist critics such as Maria Tatar (1987, 1992), Ruth Bottigheimer (1986, 1987), and Marina Warner (1994) have examined the stories as being emblematic of women's place in earlier cultures and have examined the way women are presented in popular contemporary versions, such as Disney's.

European Folk Tales in the United States

European folk tales came to North America with many of the colonists who settled the continent. In some regions, stories remained largely unchanged, but in parts of the United States, folk tales clearly show the influence of the new land and culture. The most notable examples of this are in the Appalachian Mountains, where, over time, settlers adapted stories from their homelands into what seem at first glance to be very different stories but that are in fact closely related to the older, European tales. The first collector of these stories was the U.S. folklorist and storyteller Richard Chase, who published *The Jack Tales* (1943), *Grandfather Tales* (1948), and *American Folk Tales and Songs* (1956). *The Jack Tales* are primarily English in origin, with the best-known story being "Jack and the Bean Tree." The Appalachian version has Jack stealing a rifle, a knife, and a coverlet with bells on it from the giant instead of the usual bag of gold, hen that lays golden eggs, and singing harp. Other stories in the collection show Jack succeeding through cunning and trickery (Chase, 1943). *Grandfather Tales* has Appalachian versions of stories from all over Europe, but they are adapted from versions from England. "Ashpet" is Cinderella, with the name coming from the German "Aschenputtel." She is a hired girl, rather than a stepdaughter, and she meets the King's son at a church meeting rather than a ball

(Chase, 1948). Other stories also were adapted to their new locations. *Moss Gown*, by William H. Hooks (1987), is a variation on "Love Like Salt" set in the southern United States, with plantations and a gris-gris woman (an African woman believed to have magical powers) rather than European kings and palaces.

Book cover from *Little Red Riding Hood* retold and illustrated by Trina Schart Hyman. Copyright © 1983. Used by permission of Holiday House.

The most famous American adaptations of European fairy tales are undoubtedly those made by Disney into animated films, beginning with *Snow White and the Seven Dwarfs* in 1937. *Cinderella* (1950), *Sleeping Beauty* (1959), *The Little Mermaid* (1989), and *Beauty and the Beast* (1991) followed, along with adaptations from other cultures, such as *Aladdin* (1992), and stories with little connection to folk tales and fairy tales, such as *Dumbo* (1941) and *Pocahontas* (1995). Much has been written about Disney's treatment of classic folk tales, from Walt Disney's early selection of passive heroines to later movies (after Walt Disney's death) that attempted to respond to some of the charges from feminists by featuring much more active female characters. What bothers many scholars and critics about the Disney interpretations of fairy tales is that they become the only versions many people know, and therefore other variations may remain largely unknown (Schickel, 1968; Stone, 1975; Warner, 1994). The text of the books adapted from the Disney films is also generally considered to be far inferior to most retellings available in picture book or other form.

Another form of adaptation of folk tales and fairy tales that has become quite popular in the United States is the "fractured fairy tale" or fairy tale parody. These stories take traditional tales or elements of tales that are well known and retell the stories with a variety of twists on the folk tale. (For more about fractured tales, refer to chapter 17 of this book.) One of the best known is *The True Story of the 3 Little Pigs by A. Wolf* (Scieszka, 1989), in which the wolf contends that the whole story of him killing pigs and destroying houses has been blown out of proportion—he was just trying to borrow a cup of sugar to bake his grandmother a cake. Others, such as *Princess Smartypants* (Cole, 1986) and *Cinder Edna* (Jackson, 1994), take a feminist approach to the idea of the helpless heroine who needs a man to save her. *Sleeping Ugly* (Yolen, 1981) plays with the notion that beautiful princesses are automatically wonderful people. What all these stories have in common is the assumption that their readers are familiar with the traditional stories. This may not always be the case, but the best of the parodies have humor that is accessible even to readers who don't know the folk tale (Greever, 1995).

Over the second half of the 20th century, the most common form for the folk tale and fairy tale in the United States became the picture book, often lavishly illustrated. Perhaps this is the final step in the process of taking stories that were once en-tertainment for everyone and making them the exclusive property of children. The folk tale picture book, like the folk tale movie, removes any need for the readers/viewers to envision the story themselves, once an important element in listening to a storyteller or reading unillustrated texts. Although this is certainly a loss, the picture book format also provides new opportunities for reading and enjoyment. Because the illustrations are so much a part of the story in a picture book, the illustrator has enormous influence and opportunity in imagining the story. Comparisons of different editions also provide possibilities for study by students of all ages. Whether conveyed by picture book retellings, collections with occasional illustrations, or live storytellers, folk tales offer rich and varied opportunities to engage children in oral, written, and visual experiences that can expand and deepen their response to the stories.

Using Folk Tales in the Classroom

Retelling

Teachers and librarians can involve even children in the primary grades in simple retellings of a story (Roney, 2001). Having listened to an adult either tell or read a folk tale, and having been guided in group discussion to recall important qualities of characters and plot events, children can then use their own oral language to recreate the tale for a listener. Pair the children together and have them take turns telling the story. After the first teller has retold, the two children switch roles and the teller becomes the listener. After children gain confidence, they can retell stories to larger groups. Intermediate-grade and middle school students can gain confidence and the ability to use language fluently, incorporating such paralinguistic elements as pitch, stress, and juncture, by telling tales they have practiced to children in lower grades. Baker and Greene (1987) include a useful section on the values and techniques in retelling traditional tales as well as literary folk tales.

Generating Dialogues

Drama experts describe the benefits of developing children's oral fluency through engaging them in learning to think and talk like a character. Rather than attempting to engage students in putting on an entire play version of a story, such writers as Heinig (1993) recommend selecting a part of the story in which characters interact and having students make up likely dialogue between characters.

In pairs, children could generate dialogue between

- the princess and the prince from *The Princess and the Pea* (Duntzee, 1984) the next morning when she comes down to breakfast, having tried to sleep on the pea;

- the wolf in *Little Red Riding Hood* (Hyman, 1983) when he tries to convince Grandmother to let him into the house; and

- the witch when she tries to lure *Hansel and Gretel* (Lesser, 1984) into her candy house.

All the children can work on the same scene, with you emphasizing that you value the differences that will emerge because of children's varying ideas about what the characters might say. To ensure success in this, as in most oral activities, begin with a small audience. One pair can present to just one other pair, rather than being asked to present to the entire class. Language that is fluent and imaginative to a small audience can easily turn "wooden" if students move too quickly to larger audiences.

Oral Interviews

Try setting up a situation in which pairs of students work together, one as an interviewer and the other as a folk tale character being interviewed. Children are usually familiar with the interview format through their exposure to radio and television. This is essentially a story retelling task in a different context.

Have children generate a list of questions an interviewer might ask. Use *The Shoemaker and the Elves* (Plume, 1991) and have children make up questions a reporter might ask in order to write a newspaper story about the mysterious appearance of not one, but several, pairs of shoes on successive nights. The writer could be doing a story interviewing Antonio the shoemaker, his wife Bettina, or one of his satisfied patrons.

Becoming the Character

Because folk tales are typically told by a third-person omniscient narrator, retelling as one of the characters is an interesting writing challenge for students. Wagner (1998) is one of several drama experts who point out the many benefits that accrue when children engage in such role playing. This type of activity can be begun in the primary grades, when retellings will at first be fragmentary. By providing repeated opportunities to do this with different stories, though, you are laying the foundation on which later written work can be based. By the intermediate grades, students should be able to explore point of view, the characters' perspective on events, and why the events happened.

Probably the most widely known exploration of point of view is Jon Scieszka's *The True Story of the 3 Little Pigs by A. Wolf* (1989), which has proved exceptionally popular with child readers. Ostensibly retold by the wolf, rather than the usual third-person narrator, this could be used as an introduction to the retelling of another tale from a different character's perspective.

Select a tale, for instance, *Cinderella* (Le Cain, 1973). Encourage children to think and talk about how the characters felt about what happened. In addition to the major characters, do not overlook the writing possibilities in minor characters. For instance, how did one of the sisters, the fairy godmother, the prince, or the transformed mice feel about the story events?

In the story *The Emperor's New Clothes* (Onish, 1996), you could explore with children how the tricksters, the king's minister, someone in the crowd, or the little boy felt about the events in the story.

Or, as a slight variation on this task, children can become the character some years after the story. For example, use Barbara Rogasky's retelling of *Rapunzel* (1982). Have children assume the role of either Rapunzel or the prince, and have them tell the story and details of the intervening years to the couple's children when they are grown. Does the couple feel any differently then, as contrasted with how they might have felt immediately after they were happily reunited in the wilderness?

Extending

What happens next? This question can intrigue child writers. Use Diane Stanley's *Rumpelstiltskin's Daughter* (1997) to show children how an adult author has explored this question. After children have enjoyed the original Rumpelstiltskin tale, generate writing prompts using Paul Zelinsky's (1986) finely crafted art in his Caldecott Honor-winning retelling of the story: Where did they go? What did they do? Whom did they meet?

The answers to such questions might be quite different in response to Zelinsky's compellingly serious treatment of the story, compared to the tongue-in-cheek treatment by Jonathan Langley (1991). You could use these two books to talk with students about the concept of tone in a story retelling. A seriousness comparable to Zelinsky's is found in Judith Viorst's *Sad Underwear and Other Complications* (1995). This usually very funny writer has written a serious poem titled "And When the Queen Spoke Rumpelstiltskin's name." In it, she captures the feelings, many years later, of the now-aged queen, reflecting on how she might have, with compassion, saved the dwarf from his greediness. The book, with poems on a variety of other topics, includes five poems of varying lengths that provide Viorst's responses to well-known fairy tales.

Or, after reading *The Bremen-Town Musicians* (Plume, 1980) with the class, ask students to create another adventure for the four friends: the donkey, the dog, the cat, and the rooster. At the end of this Caldecott Honor-winning book, the four have settled down in the comfortable house they appropriated after scaring away the robbers. Ask students, Did adventures come to them, perhaps in the shape of visitors to the house who presented some problem to be solved? Or did they venture forth in search of other adventures, working together to solve a problem as they did in the original story? Children could indeed do some interesting extending of this story.

Adding a Character

Another story retelling possibility involves adding a character. For example, how would *Mother Holly's* pet cat report the events that went on as Rose and her sister Blanche respond quite differently to their tasks (Stewig, 2000)? How would the cat describe Rose's good-natured, tireless, and indeed cheerful acceptance of her duties? What would the cat's attitude be toward slothful Blanche and her refusal to learn how to do even simple household tasks? How might Mother Holly herself report to a good friend her feelings about the two girls?

Introduce this idea by showing how Jonathan Langley added the Royal Crocodiles to his version of *Rumpelstiltskin* (1991). They are not in other versions of the tale, but children could retell the story from their point of view.

Retelling in a Different Time

Recasting a story into a different era offers interesting possibilities. Provide some examples of models for middle school writers. Use a traditional version of "Little Red Riding Hood" such as *Little Red Cap* (Crawford, 1983), and contrast that with *Ruby* by Michael Emberley (1990). On a chart, help children note all the changes Emberley made.

Or use a traditional variant of *Snow White* (Heins, 1974) and contrast this with Fionna French's *Snow White in New York* (1986). With this sort of background, middle school students should be able to write imaginative recastings of some traditional tales into a different time. This could be tied in with a history or social studies unit. Students could research the types of clothing, housing, and transportation used in an era, then recast the fairy tale into that time.

Oral or Written Response

For children who have an extensive background with story and with generating their own writing, you can adapt British drama expert Dorothy Heathcote's brotherhood idea (Wagner, 1999). In this approach, Heathcote helps children identify a particularly salient aspect of a character. She then challenges students to think laterally, coming up with completely different characters in dissimilar settings and times, who share this characteristic. Rather than doing a simple story drama, the children create an entirely new story embodying this characteristic as the core of the problem (Stewig, 1985). For example,

- *Cinderella* (Goode, 1996) is in the brotherhood of all those who are abused by siblings.
- *Snow White* (Santore, 1996) is in the brotherhood of all those who don't listen to wise advice.
- Reneé in *Toads and Diamonds* (Huck, 1996) is in the brotherhood of all who do a kindly act for a stranger and are given a reward.
- Princess Briar Rose in *The Sleeping Beauty* (Hyman, 2002) is in the brotherhood of all those whose lives are interrupted by something beyond their control.

Comparing Texts

Children come to understand the rich diversity evident in tale variants when you help them examine texts. This can be done on at least two levels. First, at the word level, you can help children take note and keep track, often in a group-constructed chart, of the differences in vocabulary used. You could use *Cinderella* by Nonny Hogrogian (1981), retold from the Grimm Brothers' version of the tale. This can be contrasted with the variant by Lynn Roberts (2001), based on the Charles Perrault source. The differences are apparent immediately: Hogrogian begins with "Once upon a time..." and Roberts opens with "In a time not too long ago and in a land much like our own...." Reading Hogrogian acquaints children with such words as *maiden*, *goose* (meaning a person), and *clogs* and includes such interesting images as "white with rage." In Roberts, children process such words as *straightaway*, *frock*, *muttered*, and *smugly*.

Comparisons also can be made at the episode level, as children will notice such differences as the number of trips to the ball (three in Hogrogian but only one in Roberts) and the slippers Cinderella wears (silver, embroidered, and golden slippers in Hogrogian, and glass ones in Roberts). Hogrogian features the lesser known hazel twig and dove, and Roberts uses the better-known fairy godmother as the device to get Cinderella ready for the ball.

Additional understanding of text can be accomplished by using with middle school students a poem from *Trail of Stones* by Gwen Strauss (1990). The collection presents 12 fascinating poems, each of which is a further commentary on a well-known folk tale. In her poem "Cinderella," Strauss recasts the most important elements of the story into eight poem stanzas of three lines each.

Responding to the Visuals

Because many folk tales are available in picture book format, you have a plethora of visual materials to help children learn how artists add meaning to a reteller's words. You can use a pair of variants (or several, with older students) and explore the way illustrators use visual elements such as line, color, shape, space, and proportion (Stewig, 1995).

Using a pair of books, you can work with students to examine the very different looks artists create for the same tale. Do this by framing such dichotomous questions as

- Are there a lot of different colors, or only a few?
- Are the lines all the same, or do they vary from thick to thin?
- Do the shapes seem to be rounded (three-dimensional) like objects in real life, or are they flat (two-dimensional)?
- Did the artist create the illusion of deep space we can "walk into with our eyes," or is everything shown up near the front of the page, with no space apparent?
- Are the objects shown in the "right" size (in relation to other objects), or are some things exaggerated in size to show what is more important?

Such questions as these, called selective questions by Hewett and Rush (1987), are critical in helping children study art in books with care.

You might, for example, contrast the exceptional illustrations that Fred Marcellino did for *Puss in Boots* (1990) with the completely different visual treatment provided by Ian Beck for *The Adventures of That Most Enterprising Feline Puss in Boots* (Pullman, 2000). Beginning with the close-up, head-only portrait of Puss, Marcellino strokes on richly layered, subtle gradations of realistic color in art that emphasizes the many different perspectives he takes on the different scenes. In contrast, Beck varies page layout, providing many different-sized illustrations, placed above, below, beside, and between text. The most pervasive element here is the discontinuous pen line, which provides texture over his watercolors.

In *Ruby* (Emberley, 1990) and *Snow White in New York* (French, 1986), both the words and the pictures sometimes clearly set the story in a different time than the original story's era. At other times, the text remains essentially unmodified, and only the art signals the time. With middle school students, you could compare the *Cinderella* by Christine San Jose (1994) with the one by Lynn Roberts (2001). In the first, Debrah Santini provides a richly detailed Victorian setting, and for the second, David Roberts does a campy version of the 1920s in art deco style (he was a runner-up in 1999 for the prestigious British Mother Goose award for children's illustration).

You also can help children learn to notice and respond to details of picture book format, such as book size, shape, axis orientation, page layout, and font size and design (Stewig, 2002). For example, you might use John Howe's edition of *The Fisherman and His Wife* (1983), which contains eerie art full of super-realistic detail, replete with subtle and ominous exaggerations of scale. Help children notice how the text is always distinctly separated from the art, appearing on a pale cream background and firmly detached from the art by thin black rules (lines) that serve as borders. In contrast, a retelling by Randall Jarrell (1980), with art by Margot Zemach, presents a quite different visual effect. Peopled with Zemach's usual homely faces and lumpy bodies, done in watercolor with a sketchy black pen line, the art is placed in many different locations on the page. The unbordered text is placed above or below the pictures, on the left, right, or both pages.

You can help children become aware of such details in order to move them beyond the usual use made of pictures in many reading programs. Teachers frequently ask children to read a piece of text and then to look at the accompanying picture to verify their comprehension of the words. Once the child has done that to the teacher's satisfaction, the teacher moves on. This overlooks the richness that can result when viewers study not simply what is in the pictures, but how the art was done. Attending to book format details adds another valuable component to a study of folk tales in picture books.

Reading About Folk Tale Creators

Biographies and autobiographies of children's authors and illustrators have become more commonplace recently, and they can serve two purposes. First, they provide teachers and librarians with useful information that can be shared informally with students as part of a literature unit of study. Second, some are written at a level that can be read by fluent child readers themselves.

Until now, biographies of folk tale collectors have not been available. But *The Brothers Grimm: Two Lives, One Legacy* by Donald R. Hettinga (2001) provides an admirable example that could be followed by writers in creating biographies of other folk tale collectors and retellers. Hettinga's style is pleasantly relaxed, drawing in child readers from the first sentence. He manages to include a lot of specific detail about the brothers' childhood, university student years, and subsequent mature years spent gathering tales, but readers never get bogged down in minutiae. Rather, the story moves ahead swiftly from location to location and from one writing task to another, propelled by well-integrated, brief descriptions of turbulent national events and personal intrigues that complicated their lives. The end-of-book material is intended for adult readers, although the timeline in two columns juxtaposing world events against the lives of the brothers should interest children as well.

Reading at Length

A pervasive characteristic of folk tales is their spare quality. With formulaic beginnings and endings, minimal descriptions of setting, and stock characters that often exemplify a single, strong attribute, these tales are told in few words, getting directly to the point and quickly moving the action to a conclusion and resolution. This reflects the stories' origins in the oral tradition. Today, the storyteller's words fit comfortably in the tightly constrained format of the picture book.

An interesting recent development has been the work of several authors who spin these skeletal tales out to novel-length recreations. Examples include Donna Jo Napoli's *Beast* (2002), in which the author adds the exotic quality of Persia and a journey across Europe to France by Prince Orasyn, extending the tale to 225 pages told in first-person narration. Told in the third person, Robin McKinley's *Spindle's End* (2000) develops the tale of Princess Briar Rose to a total of 422 pages. Other examples include Gail Carson Levine's *Ella Enchanted* (1997), an elaboration of the Cinderella tale, and *The Magic Circle* (Napoli, 1993), a novelization of the story of Hansel and Gretel from the point of view of the witch.

For teachers and librarians, knowing about works such as these is useful to keep alive the love for folk tales as young readers move into middle school. Focusing on the craft of language, these writers give beautifully detailed setting descriptions, thoroughly developed characterizations, and elaborate plot twists not found in the original stories. Thus, they appeal to some fluent child readers and can be recommended on an individual basis to those students who you think will respond to them.

Conclusion

European folk tales were the first ones collected in written form, and they were made available to U.S. teachers and librarians through the work of publishers who produced a wide array of collections and single edition tales in picture book format. More recently, publishers have sought out, and made available, tales from many different cultures drawn from the far reaches of the world.

It is important to expose students to such tales from lesser known cultures and peoples. But it remains equally critical that teachers and librarians continue to see the extensive body of European folk tales, described only briefly here, as an important heritage for all children. Such tales need to be a central part of the literature strand of a total literacy program.

REFERENCES

Aarne, A., & Thompson S (1971) *The types of the folktale: A classification and bibliography; translated and enlarged by Stith Thompson*. New York: B. Franklin.

Anderson, G. (2000). *Fairytale in the ancient world*. London: Routledge.

Avery, G., & Bull, A. (1965). *Nineteenth century children: Heroes and heroines in English children's stories, 1780–1900*. London: Hodder & Stoughton.

Baker, A., & Greene, E. (1987). *Storytelling: Art and technique*. New York: Bowker.

Bettelheim, B. (1976). *The uses of enchantment: The meaning and importance of fairy tales*. New York: Knopf.

Bottigheimer, R. (1986). *Fairy tales and society: Illusion, allusion, and paradigm*. Philadelphia: University of Pennsylvania Press.

Bottigheimer, R. (1987). *Grimms' bad girls and bold boys: The moral and social vision of the tales*. New Haven, CT: Yale University Press.

Greever, E.A. (1995). Fractured fairy tales: Parody in literary fairy tales for children (Doctoral dissertation, University of North Carolina at Chapel Hill). *Dissertation Abstracts International, 56*, 3863A.

Hearne, B. (1989). *Beauty and the beast: Visions and revisions of an old tale*. Chicago: University of Chicago Press.

Heinig, R. (1993). *Creative drama for the classroom teacher*. Englewood Cliffs, NJ: Prentice Hall.

Hewett, C.J., & Rush, J.C. (1987). Finding buried treasures: Aesthetic scanning with children. *Art Education, 40*(1), 41–43.

Luthi, M. (1970). *Once upon a time: On the nature of fairy tales* (P. Gottwald, Trans.). New York: Frederick Ungar.

Propp, V. (1968). *Morphology of the folktale* (2nd ed.) (L. Scott, Trans.). Austin: University of Texas Press.

Roney, R.C. (2001). *The story performance handbook*. Mahwah, NJ: Lawrence Erlbaum.

Schickel, R. (1968). *The Disney version: The life, times, art, and commerce of Walt Disney*. New York: Simon & Schuster.

Silvey, A. (Ed.). (1995). *Children's books and their creators*. Boston: Houghton Mifflin.

Stewig, J.W. (1985). Building bridges from story drama to improvisation through brotherhoods. *Children's Theatre Review, 34*(1), 11–12.

Stewig, J.W. (1995). *Looking at picture books*. Ft. Atkinson, WI: Highsmith.

Stewig, J.W. (2002). Get the picture? *The Newbery and Caldecott awards: A guide to the medal and honor books*. Chicago: American Library Association.

Stone, K.F. (1975). Things Walt Disney never told us. *Journal of American Folklore, 88*, 42–50.

Tatar, M. (1987). *The hard facts of the Grimms' fairy tales*. Princeton, NJ: Princeton University Press.

Tatar, M. (1992). *Off with their heads! Fairy tales and the culture of childhood*. Princeton, NJ: Princeton University Press.

Thompson, S. (1955–1958). *Motif-index of folk-literature: A classification of narrative elements in folktales, ballads, myths, fables, mediaeval romances, exempla, fabliaux, jestbooks, and local legends*. Copenhagen, Denmark: Rosenkilde and Bagger.

Wagner, B.J. (1998). *Educational drama and language arts: What research shows*. Portsmouth, NH: Heinemann.

Wagner, B.J. (1999). *Dorothy Heathcote: Drama as a learning medium* (Rev. ed.). Portsmouth, NH: Heinemann.

Warner, M. (1994). *From the beast to the blonde: On fairy tales and their tellers*. New York: Farrar, Straus & Giroux.

Zipes, J. (1979). *Breaking the magic spell: Radical theories of folk and fairy tales*. Austin: University of Texas Press.

Zipes, J. (1983a). *Fairy tales and the art of subversion: The classical genre for children and the process of civilization*. New York: Wildman.

Zipes, J. (1983b). *The trials and tribulations of Little Red Riding Hood: Versions of the tale in sociocultural perspective*. South Hadley, MA: J.F. Bergin.

Zipes, J. (1988). *The Brothers Grimm: From enchanted forests to the modern world*. New York: Routledge.

Zipes, J. (1992). Once there were two brothers named Grimm. In J. Zipes (Ed.), *The complete fairy tales of the Brothers Grimm*. New York: Bantam.

Zipes, J. (1997). *Happily ever after: Fairy tales, children, and the culture industry*. New York: Routledge.

Zipes, J. (Ed.). (2000). *The Oxford companion to fairy tales*. Oxford, UK: Oxford University Press.

CHILDREN'S BOOKS CITED

Chase, R. (1943). *The Jack tales: Told by R.M. Ward and his kindred in the Beech Mountain section of western North Carolina and by other descendants of Council Harmon (1803–1896) elsewhere in the southern mountains; with three tales from Wise County, Virginia*. Boston: Houghton Mifflin.

Chase, R. (1948). *Grandfather tales: American-English folk tales*. Boston: Houghton Mifflin.

Chase, R. (1956). *American folk tales and songs*. New York: New American Library.

Cole, B. (1986). *Princess Smartypants*. New York: Putnam.

Crawford, E.D. (1983). *Little red cap*. New York: Morrow.

Duntzee, D. (1984). *The princess and the pea*. New York: North-South.

Emberley, M. (1990). *Ruby*. Boston: Little, Brown.

French, F. (1986). *Snow White in New York*. New York: Oxford University Press.

Goode, D. (1996). *Cinderella*. New York: Knopf.

Heins, P. (1974). *Snow White*. Boston: Little, Brown.

Hettinga, D.R. (2001). *The Brothers Grimm: Two lives, one legacy*. New York: Clarion.

Hogrogian, N. (1981). *Cinderella*. New York: Greenwillow.

Hooks, W.H. (1987). *Moss gown* (D. Carrick, Illus.). New York: Clarion.

Howe, J. (1983). *The fisherman and his wife*. Mankato, MN: Creative Education.

Huck, C. (1996). *Toads and diamonds* (A. Lobel, Illus.). New York: Greenwillow.

Hyman, T.S. (1983). *Little red riding hood*. New York: Holiday House.

Hyman, T.S. (2002). *The sleeping beauty*. Boston: Little, Brown.

Jackson, E. (1994). *Cinder Edna*. New York: Lothrop, Lee & Shepard.

Jarrell, R. (1980). *The fisherman and his wife* (M. Zemach, Illus.). New York: Farrar, Straus & Giroux.

Langley, J. (1991). *Rumpelstiltskin*. New York: HarperCollins.

Le Cain, E. (1973). *Cinderella*. New York: Bradbury.

Lesser, R. (1984). *Hansel and Gretel*. New York: Dodd, Mead.

Levine, G.C. (1997). *Ella Enchanted*. New York: HarperCollins.

Marcellino, F. (1990). *Puss in boots*. New York: Farrar, Straus & Giroux.

McKinley, R. (2000). *Spindle's end*. New York: Putnam.

Napoli, D.J. (1993). *The magic circle*. New York: Dutton.

Napoli, D.J. (2002). *Beast*. New York: Atheneum.

Onish, L.B. (1996). *The emperor's new clothes*. New York: Ladybird/Penguin Putnam.

Plume, I. (1980). *The Bremen-town musicians*. New York: Doubleday.

Plume, I. (1991). *The shoemaker and the elves*. San Diego: Harcourt.

Pullman, P. (2000). *The adventures of that most enterprising feline Puss in boots*. New York: Knopf.

Roberts, L. (2001). *Cinderella* (D. Roberts, Illus.). New York: Abrams.

Rogasky, B. (1982). *Rapunzel*. New York: Holiday House.

San Jose, C. (1994). *Cinderella* (D. Santini, Illus.). Honesdale, PA: Boyds Mills Press.

Santore, C. (1996). *Snow White*. New York: Park Lane/Random House.

Scieszka, J. (1989). *The true story of the 3 little pigs by A. Wolf* (L. Smith, Illus.). New York: Viking.

Stanley, D. (1997). *Rumpelstiltskin's daughter*. New York: HarperCollins.

Stewig, J.W. (2000). *Mother Holly* (J. Westerman, Illus.). New York: North-South.

Strauss, G. (1990). *Trail of stones* (A. Browne, Illus.). New York: Knopf.

Viorst, J. (1995). *Sad underwear and other complications* (R. Hull, Illus.). New York: Atheneum.

Yolen, J. (1981). *Sleeping Ugly* (D. Stanley, Illus.). New York: Coward-McCann.

Zelinsky, P.O. (1986). *Rumpelstiltskin*. New York: Dutton.

CHAPTER 10

Jewish Folk Tales: From Elijah the Prophet to the Wise Men of Chelm

Evelyn B. Freeman

rowing up in a home with parents who were first-generation Americans, I was immersed in the culture of eastern European Jewry. Both my parents spoke fluent Yiddish, and my mother had spent her childhood and young adult years in Manhattan, the cultural center for American Jews. I cherish my father's copy of *A Treasury of Jewish Folklore* (Ausubel, 1948), from which he would read aloud stories, my favorite being the tales of the "wise men" of Chelm. I remember laughing aloud at their antics and marveling at their stupidity. As a child, I was unaware that noodlehead stories exist in all cultures, those tales of nonsense and absurdity that often feature a fool who quite literally interprets a request or advice.

The body of Jewish folklore is vast, and only a small fraction of this literature has been selected, retold, and published specifically for children. This chapter discusses Jewish folk tales for children and provides a sampling of books that retell these tales of the Jewish people from all over the world. Traditional versions of biblical stories are not included in this chapter, although folk legends based on biblical characters are.

Characteristics of Jewish Folk Tales

Jewish folklore reflects the religion, culture, and customs of a people who have always been a religious minority and who have been the victims of historical events such as the Spanish Inquisition and the Holocaust. Jewish history dates back to the biblical story of Abraham, a story believed by Jews to have occurred more than 5,000 years ago.

Jewish folklorist Howard Schwartz (1986) describes the evolution of Jewish folk tales as follows:

> The earliest tales that can be identified as Jewish folk tales are found in the Talmud, and more are found scattered in the Midrash. But it is in the Middle Ages that the genre attained its fullest expression. Here, long and elaborate narratives blending elements of the traditional folk tale were not only retold as part of the oral tradition, but were written down and published, especially in Constantinople, in the 16th century. (p. xxvi)

The Talmud includes both a comprehensive accumulation of Jewish law, covering areas such as festivals, the Sabbath, marriage, civil and criminal matters, food, and the like, as well as the rabbinic interpretation of and commentary on that law. *Midrash* refers to the method used by the rabbinic sages to orally transmit the teachings of the Torah (the Five Books of Moses) through a story or sermon.

Dov Noy (1986), noted Jewish folklorist, describes four elements that characterize a folk tale as Jewish: time, place, acting characters, and message. The time of the story occurs within the Jewish life cycle or calendar and may occur during the Sabbath, holidays, or other important life cycle events. An example of a Jewish setting/place might be the synagogue, the home, or the land of Israel. The central character of the Jewish folk tale may be a historical figure, the local rabbi, or a folk hero such as Elijah the Prophet. The message of the folk tale, its lesson or moral, is especially distinctive in the Jewish folk tale. Noy points out, "The Jewish folktale has as its clear and manifest *raison d'etre* a lesson—sometimes about life, but more often about man's duty to God, to his fellow man and to his people" (p. xviii).

Ausubel (1948) identifies other features of Jewish folklore, such as its "poetical and introspective nature" (p. xx) and its wit and irony. He further asserts, "despite the tragedy of their historical experiences, Jews have always been life-affirming or they could not possibly have survived the ordeals they had to go through as a people" (p. xx). In addition, Jewish folk tales often include supernatural motifs and magic.

Humor has been a distinctive feature of Jewish culture and a mainstay of Jewish life throughout the ages. As Ausubel (1948) explains,

> Jews are skillful at joke-making because they are also virtuosi in the art of pathos. They have been tempered by necessity to take life passionately—with gaiety as well as with sober earnestness. This dual capacity for weeping and laughing at the same time, from which was coined the Yiddish expression "laughter through tears," has had its origin in the chaos of life. (p. 264)

Although many people associate Jewish folk tales with Israel and eastern Europe, tales exist from around the world, wherever Jews have lived. For example, *The Sabbath Lion*, retold by Howard Schwartz and Barbara Rush (1992), is a folk tale from Algeria with many distinctive Jewish elements. A poor Jewish widow with seven children learns that her husband's uncle has willed her his fortune. But he lived in Cairo, far from the family's native city of Algiers. Although only 10 years old, Yosef, the oldest child, volunteers to embark on the dangerous journey across the desert. A devout Jew, Yosef refuses to travel on the Sabbath and is left behind by the caravan with which he was traveling. The spirit of the Sabbath, the Sabbath Queen, sends a lion to protect Yosef, carry him safely to Cairo to retrieve his great-uncle's fortune, and return him home to his family.

The Israel Folk Tale Archives, established at the University of Haifa in 1955 by Professor Dov Noy, collects and preserves Jewish folk tales. The archives include folk tales from countries such as Morocco, Iran, Tunisia, and Afghanistan as well as Poland and Israel. Jewish storyteller Penina Schram (as cited in Musleah, 1992) points out, "If you take all our folk tales together, you have a wonderful portrait of the Jewish people" (p. 42).

Talmud/Midrash Tales

The Talmud and Midrash are strong sources of Jewish folklore, and many tales have been retold in versions for children.

The Talmud tells us that in every generation there are at least 36 righteous people, the Lamed-vavniks, who hide their virtue by living humbly, in poverty, or through a disguise of ignorance. In *You Never Know: A Legend of the Lamed-Vavniks*, Francine Prose (1998) recounts how Schmuel, the poor, ignorant shoemaker, saved his town from flooding after 40 days and nights of constant rain. Although the rabbi, lawyer, doctor, butcher, baker, and candlestick maker all prayed, the rain would not cease to fall. Yet when Schmuel prayed to God, the rain stopped and the sun came out. Through a dream, the rabbi realized that Schmuel was a Lamed-vavnik and hurried to his cobbler shop, but Schmuel was already gone. "If you are one of the thirty-six Lamed-vavniks, it must remain a secret. If anyone discovers who you really are, you will lose your special powers" (Prose, 1998). Gouache and colored pencil illustrations by Mark Podwal create a Jewish setting and highlight cultural elements.

Eric Kimmel retells *Onions and Garlic* (1996), derived from a Talmudic story. In this delightful tale, Getzel, the youngest son of a merchant, is considered foolish because he can't make profitable trades. He sets sail with a bag of onions and finds himself shipwrecked in a land covered with diamonds, but where onions do not exist. To Getzel's amazement, the king of the land finds onions a delicacy, more valuable than diamonds. He eagerly trades diamonds for Getzel's onions, and Getzel returns home victorious. Colorful illustrations rendered in acrylic and watercolor by Katya Arnold extend across both pages of each double-page spread and lend a light-hearted, comic tone to the story.

In her introduction to *Clouds of Glory*, Miriam Chaikin (1998) explains,

> There is a vast body of Jewish literature that is little known even among Jews. It is called Midrash. The Hebrew word means "search and explain." Ancient rabbis, who originated the Midrash stories, believed that the Bible held the answer to all questions.... To qualify as a Midrash, a story must answer a question that the Bible raises, and it must be based on Bible teachings. (pp. 1–2)

The book contains 21 stories, each considered a Midrash, that originated in a biblical teaching and/or a legend. Woodcuts by David Frampton are interspersed throughout the book.

Tales of the Golem

The legend of the Golem dates back to 16th-century Prague and an actual historical time when the Jews faced intense persecution. *Golem* is the Hebrew word for "shapeless mass." Rabbi Judah Loew ben Bezalel, who in the story created the Golem from clay, was actually chief rabbi of Prague in the late 16th century; his statue stands in front of the Prague town hall today. The Golem, a giant who saved the Jews of Prague, is, of course, a fictitious character, but evidence of the Golem as a folk hero of Prague appears in various forms throughout the city. Although there are several theories, no one knows for certain how Rabbi Loew became connected with this legend, which recounts how the rabbi, through magical powers, creates a Golem from the mud of the river. This giant guards the Jews of the ghetto who have experienced persecution. When an angry mob attacks the ghetto, the Golem protects the Jews with rage and force, causing massive destruction of people and property. Through his prayers, the rabbi causes the Golem to stop the massacre and return to the Earth from whence he came. In recent years, this legend has become popular in children's literature and many versions have been published.

Barbara Rogasky's *The Golem* (1996) is a chapter book with illustrations by Caldecott Medal-winning artist Trina Schart Hyman. In her author's note, Rogasky points out that the idea of a golem is an old one: "Adam in the Bible is called *golem* until God breathed a soul into him that gave him the power of speech, which made him fully human. Through the centuries, stories of such a creation appear again and again" (p. 91). Similarly, Isaac Bashevis Singer's version, *The Golem* (1982), with illustrations by Uri Shulevitz, is also written in a novel format.

Two picture book versions of the legend have also appeared: *Golem: A Giant Made of Mud*, retold and illustrated by Mark Podwal (1995), and *Golem* by David Wisniewski (1996), which was awarded the Caldecott Medal. In Wisniewski's version, the Jews of Prague are being persecuted for the "Blood Lie," the falsehood believed by many that Jews mixed the blood of Christian children with the flour and water of matzah. Through mystical powers, the rabbi turns a mound of clay into a giant man. When the mob attacks the ghetto, the Golem grows taller and taller. When the emperor guarantees the safety of the Jews, the Rabbi destroys the Golem, who "collapsed into clay." The magnificent paper cut collage illustrations powerfully convey the story, with its universal themes of good versus evil, the limits of human power, and the unfair persecution of groups of people.

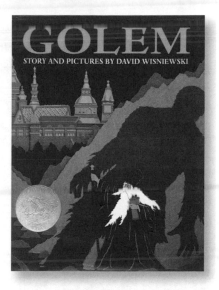

Tales of Elijah the Prophet

Elijah the Prophet first appears in the Bible in Kings (17:1) during the reign of King Ahab. He is considered a messenger from God. Isaac Bashevis Singer retells the story in *Elijah the Slave* (1970), which received the U.S. National Book Award. In this tale, Elijah comes to Earth to be the slave of a scribe who has lost his means of livelihood due to an illness affecting the use of his hand. Through magic, Elijah restores the man's hand movement and shows a rich merchant how he can build a magnificent palace. The scribe sells Elijah to the merchant and becomes a wealthy man. With the help of angels, Elijah builds the merchant his palace before returning to heaven. The book is beautifully illustrated with colorful woodcuts by Antonio Frasconi.

Two Elijah stories from Turkey, "Katanya" and "The Magic Sandals of Abu Kassim," appear in the collection *The Diamond Tree* (Schwartz & Rush, 1991). In "Katanya," Elijah returns to Earth in the form of a kind old man who assists a poor widow. When the old woman begs for food, he gives her a date, out of which comes a very tiny girl who will be her daughter. He also provides the woman a gold coin with which she can buy food. Katanya, which in Hebrew means "God's little one," has a beautiful singing voice and spreads joy whenever she sings. When the prince rides by and hears the singing, he falls in love and marries Katanya. This story is a Jewish variant of the Tom Thumb/Thumbelina tale.

In the second story, Abu Kassim, a poor rag seller, shows kindness to an old man by offering him a piece of bread. The old man, actually Elijah the Prophet, rewards Abu Kassim for his generosity with a wish. Abu Kassim asks for a pair of sandals, which by magic appear in his rag sack. The magic sandals result in a change of luck for Abu Kassim, who becomes a wealthy man.

Demon Tales

One group of Jewish folk tales may be described as demon tales, those stories that focus on evil spirits and Jewish superstitions about them. A famous kind of spirit is a dybbuk, the soul of a sinner, which after the person's death transmigrates into the body of a living person. Francine Prose retells *Dybbuk: A Story Made in Heaven* (1996), a story about the love between Leah and Chonon. Because Chonon is a poor student, Leah's parents have other plans for her marriage. They want her to wed Old Benya, the most powerful man of the village. On her wedding day to Benya,

Book cover from *Dybbuk: A Story Made in Heaven*, written by Francine Prose, illustrated by Mark Podwal. Copyright © 1996. Used by permission of HarperCollins Publishers.

Leah's voice changes and becomes that of Chonon. Leah has become possessed by a dybbuk. With humor and magic, Prose describes how the rabbis drive out the dybbuk and Leah is able to marry Chonon. Mark Podwal's gouache and colored pencil illustrations vibrantly portray the village and its inhabitants.

"The Demon in the Wine Cellar" (Schwartz & Rush, 1999), a folk tale from Yemen, takes place during the reign of King Solomon. A demon drinks the wise king's wine and turns it to vinegar. When the demon is captured, King Solomon tricks him into turning into a puff of smoke and entering one of the empty wine bottles. The bottle is cast into the sea and is washed ashore hundreds of years later. A poor man finds the bottle, opens it, and to his surprise a giant demon appears, demanding food. When the poor man says he has no food to give, the demon threatens to eat him. But the demon does agree to appear before a judge who will decide the case. After many judges agree that "the man must either return the demon to the bottle or feed it" (p. 24), the man runs as fast as he can with the demon in pursuit. In the forest, they come upon a fox who tricks the demon into turning into smoke again and reentering the bottle. Quickly, the man seals the bottle and throws it back into the sea. "And, for all we know, the bottle—and the demon—are still there" (p. 25).

Tales of Chelm

Chelm is an actual town in Poland with a Jewish community dating back to the 12th century. No one knows why this town became the fictional setting for many beloved folk tales about its inhabitants. These tales are the Jewish version of noodlehead stories (see chapter 2 for a general discussion of this type of story). Ausubel (1948) points out, "There is no body of humorous folk-literature more widely disseminated among Yiddish-speaking Jews than the stories about the fools (or 'sages' as they are scoffingly called) of Chelm" (p. 320).

Francine Prose explains the origin of the town in her retelling of *The Angel's Mistake: Stories of Chelm* (1997). In this book, two angels are instructed to populate the towns and cities with souls—one has a bag full of intelligent souls, and the other carries the bag of "souls that were...not so clever" (n.p.). The angel with the bag of stupid souls hits a jagged peak, the bag breaks, and all the souls land in one town, Chelm. "Of course, the people of Chelm were too stupid to know that they were stupid. They called themselves the wise men and wise women of Chelm, the smartest town in the world" (n.p.). Gouache and colored pencil illustrations by Mark Podwal compliment the text of this hilarious retelling.

In the introduction to her retelling of *It Happened in Chelm: A Story of the Legendary Town of Fools*, Florence Freedman (1990) explains, "Chelm is a town of fools, but they are lovable fools. They are never mean; they don't play tricks on people; they never lie. They always work together to solve their problems.... Maybe we enjoy these stories because there is a little bit of Chelm in each of us" (n.p.).

Many Chelm tales focus on the Jewish holiday of Chanukah. In *Chanukah in Chelm*, David Adler (1997) recounts how Mendel, the synagogue's caretaker, is asked by the rabbi to set up a table for Chanukah. In true Chelm style, Mendel makes this task much harder than it needs to be. Kevin O'Malley's cartoon-like illustrations rendered in oil wash on pen and ink portray the hilarity of Mendel's situation and reveal wonderful facial expressions of the characters.

In *The Jar of Fools: Eight Hanukkah Stories From Chelm*, Kimmel (2000b) retells several traditional tales but also writes some original stories set in Chelm. In his author's note, he explains,

> Chelm is the traditional town of fools. However the people of Chelm are not stupid. Their reasoning is precise and their arguments are inspired. Unfortunately, they are nearly always wrong.... Writing a good Chelm story is a challenge. You almost have to think like a Chelmer to do it. (p. 56)

This volume is illustrated with Mordicai Gerstein's whimsical and colorful ink drawings.

Tales With Droll Characters

Ausubel (1948) introduces this term in his section of folklore about comical people. Kimmel has retold stories about his favorite droll character, Hershel of Ostropol. Kimmel points out in *The Adventures of Hershel of Ostropol* (1995) that Hershel was a real person who lived in the Ukraine in the first part of the 19th century and was "an exceptionally witty man" (p. 6). He further notes about this collection,

These stories reflect the values and cultural traditions of the Jewish communities of Eastern Europe. However, one does not have to be Jewish to enjoy them. Hershel, like Coyote, Anansi, B'rer Rabbit, and Tyll Eulenspiegel, belongs to all of us. (p. 7)

Hershel is also featured in Kimmel's retelling of *Hershel and the Hanukkah Goblins* (1989), which garnered a Caldecott Honor award for artist Trina Schart Hyman (who illustrated both of these books).

Another droll character is Chusham, the traditional fool in Middle Eastern Jewish folklore. In "Chusham and the Wind" (Schwartz & Rush, 1991), a folk tale from Iraq, Chusham, a young boy, is asked by his mother to buy food for his sister's wedding party. Although Chusham means well, his logic is quite faulty, which leads to the chickens flying away, the eggs being broken, and the flour being blown home by the wind. Grandmother laughs, "You may get things mixed up, but you are our own dear Chusham. We love you just the way you are" (p. 33). This tale is reminiscent of the British tales about Lazy Jack.

Book cover from *Hershel and the Hanukkah Goblins*, written by Eric Kimmel, illustrated by Trina Schart Hyman. Copyright © 1989. Used by permission of Holiday House.

Holiday Folk Tales

Many Jewish folk tales take place during the holidays. A fine collection of holiday folk tales from Jewish communities around the world is *The Day the Rabbi Disappeared: Jewish Holiday Tales of Magic*, retold by Howard Schwartz (2000) and illustrated by Monique Passicot. These tales from Afghanistan, the Balkans, eastern Europe, Germany, Israel, Kurdistan, Morocco, Persia, and Syria each share elements of magic and miracles in conjunction with one of the Jewish holidays. Nina Jaffe has collected seven stories around the Jewish Sabbath, *Tales for the Seventh Day: A Collection of Sabbath Stories* (2000).

Kimmel retells the tale of *Gershon's Monster: A Story for the Jewish New Year* (2000a). Based on a Hasidic legend and on the Jewish custom of casting one's sins into the sea on Rosh Hashanah, the Jewish New Year, this story describes how Gershon never regrets his sins; rather, he bags them and throws them in the sea each Rosh Hashanah but never really feels repentant. Finally, when his sins and lack of repentance may cause the death of his beloved twin children at the hands of a monster, Gershon truly repents, the twins are spared, and he gives thanks to God for his mercy. Full-page watercolor illustrations by John J. Muth closely follow the plot line and portray the characters' emotions.

A Jewish variant of Cinderella, *Raisel's Riddle* (Silverman, 1999), takes place during the Jewish holiday of Purim in Poland. Raisel lives with her grandfather, a learned but poor man. When he dies, Raisel leaves her village and sets out for the city to find work. The mean cook of a distinguished rabbi hires her to do menial house-work and treats her cruelly. When it is time for the Purim play, an old lady magical-ly transforms Raisel into Queen Esther. Instead of a glass slipper, she leaves the rabbi's son with a riddle that must be answered. The story ends happily with Raisel marrying the rabbi's son.

Classroom Applications

Many versions of Jewish folk tales have received awards for their literary merit and the quality of their illustrations. In the curriculum, they can support and enrich con-tent areas, themes of study, and literacy development. Jewish folk tales are wonderful choices for reading aloud to children. A fine example of such a book is the Caldecott Honor book *It Could Always Be Worse*, written and illustrated by Margot Zemach (1977). In this hilarious retelling of a Yiddish folk tale, a man goes to the rabbi to seek advice for how to cope with an overcrowded house. The rabbi's surprising sugges-tion leads to more laughter and the ultimate moral of the story: It could always be worse.

If the class is engaged in a genre study of folk tales, Jewish tales can be incor-porated as part of the unit. When exploring specific genres, students often compare and contrast books and stories, such as variants of folk tales such as Tom Thumb/Thumbelina, or Cinderella. The Jewish versions of these tales can be included in these comparisons. Students also would enjoy investigating noodlehead stories from around the world, including those about Chelm. Students also may compare and con-trast versions of a distinctively Jewish tale, such as the variants of the Golem story.

As students learn about the holidays and festivals of various cultures, they can enjoy the Jewish folk tales that take place during a Jewish holiday being studied. The stories can be shared in concert with other books about the holidays that provide information about each holiday's meaning, customs, and traditions. *The Family Treasury of Jewish Holidays* (Drucker, 1994) is a fine source for such information.

Some collections of Jewish folk tales provide models for children to write their own folk tales based on their own family stories and traditions. (See chapter 15 for ideas for helping students collect family lore.) In the Newbery Honor book *When Shlemiel Went to Warsaw*, Isaac Bashevis Singer (1968) retells folk tales that his moth-er told him as well as creating original stories in the folk tale tradition. Adèle Geras retells 10 Russian stories in *My Grandmother's Stories: A Collection of Jewish Folk Tales* (1990). Her format involves a first-person narrative from the perspective of a young girl visiting her grandmother. In each chapter, the grandmother retells a dif-ferent traditional folk tale to her granddaughter.

Conclusion

The oral storytelling tradition has historically been integral to the fabric of Jewish life. For thousands of years, Jews around the world have shared stories with each other and have passed these tales on from generation to generation. They have preserved the heritage of the Jewish people, and storytelling is still very much a part of Jewish tradition today. By sharing Jewish folk tales with their students, teachers provide them a glimpse into the religion, history, culture, wisdom, ethics, and humor of the Jews. In classrooms, this body of literature serves as a rich resource for teachers in diverse ways—stories to read aloud, illustrations to prompt students' own retellings, links to content and interdisciplinary studies, and models for writing.

Jewish folk tales reflect both universal elements of folk literature and specific themes, motifs, and characteristics that render them specifically Jewish. Jewish folk tales are not confined to one location but have emerged throughout the world, wherever Jews have lived. Many tales, therefore, also may share features with their country of origin and have become part of that folk literature. For example, references to the Golem are included in various Prague travel guidebooks.

Ausubel (1948) describes Jewish folklore as

> richly varied and colorful with the imprint of the many diverse cultures that Jews have assimilated everywhere through the many centuries. Nonetheless, despite the absorption and adaptation of non-Jewish elements from without and despite the consequences of more than twenty-five centuries of wide dispersion in almost every part of the world, Jewish folklore probably possesses an over-all unity greater than that of any other. (p. xviii)

This chapter has highlighted a small sampling of Jewish folk tales that have been retold especially for a child audience and has generated some ideas for using these stories in classrooms with elementary and middle school students. These tales are filled with humor, pathos, magic, and supernatural beings. They tell of faith, justice, mercy, and kindness. Although these tales have distinctive Jewish elements, they share themes that are universal and touch the hearts of all children.

The author gratefully acknowledges Rabbi Gary Huber, Congregation Beth Tikvah, Worthington, Ohio, for reviewing this chapter to ensure its accuracy.

REFERENCES

Ausubel, N. (Ed.). (1948). *A treasury of Jewish folklore*. New York: Crown.

Musleah, R. (1992, September 21). Rediscovering the Jewish folktale. *Publishers Weekly*, 42–43.

Noy, D. (1986). What is Jewish about the Jewish folktale? In H. Schwartz (Ed.), *Miriam's tambourine: Jewish folktales from around the world* (pp. xi–xix). New York: Free Press.

Schwartz, H. (1986). *Miriam's tambourine: Jewish folktales from around the world* (L. Bloom, Illus.). New York: Free Press.

CHILDREN'S BOOKS CITED

Adler, D.A. (1997). *Chanukah in Chelm* (K. O'Malley, Illus.). New York: Morrow.

Chaikin, M. (1998). *Clouds of glory* (D. Frampton, Illus.). New York: Clarion.

Drucker, M. (1994). *The family treasury of Jewish holidays* (N. Patz, Illus.). Boston: Little, Brown.

Freedman, F.B. (1990). *It happened in Chelm: A story of the legendary town of fools* (N. Krevitsky, Illus.). New York: Shapolsky.

Geras, A. (1990). *My grandmother's stories: A collection of Jewish folk tales* (J. Jordan, Illus.). New York: Knopf.

Jaffe, N. (2000). *Tales for the seventh day: A collection of Sabbath stories* (K.S. Sutherland, Illus.). New York: Scholastic.

Kimmel, E.A. (1989). *Hershel and the Hanukkah goblins* (T.S. Hyman, Illus.). New York: Holiday House.

Kimmel, E.A. (1995). *The adventures of Hershel of Ostropol* (T.S. Hyman, Illus.). New York: Holiday House.

Kimmel, E.A. (1996). *Onions and garlic* (K. Arnold, Illus.). New York: Holiday House.

Kimmel, E.A. (2000a). *Gershon's monster: A story for the Jewish New Year* (J.J. Muth, Illus.). New York: Scholastic.

Kimmel, E.A. (2000b). *The jar of fools: Eight Hanukkah stories from Chelm* (M. Gerstein, Illus.). New York: Holiday House.

Podwal, M. (1995). *Golem: A giant made of mud*. New York: Greenwillow.

Prose, F. (1996). *Dybbuk: A story made in heaven* (M. Podwal, Illus.). New York: Greenwillow.

Prose, F. (1997). *The angel's mistake: Stories of Chelm* (M. Podwal, Illus.). New York: Greenwillow.

Prose, F. (1998). *You never know: A legend of the Lamed-vavniks* (M. Podwal, Illus.). New York: Greenwillow.

Rogasky, B. (1996). *The Golem* (T.S. Hyman, Illus.). New York: Holiday House.

Schwartz, H. (2000). *The day the rabbi disappeared: Jewish holiday tales of magic* (M. Passicot, Illus.). New York: Penguin Putnam.

Schwartz, H., & Rush, B. (1991). *The diamond tree: Jewish tales from around the world* (U. Shulevitz, Illus.). New York: HarperCollins.

Schwartz, H., & Rush, B. (1992). *The Sabbath lion: A Jewish folktale from Algeria* (S. Fieser, Illus.). New York: HarperCollins.

Schwartz, H., & Rush, B. (1999). *A coat for the moon and other Jewish tales* (M. Iofin, Illus.). Philadelphia: Jewish Publication Society.

Silverman, E. (1999). *Raisel's riddle* (S. Gaber, Illus.). New York: Farrar, Straus & Giroux.

Singer, I.B. (1968). *When Shlemiel went to Warsaw* (M. Zemach). New York: Farrar, Straus & Giroux.

Singer, I.B. (1970). *Elijah the slave* (A. Frasconi, Illus.). New York: Farrar, Straus & Giroux.

Singer, I.B. (1982). *The Golem* (U. Shulevitz, Illus.). New York: Farrar, Straus & Giroux.

Wisniewski, D. (1996). *Golem*. New York: Clarion.

Zemach, M. (1977). *It could always be worse*. New York: Farrar, Straus & Giroux.

CHAPTER 11

Exploring Latino Culture Through Folk Tales

Lynn Atkinson Smolen and Victoria Ortiz-Castro

This chapter provides an overview of the history and development of Latino folk literature in the Americas and introduces readers to some of the quality picture books and collections that represent this impressive oral tradition in written form. The discussion of the books is organized into the following categories: origin tales, legends and tales based on historical facts, magic and wonder tales, trickster tales, noodlehead tales, cumulative tales, and folk tale collections. The chapter also describes activities that can be used with the books, including linking the folk tales with information books and technology, developing comparison charts, creating a codex with hieroglyphics, performing Readers Theatre, storytelling with masks, and making a book cube.

Children face many challenges in the 21st century. One of the greatest is that schools, as well as society, have become much more culturally and linguistically diverse than in the past (Schultz, 1997; Villegas, 1991). Teachers, consequently, have the task of preparing students to deal with this diversity. One way to enhance student involvement in the curriculum is to actively engage students in reading and discussing multicultural literature (Dietrich & Ralph, 1995). Multicultural literature develops understanding, appreciation, and respect for differences and thereby combats the racism and bigotry that can sometimes pervade modern society (Cangemi & Aucoin, 1996). Through studying literature from a variety of cultures, students increase their awareness of sociological changes, expand their knowledge and understanding of geography, and deepen their literary appreciation of authors from different cultural backgrounds (Norton, 1990).

Updated from "Dissolving borders and broadening perspectives through Latino traditional literature" published in *The Reading Teacher*, 53, April 2000.

This chapter focuses on one aspect of multicultural literature, Latino folklore. It explores folk tales recently published in books for children and adolescents in both English and Spanish in the United States. The folklore comes from a broad geographical area, including Mexico, Central America, the Caribbean, South America, and the southwestern United States. Teachers can use these stories in the classroom to broaden students' knowledge and appreciation of the rich history and heritage of Latinos within the United States as well as in neighboring countries. Through reading these stories, children learn about cultures different from their own and thereby come to realize that they share many things in common with others they perceive as different (Smolen & Ortiz-Castro, 1997). They also develop understanding, respect, and appreciation for the Spanish language and Latino peoples, who have recently become the largest minority group in the United States (Lewis, 1998). Furthermore, this literature affirms Latino children's heritage by providing them with opportunities to see the world of their ancestors represented in books. It thereby empowers them with a strong sense of self-identity and pride in their culture. In fact, Latino traditional literature is an excellent vehicle for dissolving borders and broadening perspectives of the world for all students.

Latino folk literature contains rich, expressive language as well as magic, humor, and adventure. Reading and discussing this literature contributes to children's language and literacy development. With teacher guidance, students can develop literary analysis skills, reading comprehension, and critical thinking skills through the study of this folk literature (Bosma, 1992).

The books discussed in this chapter range in reading difficulty and complexity of thought. For example, Alma Flor Ada's *The Rooster Who Went to His Uncle's Wedding* (1993) has repetitive language and predictable narrative patterns, making it accessible to early readers. Legends and myths in Lulu Delacre's collection *Golden Tales* (1996) have more complex plots, longer paragraphs with descriptive narrative, and sophisticated themes, making them appropriate for upper elementary and middle school students. Such a range in reading levels makes these books ideal for almost any age group. (Note: In writing this chapter, we have attempted to honor individual choices for the use of accent marks on Spanish names. The names of authors, illustrators, and characters are shown in this chapter the way they appear in the actual books.)

Latino folk tales invite students to explore related concepts and integrate literature with different content areas. For example, the stories inspire children to learn about the history and culture of Latino peoples, the geography of Latin America, and the ecology of the animals featured. In fact, it is important for these stories to be presented within their historical, social, and geographical context to avoid the potential of reinforcing Latino stereotypes (Perez-Stable, 1997). The section on activities describes how the classroom can be set up to maximize integration across the curriculum.

A Historical Perspective of Latino Folkloric Literature

Many of the myths and legends described in this chapter come from the indigenous peoples of the Americas. The four main groups included are the Aztecs, the Incas, the Maya, and the Taínos. From the 14th through 16th centuries, the Aztecs formed a great empire that included a large portion of central and southern Mexico. Some of their finest achievements included the building of magnificent cities and pyramids, as well as an impressive knowledge of astronomy (PBS Online, 1997a). Between the mid-15th and mid-16th century, the Incas Empire expanded from a single river valley to a territory of more than 1 million square kilometers, stretching from southern Colombia to southern Chile and across the Andes mountains. The Incas had a highly developed technology and architecture as well as extensive agricultural know-how (*Encyclopaedia Britannica*, 1987). The Maya lived in present-day southern Mexico and Central America, where they built splendid temples and pyramids. Their civilization, which peaked in the 8th century, included achievements in mathematics, architecture, and agriculture (PBS Online, 1997b). The Taínos occupied the Caribbean islands more than 2,000 years ago. They forged a highly organized society consisting of political divisions similar to states known as *caciques*. In 1492, they were among the first groups to welcome Columbus to the New World (PBS Online, 1997c).

These indigenous peoples had a well-established, rich traditional literature when the Spaniards arrived on the shores of the Americas. The Spaniards brought with them an important legacy: the Spanish language, the Catholic religion, and their European culture (Delacre, 1996). Later, Africans were transported as enslaved people to the Americas. Unable to bring their worldly goods, they carried with them their customs, beliefs, and rich oral traditions. As time went on, the Spaniards and Africans intermingled with each other and with the indigenous peoples to varying degrees, depending on the geographic location. This cross-cultural merging and mixing of peoples are mirrored in the traditional stories of the Americas. As Anaya points out, the folklore of the Latino peoples reflects

> a history of thirteen centuries of cultural infusing and blending in the Hispano *mestizaje* (mixing), from the Moors and Jews in Spain, to the Orientals in the Philippines, Africans in the Caribbean, and the Indians in America—be they Aztec, Apache or Pueblo. (1980, p. 4)

For centuries during which the printed word was rare, the oral tradition was strong among the peoples of the Americas. These stories helped to sustain their imagination and form their identities (Anaya, 1980). For the indigenous peoples, folk tales served three main purposes: They taught lessons, they passed on tribal history, and they helped to explain natural phenomena. In post-Colombian times, the oral tradition helped to underscore religious practices, celebrate heroes, explain unusual events, and entertain (Barlow, 1972).

The books discussed in this chapter draw from the best of Latino folklore in print. Among the authorities on multicultural literature is the Américas Book Award List. According to the Consortium of Latin American Studies Programs (see www.uwm.edu/Dept/CLACS/outreach_americas.html), the award is given

> in recognition of U.S. works of fiction, poetry, folklore, or selected non-fiction (from picture books to works for young adults) published in the previous year in English or Spanish that authentically and engagingly portray Latin America, the Caribbean, or Latinos in the United States.

The selections in this chapter include books written in English only, books with separate English and Spanish editions, and bilingual books with alternating passages in English and Spanish.

It is important that teachers, librarians, and parents select Latino literature carefully. A number of authorities on children's literature have raised the concern that, far too often, Latinos have been stereotyped and their language and culture misrepresented in children's books (Barrera, Liguori, & Salas, 1993; Miller-Lachmann, 1992; Nieto, 1993; Schon, 1993): We have used the following criteria—adapted from the Américas Book Award; Barrera, Liguori, and Salas (1993); Carrasquillo (1994); Cullinan and Galda (1994); Schon (1991); and Yokota (1993)—in selecting the folk literature discussed in this chapter. The criteria also will be useful to you in choosing other Latino folk literature with your students.

- Literary quality

  Is the story well written? Will it capture the interest and imagination of readers from a wide variety of backgrounds?

  Are the illustrations attractive and appealing to readers? Do they extend the narrative and provide the reader with a context for the story?

- Cultural authenticity

  Do the text and illustrations represent the specific Latino culture accurately and nonstereotypically?

  Are the time, place, architecture, artifacts, and people of the period represented authentically?

- Cultural detail

  Do the author and illustrator provide rich details of the culture to help the reader form a picture of the culture?

  Does the author provide information about the folk tale and its culture in the book's introduction or in notes at the back of the book?

- Language

    Is the dialogue (whether in English and/or in Spanish) representative of how people in the particular culture and region speak?

    Is the language, both in the original and in translation, written in a fluent, rich, and natural way?

    Are the Spanish words spelled correctly, and do they have the appropriate accent marks?

Categories of Tales

Origin Tales

Folklore has been described by Zena Sutherland and May Hill Arbuthnot (1991) as a "mirror of a people" (p. 182), revealing their attempts to explain natural phenomena that they do not understand. This is particularly evident with origin tales. By far the largest number of books containing Latino folklore relate to the origins of things. (More about origin stories, also called pourquoi tales, can be found in chapter 2.) Some stories describe how the world was created; others explain the origins of a particular phenomenon such as music, or why an animal has a particular characteristic. Most of these myths originated from the indigenous groups who have lived for thousands of years in the Americas.

The Fifth and Final Sun by C. Shana Greger (1994) is a beautifully illustrated retelling of the Aztec sun creation myth. The human-like gods allow jealousy to disrupt the reign of the First Sun when Tezcatlipoca, the God of Night, is deposed by Quetzalcoatl, the God of Wind. A mighty struggle causes three more Suns, each ruled by a different god, to come and go with various positive and negative effects on the Earth. In the end, it is the willing sacrifice of a small, unsung god that establishes the Fifth and Final Sun. The border designs on the book's pages are based on Aztec patterns, and the design of the initial capital letter at the beginning of each section comes from the Aztec calendar. These details lend authenticity and cultural richness to this tale. This myth also is retold in *How We Came to the Fifth World* by Harriet Rohmer and Mary Anchondo (1976). Greger retells the story from the point of view of the gods, whereas Rohmer and Anchondo recount the tale from the perspective of the people.

The Lizard and the Sun is a Mexican creation tale retold in Spanish and English by Alma Flor Ada (1997) and translated by Rosalma Zubizarreta. The story is set in a time long, long ago, when the sun disappears and the world is cast in darkness. All the animals search for the sun, but eventually all of them give up looking except for a lizard. The lizard finally comes across a rock, shining "so brightly that is seemed to glow" (Ada, 1997, n.p.). He seeks counsel from the emperor, who orders him to move the rock. The lizard is unable to do so, and the emperor and a woodpecker go to his aid. The woodpecker breaks the rock with its beak, releasing the sun, who is fast asleep. The sun refuses to wake up until a group of musicians and dancers play their liveliest music. Finally, the sun ascends into the sky to bring light again to the world. The eloquent language of this tale is complemented by Felipe Dávalos's richly detailed illustrations that set this story in the time of the Aztecs.

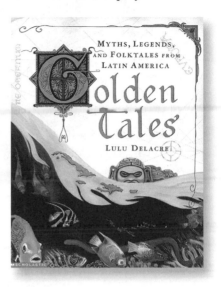

How Music Came Into the World by Hal Ober (1994) is a myth that tells how Quetzalcoatl, the God of Wind, captures musicians and singers from the House of the Sun and brings them to the silent Earth to fill it with beautiful melodies. This myth comes to life with Carol Ober's striking illustrations reminiscent of pre-Colombian motifs found on Aztec and Mayan artifacts, thus lending cultural authenticity to this book. Gerald McDermott retells this same myth in *Musicians of the Sun* (1997). In both versions, the musicians bring music and color to the silent, gray Earth; however, in McDermott's version there is more emphasis in both the text and illustrations on how the musicians brighten the world with color.

From *Golden Tales: Myths, Legends, and Folktales From Latin America* by Lulu Delacre. Published by Scholastic Press, a division of Scholastic, Inc. Copyright © 1996 by Lulu Delacre. Used by permission.

In *The Golden Flower: A Taino Myth From Puerto Rico*, Nina Jaffe (1996) retells the story of how Puerto Rico was created and how the sea began. The tale begins in a primal land with no water, plants, or trees. One day a young boy plants some seeds from which a large pumpkin sprouts. Two men fight over the pumpkin, each claiming it for himself. As they push and pull, the vine severs and the pumpkin rolls down the side of the mountain, breaking apart. The sea with all its creatures—whales, dolphins, crabs, and sunfish—bursts forth from the pumpkin and covers the desert plains. This myth, illustrated with glowing colors, is typical of creation stories of Latin America and the Caribbean that tell of the sea hidden inside a pumpkin. In another flood myth, *The Llama's Secret* (Palacios, 1993), a llama saves the people of the Andes from a flood. The story thus explains the llama's value to Peruvian culture.

Food plays a key role in a number of Latino legends and myths. *People of Corn: A Mayan Story*, retold by Mary-Joan Gerson (1995), is a creation tale about the importance of corn in Mayan culture. To the Maya, corn is much more than food; it is the very foundation of their culture and the spirit of life itself. In this ancient story, Plumed Serpent and Heart of Sky create the Earth. They then try to create people to sing their praises. Their first attempt fails, but finally they succeed when they fashion people out of white and yellow corn. Carla Golembe's luscious gouache paintings enrich this beautiful story. The authenticity of the tale is enhanced by the borders and patterns on woven fabric, which were derived from ancient Mayan glyphs and cloth.

The Tree That Rains: The Flood Myth of the Huichol Indians of Mexico, retold by Emery Bernhard and illustrated by Durga Bernhard (1994), explains the cycle of life and the vital role rain plays in growing crops. Great Grandmother Earth warns Watakame that a great flood will come because the people have forgotten the gods. The Earth then endures floods for five years. When the waters finally recede, Watakame settles down near Lake Chapala where he plants corn, beans, squash, and a magic fig tree that showers rain on the fields. In this green paradise, he and his wife have children, and soon afterward the Earth becomes repopulated. The author's note at the end of the book explains that every year the Huichol shamans recite this flood myth at the Harvest Festival of the New Corn and Squash in the Sierra Madre of western Mexico. The bold illustrations painted in gouache on watercolor paper are reminiscent of Huichol Indian yarn painting and provide a rich cultural context for the myth.

Another creation myth that features a tree as the source of water is *When Woman Became the Sea* by Susan Strauss (1998). In this Costa Rican myth, Sibu, the creator, seeks to complete the creation of the world. He creates Sea, the first woman, whom Thunder takes as his wife. Sea defies the dictates of both Sibu and Thunder, and, as a result, her walking stick turns into a venomous snake that bites her. Before she dies, a magnificent tree sprouts from her belly, from which all the waters of the world gush forth, thus completing Sibu's creation of the world. Cristina Acosta's exuberant and brightly colored paintings emphasize the lushness of the rainforest. In her introduction to the book, Strauss points out that early people's observations of nature often were preserved in "sacred stories we now call myths" (n.p.). The parallel the author draws between myth and science could inspire interesting classroom discussions and explorations of other myths that may have scientific connections.

George Crespo's retelling of *How the Sea Began: A Taino Myth* (1993) is an allegory of a people adapting from a hunting-based society to a fishing-based society. When Yayaél, a great hunter among Puerto Rico's Taíno people, dies in a hurricane, his parents place his bow and arrows in a gourd and hang it from the ceiling of their hut. Having lost their main hunter, the tribe soon experiences serious food shortages. One day some boys carelessly break open the gourd and out gushes sea water, flooding the periphery of the mountain of Boriquén (the Taíno name for Puerto Rico). The sea, filled with fish, provides the hungry people with a new source of food. The brightly colored oil paintings are an excellent complement to the text.

The Two Mountains: An Aztec Legend by Eric Kimmel (2000b) explains the formation of two mountains overlooking the Valley of Mexico. Ixcocauqui, son of the sun god, meets and falls in love with Coyolxauhqui, daughter of the moon goddess. When Ixcocauqui's father learns of the relationship, he is furious and will not agree to their marriage unless they promise never to leave the heavens. Despite the sun god's warning that they will lose their immortality if they break their oath, the two lovers' curiosity causes them to transgress. As a result, they are banished from the heavens to live forever on Earth. When Coyolxauhqui falls gravely ill, her husband takes her to the mountaintop, vowing never to leave her side. The gods then transform "the two young lovers into two mountains" (n.p.). Students will be fascinated with how the theme of temptation leading to transgression parallels the Adam and Eve story. They also will be intrigued to learn that the indigenous peoples of Mexico created legends to explain the geological formations of the region. Leonard Everett Fisher's bold, bright acrylic paintings help make this story powerful and appealing. A pronunciation key accompanies the text. Kimmel's *Montezuma and the Fall of the Aztecs* (2000a) is a companion to this tale, and the two books would be excellent additions to a social studies unit on Mexico.

Legends and Tales Based on Historical Facts

Legends from Latino cultures reflect the intermingling and exchange of ideas between the Europeans and the indigenous peoples of the New World during the post-Colombian period.

Miro in the Kingdom of the Sun by Jane Kurtz (1996) is a retelling of an ancient legend of the Incas. The king's son is dying, and nothing will cure him except water from a distant lake. Two young men set out to find the water, but when they are unable to find it they return with ordinary water that they pretend is the magic potion. When their deception is discovered, they are imprisoned. Their sister, Miro, a strong and spirited young girl, then sets out on a quest for the curative waters to save her brothers and the ailing prince. In the end, she triumphs as a result of her bravery and her friendship with the birds. David Frampton's painted woodcuts provide details of the Inca architecture and decorative arts, evoking the mystery and wonder of this ancient Indian culture.

The Magic Bean Tree: A Legend From Argentina, retold by Nancy Van Laan (1998), is another quest story from Latin America that emphasizes the importance of the rain to an agrarian people. One summer, no rain falls on the pampas, and the land is parched. Despite the dangers of exposure to the strong sun, brave little Topec sets off to find the rain. On his way, the North Wind swirls him across the pampas and flings him under a moist, green carob tree. There he learns that the Great Bird of the Underworld sits on the tree's top branches, blocking the way for the rain to come.

Topec then leads a procession of village noisemakers who frighten the bird away, bringing the rain. Van Laan weaves a beautiful, dramatic tale using literary devices such as onomatopoeia and alliteration. Beatriz Vidal's folk-art illustrations with warm earth tones complement the retelling. This tale would be excellent for reading aloud or storytelling.

In *Maya's Children: The Story of La Llorona*, Rudolfo Anaya (1997) retells the ancient Mexican story of the crying woman who "is the best-known character in the Latino oral tradition" (Anaya, 1999, p. 13). Maya is born with a birthmark signifying that she is the daughter of the sun god and destined to be immortal. Her extraordinary circumstances anger Señor Tiempo, Mr. Time, who allots a specific amount of time to each person on Earth. Vowing to prevent her from passing on her immortality to her children, one day he tricks Maya and steals her children. Inconsolably crying, she searches the lake for her beloved children. She becomes known as "La Llorona," the ghostly woman who cries for her lost children, frightening those who hear her wailing. Maria Baca's gouache illustrations with dark blue and green backgrounds evoke the haunting quality of this tale. In an author's note, Anaya explains that he wrote the tale for young children and therefore does not have Maya kill her children as she does in the original legend.

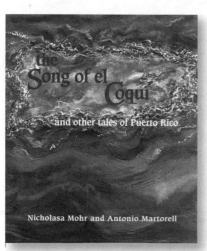

Book cover from *The Song of El Coqui and Other Tales of Puerto Rico* by Nicholasa Mohr and Antonio Martorell, copyright © 1995 by Nicholasa Mohr and Antonio Martorell, illustrations. Published by Viking, A Division of Penguin Young Readers Group, A Member of Penguin Group (USA) Inc., 345 Hudson Street, New York, NY 10014. All rights reserved.

The Legend of El Dorado: A Latin American Tale by Beatriz Vidal (1991) is a story from the Chibcha Indians of Colombia. For centuries, El Dorado (the gilded one) has symbolized the quest for gold that brought Spanish conquistadors to the New World. This story is set in a resplendent land near the enchanted Lake Gatavita, where a king lives happily with his people. One day an emerald sea serpent casts a spell on the king's wife and daughter, luring them into the depths of the lake. The grief-stricken king then learns that he must wait to be reunited with his loved ones. He establishes a ceremony in which he covers himself with gold dust and rides regally on a raft casting gold and jewels into the lake. The lustrous paintings enhance the ethereal feeling of this story.

The Woman Who Outshone the Sun: The Legend of Lucia Zenteno/La mujer que brillaba aún más que el sol: La leyenda de Lucía Zenteno by Alejandro Cruz Martinez (1991) is a powerful story from the Zapotec Indians of Oaxaca, Mexico. In this Spanish-English retelling, Lucía Zenteno, a woman with extraordinary bonds with nature, comes into a village where her exceptional beauty causes the river to fall in love with her. However, this newcomer is feared by the villagers, who eventually drive her away. The river departs with her, leaving behind parched earth. The villagers soon learn the consequence of their intolerance and beg her to return. The striking bold paintings, recalling primitive folk art, evoke the rugged Mexican landscape and portray Lucía as a large, strong woman with noble features. A note at the end of the story tells that Cruz Martinez was killed while organizing the Zapotec people to regain their lost water rights. This book would be excellent to use in classroom discussions on social issues such as natural resources and intolerance.

The legend *The Invisible Hunters/Los cazadores invisibles*, retold by Harriet Rohmer, Octavio Chow, and Morris Vidaure (1987), documents the first contact between the Miskito Indians of Nicaragua and the Spaniards. It is a metaphor for what has happened to many of the indigenous groups in the Americas. With the help of the Dar, a magical vine, three brothers gain special powers and become famous hunters among their people. One day they meet some European traders who convince them to betray their people and give up their traditional ways. Despite their promises to the Dar, they sell the meat from the wild pigs they have killed and refuse to share it with the people. As a punishment, the Dar makes the greedy hunters permanently invisible. Brilliantly colored collage illustrations dramatically accompany the bilingual text.

The Song of el Coquí and Other Tales of Puerto Rico by Nicholasa Mohr and Antonio Martorell (1995) is an exquisitely illustrated collection of three tales that celebrate the history and heritage of Puerto Rico in both English and Spanish. Each story features an animal that reflects one of the three most important influences in Puerto Rican culture. The first story features the coquí, a tiny tree frog native to Puerto Rico. This creature represents the Taíno, the indigenous people of the island. The second story features a guinea hen that symbolizes the Africans who were brought as slaves to the island. In the last story, a parable about the Spanish who conquered the island, a mule is mistreated and worked to near exhaustion by Spanish bandits. This book beautifully illustrates the mixing and blending of cultures that have occurred in many Latin American countries.

Magic and Wonder Tales

Starting in the 1500s, the Spanish brought their folktales, or *cuentos*, to the Americas. According to Anaya (1999), the two largest categories of these *cuentos* brought to the southwestern United States are tales of the *pícaro*, or rogue, and tales of enchantment, involving magic or incantations. These tales of magic have been published in English in collections as well as some picture books. Recently, three different versions of the Cinderella tale have appeared in picture books. Two of these tales are from the U.S. Southwest and one is from Mexico.

Domitila: A Cinderella Tale From the Mexican Tradition by Jewell Coburn (2000) tells the story of a young, loving girl who finds work as a cook at the governor's man-

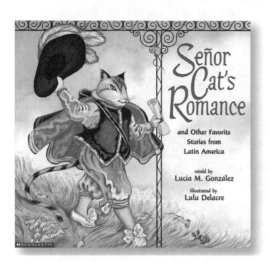

Illustration by Lulu Delacre from *Señor Cat's Romance and Other Favorite Stories From Latin America* by Lucia González. Published by Scholastic Press, a division of Scholastic, Inc. Copyright © 1996 by Lulu Delacre. Used by permission.

sion in Hidalgo. Her culinary expertise wins the attention of Timoteo, the governor's son, but soon she is called home to be with her dying mother. Determined to find her, Timoteo sets off on his horse with only a beautifully tooled leather strap from her sandal as a clue to her whereabouts. After searching throughout the land, he finally finds her and they fall in love and marry. The story is replete with elements of the familiar Cinderella tale, including the evil stepmother who schemes to present her lazy daughter to the handsome Timoteo. Connie McLennan's luminous oil paintings illustrate the stark beauty of the desert. Decorative borders depicting the crafts and flora of the region embellish each page and include proverbs (*dichos*) in both English and Spanish.

Robert D. San Souci's *Little Gold Star: A Spanish American Cinderella Tale* (2000) is an excellent example of the influence of Roman Catholicism in many of the *cuentos* from the U.S. Southwest and Mexico. Sweet Teresa's life becomes miserable when her father, Tomás, marries an opportunistic widow with two vain daughters. One day the stepmother sends Teresa to wash a lamb's fleece in the river. When the fleece is snatched by a fish, a woman in blue appears who promises to get it back if Teresa will care for an old man and a baby. Unbeknownst to Teresa, the three are the Virgin Mary, Joseph, and the baby Jesus. The reward for her kindness is a gold star planted on her forehead. Seeking the same results for her daughters, the stepmother sends them to wash the fleece. Instead, their unkind behavior earns them goat horns and donkey ears. The expected Cinderella ending occurs when Teresa meets a wealthy young man at a fiesta. Sergio Martinez's watercolor paintings complement the beauty of this tale and provide accurate details of colonial Spanish buildings, furniture, and clothing.

In a similar version of the Cinderella tale, Joe Hayes retells *Estrellita de oro/Little Gold Star* (2000) in Spanish and English. In this version, a hawk replaces the Virgin Mary as the one who places a gold star on Arcía, the Cinderella character, and a donkey ear and cow's horn on her stepsisters. In both San Souci's and Hayes's versions, a talking cat helps Cinderella's suitor locate her whereabouts. The acrylic-on-art-board illustrations, painted in a folk-art style using vivid colors and strong lines, add a touch of humor to Hayes's tale. Children will delight in comparing the three Latino versions of the Cinderella tale.

In *The Three Golden Oranges*, a classic Spanish folktale retold by Alma Flor Ada (1999), three brothers wish to marry and seek the advice of an old woman. She tells them that if they travel to a distant castle, pick three golden oranges, and return them to her, they will have the brides they desire. She warns, however, "Woe to you if you do not follow my advice" (n.p.). The two older brothers fail to follow her advice and in the end remain brideless. Matías, the youngest brother, the only one who complies, wins the hand of Blancaflor, and with her help liberates her family who has been under a sorcerer's spell. The transformations that occur in this tale fascinate the reader. For example, when Matías removes a thorn from a white dove it transforms into Blancaflor, a beautiful young woman. The moral that one should work together with and follow the advice of elders is clearly spelled out in this tale. Reg Cartwright's stylized, bold oil paintings enliven the story and bring the Spanish countryside to life.

Trickster Tales

Trickster tales are among children's favorite stories. Children delight in reading tales about how a smaller, weaker creature outwits a larger and more powerful one. (See chapter 2 for more about trickster tales.) Many of these tales were brought to the Americas by African slaves and were adapted to their new surroundings. Other trickster tales originated from the indigenous peoples of Mexico, Central America, and South America.

A beautifully told trickster tale, "How Uncle Rabbit Tricked Uncle Tiger," appears in Lucía González's collection *Señor Cat's Romance and Other Favorite Stories From Latin America* (1997). In this story, the cunning and clever Tío Conejo (Uncle Rabbit) uses his wit to outsmart the more powerful Tío Tigre (Uncle Tiger). He convinces Tío Tigre that the sweet, soft *guama* fruit that he is eating is really his own rabbit tail. Tío Tigre tastes Tío Conejo's "tail" and is so enthralled with its sweetness that he allows the rabbit to tie his own tail in knots, anticipating that it also will taste delicious. When Tío Tigre discovers that he has been deceived by this smaller creature, he explodes in a rage and seeks revenge. However, the quick, sly Tío Conejo disappears into the jungle to elude his rival.

Rabbit as trickster also appears in Tony Johnston's engaging book *The Tale of Rabbit and Coyote* (1994). In this story, the mischievous Rabbit uses his cunning and wit to dupe his less astute rival, Coyote. Rabbit engages Coyote in a variety of hilarious escapades in which Coyote turns out to be the butt of the joke. In the end, to escape Coyote's rancor, Rabbit climbs a ladder to the sky and becomes forever embedded in the moon. The tale thus explains the Mexican legend that a rabbit lives there, not a man. Tomie dePaola's vibrant prints capture the liveliness and humor of this tale from Oaxaca, Mexico.

A lamb appears as a trickster in *Borreguita and the Coyote*, Verna Aardema's (1991) retelling of a Mexican folk tale. Coyote is eager to eat Borreguita, a little ewe, but each time he tries, she manages to escape by deceiving him. She keeps him at bay by tricking him into chasing after a round of cheese that is really the reflection of the moon in a pond and by beguiling him into holding up a mountain she claims will fall without his support. In the end, Borrequita rams her head inside his mouth and gives him such a toothache that he learns never to bother her again. The bold, vivid illustrations capture the cleverness of the lamb and the gullibility of her hungry antagonist.

The trickster Anansi, who originated from the Ashanti people of West Africa (see chapter 7), takes on a modern twist in De Sauza's *Brother Anansi and the Cattle Ranch* (1989), a Nicaraguan tale that includes cattle ranching and the lottery. When Brother Tiger wins the lottery, Brother Anansi convinces him to use his fortune to buy a cattle ranch so that the two of them can start a cattle raising business. After a few years, the business begins to boom, and Anansi contrives a plan to trick Brother Tiger into giving up all his cattle. The gullible Brother Tiger agrees to the plan but later discovers he has been duped. In disgust he warns Anansi he will get even with him next time. The bilingual text is complemented by bold, colorful paintings done in acrylics and colored pencils.

John Bierhorst's *Doctor Coyote: A Native American Aesop's Fables* (1987) is a collection of Old World stories that were transformed by the Aztecs into trickster tales and thus exemplify the infusion of Aztec and European cultures. In the beginning of the book, readers find Coyote young and ready to trick anybody he comes across with cunning and malice. His pranks often get him into trouble. Throughout the story, Coyote grows older, wiser, and sometimes kinder. At the end of the book, Coyote is old and dying. Having lost most of his worldly possessions as a result of his profligate and evil ways, he finds that his only remaining belonging is his cornfield. Wendy Watson's illustrations provide an interesting modern spin on the tales by setting them in the U.S. Southwest in the 20th century, complete with pickup trucks, a gas station, adobe houses, and shotguns.

Noodlehead Tales

Stories about the adventures of a fool exist throughout the Spanish-speaking world. Juan Bobo, or Foolish John, is one of the most prevalent fools in Latino noodle-head tales. In Puerto Rico, he is the most popular folk hero and is tied to the humor and wisdom of the jibaros, country folk who have Spanish, African, and native Taíno roots. His apparent stupidity often is used to point out the foibles of others or to teach a lesson (González, 1997; Montes, 2000; Pitre, 1993). The hilarious antics of this lovable fool appear in a number of picture books and collections.

In *Juan Bobo Goes to Work: A Puerto Rican Folktale*, retold by Marisa Montes (2000), Juan Bobo sets out on repeated trips to find a job, first with a farmer and then with a grocer. Despite the clear instructions given by his mother and the simple tasks given by his employers, the well-intentioned fool always bungles what he is asked to do. As in many Juan Bobo tales, he uncannily ends up with luck on his side. He is rewarded for making the ill daughter of a rich man laugh. Joe Cepeda's oil paintings provide details that place this humorous tale in the countryside of Puerto Rico. Spanish words and phrases are interspersed throughout the text, giving the story authenticity. A glossary assists the reader with pronunciation and definitions of Spanish terms. Felix Pitre's *Juan Bobo and the Pig* (1993) portrays Juan Bobo as equally foolish. In this tale the fool dresses a pig in women's clothes and jewelry to go to church. This tale has permeated the Puerto Rican culture to such an extent that it has influenced the idiomatic language of Puerto Rico: The expression "dressed like Juan Bobo's pig" means a person is wearing too many accessories or too much make-up or is overdressed for the occasion.

"Juan Bobo and the Three-Legged Pot" appears in Lucía González's *Señor Cat's Romance and Other Favorite Stories From Latin America* (1997). In this story, Juan Bobo goes to his grandmother's house to get a three-legged iron pot to prepare dinner and ends up having a race with the pot. He kicks it down the hill with such a strong blow that the pot wins the race. Lulu Delacre uses the vivid pink wash that covers the facades of many Caribbean homes for the interior of Juan Bobo's house. She also includes her own recipe for *arroz con pollo*, a favorite dish in Spanish-speaking countries.

Cumulative Tales

Cumulative tales that are built up by repeating lines and adding to them exist in Latino cultures as in all cultures around the world. These tales repeat actions, characters, or speeches sequentially, often in an amusing way, until a climax is reached. Most tales endow the main character with intelligence and the ability to reason. Young children enjoy being told these stories because the repeating structure allows them to join in as each event occurs (Norton, 2003).

A delightful example of this type of tale is *The Bossy Gallito/El gallo de bodas* by Lucía González (1994). In this bilingual book, a bossy and perfectly groomed rooster sets out early one morning to attend his uncle's wedding. On the way, his beak becomes covered with mud and he implores the velvety grass to help him clean it. When the grass refuses to help, he appeals to a goat to eat the grass so he can go to his Tío Perico's wedding. He continues to appeal to one contrary character after another until the sun agrees to help and reverses the sequence of events. Finally, the rooster's beak is cleaned and he can proceed to his uncle's wedding. Both the Spanish and

English versions of this tale are well written. The rhythmic repetition in both languages makes this story particularly good for oral reading activities. The tale is greatly enhanced by Delacre's gorgeous watercolor illustrations. The author/artist places this story in the Cuban section of Miami. Such details as the portrayal of colorful, native exotic birds and scenes of Cuban American life bring authenticity and cultural detail to this engaging tale. Another charming version of this story is *The Rooster Who Went to His Uncle's Wedding: A Latin American Folktale* by Alma Flor Ada (1993).

Folk Tale Collections

A number of folklore collections of Latino traditional literature have been published for readers in upper elementary school, middle school, and high school. In these collections, readers can read a rich variety of tales from the indigenous groups as well as those that originated from Europe. When reading these tales, they can explore in more depth the values, beliefs, and customs of the peoples of Latin America. Many of the books have introductions and notes that provide insight into the origins of the tales and important historical and geographic facts related to them.

Delacre's *Golden Tales: Myths, Legends, and Folktales From Latin America* (1996) is a treasury of 12 classic tales from 13 countries. The author/illustrator devotes a section of the book to each of the following indigenous groups: the Taínos of Puerto Rico, the Muisca of Colombia, the Inca of Peru, and the Zapotec of Mexico. Each of the sections has an introduction that provides insight into the history and culture of the particular group. Four of the stories are creation myths. Delacre's luminous oil paintings enhance the beauty, complexity, and depth of these compelling stories and authentically portray the foods, architecture, clothing, and artifacts of these four ancient peoples. Delacre also includes a map indicating the locations of the tribes, detailed notes on the stories and artwork, sources for each tale, and a pronunciation key. The book is available in both English and Spanish editions.

Another illustrated collection of myths from Latin America that offers early Americans' explanations of natural phenomena is Natalia Belting's *The Moon Was Tired of Walking on Air* (1992). This book focuses exclusively on the continent of South America and includes 14 creation myths from 10 indigenous groups.

When Jaguars Ate the Moon is a collection of beautifully illustrated stories about the origins of animals and plants indigenous to the Americas. The stories, retold by María Cristina Brusca and Tona Wilson (1995), are written in ABC format. On each page, the authors feature a tale about a particular animal or plant and identify the people and geographic area where the story originated. Many of the tales provide explanations for the origins of things, such as the origin of dance, the origin of death, and how howler monkeys came to live in trees. The reading level is easier in this book than in some other collections mentioned here, making it accessible to younger readers. The rich information on plants and animals makes this book an excellent choice for a social studies unit exploring the ecology of Latin America.

Fiesta Femenina is a collection of eight folk tales retold by Mary-Joan Gerson (2001) that celebrate the courage and strength of women in Mexican folk tales. This cornucopia of tales features a variety of women. Some are extraordinarily strong, such as Rosha in "Rosha and the Sun," who rescues the sun, saving her people from eternal darkness. Some are complex and controversial, such as Malintzin, an Aztec princess who helps Cortés in his conquest of her own people but later regrets her actions and becomes a mythical protector of the Mexican people. Unique among these extraordinary women is the Virgin of Guadalupe, patron saint of Mexico and spiritual protector of the Mexican people, who has the power to perform miracles. "These remarkable women, through their inner strength and creativity, are able to overcome the forces of opposition" (p. 6). Gerson's writing is com-

Book cover from *Fiesta Femenina: Celebrating Women in Mexican Folktale*, first published in 2001 by Barefoot Books, Inc. Text copyright © 2001 by Mary-Joan Gerson. Illustrations copyright © 2001 by Maya Christina Gonzalez.

pelling and engaging, making the women she writes about believable. Maya Christina Gonzalez's acrylic paintings with their vibrant, bold colors enhance the stories, helping to make this book a treasure that should be included in any literature collection. Gerson includes detailed notes on the sources of the tales, a pronunciation guide, and a glossary of Spanish words and phrases.

Plays From Hispanic Tales by Barbara Winther (1998) includes 11 royalty-free, one-act plays that draw their themes from traditional folk tales from the Caribbean, Central America, Mexico, South America, and Spain. The collection features a variety of story types including a ghost tale, trickster tales, folk tales featuring talking animals, and Aztec and Mayan legends. In "Pedro De Urdemalas," readers meet one of Latin America's favorite tricksters, who is related to Juan Bobo but is less simple-minded. "El Caballito of Seven Colors" tells the tale of a magical horse that grants wishes to the youngest son of a farmer and helps him win the hand in marriage of the mayor's daughter. Each play has an introduction that provides background information on the story and helpful cultural and historical details. An extensive glossary also is included.

The Emerald Lizard, retold by Pleasant DeSpain (1999), is an anthology of folk tales from 15 Latin American countries and cultures retold in English and Spanish. The collection includes "The Emerald Lizard" from Guatemala, about a lizard that magically turns into emerald and brings good health and good fortune to a poor man's family, and "The Crocodile Man" from Colombia, about a humble man who transforms himself into a crocodile to be near his lover. Motifs include an obstinate wife, a quest for healing water, the flooding of the world, a horseman who refuses to give a ride to a peasant, and Juan Bobo dressing a pig for church. The tales are short and would be excellent for storytelling. DeSpain provides detailed source notes that give motifs and information on where to find other versions of the tales.

Anaya's *My Land Sings: Stories From the Rio Grande* (1999) is a collection of five traditional tales and five original stories. Almost all set in New Mexico, the *cuentos* fall into three broad categories: (1) stories about animals, riddles, humorous tales, and stories with a moral; (2) tales of enchantment; and (3) *pícaros*, tales of rogues who usually are involved with the devil. As Anaya (1999) points out, "Some of these categories are combined in many stories" (p. 10). The stories with a moral incorporate themes such as respect for elders, the importance of the Catholic faith, and the dangers of disavowing traditional mores. In "Dulcinea," for example, a beautiful, young girl disobeys her father and ignores warnings when she goes to meet a handsome stranger at a dance. The results of this encounter are devastating when Dulcinea learns that she has been dancing with the devil himself.

More advanced readers will enjoy *Latin American Folktales: Stories From Hispanic and Indian Traditions*, edited by John Bierhorst (2002), a collection of 100 folk tales gathered from 20 countries, including the United States. Bierhorst, a folklore specialist, provides an introduction that explains the historical development of the tales, oral storytelling traditions, and the manner in which the stories were recorded by folklorists and anthropologists. The collection begins with early colonial legends of the conquest of Mexico and Peru told from the perspective of the indigenous peoples, who reveal that "the entire disastrous episode was foreordained" (p. 20). The anthology includes stories about magical objects, tricksters, witches, ghosts, beautiful maidens, animals with magical powers, ogres, amorous men, and the devil. The collection is ambitious in scope and size. A glossary and list of motifs are included.

Classroom Activities

A wide variety of activities can be used with the books described in this chapter, such as comparing different versions of a story, engaging in storytelling, performing Readers Theatre, and writing folk tales based on the themes found in these tales. This section describes in detail a variety of activities that can be used with these books in the classroom to foster literacy and to make powerful connections with content areas across the curriculum.

Setting the Stage

To introduce these stories to children, set up a learning center that includes a display of Latino folk tales with an attractive background of posters showing the landscapes of Central America, Mexico, Puerto Rico, and South America. The center also could include maps of the different regions and information books on the ancient peoples of these regions. Some excellent examples are *Aztecs and Incas* by Penny Bateman (1988); *The Art of Ancient Mexico* by Shirley Glubok (1968); *The Mystery of the Ancient Maya* by Carolyn Meyer and Charles Gallenkamp (1995); and *They Lived Like This: The Ancient Maya* by Marie Neurath (1996). As the students read the literature, they can illustrate the stories in a group-created mural and mark the country of origin for each tale on a map.

Multimedia

Multimedia activities can enrich students' experiences with the beautiful literature of Latino cultures. The *Legends of the Americas* CD-ROM program (Patrissi & Spatz, 1995) is an exciting resource for students to learn more about the folklore and culture of Brazil, Guatemala, Mexico, and Peru while applying their literacy and research skills. Students can read, or listen to and read, a story in English or Spanish using the Read-A-Legend feature, or they can research interesting historical, geographic, and cultural facts about the country in which a tale originates with the Explore-A-Legend feature. Four books accompany the program, including *The Llama's Secret* (Palacios, 1993).

Another resource that students in middle school or high school can use to broaden their knowledge is the PBS four-part video series *Spirits of the Jaguar* (Reddish & Jacobs, 1997), a visually dazzling presentation of historical, cultural, and geographic content. The first video gives a geological overview of how the Caribbean Islands and Central America were formed. Each of the other three episodes focuses on a people: the Aztec, the Maya, and the Taínos. The episode on the Taínos explains how these ancient people sailed from Central America to the Caribbean Islands, and provides children with a historical context for *How the Sea Began* (Crespo, 1993) and *The Golden Flower* (Jaffe, 1996), two picture book versions of a myth about a culture's shift from an agricultural to a fishing society. The series provides a more adult version of the myth and can be used by older readers to compare and contrast how stories are adapted for different age levels. They also can explore how ecological necessities shape a culture and a literature. There is a website that has more information and links to other websites (www.pbs.org/wnet/nature/spirits/html/body_intro.html).

Comparison Charts

Students can compare various elements of similar tales to promote critical reading and thinking. For example, students can compare different flood myths, as illustrated in Table 11.1. In cooperative groups, students can write the story's title, the setting, the causes of the flood, the events following the flood, what the myth explains, and the values taught. They can write these items on cards that can be placed in a pocket chart and then later use the cards to retell the events in their tale, as suggested by Young and Ferguson (1995).

Table 11.1					
Comparison of Latino Flood Myths					
Myth	**Setting**	**What Causes the Flood?**	**What Happens After the Flood?**	**What Does the Myth Explain?**	**What Values Are Emphasized?**
The Tree That Rains (Bernhard, 1994)	Sierra Madre, Mexico, near Lake Chapala (Huichol Indians)	The people forget the gods	The world becomes green; a tree that rains springs forth	The importance of Great Grand-mother Earth for growing crops	The importance of rain for growing crops
How the Sea Began (Crespo, 1993)	Boriquén—now Puerto Rico (Taínos)	The gourd holding Yayael's bow and arrows splits open and the sea gushes out	Boriquén becomes an island	How the sea began and how Boriquén became an island	The importance of the sea as a source of food
The Golden Flower (Jaffe, 1996)	Boriquén—now Puerto Rico (Taínos)	The pumpkin bursts apart and the sea gushes out	Streams flow throughout the land and a sea surrounds Boriquén	How Boriquén was created	The importance of streams and the sea for fishing and growing crops
The Llama's Secret (Palacios, 1993)	Andes Mountains, Peru (Incas)	Mamacocha, the sea, becomes angry	The waters recede, then people and animals descend the mountaintop	How the llama saved the people and animals from a great flood	The importance of the llama for Peruvian people

Where

Come visit the land
of the gods in the
Yucatan Peninsula
in Mexico.
Come see magical
cornfields, sparkling
waters, and
deep blue skies!

When

Travel back in time
to when the gods
first created
the world.
Come see what the
world was like
a really, really
long time ago.

Wondrous Sights

Plumed Serpent and
Heart of Sky
creating people
out of corn.
Grandmother of Light
weaving the cloth
of light.
The deep, dark silence
that came before
there was a world
And many more...

Travel Brochure

Children enjoy using their artistic abilities to express what they find interesting in books. They could design and illustrate a travel brochure for the setting in one of the myths, using an 8 $\frac{1}{2}$" × 11" piece of paper folded in thirds. In their descriptions, they could use persuasive language to entice visitors to explore the sights and sounds of the imaginary place. Figure 11.1 shows an example from the Mayan myth *People of Corn* (Gerson, 1995).

Codex With Hieroglyphics

The Aztecs and other peoples of Mexico wrote on bark pages connected together in one long accordion-folded piece. These "books," called codices, were written in hieroglyphics and contained records of history, calendars, and daily life. Students could make a codex by cutting a strip of tagboard 4" wide by 36" long and then folding it accordion-style as shown in Figure 11.2. They could then write their own version of a myth or legend based on an Aztec story such as *The Fifth and Final Sun* (Greger, 1994) and copy it onto the codex. To add authenticity, students could include Aztec hieroglyphics. Information on how to draw the Aztec calendar symbols for each month is available on the Internet at www.ai.mit.edu/people/montalvo/ Hotlist/aztec.html.

Figure 11.2
Sample Codex With Aztec Hieroglyphics

Circular Story Map

A circular story map is a graphic display that often is used to illustrate the sequence of events in a cumulative tale. Using the story map helps young readers with comprehension by directing their attention to the circular pattern within each level of a cumulative story. Students can use the story map as a prompt for retelling. As a child retells the story, the characters that are placed in a circle on the story map can remind him or her of the repeating sequence of events. Students can make a story map by drawing figures that represent the chain of events in a story. The figures can be cut out and glued onto a large piece of poster board in the shape of a circle. They should be glued clockwise to show the sequence of events. Figure 11.3 provides an example of a story map for *The Rooster Who Went to His Uncle's Wedding* (Ada, 1993).

Readers Theatre

Readers Theatre, a form of drama in which children read with expression from a script, is excellent for developing children's oral reading skills, confidence level with reading, and enthusiasm for literature. Many of the Latino folk tales are easily adaptable to Readers Theatre, as shown in this brief excerpt from *Musicians of the Sun* (McDermott, 1997):

Wind: Musicians of the Sun, I am coming to free you!

Narrator 1:   The musicians heard the voice of Wind. They yearned to be free, but Sun made them more fearful.

Narrator 2:   The musicians continued to play.

Sun: Go away, Wind, or I will destroy you.

Narrator 2:   Wind went closer still and called out again.

Wind: Musicians of the Sun, come with me!

Sun: Ignore him. Play on.

Narrator 3:   Sun burned more fiercely and the musicians played louder than before.

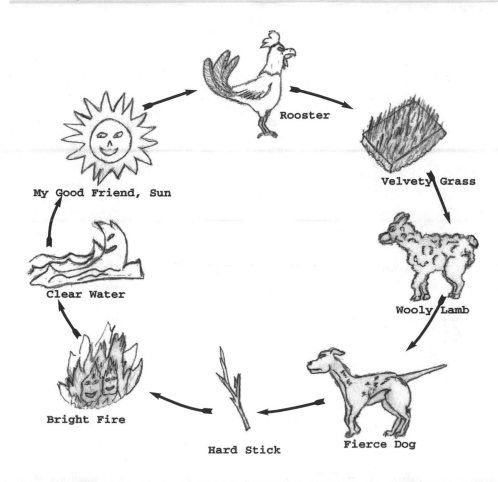

Shadow Puppets

An excellent way to involve children in the dramatic retelling of a story is through puppetry. Children can make their own shadow puppets by cutting animal shapes or human figures from poster board and attaching sticks to them. For example, for *Borreguita and the Coyote* (Aardema, 1991), students can cut out large shapes of a lamb and a coyote and use the puppets to dramatize the story, as illustrated in Figure 11.4. A dramatic effect can be created by having the actors hide behind a large, overturned table with a sheet in the background serving as a screen. A light positioned behind the actors will make the puppet figures look like shadows.

Figure 11.4
Sample Shadow Puppets for *Borreguita and the Coyote*

Storytelling With Masks

Another excellent way to involve students dramatically with Latino folklore is through storytelling. Students could portray some of the strong, brave women in *Fiesta Femenina* (Gerson, 2001) or powerful male figures such as Montezuma in *Latin American Folktales* (Bierhorst, 2002). To prepare for the storytelling, students should read the tales carefully to become familiar with the language, characters, and plot. Guide the students by emphasizing important aspects of storytelling, such as using intonation, stress, and pitch effectively to convey a message; memorizing key phrases to preserve the tone of the folk tale; and using effective eye contact and expressive body movements (Bosma, 1992). Students can make masks of the faces of the characters they will portray, using tagboard, colored markers, felt pieces, sequins, and other art materials. They can staple their masks onto an art stick or tongue depressor so the masks can be held like a fan. Students can practice their parts and then perform them in front of their classmates or in front of another class. Backdrops of scenes of pyramids and temples can add to the effect.

Book Cube

A book cube is a great way for students to write about a book and to focus on story structure using a three-dimensional form. Give students six pieces of 8" × 8" sheets of poster board. On the sides of the cube, have them draw illustrations from the story and write information about setting, plot, theme, their favorite parts, and examples of descriptive language. Students can then form a cube by gluing or stapling together the edges of the pieces. Figure 11.5 shows an example from *The Invisible Hunters* (Rohmer, Chow, & Vidaure, 1987).

Figure 11.5
Sample Book Cube for *The Invisible Hunters*

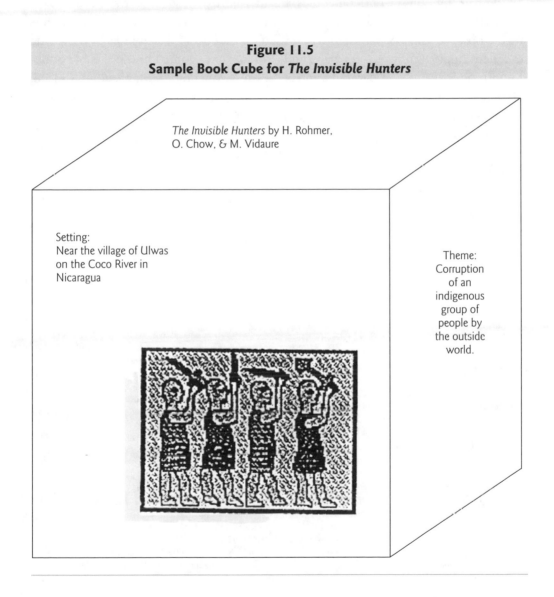

The Invisible Hunters by H. Rohmer, O. Chow, & M. Vidaure

Setting:
Near the village of Ulwas on the Coco River in Nicaragua

Theme:
Corruption of an indigenous group of people by the outside world.

Conclusion

In this chapter, we have provided a glimpse of the traditional Latino literature that has blossomed with the blending of races, cultures, religions, and languages in the Americas. This rich oral literature echoes the history and heritage of Latin America and is the voice of the Latino peoples. As society continues into the 21st century, educators are seeing the emergence of quality picture books and collections representing this impressive oral tradition in written form. It is crucial to spread the word about these marvelous books to parents, teachers, and librarians. These books have the power to build bridges across cultural boundaries by helping students learn to value the contributions of Latino peoples. Furthermore, by reflecting their cultural experiences and the history of their peoples, these books can empower Latino students with a positive sense of self-identity and self-confidence. These books also provide excellent opportunities for teachers and students to become knowledgeable about Latino cultures and to integrate Latino literature throughout the curriculum. Indeed, along with the folk tales of Grimm and Perrault, these stories belong in U.S. mainstream classrooms to be loved, cherished, and appreciated.

The authors gratefully acknowledge Justin Smolen for his assistance in drawing the examples for the activities in this chapter.

REFERENCES

Anaya, R. (1980). *Cuentos: Tales of the Hispanic southwest*. Santa Fe, NM: Museum of New Mexico Press.

Barlow, G. (1972). Latin American folklore and the folktale. In R.K. Carlson (Ed.), *Folklore and folktales around the world* (pp. 25–39). Newark, DE: International Reading Association.

Barrera, R.B., Liguori, O., & Salas, L. (1993). *Ideas a literature can grow on: Key insights for enriching and expanding children's literature in grades K–8*. Norwood, MA: Christopher-Gordon.

Bosma, B. (1992). *Fairy tales, fables, legends, and myths: Using folk literature in your classroom* (2nd ed.). New York: Teachers College Press.

Cangemi, J.A., & Aucoin, L. (1996). Global thematic units are passports to learning. *Social Education, 60*(2), 80–81.

Carrasquillo, A.L. (1994). A rationale for Hispanic representation in instructional materials. *Journal of Educational Issues of Language Minority Students, 14*, 115–126.

Cullinan, B.E., & Galda, L. (1994). *Literature and the child* (3rd ed.). New York: Harcourt Brace.

Dietrich, D., & Ralph, K.S. (1995). Crossing borders: Multicultural literature in the classroom. *Journal of Educational Issues of Language Minority Students, 5*(15), 65–73.

Encyclopaedia Britannica. (1987). Vol. 6, s.v. Inca.

Lewis, A.C. (1998). Growing Hispanic enrollments: Challenge and opportunity. *Phi Delta Kappan, 80*(1), 3–4.

Miller-Lachmann, L. (1992). *Our family, our friends, our world: An annotated guide to significant multicultural books for children and teenagers*. New Providence, NJ: R.R. Bowker.

Nieto, S. (1993). We have stories to tell: A case study of Puerto Ricans in children's books. In V.J. Harris (Ed.), *Teaching multicultural literature in grades K–8* (pp. 171–201). Norwood, MA: Christopher-Gordon.

Norton, D.E. (1990). Teaching multicultural literature in the reading curriculum. *The Reading Teacher, 44*(1), 28–40.

Norton, D.E. (2003). *Through the eyes of a child: An introduction to children's literature* (6th ed.). Upper Saddle River, NJ: Prentice Hall.

Patrissi, N. (Designer, Producer, Director), & Spatz, J. (Executive Producer). (1995). *Legends of the Americas: A Troll interactive multimedia CD-ROM for Macintosh and Windows* [CD-ROM]. Mahwah, NJ: Troll.

PBS Online. (1997a). *Aztecs: Fierce Wanderers*. [Video recording]. New York: WNET. Available: http://www.pbs.org/wnet/nature/spirits/html/body_aztec.html

PBS Online. (1997b). *Maya: Children of corn*. Video recording]. New York: WNET. Available: http://www.pbs.org/wnet/nature/spirits/html/body_maya.html

PBS Online. (1997c). *Taino: Voices from the past*. [Video recording]. New York: WNET. Available: http://www.pbs.org/wnet/nature/spirits/html/body_taino.html

Perez-Stable, M. (1997). Keys to exploring Latino cultures: Folktales for children. *Social Studies, 88*(1), 29–34.

Reddish, P. (Series Producer), & Jacobs, M. (Producer). (1997). *Spirits of the Jaguar* [Video recording]. (Available from WNET Video Distribution, 800-336-1917, or WNET Video Distribution, PO Box 2284, South Burlington, VT 05407, USA.)

Schon, I. (1991). Recommended and not recommended books in Spanish for children and adolescents. *Teacher Education Quarterly, 18*(4), 73–83.

Schon, I. (1993). Good and bad books about Hispanic people. *Multicultural Review, 2*(1), 28–31

Schultz, F. (1997). The social contexts of multicultural education. In F. Schultz (Ed.), *Multicultural education 97/98: Annual editions* (pp. 4–5). Guilford, CT: Dushkin/McGraw-Hill.

Smolen, L.A., & Ortiz-Castro, V. (1997). Bridges across borders: Infusing Latino literature into the curriculum. *Ohio Journal of the English Language Arts, 38*(1), 54–64.

Sutherland, Z., & Arbuthnot, M.H. (1991). *Children and books* (8th ed.). New York: HarperCollins.

Villegas, A.M. (1991). *Cultural responsive teaching*. (Educational Testing Service, The Praxis Series: Professional Assessments for Beginning Teachers.) Princeton, NJ: Educational Testing Service.

Yokota, J. (1993). Issues in selecting multicultural children's literature. In M.F. Opitz (Ed.), *Literacy instruction for culturally and linguistically diverse students*. Newark, DE: International Reading Association.

Young, T.A., & Ferguson, P.M. (1995). From Anansi to Zomo: Trickster tales in the classroom. *The Reading Teacher, 48*, 490–503.

CHILDREN'S BOOKS CITED

Aardema, V. (1991). *Borreguita and the coyote* (P. Mathers, Illus.). New York: Knopf.

Ada, A.F. (1993). *The rooster who went to his uncle's wedding: A Latin American folktale* (K. Kuchera, Illus.). New York: G.P. Putnam's Sons.

Ada, A.F. (1997). *The lizard and the sun/La lagartija y el sol* (F. Dávalos, Illus.). New York: Bantam Doubleday Dell.

Ada, A.F. (1999). *The three golden oranges* (R. Cartwright, Illus.). New York: Atheneum.

Anaya, R. (1997). *Maya's children: The story of the La Llorona* (M. Baca, Illus.). New York: Hyperion.

Anaya, R. (1999). *My land sings: Stories from the Rio Grande* (A. Córdova, Illus.). New York: Morrow.

Bateman, P. (1988). *Aztecs and Incas: AD 1300–1532*. New York: Franklin Watts.

Belting, N.M. (1992). *The moon was tired of walking on air: Origin myths of South American Indians* (W. Hillenbrand, Illus.). New York: Houghton Mifflin.

Bernhard, E. (1994). *The tree that rains: The flood myth of the Huichol Indians of Mexico* (D. Bernhard, Illus.). New York: Holiday House.

Bierhorst, J. (1987). *Doctor Coyote: A Native American Aesop's fables* (W. Watson, Illus.). New York: MacMillan.

Bierhorst, J. (Ed.). (2002). *Latin American folktales: Stories from Hispanic and Indian traditions*. New York: Pantheon.

Brusca, M.C., & Wilson, T. (1995). *When jaguars ate the moon and other stories about animals and plants of the Americas*. New York: Henry Holt.

Coburn, J.R. (2000). *Domitila: A Cinderella tale from the Mexican tradition* (C. McLennan, Illus.). Auburn, CA: Shen's Books.

Crespo, G. (1993). *How the sea began: A Taino myth*. New York: Clarion.

Cruz Martinez, A. (1991). *The woman who outshone the sun: The legend of Lucia Zenteno* (F. Olivera, Illus.). San Francisco: Children's Book Press.

Delacre, L. (1996). *Golden tales: Myths, legends, and folktales from Latin America*. New York: Scholastic.

De Sauza, J. (1989). *Brother Anansi and the cattle ranch/El hermano Anansi y el rancho de ganado* (S. Von Mason, Illus.). San Francisco: Children's Book Press.

DeSpain, P. (1999). *The emerald lizard: Fifteen Latin American tales to tell in English and Spanish/La lagartija esmeralda: Quince cuentos tradicionales Latinoamericanos*. Little Rock, AR: August House.

Gerson, M.-J. (1995). *People of corn: A Mayan story* (C. Golembe, Illus.). Boston: Little, Brown.

Gerson, M.-J. (2001). *Fiesta femenina: Celebrating women in Mexican folktale* (M.C. Gonzalez, Illus.). New York: Barefoot Books.

Glubok, S. (1968). *The art of ancient Mexico* (A.H. Tamarin, Photog.). New York: Harper & Row.

González, L.M. (1994). *The bossy gallito/El gallo de bodas* (L. Delacre, Illus.). New York: Scholastic.

González, L.M. (1996). *Señor Cat's romance and other favorite stories from Latin America* (L. Delacre, Illus.). New York: Scholastic.

Greger, C.S. (1994). *The fifth and final sun: An ancient Aztec myth of the sun's origin*. Boston: Houghton Mifflin.

Hayes, J. (2000). *Estrellita de oro/Little gold star* (G. Osuna Perez & L.A. Perez, Illus.). El Paso, TX: Cinco Puntos Press.

Jaffe, N. (1996). *The golden flower: A Taino myth from Puerto Rico* (E.O. Sánchez, Illus.). New York: Simon & Schuster.

Johnston, T. (1994). *The tale of rabbit and coyote* (T. dePaola, Illus.). New York: G.P. Putnam Sons.

Kimmel, E.A. (2000a). *Montezuma and the fall of the Aztecs* (D. San Souci, Illus.). New York: Holiday House.

Kimmel, E.A. (2000b). *The two mountains: An Aztec legend* (L.F. Fisher, Illus.). New York: Holiday House.

Kurtz, J. (1996). *Miro in the kingdom of the sun* (D. Frampton, Illus.). Boston: Houghton Mifflin.

McDermott, G. (1997). *Musicians of the sun*. New York: Simon & Schuster.

Meyer, C., & Gallenkamp, C. (1995). *The mystery of the ancient Maya*. New York: Margaret K. McElderry.

Mohr, N., & Martorell, A. (1995). *The song of el Coquí and other tales of Puerto Rico*. New York: Viking.

Montes, A. (2000). *Juan Bobo goes to work* (J. Cepeda, Illus.). New York: HarperCollins.

Neurath, M. (1966). *They lived like this: The ancient Maya*. New York: F. Watts.

Ober, H. (1994). *How music came into the world: An ancient Mexican myth* (C. Ober, Illus.). Boston: Houghton Mifflin.

Palacios, A. (1993). *The llama's secret: A Peruvian legend* (C. Reasoner, Illus.). Mahwah, NJ: Troll.

Pitre, F. (1993). *Juan Bobo and the pig* (C. Hale, Illus.). New York: Dutton.

Rohmer, H., & Anchondo, M. (1976). *How we came to the fifth world/Como vinimos al quinto mundo*. San Francisco: Children's Book Press.

Rohmer, H., Chow, O., & Vidaure, M. (1987). *The invisible hunters: A legend from the Miskito Indians of Nicaragua/Los cazadores invisibles: Una leyenda de los Indios Miskitos de Nicaragua* (J. Sam, Illus.). San Francisco: Children's Book Press.

San Souci, R.D. (2000). *Little gold star: A Spanish American Cinderella tale* (S. Martinez, Illus.). New York: HarperCollins.

Strauss, S. (1998). *When woman became the sea* (C. Acosta, Illus.). Hillsboro, OR: Beyond Words.

Van Laan, N. (1998). *The magic bean tree: A legend from Argentina* (B. Vidal, Illus.). Boston: Houghton Mifflin.

Vidal, B. (1991). *The legend of El Dorado: A Latin American tale*. New York: Alfred A. Knopf.

Winther, B. (1998). *Plays from Hispanic tales: One-act, royalty-free dramatizations for young people, from Hispanic stories and folktales*. Boston: Plays.

CHAPTER 12

Open Sesame! Middle Eastern and Indian Subcontinent Folk Literature

Marcia Baghban

Ancient Turkish, Arabian, Persian, and Indian cultures offer their folk tales, epics, legends, fables, and tricksters not only to help us understand human nature but also to help us understand the countries that have nurtured these genres of folk literature. This chapter begins by making a contemporary connection to the region through Disney's Aladdin and then leads into a discussion of the adaptations of *The Thousand and One Nights* in books for children and young adults. Since storytelling involves training, children will be interested in the next section, which describes how oral literature is passed from one generation to another to create a storyteller. Because the tellers move, stories also move from place to place.

One possibility for the movement of oral literature in this region has been east and west travel on the Silk Road. Through a discussion of genres in the region, the chapter travels from west to east with Turkish folk tales, next Iranian tales, and then Indian tales. Once in India, the world famous epics of the *Mahabharata* and the *Ramayana* dominate folk literature. The chapter then moves from east to west, back to Mesopotamia and the epic of *Gilgamesh*. The chapter also includes legends, fables, and tricksters from the region; classroom applications; and finally children's books that support teachers' understanding of contemporary traditions from the region.

For now, let us return to the beginning of our discussion with a shout of "Open Sesame!"

The Thousand and One Nights

"Open Sesame!" is one of the most famous passwords in all of folk literature and perhaps even in all of Disney's films. In *Aladdin and the King of Thieves*, the third installment of Disney's Aladdin movies, Aladdin struggles to find his father, who is the king of thieves. The thieves have hidden a treasure in a sealed magic cave that opens to the password "Open Sesame." But did you know that Ali Baba, not Aladdin, is the character who appears in the original story with the thieves and discovers the famous password that opens the cave? And his story is but one tale in the world-famous *The Thousand and One Nights*.

This collection of approximately 200 folk tales from Arabia, Egypt, India, and Persia is probably the most famous piece of literature translated from Arabic for Westerners. An overall tale holds all these folk tales together. It begins with King Shahriyar, who is betrayed by his first wife. He orders her killed and promises to marry a different maiden every night and have her executed the following morning. Sheherezade, the intelligent daughter of a court official, insists on becoming one of his brides because she believes that she can end his tyranny. She tells her sister to come to the bedchamber on the wedding night and ask permission for Sheherezade to tell one last story. Her sister visits, praises Sheherezade's talent for storytelling, and the king agrees. By beginning one exciting tale every evening but withholding the ending, Sheherezade not only creates the concept of the cliffhanger but also convinces the enthralled king to spare her life for another day until the next night's installment. After 1,001 nights, or three years, she has saved her life forever.

Brian Alderson presents a few dozen of her stories from Arabia, India, and Persia in *The Arabian Nights, or, Tales Told by Sheherezade During a Thousand Nights and One Night* (1995). This collection for children ages 9–12 includes episodic stories of Sinbad, Ali Baba and the 40 thieves, Aladdin, and the City of Brass as well as individual tales and fables. Alderson's version maintains the familiar formulas of the original, as well as the earthiness in language and culturally appropriate references to his Majesty and the Mystery of Allah. Readers also can journey back to the magic days of romance, suspense, mystery, and adventure with sultans and caliphs, djinns, sorcerers, and crafty mothers in another collection for ages 9–12 by N.J. Dawood, *Aladdin and Other Tales From the Arabian Nights* (1997). Like Alderson's, this version does not reflect contemporary versions of the stories but seeks to be faithful to authentic Arabic sources. The author was born in Baghdad and achieved a reputation as a scholar during his university education in London. These stories are clearly Arabic in character, and Islam is a dominant theme throughout. Although health, wealth, wine, and women are bestowed as the blessings of Allah for obedience, the stories still capture the Western imagination. Readers are definitely taken to another world.

A Common Formula: Tale Within a Tale

Because Sheherezade tells one tale after another within a larger framework (Bueler, 2001), it is also possible to locate books that present just one of her stories, in addition to the many collections of her stories that are available. John Yeoman retells for readers ages 9–12 only the tales of Sinbad in *The Seven Voyages of Sinbad the*

Sailor (1997). In the stories, Sinbad explains how he got his wealth through seven voyages of disaster, horror, and adventure that eventually led him to happiness. Well-known illustrator Quentin Blake presents cartoon-like drawings that seem appropriate for giants, hungry serpents, and wild sea storms. For younger readers ages 6–8, Eric Kimmel presents *The Tale of Ali Baba and the Forty Thieves: A Story From the Arabian Nights* (1996) as a picture book of one tale. Kimmel captures the flavor and excitement of *The Thousand and One Nights* in his retelling of the story of Ali Baba, who finds a treasure that leads to his greedy brother's death. With the help of a clever slave girl, he gives his brother a proper burial and avenges his brother's death by outwitting the thieves for their treasure, which is hidden in a cave, through the discovery of the famous password, "Open Sesame."

The Preservation and Transmission of Tales

But storytellers do not just live in palaces. For centuries, traditions of storytelling have not only endured but also flourished in Afghanistan, Algeria, Bangladesh, Egypt, India, Iran, Iraq, Jordan, Lebanon, Libya, Morocco, Pakistan, Saudi Arabia, Syria, Tunisia, and Turkey. Although large, extended families always have at least one good storyteller who tells stories for the family's amusement, certain public contexts in which readers may find storytellers appear in children's picture books. Ted Lewin's *The Storytellers* (1998) shows a day in the life of professional storytellers in Fez, Morocco. Abdul and his grandfather walk to work through the market streets of spice merchants, saddle makers, wool dyers, carpet sellers, and carpenters. They spread a carpet on the ground and wait for a crowd to gather. Finally, the grandfather opens his story with the formulaic beginning, "This happened, or maybe it did not. The time is long past, and most is forgot." Such formulaic beginnings generally excuse the teller's variations on what is most likely a previously heard story. In Afghanistan, the formula, "Tonight is my turn to tell lies," is extreme enough not only to excuse the storyteller but also to totally remove the story from reality.

Lewin's book, in addition, without clearly indicating any formal teaching, demonstrates that Abdul's observation of his grandfather, participation in the day, and listening to the same stories again and again are preparing Abdul to become a professional storyteller. Such informal educational strategies preserve oral traditions. It is clear that Abdul is a storyteller in training. After Abdul and his grandfather spread their carpet, his grandfather releases a white pigeon that immediately flies to sit on Abdul's head. Grandfather then leans an old photo of himself for all to see against a silver teapot. In it, he is as young as Abdul, and a white pigeon sits on his head. This predestination suits Abdul just fine. He already likes his craft. As he passes through the copper and metalworkers' street and sees boys pounding metal into huge bowls, he tells his grandfather, "What noisy work. Not like ours." As they pass the wool dyeing street, he tells his grandfather, "What hard work. Not like ours." He is happy to work where the air is fresh and where he can see the sky.

Moreover, storytellers do not always stay in one location. Many theories exist about why human beings have familiar themes in their stories around the world (Dundes, 1965; Propp, 1985; Thompson, 1967). Some theorists propose that common themes come from common human experiences and are accidental. Other scholars note that travel has played a great part in spreading folk tales around the world. Following this theory, one of the most famous routes for commerce and for tales has been the Silk Road. This famous caravan trail stretched from Persia to China and was used from 200 B.C. to the 14th century. Travelers told stories as they moved along the route to the east or west and when they camped during the journey. In seven stories, Cherry Gilchrist's *Stories From the Silk Road* (1999) for ages 9–12 rekindles the lively spirit of travel with retellings from humorous to creepy and with an assortment of kind and vengeful gods, spirits, animals, and human travelers. Generosity and kindness are rewarded; greed is punished. In addition, an introduction provides information about the Silk Road and maps to detail the route.

Folk Tales Along the Route

The Silk Road may have been one way in which stories traveled (Preston, 1995). If we begin in the Middle East, we may be able to follow the Road and reach India. Let's start with the edge of Europe. Barbara Walker presents *A Treasury of Turkish Folktales* (1998) for children ages 4–8. Next, in old Baghdad, a caliph and his vizier are transformed into storks by an evil spell. With the help of a beautiful princess, they reverse the spell in Aaron Shepard's retelling of *The Enchanted Storks: A Tale of the Middle East* (1995a). In Persia, the royal treasure has been stolen and no fortuneteller can find it. A young man name Ahmed, tired of his poverty, sits in the marketplace to tell fortunes. He locates a missing ring by pure luck, and the king turns to him to find the royal treasure in Shepard's *Forty Fortunes: A Tale of Iran* (1999) for ages 4–8. Ahmed knows that he has no fortunetelling skills, and with 40 days to find 40 fortunes, he must use his wits to fool the real thieves.

Numerous Iranian folk tales appear in a collection translated by Idries Shah. Outstanding among the collection are *The Silly Chicken* (2000b) and *The Magic Horse* (1998), both for readers ages 4–8. Silly Chicken struts through village streets repeating, "Tuck-tuck-tuck-tuck-tuck." No one knows what it means. When the chicken learns to talk, it squawks, "The Earth is going to swallow us up." The villagers try to escape and then realize it is a trick. When they ask the chicken why he tried to fool them, the chicken replies, "You think a chicken knows something because he can talk?" The comical story emphasizes to young readers that it is important not to believe everything you hear. In the second book, from a story that has been told for more than 1,000 years in central Asia and the Middle East, a magical wooden horse carries a young boy named Prince Tambal to wondrous places to achieve his heart's desire. A simple tale of generosity for readers 4–8 years old appears in *The Little Brown Jay: A Tale From India* by Elizabeth Claire (1994). With the collection *Folk Tales of Bangladesh* by P.C. Roy Chaudhury (1995), we have arrived at the end of the Silk Road in our geographic area of concern.

In addition to city marketplaces and caravan trails, readers may notice yet another outdoor venue for folk performance in Barbara Bash's *In the Heart of the Village: The World of the Indian Banyan Tree* (1996). The enormous Indian fig tree called a banyan is also referred to as the many-footed one because of its many self-rooting branches that form pillars when they touch the ground. This particular banyan tree is in the heart of an Indian village, and the book shows activity around the tree from sunrise to sunrise. One time after another, it becomes the place for birds to nest, villagers to barter, children to play, monkeys to frolic, bats to feed, elders to meet, and folk performances to occur. Villagers gather in front of a simple stage set up under the banyan tree. Far into the night, costumed dancers act out ancient stories with graceful hand movements and intricate footwork. The tree becomes a theater, a place of imagining, for storytelling.

Stories for all ages from the Indian subcontinent depict clever, vengeful, loving, modest, beautiful, or fierce heroines in Uma Krishnaswami's *Shower of Gold: Girls and Women in the Stories of India* (1999). This anthology contains 18 tales that come from Hindu and Buddhist mythology, oral tradition, legends, literary masterpieces, and the author's own memory. The stories are reincarnation tales, a romance from 15th-century India, tricks of magical and powerful Hindu goddesses, and traditional male-dominated stories told from the female point of view. Rather than heroines who marry the prince and become rich, these heroines achieve intangible rewards. In one tale, a young princess comes to realize that strength and duty are more important than looks and marriage. In another, a group of royal ladies survives physical deprivation to convince the Buddha that they are spiritually prepared to become disciples. Krishnaswami's introduction discusses the movement of stories from culture to culture, place to place, and time to time and includes women's roles in the stories she has chosen.

Famous Epics

Long poems that tell stories, particularly of historical events, are beloved in cultures with strong oral traditions. These epics provide a shared past for the people who live in such cultures (Narayan, 1989). Many of the best-loved stories from India come from two great epic poems: the *Mahabharata* and the *Ramayana*.

The word *Mahabharata* means *Great King Bharata*. This poem was transcribed into Sanskrit about 2,000 years ago after a long life in oral tradition. According to tradition, a wise man dictated it to the god of wisdom, but it is actually a collection of writings by several authors who lived at different times (Honko, 2000). Parts of it may be as old or older than 2,500 years (White, 2002a). The epic demonstrates the futility of war and tells the story of King Bharata through two families who once lived in northern India. The Pandava brothers lose their kingdom to their cousins and struggle to gain it back. Some of the poem's heroes are taken from history, and some characters represent gods and human ideals.

Book cover from *The Storytellers* by Ted Lewin. Copyright © 1998. Used by permission of HarperCollins Publishers.

Following the familiar tale within a tale formula, the *Mahabharata's* main story line often is interrupted by other stories. For an easy, smooth retelling of one such story aimed at readers ages 4–8, look at *Savitri: A Tale of Ancient India* by Aaron Shepard (1992). In this story, the wise and beautiful princess Savitri seeks a husband of her own choosing. Her father agrees and encourages her to go out into the world and find a man worthy of her. In the company of servants and counselors, she travels from place to place until she comes to a monastery. There she sees Prince Satyavan guiding his old and blind father. The eldest teacher tells Savitri that the young man's name means "Son of Truth" and that no man is richer in virtue. When Savitri arrives home, her father is sitting with a holy seer. She tells her father that she has selected the impoverished son of a conquered king. The seer prophesies that Satyavan will die in a year. Although her father tells her to pick someone else, she marries him anyway, determined to share his life, short or long. When Yama (or Death) appears, Savitri outwits him through a series of bargains. She manages to regain her husband's life, and she restores her father-in-law's kingdom.

A small part of the *Mahabharata* is called the *Bhagavad-Gita*, and it also may be found in a children's book. Jean Griesser's *Our Most Dear Friend: Bhagavad-Gita for Children* (1996) for ages 9–12 begins in long-ago India. The story is presented as a conversation between Arjuna Pandava and Lord Krishna, who appears in human form as Arjuna's friend and chariot driver. Their conversation takes place on a battlefield at the beginning of a war between Arjuna and members of his own family. Arjuna faces a difficult decision. As a warrior, he should defend his brother, who is the king. However, he has cousins and teachers on the opposite side. Arjuna asks Lord Krishna for advice. Krishna describes the workings of the spiritual world and teaches him that people can achieve freedom by following their prescribed duty. He also describes the soul's presence in every living thing and teaches that all living things are part of the Creator. He introduces reincarnation but does not use the specific term.

The other major ancient epic in Hindu culture, the *Ramayana*, dates from about 500 B.C. (White, 2002b). Rama, its hero, is a human form of the god Vishnu. He is the son and heir of an Indian king. In the story, Rama lives in a kingdom in northern India. His father exiles him for 14 years because of a dispute over the throne. The main conflict, though, is between Rama and Ravana, a demon king who kidnaps Rama's wife and takes her to his kingdom on the island of Lanka. Rama rescues his wife and kills Ravana with an arrow. At the end of Rama's exile, he and his wife return home, and Rama becomes king. Their story represents high standards for human behavior and devotion to duty, and Rama serves as a model of a brave and devoted husband.

Erik Jendresen and Joshua Greene (1998) present one of the many stories within the overall *Ramayana* story. The monkey-human hero Hanuman appears in their book *Hanuman: Based on Valmiki's Ramayana* (for readers ages 4–8). Here Hanuman tells how he once leaped all the way to the sun but suffered for it. Now grown up, he uses his forgotten powers of long ago in his devotion to Prince Rama. In the cosmic battle to save Princess Sita, Rama's wife, from the Ravana, the 10-headed beast who kidnapped her, good triumphs over evil.

Nizami, the 12th-century Persian poet, wrote the epic *Haft Paykar* or *Seven Beauties*. Translated for the first time, the poem becomes the collection of tales in *The Seven Wise Princesses: A Medieval Persian Epic* (Tarnowska, 2000) for readers ages 9–12. In the book, Shah Bahram invites seven princesses to leave their homelands to live at his palace, each in a different-colored pavilion. He visits each princess on a day ruled by the appropriate planet, and each princess tells him one wise tale to demonstrate the seven ideals of sovereignty: truth, patience, perseverance, forgiveness, humility, wisdom, and love.

Another of the oldest epics in world literature is the epic of Gilgamesh. The earliest verses come from 2000 B.C. in Mesopotamia, although fragments of manuscripts were found in Syria and Turkey even earlier (Lindahl, 2002). The epic centers around Gilgamesh, a powerful king who oppresses his people in ancient Sumeria. When the people pray for help, the gods create a champion, Enkidu, to meet Gilgamesh in battle. Instead of destroying each other, the two men become friends and share many adventures until Enkidu dies. Gilgamesh then searches for the secret of immortality (Lindahl, 2002). Ludmilla Zeman (1998a, 1998b, 1998c) retells this long epic in three books for children. In the first, *Gilgamesh the King* (1998a), Zeman introduces the ancient king to readers ages 9–12. The character is part man and part god. In his loneliness he becomes a cruel tyrant. To impress the citizens of Uruk, he orders a great wall built and drives his people to despair and exhaustion. They cry to the Sun God for help, and the Sun God sends Enkidu, who will eventually meet Gilgamesh. Enkidu lives among the animals to learn kindness and falls in love with Shamhat, a singer from the temple, following her back to Uruk. There Enkidu fights Gilgamesh to save the people of Uruk. Enkidu spares Gilgamesh's life. From Enkidu, Gilgamesh learns what it means to be human.

In the second book of Zeman's trilogy, *The Revenge of Ishtar* (1998c), the goddess Ishtar become angry because Gilgamesh and Enkidu slay monsters that threaten the city of Uruk. While striving to kill Humbaba, one of the monsters, Gilgamesh rejects the advances of the goddess Ishtar. In revenge, she causes Enkidu's death. Gilgamesh vows that he will destroy death, the last monster. Gilgamesh mourns the death of his friend in *The Last Quest of Gilgamesh* (1998b), the third book in this award-winning trilogy. However, the journey to immortality is dangerous. Gilgamesh must fight serpents and lions. He travels through cold caves, across burning deserts, and over the fatal waters of the Sea of Death. Finally, he arrives at the palace of Utnapishtim, the only human who knows the secret of immortality. He gives Gilgamesh a test and wants him to stay away for six days and seven nights, but Gilgamesh fails. Ishtar reappears and eats the flower of eternal youth, Gilgamesh's last hope. Finally, Enkidu comes from the underworld to show Gilgamesh his true immortality: The king will be remembered for his good deeds, his courage, and his love for his people. Through all three books, Zeman tells this complex epic simply, and her illustrations reflect the flavor of ancient Mesopotamia.

Legends as Inspiration for Children's Books

Legends tell the history of places, objects, and famous people (for more on legends, see chapter 5). If we think back to Disney's film *Aladdin*, we remember seeing Aladdin traveling on a magic carpet. Such carpet rides are actually a famous part of Middle Eastern folklore. Tomie dePaola retells *The Legend of the Persian Carpet* (1993) for children ages 5–8. In the book, King Mamluk has a prize diamond that fills his palace with the light and color of a "million rainbows." When a stranger steals the jewel and it is shattered, the king is in despair. Accustomed to living in a beautiful light-filled room, he takes to simply staring at the fragments and forgets about his subjects. A young apprentice weaver organizes the other apprentices to weave a spectacular carpet with vibrant colors and intricate patterns to interest the king and get him back on his throne.

An Arab legend demonstrates both culture contact and the origin of paper. In *The Cloudmakers* by James Rumford (1996), a story for readers ages 6–9 years, a Chinese grandfather and his grandson are captured by the great sultan of Samarkand in a battle that the Chinese lose to the Arabs. Young Wu and his grandfather bargain for their freedom. It is agreed that if the old man can "make clouds," they will be set free. The Sultan gives them seven days to produce this miracle. Using wood ash and hot water, they pound their wet hemp shoes into fiber. Next, they dry the solution on a frame made from the grandfather's cane and a worn sack. When they show the Sultan the dry piece of paper and it drifts through the air, the boy declares it a cloud. The Sultan recognizes that it is paper and is eager to learn the secret of papermaking for his own subjects. The legend demonstrates how knowledge spreads throughout the world.

A Sufi legend about names recounts the story of a boy whose parents are told not to name him when he is born. Idries Shah tells his tale in *The Boy Without a Name* (2000a), for children ages 4–8 years. Because of a wise man's visit on the day of his birth, the boy grows up without a name. He asks his friend Anwar for a name, but Anwar has only one name and cannot give it away, so together they go to see the wise man. The wise man opens a magic box full of names. One name, "Husni," creeps into the boy's ears. Anwar gets a gift, too: The wise man opens a box full of dreams, and the dreams enter both boys' ears to give them sweet dreams. The book is based on the birth story of a great Islamic mystic, but its themes are more universal ones of peace and happiness.

Fables Retold in Children's Books

A fable is generally an animal story with a moral lesson. (Fables are further discussed in chapter 3.) Famous fables in Asia come from previous lives of the Buddha and are called *jatakas*. Some jatakas are found in India. Paul Galdone captures *The Monkey and the Crocodile: A Jataka Tale From India* (1987) in a picture book for children ages 4–8 years. In this fable, Buddha appears as a clever monkey who twice defeats the attempts of a crocodile to capture him. *The Brave Little Parrot* by Susan Gaber (1998) with illustrations by Rafe Martin (for children 4–8 years) retells another jataka. This time a brave little gray parrot works against a forest fire. The parrot asks every animal to help put out the fire. They tell her it is hopeless and to save herself. Her valiant efforts come to the attention of a god disguised as an eagle. The eagle weeps compassionate tears, which fall in torrents and save the forest and the animals. The tears also change the parrot's feathers into flaming colors as a remembrance of the event.

Famous Comics and Tricksters

Perhaps the most famous foolish man in the Middle East is Mullah Nasrudin. His stories actually appear in oral traditions from the Middle East to Greece, Russia, France, and even China. Many nations claim Nasrudin, but no one really knows his origin.

According to one legend from the 13th century, he was snatched as a school-boy from the clutches of the "Old Villain," who represents the unrefined thought that traps human beings. Mullah is supposed to show all of us how to escape such think-

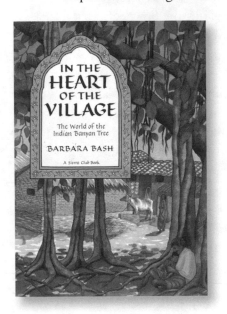

Book cover from *In the Heart of the Village* by Barbara Bash. Copyright © 1996. Published by Sierra Club Books.

ing. He was chosen because he could make people laugh and because humor helps even rigid thinkers loosen up. For many centuries, his tales have been studied in Sufi circles for hidden wisdom. They are used as teaching exercises in which familiar states of mind might be recognized.

The key to their philosophical significance appears in Idries Shah's book *The Sufis* (1964), which also presents a complete system of mystical training based on the tales. For example, in *The Pleasantries of the Incredible Mulla Nasrudin* by Idries Shah (1993), Mulla tells a group of followers who have approached him to ask for the Value of Truth that if they want the truth they must pay for it. When they ask him why anyone would have to pay for something like the Truth, he tells them that the scarcity of a thing determines its value.

In an educational yet humorous collection, Barbara Walker presents *Watermelons, Walnuts and the Wisdom of Allah: And Other Tales of the Hoca* (1991), 18 standard tales feature Nasreddin Hodja as a Turkish teacher. *Nasreddin Hodja*, a light collection for children ages 4–8 by Meriam Sinclair (1997), offers 19 humorous tales. Here, readers can find out why Hodja rides his horse backward and wants to be buried upside down.

"Toontoony Pie" tells the story of a shrewd bird named Toontoony. He moves some of the king's gold to his nest. When the king finds it and takes it back, Toontoony shames and angers the king. The king then has him trapped. One of the king's daughters saves Toontoony before he is made into a pie. She makes a pie out of frogs, which the king eats thinking that it is the bird, and Toontoony flies away. This tale and 21 more collected from the Punjab and Bengal appear in the collection *Pakistani Folk Tales: Toontoony Pie and Other Stories* (Siddiqui & Lerch, 1998) for children ages 9–12.

Also from the subcontinent is the single tale *The Gifts of the Wali Dad: A Tale of India and Pakistan* (Shepard, 1995b) for children ages 4–8. A simple grass cutter named Wali Dad gives a bracelet to the Queen of Khaistan, who gives him a gift that he sends to the King of Nekabad, who gives him a gift that he sends to the Queen. Wondering why gifts from Wali Dad keep arriving, the two rulers are tricked into meeting in a humorous conclusion.

Classroom Applications for Folk Tales, Epics, Legends, Fables, and Stories About Comics and Tricksters

The folk literature of the Middle East and Indian subcontinent offers exciting contexts for uses in classrooms. Dioramas may be constructed of the marketplaces, village squares, and palaces as the traditional places where most people heard these stories when they were being passed down orally. Bingo games and crossword puzzles can use exotic words such as *sultan*, *genie*, *djinn*, *caliph*, and *raja* as well as the names of literary forms such as epics, legends, jatakas, and fables. Research can help students locate present-day countries' names for Mesopotamia, Persia, Sumeria, and Arabia. Students can map the entire Silk Road from the Middle East to China. Using suggestions from authors such as Barchers (2000), Blau (1997), and Sierra (1996), folk tales can become Readers Theatre and full plays. Because epics are told in couplets or quatrains, students may try such literary forms to write an epic about an event in their school. And, of course, students also can retell stories and compose their own (Sawyer, 1998).

Folk literature has inspired many contemporary children's authors. Susan Fletcher in the chapter book *Shadow Spinner* (1999) takes the story of Sheherezade, and along with some advice in "Lessons for Life and Storytelling" at the beginning of each chapter, imagines what might have happened if Sheherezade had run out of stories with number 888. Here Sheherezade befriends a young girl named Marjan, a storyteller herself, who sneaks out of the palace to the marketplace to find more stories for Sheherezade and especially to find the ending of a story the sultan particularly loves. Although Fletcher provides one explanation as to how Sheherezade learned her 1,001 stories, students can write even more explanations.

Vrindavan, the famous and heartless city of widows in India, is the final setting for Gloria Whelan's chapter book *Homeless Bird* (2001). Koly is married and then widowed at age 13. She has no means to go home to her parents, who arranged what they thought would be a prosperous marriage for her. Her mother-in-law, who uses Koly's dowry to try to save her tubercular son and who then tricks Koly out of her widow's pension, takes Koly to Vrindavan and leaves her destitute on the street. Koly's excellent ability to embroider, a folk craft among women, saves her life and gives her a creative outlet to navigate her survival. Her story is full of alternatives for students to consider: What if Koly's parents had resisted pressure to marry her off at puberty? Have students imagine another life for her. What if her father-in-law, who teaches Koly to read, had lived? Have students find a way Koly could become a scholar. From Whelan's story, students can imagine and describe other roads not taken.

Picture books also provide classroom applications not only for writing but for curricular areas as well. Demi uses an exotic and beautiful context in India to instruct in *One Grain of Rice: A Mathematical Folktale* (1997). Rani, a clever village girl, performs a good deed and the local raja offers her a reward. She asks for one grain of rice, to be doubled each day for 30 days. At the end of the month, she has outwitted the raja and obtained enough food to feed the starving people of her village. The story also appears in an ancient Indian setting in David Birch's *The King's Chessboard* (1993) and in China in Helena Pittman's *A Grain of Rice* (1996).

Using Other Books in the Classroom

The folk literature of the world is certainly wonderful to hear and read, but it is also important to acquaint students with books that provide information about traditional areas of life in contemporary countries. In recent years, holiday and festival books, although not folk literature, have appeared as books of customs that tell us more about the lives of the people who live in or come from the Middle East or the Indian subcontinent. For example, Divali is the most celebrated Hindu festival, held during the fall new moon. Rashna Gilmore, in *Lights for Gita* (2000), written for children ages 4–8, tells the story of an immigrant child from India who celebrates Divali for the first time in her new home in Canada. Gita invites friends from school to celebrate Divali with her family, but an ice storm cuts off the electricity. Gita experiences anticipation, disappointment, and finally joy in learning that hope fills the darkness with light no matter where she celebrates the holiday.

Meenal Pandya describes the preparation and celebration involved in this five-day holiday in *Here Comes Diwali: The Festival of the Lights* (2000). An activity section for readers ages 4–8 includes recipes, crafts, a glossary, and a word search. Mary Matthews describes the major Muslim holiday in *Magid Fasts for Ramadan* (2000). Magid is 8 years old and wants to fast, though his parents tell him he is too young. He feeds his lunch to geese and pours his lemonade away until his sister sees him and tells his parents. His parents and grandparents recognize his strong will and allow him to fast for half of each day. The book is set in contemporary Egypt and explains the holiday to non–Muslims. It includes a brief introduction to Islam and a glossary.

For older readers, Diane Hoyt-Goldsmith presents *Celebrating Ramadan* (2001). In the book, Ibraheem, a fourth grader living in New Jersey, celebrates the holy month of Ramadan. The book begins with an introduction to Islam as faith and practice, with pictures of Ibraheem in the various positions for prayer. It then explains the five pillars of Islam in pictures and text, noting that Ramadan is one of the five pillars. During this month, God revealed the Koran to Mohammed, and Muslims celebrate with a month-long fast. Kerena Marchant, author of *Id-Ul-Fitr (Festivals)* (1998), includes full-color photos in her book of how Muslims celebrate Id, the celebration after Ramadan, all over the world.

Some popular folk customs in many Middle Eastern countries involve women who attend weddings. For example, female guests or members of a wedding party have their hands painted with traditional designs using henna. In the book *Nadia's Hands* (English, 1999), Nadia, a Pakistani-American girl, is flower girl in her Auntie Laila's traditional wedding. Nadia is thrilled until she sees the henna paste and worries that because the designs do not wash off, her classmates in school on Monday will see them and will not understand. Karen English captures Nadia's ambivalence about her important participation in the wedding and about her reluctance to be different at school. This simple picture book presents the dilemma of an immigrant child in the United States and her feelings about being caught between two cultures. It reminds us that no matter how alien a culture may seem to us, that culture's child may be in our classroom. We can only learn by seeing the world from his or her point of view.

Conclusion

This chapter began by offering that the folk literature of this region can help us not only understand human nature but also the countries that have nurtured such literature. For the Middle East and Indian subcontinent, these are clearly troubled times. Factions fight over religion, ethnicity, and politics. Families immigrate to other countries and children may not know the folk literature and traditions of their native countries. Children in the countries to which they immigrate may not have knowledge of any aspect of life in such countries. While the literature of any region helps us develop the awareness that aids understanding, it also reminds us of our common humanity and humaneness. Perhaps no other region so desperately needs such awareness.

REFERENCES

Barchers, S.I. (2000). *Multicultural folktales: Readers Theatre for elementary students*. Englewood, CO: Teacher Ideas Press.

Blau, L. (1997). *Favorite folktales and fabulous fables: Multicultural plays with extended activities*. New York: One From the Heart.

Bueler, L.E. (2001). *The tested woman plot: Women's choices, men's judgments, and the shaping of stories*. Columbus, OH: Ohio State University Press.

Dundes, A. (1965). *The study of folklore*. Englewood Cliffs, NJ: Prentice-Hall.

Honko, L. (2000). *Textualization of oral epics*. Hawthorne, NY: Walter De Gruyter.

Lindahl, C. (2002). *Epic of Gilgamesh*. *World Book Online Edition*. Retrieved April 16, 2002, from http://www.aolsvc.worldbook.aol.com/wbol/wbPage/na/ar/co/224390

Narayan, K. (1989). *Storytellers, saints, and scoundrels: Folk narrative in Hindu religious teaching*. Philadelphia: University of Pennsylvania Press.

Preston, E.Y. (1995). *Folklore, literature, and cultural theory: Collected essays*. New York: Garland.

Propp, V. (1985). *Theory and history of folklore*. Minneapolis, MN: University of Minnesota Press.

Sawyer, R. (1998). *The way of the storyteller*. New York: Penguin.

Sierra, J. (1996). *Multicultural folktales for the feltboard and reader's theater*. Phoenix, AZ: Oryx.

Thompson, S. (1967). *The folktale*. New York: Holt, Rinehart and Winston.

White, C.S.J. (2002a). Mahabharata. *World Book Online*. Retrieved April 15, 2002, from http://www.aolsvc.worldbook.aol.com/wbol/wbPage/na/ar/co/338780

White, C.S.J. (2002b). Ramayana. *World Book Online*. Retrieved April 15, 2002, from http://www.aolsvc.worldbook.aol.com/wbol/wbPage/na/ar/co/458860

CHILDREN'S BOOKS CITED

Alderson, B. (1995). *The Arabian nights, or, tales told by Sheherezade during a thousand nights and one night* (M. Foreman, Illus.). New York: Morrow.

Bash, B. (1996). *In the heart of the village: The world of the Indian banyan tree*. San Francisco: Sierra Club Books.

Birch, D. (1993). *The king's chessboard* (D. Grebu, Illus.). New York: Scott Foresman.

Chaudhury, P.C.R. (1995). *Folk tales of Bangladesh*. Columbia, MO: South Asia.

Claire, E. (1994). *The little brown jay: A tale from India* (M. Katin, Illus.). New York: Mondo.

Dawood, N.J. (1997). *Aladdin and other tales from the Arabian nights*. New York: Puffin.

Demi. (1997). *One grain of rice: A mathematical folktale*. New York: Scholastic.

dePaola, T. (1993). *The legend of the Persian carpet*. New York: Putnam.

English, K. (1999). *Nadia's hands* (J. Weiner, Illus.). Honesdale, PA: Boyds Mills Press.

Fletcher, S. (1999). *Shadow spinner*. New York: Aladdin.

Gaber, S. (1998). *The brave little parrot* (R. Martin, Illus.). New York: Putnam.

Galdone, P. (1987). *The monkey and the crocodile: A Jataka tale from India*. Boston: Houghton Mifflin.

Gilchrist, C. (1999). *Stories from the Silk Road* (N. Mistry, Illus.). Cambridge, MA: Barefoot Books.

Gilmore, R. (2000). *Lights for Gita* (A. Priestley, Illus.). New York: Tilbury House.

Griesser, J. (1996). *Our most dear friend: Bhagavad-Gita for children*. New York: Torchlight.

Hoyt-Goldsmith, D. (2001). *Celebrating Ramadan* (L. Migdale, Photog.). New York: Holiday House.

Jendresen, E., & Greene, J.M. (1998). *Hanuman: Based on Valmiki's Ramayana* (L. Ming, Illus.). Berkeley, CA: Tricycle.

Kimmel, E.A. (1996). *The tale of Ali Baba and the forty thieves: A story from the Arabian nights* (W. Hillenbrand, Illus.). New York: Holiday House.

Krishnaswami, U. (1999). *Shower of gold: Girls and women in the stories of India* (M. Selven, Illus.). North Haven, CT: Linnet.

Lewin, T. (1998). *The storytellers*. New York: Lothrop, Lee & Shepard.

Marchant, K. (1998). *Id-ul-fitr (festivals)*. New York: Millbrook.

Matthews, M. (2000). *Magid fasts for Ramadan* (E.B. Lewis, Illus.). Boston: Houghton Mifflin.

Pandya, M. (2000). *Here comes Diwali: The festival of lights* (A. Mehta, Illus.). New York: Meera.

Pittman, H.C. (1996). *A grain of rice*. New York: Skylark.

Rumford, J. (1996). *The cloudmakers*. New York: Houghton Mifflin.

Shah, I. (1964). *The Sufis*. Garden City, NY: Doubleday.

Shah, I. (1993). *The pleasantries of the incredible Mulla Nasrudin*. New York: Penguin Arkana.

Shah, I. (1998). *The magic horse* (J. Freeman, Illus.). New York: Hoopoe.

Shah, I. (2000a). *The boy without a name* (M. Caron, Illus.). New York: Hoopoe.

Shah, I. (2000b). *The silly chicken* (J. Jackson, Illus.). New York: Hoopoe.

Shepard, A. (1992). *Savitri: A tale of ancient India* (V. Rosenberry, Illus.). New York: Albert Whitman.

Shepard, A. (1995a). *The enchanted storks: A tale of the Middle East* (A. Dianov, Illus.). New York: Clarion.

Shepard, A. (1995b). *The gifts of the Wali Dad: A tale of India and Pakistan* (D. San Souci, Illus.). New York: Atheneum.

Shepard, A. (1999). *Forty fortunes: A tale of Iran* (A. Dianov, Illus.). New York: Clarion.

Siddiqui, A., & Lerch, M. (1998). *Pakistani folk tales: Toontoony pie and other stories* (J. Fairservis, Illus.). New York: Hippocrene.

Sinclair, M. (1997). *Nasreddin Hodja*. New York: Selt.

Tarnowska, W. (2000). *The seven wise princesses: A medieval Persian epic*. Cambridge, MA: Barefoot Books.

Walker, B. (1991). *Watermelons, walnuts, and the wisdom of Allah: And other tales of the Hoca* (H. Berson, Illus.). Lubbock, TX: Texas Tech University Press.

Walker, B. (1998). *A treasury of Turkish folktales*. North Haven, CT: Linnet.

Whelan, G. (2001). *Homeless bird*. New York: Harper Trophy.

Yeoman, J. (1997). *The seven voyages of Sinbad the sailor* (Q. Blake, Illus.). New York: Margaret K. McElderry.

Zeman, L. (1998a). *Gilgamesh the king*. Toronto: Tundra.

Zeman, L. (1998b). *The last quest of Gilgamesh*. Toronto: Tundra.

Zeman, L. (1998c). *The revenge of Ishtar*. Toronto: Tundra.

CHAPTER 13

Tribal Stories From Native America

Debbie A. Reese

*N*ative Americans. American Indians. Indians. All these terms refer broadly to the indigenous people of the Americas. Specifically, they include well-known tribal nations such as the Navajos and Cherokees, and less familiar ones such as the Tohono O'Odhams of Arizona and the Passamaquoddys of Maine. Native Americans pass on their stories and songs through the oral tradition. Over time, these stories and songs were recorded on tape and in print form, and today many are available in picture books for children. In their efforts to provide students with a broad picture of the diversity of the United States, teachers use Native American folk tales not only as entertainment during storytime but also as instructional material in units about Native Americans.

It is in the genre of traditional literature that the bulk of stories about Native Americans are found. Hirschfelder (1993) has pointed out that the 1980s and early 1990s experienced an "outpouring of retellings of Native American stories" (p. 415). The publishing of Native traditional stories was one way in which publishing houses could meet the demands for literature about people of color.

This chapter provides a sampling of Native American folk literature and some ideas for using it in the classroom. However, my emphasis is on examining problems in folk literature about Native Americans. I will use a few popular folk tales to illuminate these problems and discuss why the problems developed. In this discussion, I will issue a caution about this body of literature and a call for change in the literature so that all children will eventually have a better understanding of who Native Americans are.

Problems in Native American Literature

At first glance, it may seem that there is a plethora of Native American folk tales from which teachers can choose. But books chosen from that plethora should be selected carefully. The literary elements (plot, setting, etc.) by which we typically evaluate a story must be combined with the knowledge that folk tales are not simple entertainment. By definition, traditional stories are the means by which a culture's view of the world is passed from one generation to the next. Given that the publishing industry is primarily composed of Euro-Americans who have their own culturally specific worldview, it is easy to see how problems with bias, outside authorship, and adaptation and authenticity arise with the retelling of Native American stories.

Bias in Native American Literature

In the United States, there is a reverence for Native American Indians. Largely due to stereotypical images in literature and popular culture, Americans believe Native Americans had some noble and admirable attributes that should be emulated in everyone's life. The careful reader will note that the verb used in the previous sentence is *had* rather than *have*. That verb choice is deliberate, for along with that admiration is an erroneous belief that Native Americans no longer exist today. They are thought of as noble chiefs, warriors, and princesses whose way of life ended. That way of life included courage in the face of adversity and a reverence for the Earth and its many resources. These are wonderful attributes, and there is much to be gained by emulating them. However, Native Americans are still with us. They live modern lifestyles that reflect modern America but also include traditions and stories that have been protected and passed down from one generation to the next. Throughout the 20th century, Native peoples became increasingly politically active and sought higher education that would allow them to work for their people in the reclamation of land, human remains, artifacts, and also story. While Native American culture presents a richness from which teachers can draw, it is important to listen to Native people who are asking that they be considered not as objects of the past but as people of the present day who have concerns about the way their culture and stories are used and presented in literature.

There are more than 500 different Native American tribal nations in the United States; each has its own creation story, homeland, form of government, religion, material culture (houses, clothing, foods), and history of interaction between the Native tribe and the Europeans with whom they first came into contact. Although there are similarities across tribes, there are also significant differences. Equally important is the basic fact that there are differences between tribes and Euro-Americans and the way they see and value the world. Within any given culture, stories are told and retold. They become familiar. Because a culture's values and ideology undergird the story, people within that culture recognize and enjoy the stories and the lessons they convey. The stories resonate with them, and they judge other stories according to that culture's standard of what constitutes a good story. Without knowing, people within that cultural group have developed a bias, or perspective, from which they view and interpret the world (Wiget, 1994). This explains the problems that can occur when an outsider attempts to retell a story from another culture.

The problem of bias is not new. It has a long history. For example, when Europeans first came to the New World and saw relatively unclothed Native people, they drew from their own cultural experience and judged the Native people's attire as indicative of a primitive and promiscuous people (Medicine, 1996). However, the coastal areas where first contacts occurred are hot and humid places. Wearing less clothing made sense; it had little to do with expression of sexuality. Moreover, highly evolved systems of government among Native peoples indicate they were far from primitive.

Essentially, the Europeans were trying to render the unfamiliar familiar. They did this by interpreting it from their worldview. In the context of folk tales, this meant that Euro-Americans who collected the stories heard and interpreted them from their own worldview. In the process of recording the stories, parts of the stories were changed so they made sense to a Euro-American audience. Anthropologists and others who collected oral stories in the 1800s and early 1900s often misinterpreted the stories they collected, filtering information through their own cultural lens rather than that of the tribal perspective from which the story emanated. Henry Rowe Schoolcraft is often cited as a major figure in the collection of Ojibwa stories, but scholar Stith Thompson noted that his work is "marred by the manner in which he has reshaped the stories to suit his own literary taste. Several of his tales, indeed, are distorted beyond recognition" (Thompson, 1929, p. xv).

Teachers and librarians may not be cognizant of the problem of bias to the degree they should be; they may not be aware that stories they share with students can sometimes reflect an author's (or folklorist's, or anthropologist's) own knowledge and world view, rather than the knowledge and worldview of the people who originally told the story.

Authors Writing Outside Their Culture

Many books about Native Americans obscure the diversity within Native American culture. For example, stories subtitled "A Native American Folktale" such as *Soft Child: How Rattlesnake Got Its Fangs: A Native American Folktale* (Hayes, 1993) are problematic because there is no "Native American" tribe. A factor contributing to problems such as this is that most of the Native American folk tales published today for children are written by authors such as Joe Hayes who are not themselves Native American. Native Americans consider tribe as a significant piece of information and will generally specify their own tribal nation in their writing and personal interactions. Typically, Native American authors specify the tribe from which a story originates. This can be seen later in this chapter, in the recommended books section. However, most of the folk tales available today are not written by Native American authors.

This can be seen by examining the recommended lists of folk tales in many children's literature textbooks. For example, Sutherland's *Children and Books* (1997) includes 30 Native American folk tales, only 1 of which was written by a Native author. Similarly, *Children's Literature in the Elementary School* (Huck, Hepler, Hickman, & Kiefer, 2001) lists 58 Native American stories, only 8 of which are by Native authors. It is clear that Native American voices are not in the majority in telling Native American stories. This means that most of the books are written by authors who are writing outside of their own cultural experience, and in many cases the result is a book that conveys erroneous information about Native Americans.

Adaptation and Authenticity

In their retellings, some authors intentionally adapt or change the original stories to make them more accessible to a Euro-American audience. When researchers talk about whether or not a story accurately reflects the culture it is about, they refer to this as an issue of authenticity.

In *Children's Literature in the Elementary School*, Huck et al. (2001) note that questions often arise about which version of a folk tale is authentic. They go on to say,

> From a folklorist's point of view, a tale is recreated every time it is told and therefore every retelling is correct in its own way. A great deal of variation is also acceptable in print versions, where literary style carries the same uniqueness as the teller's voice. Authors and illustrators may also add original twists, customize their stories for a chosen audience, or adapt a familiar tale to an unfamiliar setting, as oral storytellers do. There might be a problem, however, when a print version suggests by its title, or lack of an author's note, that it represents a tale derived directly from a previously printed source. (p. 233)

By way of example, Huck et al. (2001) conclude by stating that readers of a story that has been identified as being recorded and published by the Grimm brothers have a right to find out if the tale they are reading remains true to the original, without major additions, omissions, or distortions.

The Huck et al. (2001) statement uses Grimm's retellings as an example, but it applies to any story. Authors can use the author's note to describe the ways their retelling differs from the original. In 1993, Betsy Hearne, the noted children's book author and folklore scholar, published an article titled "Cite the Source: Reducing Cultural Chaos in Picture Books." In it, Hearne discusses problems that can occur when authors retell stories. She developed a rubric consisting of five categories teachers can use when evaluating source notes. First is the "model source note," which cites specific source(s), provides a description of the cultural context in which a story was originally told, and provides a description of any changes the author made. Second is the "well-made source note," which cites the specific source(s) in a highly visible manner and may include details about the context and details of the story's original telling. The third category, "fine-print source notes," are those that cite specific source(s) in small print, typically on the page facing the title page. Hearne's last two categories describe source notes that are essentially useless. The fourth category is the "background-as-source note" that gives general information about the culture from which the story originates, and which may include details about the story but does not cite a specific printed source. The final category, the "nonexistent source note," provides no information on sources at all other than a subtitle, such as "A Korean Tale."

In a more recent article titled "Swapping Tales and Stealing Stories," Hearne (1999) applies the rubric to the source notes for two Native American folk tales: *The Windigo's Return: A North Woods Story* (Woods, 1996) and *The Legend of the Windigo: A Tale From Native North America* (Ross, 1996). In her analysis, Hearne finds Ross's source note more useful to readers who want to know more about the windigo and the process Ross went through in selecting and changing the story she retells in her book. Knowledge of Hearne's rubric can help teachers and librarians select folk tales.

Selecting Native American Folk Tales

Teachers use literature in the classroom for a variety of reasons, but given the schools' educational mission, a prime reason teachers use story is to educate (Huck et al., 2001). In the context of multicultural literature, Sims Bishop (1997) has identified five functions of a story:

1. to provide knowledge or information
2. to expand how students view the world by offering varying perspectives
3. to promote or develop an appreciation for diversity
4. to give rise to critical inquiry
5. to illuminate human experience

Given this educational use, teachers and librarians can do the following: read the critical literature (articles and books) written by scholars and critics who write about Native American literature, adopt a critical stance when selecting and using multicultural literature, and employ a strategy in which they become an expert on a single tribe and apply that expertise to their selection process.

Read the Critical Literature

A number of excellent print and online resources about Native American literature have been published since the early 1990s. Reading these resources will help teachers develop the critical stance and expertise necessary to make informed decisions about folk tales they are considering for their classrooms. The end of this chapter includes a list of resources, a few of which are described here. Additional resources are available at www.scils.rutgers.edu/~kvander/ChildrenLit/native.html.

One of the best resources is *Through Indian Eyes: The Native Experience in Books for Children* (Slapin & Seale, 1998). It contains essays written by Native Americans who describe the struggles they experienced in school as they endured reading biased literature, participating in school pageants and plays, and taking part in arts and crafts activities. Approximately half the book is dedicated to critical reviews of children's books about Native Americans. In addition to coediting the book, Slapin maintains Oyate, a Native organization that works to see that the lives and histories of Native peoples are portrayed honestly. The Oyate website (www.oyate.org) includes critical book reviews and distributes children's, young adult, and teacher books and materials about Native Americans. Slapin and Seale are completing a second book, *The Broken Flute*, that will contain critical reviews.

American Indian Stereotypes in the World of Children: A Reader and Bibliography (Hirschfelder, Molin, & Wakim, 1999) begins with chapters that critically examine a range of media, from textbooks and children's books to toys and movies. It concludes with an extensive bibliography of more than 250 articles and books on stereotyping, followed by several pages of items such as videos, newspapers, critical essays, catalogs, and websites teachers can use to develop better instructional materials about Native Americans.

The website for the American Indian Library Association contains an article written by Naomi Caldwell-Wood and Lisa Mitten titled "I Is Not for Indian: The Portrayal of Native Americans in Books for Young People" (www.nativeculture.com/lisamitten/aila.html). The article begins with an introduction to this body of literature and is a selected bibliography of recommended books and books to avoid. Mitten also was involved in a project at the Anthropology Outreach Office of the Smithsonian Museum. The project resulted in an extensive online bibliography in which annotated books are categorized according to geographical area. (See http://nmnhwww.si.edu/anthro/outreach/Indbibl/bibliogr.html.)

An excellent online resource is Paula Giese's "Native American Books." Giese maintained a website about Native American culture that included reviews of children's books. Upon her death in 1997, the site was moved to Karen Strom's website about Native Americans (www.kstrom.net/isk/books/all_idx.html). It has not been updated since Giese's death, but it contains nearly 100 reviews of folk tales.

Take a Critical Stance

The critical stance means questioning the accuracy and authenticity of the story under consideration. Some refer to this stance as "reading against the grain," which is a way to "examine the unexamined, question the unquestioned, and hold up to scrutiny the unspoken assertions the text is making about the way lives are lived in society" (Temple, Martinez, Yokota, & Naylor, 1998, p. 43). Some questions teachers can ask when considering a book for use in the classroom are as follows:

Who wrote the story? Is it someone from the tribal nation the story is about? This information is usually contained on the inside flap of the book jacket, or inside the book itself. If little, or ambiguous, information is included, teachers may want to do an Internet search to see what they can learn about the author. If the author is not from the tribe, is there any indication that he or she has some expertise on that tribe or has consulted with people of that tribe in the development of the story?

Does the book include a source note that specifies the source for the story? If it was taken from a book, does the author provide the title of the book and its author? If the author heard the story told orally, does he or she list details about where and when he or she heard the story, and whether or not he or she asked permission to retell it? Does the source note include details about how and why the author changed the original story?

Who reviewed or recommended the story? Is it someone who has specific expertise in the evaluation of literature by and about Native Americans? Mainstream literary review journals often lack reviewers with enough background knowledge to identify problematic books (see Atleo et al., 1999), but there are other journals and organizations whose reviewers have this expertise. See, for example, *Multicultural Review* and *CCBC Choices*, published by the Cooperative Children's Book Center (CCBC) located in Madison, Wisconsin.

Become an Expert

The expertise strategy involves identifying a single tribe on which to focus. It can be a tribe currently located near the school or one that was there prior to contact and removal that occurred as the United States was settled. Having selected a single tribe, the teacher then can read the works of critics and scholars who write about that tribe. To get started, teachers can begin by reading relevant information in two edited encyclopedias that are widely recognized for their accuracy: Mary Davis's *Native America in the Twentieth Century: An Encyclopedia* (1996) and Frederick Hoxie's *Encyclopedia of North American Indians* (1996). Each entry includes sources teachers can turn to for further reading. Equally useful are Duane Champagne's *Native America: Portrait of the Peoples* (1994b) and *Chronology of Native North American History* (1994a). Using these readings as a guide, a teacher can develop a unit about the selected tribe. The unit can begin with a read-aloud of a folk tale about the tribe, with discussion focusing on the literary merits of the story. Next, the teacher can begin the instructional unit. As the students gain mastery of the information, they can revisit the folk tale to compare how well it does or does not present the tribe.

To illustrate how this depth of knowledge can help teachers select and use Native American folk tales, I will focus on Pueblo Indians and on two folk tales about Pueblo Indians. First, some basic information about Pueblo Indians: There are currently 19 Pueblo Indian nations in New Mexico and 13 in Arizona among the Hopi Nation (their villages also are called pueblos). Each Pueblo is unique, but common to all are the adobe brick, multistoried buildings arranged around a plaza and a kiva (similar to a church). Some Pueblos have one kiva; others have two. The Pueblo people raise corn, beans, and squash and also hunt deer. Extended family, kinship systems, and a strong sense of supportive community characterize the social organization. In the early 1600s, Spanish colonization began. The Pueblo people fought to defend their land and way of life, but overwhelmed by a larger and better-equipped force, they endured years of torture. Their ceremonies and rituals were suppressed and they were forced into manual labor to support Spanish landowners. The Pueblo Revolt of 1680 drove out the Spanish. Reconquest occurred in 1695, but the Spanish allowed the Pueblo people to practice their religion. Those practices, which include traditional dance, song, and story, continue today. Among their stories are many that explain land formations and the significance of place to the Pueblo people. Although the Pueblos are careful to protect their ceremonies from being recorded and appropriated by outsiders, some have collaborated on projects through which their stories were recorded in print format. One example of this is a collection of stories told by storytellers at Zuni Pueblo. The collection is titled *The Zunis: Self-Portrayals* (Zuni People, 1972).

OLD FATHER STORY TELLER BY PABLITA VELARDE

Book cover from *Old Father Story Teller* by Pablita Velarde. Copyright © 1993. Used by permission of Clear Light Publishing, Santa Fe, New Mexico, www.clearlightbooks.com.

With this background knowledge, a teacher and his or her students can apply the knowledge to two popular children's folk tales about Pueblo Indians: Gerald McDermott's *Arrow to the Sun: A Pueblo Indian Tale* (1974) and Penny Pollock's *The Turkey Girl: A Zuni Cinderella Story* (1996). *Arrow to the Sun* won the Caldecott Medal in 1975. In the story, a young boy searches for his father, but before he can claim the Sun as his father, he must prove his worthiness by passing through the kiva of lions, the kiva of snakes, the kiva of bees, and the kiva of lightning. Analysis of the story reveals several problems. Of primary concern is McDermott's presenta tion of kivas. In Pueblo culture, kivas are places of ceremony and instruction, not places of trial. Because of their newly acquired knowledge about kivas, the children will be able to spot the error on their own or with guidance by the teacher. They also may wonder which Pueblo the story is from.

The Turkey Girl was published in 1996 and was favorably reviewed by major children's literature review journals such as *Kirkus*, *Horn Book*, and *Booklist*. In 1996, *The Turkey Girl* was listed among the Aesop Accolades by the American Folklore Society. Among the criteria for the award is that the book accurately reflect the culture and worldview of the people whose folklore is the focus of the book.

Most North Americans are familiar with the Cinderella story told by Perrault, the Brothers Grimm, or Walt Disney. The plot of the story across these versions is similar: The girl's mother dies; her father remarries and brings into the home two stepsisters; stepmom and stepsisters mistreat the girl; father is indifferent or absent; girl performs menial tasks, and works and lives in the ashes; girl is prevented from going to the ball; girl is aided by a magical helper; helper improves the girl's condition; helper issues interdiction; girl goes to the ball; girl meets a man she will marry; girl ignores interdiction and returns to former condition; the shoe-test is employed to locate the girl; girl is located and marries prince (Goldberg, 2000). There are many other versions of the Cinderella story. Huck et al. (2001) write that "the Cinderella story is found throughout the world, with nearly five hundred variants in Europe alone" (p. 230).

The Turkey Girl is a Native American variant of the Cinderella story. The differences between Pollock's version and the familiar Disney version are as follows: Instead of a stepmother and stepsisters treating the protagonist badly, the girl lives alone and it is an entire Pueblo Indian village that rejects and belittles her. Instead of a fairy godmother, it is a flock of turkeys who transform her clothing and warn her to return to them at a specified time. Like Cinderella, Turkey Girl loses track of time and returns late, and her clothes turn back to rags. Pollock's story ends there, while Disney's continues and ends with the girl getting the prince.

With their background reading about Pueblo culture, students may note some things in the Pollock retelling that are not in the version the Zuni people tell, which is in *The Zunis: Self Portrayals*. In the author's note, Pollock says that anthropologist Frank Hamilton Cushing's (1931/1986) collection of Zuni folk tales is the source for her retelling. A comparative analysis of these versions (Reese, in press) found several problems with Pollock's retelling. It mirrors Cushing's to a great extent, but Pollock inserts elements not found in the Cushing or Zuni versions that align it more closely with the Disney version. These inserted elements fundamentally alter the story and misrepresent Zuni culture and values. Pollock's style and tone present the Zuni people in a romantic, stereotypical manner that dovetails with popular culture rather than an accurate and realistic presentation of their lives and culture. Finally, Pollock's ending omits any reference to the land. Near Zuni is a spring with fossilized turkey tracks. The Cushing and Zuni versions of the story end by explaining that the turkeys flew away to a spring and left their tracks there. A major purpose of the story, as told by the Zuni people, is to explain how the tracks got there. It also indicates the significance of land and story within their culture. By omitting this, Pollock changes the story and its significance to the Pueblo people.

Recommended Selections

The most successful Native author writing for children today is Joseph Bruchac. Among his books are several picture book folk tales. *The First Strawberries: A Cherokee Story* (1993) is a pourquoi story about how strawberries came to be. Bruchac has written more than 20 picture book folk tales and collections. Teachers will readily find many of them in libraries and bookstores. Within Native American writers circles, Bruchac is well known for his mentoring of new authors. Among his coauthors is his son, James. Together they wrote *How Chipmunk Got His Stripes* (2001), which works particularly well with younger children because of its repetitive phrase, "The sun is going to rise, oooh! The sun is gong to rise, oooh!" Another coauthor is Gayle Ross, with whom Bruchac wrote *The Story of the Milky Way* (1995). In addition to his picture book folk tales, Bruchac coauthored with Michael Caduto several collections that include folk tales: *Keepers of the Earth: Native American Stories and Environmental Activities for Children* (1988), *Keepers of the Animals: Native American Stories and Wildlife Activities for Children* (1991), and *Keepers of Life: Discovering Plants Through Native American Stories and Earth Activities for Children* (1994).

Gayle Ross's picture book folk tales are exceptional for her source notes, but equally noteworthy is her storytelling style and Murv Jacobs's illustrations. Their books include *How Turtle's Back Was Cracked: A Traditional Cherokee Tale* (1995), *How Rabbit Tricked Otter and Other Cherokee Trickster Stories* (1994), and *The Legend of the Windigo: A Tale From Native North America* (1996).

Among Native folk tales for children are those that feature Coyote. The Native American trickster can be a raven, rabbit, or coyote, with coyote being most common. Coyote is always understood to be a human and can transform himself at will. Coyote can be male, female, or a hermaphrodite. Babcock and Cox (1996), noting that Coyote is most often depicted as a male, speculate this may be due to Euro-American bias of early anthropologists who collected Coyote tales.

There are two Hopi Coyote tales in which children provide the illustrations: *Coyote & the Winnowing Birds* (Sekaquaptewa, 1994) and *Coyote & Little Turtle* (Talashoema, 1994). Both are collaborative projects that involved the Institute for the Preservation of the Original Languages of the Americas, the Hopi Tribe Cultural

Preservation Office, the Hotevilla-Bacavi Community School, and the University of Arizona's Bureau of Applied Research in Anthropology. Both are stories of Coyote's greed and both include English and Hopi text.

Native American folk tales published by the National Museum of the American Indian include one about Coyote. *Coyote in Love With a Star* (De Montano, 1998), an adaptation of a Potawatomi tale, is set in the present day and explains how the reservoir in New York's Central Park came to be. In it, Coyote leaves the reservation and gets a job as a rodent control officer at the World Trade Center. Given the tragedy of September 11, 2001, some teachers may not feel comfortable using this story.

Given the difficulty in getting published by major publishing houses, many Native American authors turn to small presses. With small advertising budgets, these books depend on word-of-mouth for sales and can be hard to locate. Oyate (www.oyate.org) is the most reliable and comprehensive source for books published by small presses. Their catalog lists more than 50 books from small presses. One example is the Nanabosho (Ojibwe/Chippewa trickster) folk tales retold by Joseph McLellan. They are published by Pemmican, a small press in Canada. They include *The Birth of Nanabosho* (1989), *Nanabosho Dances* (1991), *Nanabosho: How the Turtle Got Its Shell* (1994), *Nanabosho, Soaring Eagle, and the Great Sturgeon* (1993), *Nanobosho Steals Fire* (1990), and *Nanabosho and the Woodpecker* (1995). Coauthored with Matrine

McLellan, his more recent books include *Nanabosho and the Cranberries* (1998), *Nanabosho and Kitchie Odjig* (1997), and *Nanabosho Grants a Wish* (2002). Because of the limited budget of some smaller presses, their books may not have slick production values (weight of paper, quality of binding, etc.), but the stories are excellent and deserve a place in the classroom.

During the 1930s when the U.S. Bureau of Indian Affairs was assimilating Native American children through boarding schools, a series of books were published for their use. Some were nonfiction descriptions of life, but some were retellings of traditional folk tales. Most of the books were not written by Native people, but in all books, the illustrations were done by Native artists. One of the better-known stories from this effort is *Field Mouse Goes to War/Tusan Homichi Tuwvota* (Kennard, 2000). It is the Hopi story of how a tiny field mouse saves the Mishongnovi people's chickens from a hawk. The illustrations are by Hopi artist Fred Kabotie, whose work is now highly sought after. The story is printed in English and Hopi.

Finally, teachers looking for a culturally authentic Pueblo Indian variant of the Cinderella story can turn to Pablita Velarde's *Old Father Storyteller* (1993). In the book, Velarde retells six stories told to her by her grandfather, including "Turkey Girl." Velarde, a world-renowned artist from Santa Clara Pueblo, illustrated the book herself.

Classroom Activities

Teachers will find the first chapter in *Lessons From Turtle Island: Native Curriculum in Early Childhood Classrooms* (Jones & Moomaw, 2002) helpful in determining whether or not an arts and crafts activity is appropriate. In elementary classrooms, many teachers use hands-on craft activities to supplement instruction. Popular activities are to make Indian headdresses using construction paper feathers and to make fringed vests with grocery paper bags. Students also may construct tipis with sticks and paper. I urge teachers to think carefully about these activities because they affirm stereotypical ideas that all Native peoples wore feathered headdresses or fringed buckskin or lived in tipis and hunted buffalo. Jones and Moomaw discuss the cultural insensitivity in other popular activities such as making a peace pipe, totem pole, and other Native American artifacts.

Instead of these activities, teachers can turn to the practice of companion books, in which a folk tale and a nonfiction photo essay are both used. An excellent series of photo essays is the We Are Still Here series published by Lerner. Each essay focuses on a specific tribe and a child of that tribe, and each book presents a wealth of information about the people of the tribe in a present-day context, showing the ways tradition and modernity interact. Some, such as *Children of Clay: A Family of Pueblo Potters* (Swentzell, 1992), include a traditional story. In *Children of Clay*, we learn how Pueblo people gather clay to make pottery and clay figures. A companion book could be *Old Father Storyteller* (Velarde, 1993). The art activity for this unit could be the creation of clay pots or figures.

Teachers in the Great Lakes area can focus on the Ojibwe (Chippewa) tribe. A unit on the Chippewa or Cree Indians can include the traditional story *The Legend of the Windigo* (Ross, 1996) and the photo essays *Fort Chipewyan Homecoming* (Mercredi, 1997) and *Shannon: An Ojibway Dancer* (King, 1993). Follow-up activities can include a beading activity (beading is a traditional craft of the Ojibway used on moccasins and clothing).

Virginia Stroud's book *Doesn't Fall Off His Horse* (1994) is a family story about how a great-grandfather got his name. The story is about the Kiowas and the Comanches. Companion nonfiction books include *The Kiowa Indians* (Dolan, 1993). As a follow-up writing activity, teachers can ask students to write a story from their own family history.

Concluding Thoughts

Teachers are a strong force. Because of teacher letters, Crayola, Inc., was prompted to change the name of the Indian Red crayon. If you want better books to use in your classroom, consider taking a moment to write to publishers, asking for books that include substantive author or source notes. Ask publishers to take risks and publish more books written by Native American authors and do not buy or recommend a book unless you are sure of its cultural accuracy.

REFERENCES

Atleo, M., Caldwell, N., Landis, B., Mendoza, J., Miranda, D., Reese, D., et al. (1999). Fiction posing as truth: A critical review of *My Heart Is on the Ground: The Story of Nannie Little Rose, a Sioux Girl. Rethinking Schools, 13*(4), 14–16.

Babcock, B., & Cox, J. (1996). The Native American trickster figure. In A. Wiget (Ed.), *Handbook of Native American literature* (pp. 99–104). New York: Garland.

Caldwell-Wood, N., & Mitten, L. (1991). *"I" is not for Indian: The portrayal of Native Americans in books for young people.* Available: http://www.nativeculture.com/lisamitten/ailabib.htm.

Champagne, D. (1994a) *Chronology of Native North American history.* Detroit, MI: Gale Research Inc.

Champagne, D. (1994b). *Native America: Portrait of the peoples.* Detroit, MI: Visible Ink Press.

Cushing, F.H. (1986). *Zuni folk tales.* Tucson, AZ: University of Arizona Press. (Originally published 1931)

Davis, M. (1996). *Native America in the twentieth century: An encyclopedia.* New York: Garland.

Goldberg, H. (2000). Cinderella. In J. Zipes (Ed.), *The Oxford companion to fairy tales* (pp. 95–97). Oxford, UK: Oxford University Press.

Hearne, B. (1993, July). Cite the source: Reducing cultural chaos in picture books (part 1). *School Library Journal, 39*(7), 22–27.

Hearne, B. (1999, Winter). Swapping tales and stealing stories. *Library Trends, 48*(1), 509–528.

Hirschfelder, A.B. (1993). Native American literature for children and young adults. *Library Trends, 41*(3), 414–436.

Hirschfelder, A.B., Molin, P.F., & Wakim, Y. (1999). *American Indian stereotypes in the world of children: A reader and bibliography.* Lanham, MD: Scarecrow Press.

Hoxie, F.E. (1996). *Encyclopedia of North American Indians.* Boston: Houghton Mifflin.

Huck, C.S., Hepler, S., Hickman, J., & Kiefer, B.Z. (2001). *Children's literature in the elementary school.* Boston: McGraw-Hill.

Jones, G., & Moomaw, S. (2002). *Lessons from Turtle Island: Native curriculum in early childhood classrooms.* St. Paul, MN: Redleaf Press.

Medicine, B. (1996). Women. In F. Hoxie (Ed.), *Encyclopedia of North American Indians* (pp. 685–689). Boston: Houghton Mifflin.

Reese, D. (in press). Traditional literature rewritten for an American audience: Romantic and exotic images. *American Indian Quarterly.*

Sims Bishop, R. (1997). Selecting literature for a multicultural curriculum. In V. Harris (Ed.), *Using multiethnic literature in the K–8 classroom* (pp. 1–19). Norwood, MA: Christopher-Gordon.

Slapin, B., & Seale, D. (1998). *Through Indian eyes: The Native experience in books for children.* Los Angeles: University of California, American Indian Studies Center.

Slapin, B., & Seale, D. (in press). *The broken flute.* Walnut Creek, CA: Alta Mira Press.

Sutherland, Z. (1997). *Children and books* (9th ed.). New York: Longman.

Temple, C.A., Martinez, M., Yokota, J., & Naylor, A. (1998). *Children's books in children's hands: An introduction to their literature.* Boston: Allyn & Bacon.

Thompson, S. (1929). *Tales of the North American Indians.* Cambridge, MA: Harvard University Press.

Wiget, A. (1994). Native American oral literature: A critical orientation. In A. Wiget (Ed.), *Handbook of Native American literature* (pp. 3–18). New York: Garland.

Zuni People. (1972). *The Zunis: Self-portrayals.* Santa Fe: University of New Mexico Press.

CHILDREN'S BOOKS CITED

Bruchac, J. (1993). *The first strawberries: A Cherokee story.* New York: Dial.

Bruchac, J., & Bruchac, J. (2001). *How chipmunk got his stripes* (J. Areugo & A. Dewey, Illus.). New York: Dial.

Bruchac, J., & Caduto, M. (1988). *Keepers of the earth: Native American stories and environmental activities for children.* Golden, CO: Fulcrum.

Bruchac, J., & Caduto, M. (1991). *Keepers of the animals: Native American stories and wildlife activities for children.* Golden, CO: Fulcrum.

Bruchac, J., & Caduto, M. (1995). *Keepers of life: Discovering plants through Native American stories and earth activities for children.* Golden, CO: Fulcrum.

Bruchac, J., & Ross, G. (1995). *The story of the Milky Way* (V.A. Stroud, Illus.). New York: Dial.

De Montano, M.K. (1998). *Coyote in love with a star.* New York: Abbeville Press.

Dolan, T. (1993). *The Kiowa Indians*. New York: Chelsea House.

Hayes, J. (1993). *Soft child: How Rattlesnake got its fangs* (K. Sather, Illus.). Tucson, AZ: Harbinger.

Kennard, E.A. (2000). *Field mouse goes to war/Tusan homichi tuwvota* (F. Kabotie, Illus.). Walnut, CA: Kiva.

King, S. (1993). *Shannon: An Ojibway dancer* (C. Whipple, Photog.). Minneapolis, MN: Lerner.

McDermott, G. (1974). *Arrow to the sun: A Pueblo Indian tale*. New York: Viking.

McLellan, J. (1989). *The birth of Nanabosho* (J. Kirby, Illus.). Winnipeg, Canada: Pemmican.

McLellan, J. (1990). *Nanobosho steals fire* (D. Monkman, Illus.).Winnipeg, Canada: Pemmican.

McLellan, J. (1991). *Nanabosho dances* (R. Brynjolson, Illus.). Winnipeg, Canada: Pemmican.

McLellan, J. (1993). *Nanabosho, Soaring Eagle, and the Great Sturgeon*. Winnipeg, Canada: Pemmican.

McLellan, J. (1994). *Nanabosho: How the turtle got its shell* (R. Brynjolson, Illus.). Winnipeg, Canada: Pemmican.

McLellan, J. (1995). *Nanabosho and the woodpecker* (R. Brynjolson, Illus.). Winnipeg, Canada: Pemmican.

McLellan, J., & McLellan, M. (1997). *Nanabosho and Kitchie Odjig* (L. Swampy, Illus.). Winnipeg, Canada: Pemmican.

McLellan, J., & McLellan, M. (1998). *Nanabosho and the cranberries* (L. Swampy, Illus.). Winnipeg, Canada: Pemmican.

McLellan, J., & McLellan, M. (2002). *Nanabosho grants a wish* (L. Swampy, Illus.). Winnipeg, Canada: Pemmican.

Mercredi, M. (1997). *Fort Chipewyan homecoming: A journey to Native Canada*. (D. McNally, Photog.) Minneapolis, MN: Lerner.

Pollock, P. (1996). *The turkey girl: A Zuni Cinderella story* (E. Young, Illus.). Boston: Little, Brown.

Ross, G. (1994). *How Rabbit tricked Otter and other Cherokee trickster stories* (M. Jacob, Illus.). New York: HarperCollins.

Ross, G. (1995). *How Turtle's back was cracked: A traditional Cherokee tale* (M. Jacob, Illus.). New York: Dial.

Ross, G. (1996). *The legend of the Windigo: A tale from Native North America* (M. Jacob, Illus.). New York: Dial.

Sekaquaptewa, E. (1994). *Coyote & the winnowing birds: A traditional Hopi tale/Iisaw niqw tsaayantotaqam tsiróot* (Hopi Children, Illus.). Santa Fe, NM: Clear Light.

Stroud, V. (1994). *Doesn't Fall Off His Horse.* New York: Dial.

Swentzell, R. (1992). *Children of clay: A family of Pueblo potters*. Minneapolis, MN: Lerner.

Talashoema, H. (1994). *Coyote and Little Turtle* (E. Sekaquaptewa & B. Pepper, Trans. Hopi Children, Illus.). Santa Fe, NM: Clear Light.

Velarde, P. (1993). *Old father storyteller*. Santa Fe, NM: Clear Light.

Woods, D. (1996). *The windigo's return: A north woods story.* (G. Couch, Illus.). New York: Simon & Schuster.

RECOMMENDED READING TO LEARN MORE ABOUT NATIVE AMERICANS

Ackerman, N., & Roalf, P. (1995). *Strong hearts: Native American visions and voices*. New York: Aperture.

Berkhofer, R.E. (1978). *The white man's Indian*. New York: Vintage.

Bigelow, B., & Peterson, B. (Eds.). (1998). *Rethinking Columbus: The next 500 years*. Milwaukee, WI: Rethinking Schools.

Cubbins, E.M. (1999). *Techniques for evaluating American Indian web sites*. Retrieved June 19, 2003, from http://www.u.arizona.edu/~ecubbins/webcrit.html

Deloria, P. (1998). *Playing Indian*. New Haven: Yale University Press.

Reese, D.A., & Caldwell-Wood, N. (1997). Native Americans in children's literature. In V.J. Harris (Ed.), *Using multiethnic literature in the K–8 classroom* (pp. 155–192). Norwood, MA: Christopher-Gordon.

Seale, D., Slapin, B., & Silverman, C. (1998). *Thanksgiving: A Native perspective*. Berkeley, CA: Oyate.

Sneve, V.D.H. (1996). *The Cherokees* (R. Himler, Illus.). New York: Holiday House.

Sneve, V.D.H. (1997). *The Apaches* (R. Himler, Illus.). New York: Holiday House.

Stedman, R.W. (1982). *Shadows of the Indian*. Norman, OK: University of Oklahoma Press.

Thompson, M.K. (2001). A sea of good intentions: Native Americans in books for children. *The Lion and the Unicorn, 25*(3), 353–374.

Womack, C. (1999) *Red on red: Native American literary separatism*. Minneapolis, MN: University of Minnesota Press.

Celebrating Folk Literature in the Classroom

CHAPTER 14

Cinderella and Her Sisters: Variants and Versions

Ann Sloan and Sylvia M. Vardell

Cinderella is such a part of Americans' literary heritage that phrases such as "if the shoe fits," "Cinderella complex," and "until the stroke of midnight" are part of their everyday vernacular. What is it about this girl's story that has such appeal across generations of listeners and readers, and also across so many countries and cultures? How does this neglected girl and her jealous sister or sisters (or sometimes this neglected boy and his brothers) tap into our collective need for happy endings? The story of the good sister/bad sister relationship, usually known by the European name "Cinderella," has unique attributes that qualify it as a leading candidate in the study of folk tales in the classroom.

Folklorists have identified more than 3,000 stories that qualify as Cinderella variants worldwide; almost every culture, every nation, has at least one variant, one authentic tale with Cinderella-style characters and motifs. The story of Cinderella has endured for more than 1,000 years, surfacing first in a literary source in ninth-century China, said to have originated in the T'ang dynasty somewhere between 618 and 907 (Yamate, 1997). The story has been found from Asia to the interior of South America.

"Cinderella" is not a single text but an entire range of stories with the common element of a persecuted heroine who responds to her situation with defiance, cunning, ingenuity, self-pity, anguish, or grief. Because traditional tales deal with such primal human experiences and emotions, stories like "Cinderella" surface in nearly every part of the world. The variants are certainly different in setting and detail, but a fascinating sameness still exists (Tunnell & Jacobs, 2000). Seeing past the differences to discover the similarities can lead students to recognize the value of both. In studying something so familiar, students have the opportunity to explore basic story elements, unique cultural markers, and their own personal responses.

It can be said safely that no other tale has so many early, independently created, and widely scattered versions (Taylor, 1988). What is it about the story of Cinderella that is so appealing that there are so many versions in so many diverse cultures? Whatever the symbolism of the various parts may be or the fascination we have with the story, our emotions are aroused by the story of a young girl who was loved by her parents and is now being mistreated by her stepmother. Its episodes are at times obscure and only partly understood, but they grow from situations that are familiar to all of us (Jameson, 1988), including coping with death, love, and housework. There are still dangers on the dark and twisting path of life, as well as metaphorical "fairy godmothers" and "animal guides" to light the way for modern readers (Datlow & Windling, 2000).

Literary Elements in "Cinderella"

What makes a story a Cinderella story? There is general agreement that there are certain common elements in the Cinderella formula story. Many scholars have studied the Cinderella genre and identified key variables (Dundes, 1988; Philip, 1990; Tatar, 1987, 1999; Warner, 1996; Zipes, 2002). The main character is usually (although not always) a girl who is badly treated by her family. Her tormentors have few redeeming features, but she is portrayed as a good and kind person. Her goodness is rewarded by magical or supernatural intercession. She is recognized for her worth by something she has left behind (for example, a slipper). She is elevated in position by a royal person who loves her for her good qualities.

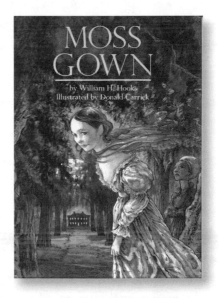

Many contemporary critics have expressed concern that folk tales most often favor active boy heroes and cast the heroines in passive roles. For example, in the classic 18th-century adaptation by Charles Perrault, retold and illustrated by Marcia Brown (1954) in her Caldecott Medal-winning version, the image of Cinderella is of a self-effacing, submissive girl; however, her ancestors were more often shrewd, resourceful characters who effected their own rescues. Protagonists and antagonists in folk tales are usually archetypes; they are symbolic of basic human traits, such as good or evil, rather than three-dimensional, dynamic characters. Psychologist Bruno Bettleheim (1989) contends that in folk tales, "figures are clearly

drawn; and details, unless very important, are eliminated. All characters are typical rather than unique" (p. 8).

In the majority of Cinderella tales, the plot can be summarized as follows: The heroine is persecuted, a supernatural being intervenes, the heroine's beauty and goodness are recognized, and she finds a significant other. Action and theme rather than character development are the focus of interest. People's discovery of the nature of human beings comes from this relationship of theme to action (Lukens, 1999). According to Bettleheim (1989),

> It is characteristic of fairy tales to state an existential dilemma briefly and pointedly. This permits the child to come to grips with the problem in its most essential form, where a more complex plot would confuse matters for him (her). The fairy tale simplifies all situations. (p. 8)

"Cinderella" is also appropriate for older children because it is a somewhat longer tale and contains elements of love and romance (Huck, Hepler, Hickman, & Kiefer, 2001).

Folk tales tend to have similar themes regardless of when or where they originated. These similar themes seem to be evidence that people create and respond to similar ideas about human nature. Important fundamental values are expressed in folk tales. Humility, mercy, kindness, perseverance, and courage are rewarded (Huck et al., 2001). Justice, in particular the punishment of evil, and the power of love are major forces in folk tales. This is very true in most versions of the Cinderella stories.

The setting of most folk tales and fairy tales serves as a backdrop to the story and is established quickly. The setting is often a vague long-ago-and-far-away time and place with specific details added. Such a setting also suggests one of the most pleasurable aspects of the folk tale: Maybe it happened here, maybe yesterday, and maybe it could happen again today (Lukens, 1999). Indeed, "Cinderella" has been reimagined in almost every conceivable setting, including modern times. There are probably more picture book versions of the Cinderella story available than any other tale, with countless possibilities for illustrating the story's setting.

Variants of the Cinderella Tale

It is important to note that calling a story a Cinderella story does not mean that the heroine is named Cinderella. Indeed, the name has many other incarnations. The names Aschenputtel, Tattercoats, and Catskins also may be somewhat familiar, but there are surely as many different names for the protagonist as there are different versions of the story. In the British Isles, for example, Cinderella goes by the name of Catskin, Mossycoat, or Rashin-Coati (Tatar, 1999). In 1891, The Folk-Lore Society in London published Marian Roalfe Cox's *Cinderella: Three Hundred and Forty-Five Variants of Cinderella, Catskin, and Cap O' Rushes*. It was the first modern, scientific study of the Cinderella body of work. Cox identified three major categories into which the Cinderella variants fall. Although they share some characteristics, each type has its own distinctive qualities (as cited in Taylor, 1988). Distinct elements of each are shown in Table 14.1.

Table 14.1
Distinct Qualities of Cinderella Stories

	Cinderella and Her Sisters Examples: Cinderella, Yeh-Shen	Runaway Cinderella Examples: Allerleirauh, Thousand Furs	Testing Cinderella Examples: Cap o' Rushes, Moss Gown
Problem	Evil stepmother and stepsisters, unkind sister	Unnatural father, marriage to undesirable partner	King Lear test of father-daughter bond
Supernatural Helper	Fairy godmother, fish, cow, bones	Magical being	Elijah the Prophet, no help needed
Means of Recognition	Shoe, other object	Golden objects	Shoe, ring, salted meat

When children learn that people all over the world share empathy for a lonely, unloved person, they realize that even though there are differences among people, there are as many important similarities among them. Through folk tales, children read and hear stories that illustrate everyone's common need for love, hope, and security and everyone's feelings of happiness, anger, pride, and loneliness. At the same time, the folk stories demonstrate how people may respond differently to emotional and environmental situations (Bosma, 1992). Children may learn tolerance along with feeling pleasure in discovering and sharing what the "Cinderella" sister stories have to offer. Although the name Cinderella brings with it the European cultural values associated with the French and German versions of a story familiar to most Western readers, values such as kindness and compassion are shared by many other cultures. The "Cinderella" sister stories representing these cultures also deserve to be explored. These variants reflect the authentic story known in the root culture, as opposed to new versions that parody or reinvent tales with new twists provided by the adapter rather than drawn from the culture. (For a discussion of a Native American variant of the Cinderella story, see chapter 13.)

Many examples of variants and versions can be found on Russell Peck's website (www.lib.rochester.edu/camelot/cinder/cinintr.htm), which has a lengthy bibliography with a wealth of information. It includes detailed summaries for many of the English and American versions, as well as African, Caribbean, Creole, African American, Asian, Mediterranean, Russian, and Middle Eastern versions, among others. And Judy Sierra's collection *Cinderella* (1992), from the Oryx Multicultural Folk Tale series, provides brief narrative versions of many Cinderella tales that are not yet available in picture book form. Although each culture has put its own imprint on this story, the basic elements can be found in all the tales. Although folk tales certainly vary from culture to culture, it is amazing how alike in form they are and how the basic literary elements are similar.

Reasons for Using "Cinderella" Sister Tales in the Classroom

Traditional literature has much to offer children and young adults. It is an excellent method for involving students in the exploration of their own experiences in finding meaning in life. Bettelheim (1989) has observed that classic folk tales and fairy tales have much to teach children "about the inner problems of human beings, and of the right solutions to their predicaments in any society" (p. 5). Folk tales have been called the "spiritual history" of humankind, the "cement of society," binding a culture together (Lukens, 1999). The endurance of these stories, their widespread and lasting popularity, suggests that they deal with issues that have significant individual and social meanings (Tatar, 1987).

Traditional literature also lays the groundwork for an understanding of literature in general (Huck et al., 2001). It provides children with a frame of reference for literature they will later encounter. Many allusions to the archetypes and motifs of traditional literature and folk tales appear in contemporary fiction and nonfiction. Many modern fantasies, such as The Lord of the Rings series (Tolkien, 1954a, 1954b, 1955), *His Dark Materials* (Pullman, 2001), *Chronicles of Prydain* (Alexander, 1999), the Earthsea trilogy (LeGuin, 1984), and *The Dark Is Rising* (Cooper, 1993), echo literary patterns found in myths and legends of traditional literature.

Folk tales can be ideal as a tool for reading instruction. Most published traditional literature is available in picture book format, with rich illustrations that help cue the reader to important story elements, as well as providing visual cultural details for the story. As we consider in this chapter the power of folk tales in telling basic human stories, it becomes apparent that these diverse "Cinderella" sister tales represent a substantial resource for instruction. There are many reasons for bringing Cinderella, her sisters, and her brothers into the classroom:

- Folk tales are a basic, formulaic story type with wide appeal.
- There are many available versions of individual tales, and they are easy to locate.
- Multiple tale variants and versions can be compared and contrasted.
- The stories provide an opportunity to discuss cultural roots and details.
- Folk tales are rich with possibilities for discussion, dramatization, and writing.

Planning a "Cinderella" Sister Tale Unit

There are scores of possible approaches to presenting folk literature in class. "Fairy tales are an inspiration for learning to read because they address questions about life and human struggle," contend Worthy and Bloodgood (1993, p. 290), providing an excellent outline of a "Cinderella unit" for the upper elementary grades. The authors also claim, "Connecting the known stories to new, structurally similar ones is a powerful tool for reading instruction and an excellent foundation for exploring other subjects through literature" (p. 290). Their approach includes the following components for the prereading, reading, and postreading stages of instruction:

Prereading instruction

- Purpose setting
- Word recognition, vocabulary, building background information

Reading and postreading instruction

- Vocabulary from context
- Story structure:
    Comparison matrix
    Venn diagram
    Sequence chart
    Character flow chart
- Literary evaluation:
    Does the book tell a good story?
    How does the author portray the characters?
    Interpretive comments on illustrations
    Illustrator and author studies
- Written response:
    Keeping response journals
    Writing poetry
    Transforming existing tales or writing new stories
- Across the curriculum:
    Making connections to the geography of the stories
    Looking at the history of the tale

The study of "Cinderella" sister stories can form a stand-alone unit or can be part of a unit that focuses on folklore in general, modern fantasy, world cultures, or gender roles. Even if students initially protest that they already know the story of

Cinderella, they will quickly learn that there are many different incarnations that will be new to them. This chapter will focus on outlining instructional possibilities for four major approaches to the use of "Cinderella" sister tales in the upper elementary grades:

Cinderella vs. Cinderella: Study of the basic Cinderella formula

Cultural Diversity: Stories from several different countries and cultures

What Makes a Hero? Stories with male Cinderellas in the usual female role

The Humorous Cindy: Creative and modern versions of the tale

An ambitious plan might even integrate all four Cinderella subthemes, beginning with major story types and examples, continuing with applying the Cinderella formula to stories across cultures, then connecting the Cinderella heroine with gender issues, and finally "spoofing" Cinderella in contemporary and humorous ways. In addition, each of these thematic approaches can include the same basic unit components from Worthy and Bloodgood (1993) for prereading, during reading, and postreading instruction, as follows.

Prereading strategies

• Have students get into groups and use clustering to brainstorm everything they know or associate with "Cinderella" and its sister tales.

• Introduce variants and versions of Cinderella; show students the covers of books, read the titles, and note the names of adapters and illustrators.

• Discuss with students any unfamiliar vocabulary, particularly any unusual names for Cinderella and other characters, features of dialect, etc.

Reading strategies

• Read the story aloud to the class.

• Have students listen to an audiotape of the story (whether commercially produced or taped by the teacher, librarian, a parent, or a student volunteer).

• Have students reread the story aloud to each other in small groups or partnered with a reading buddy.

• Have students read their own choices of individual Cinderella tales independently.

• As the class reads the books, have them create and maintain a chart that compares the stories, using the following headings:

    Title

    Author/Adapter

Illustrator

Country of Origin/Setting

Main Character (Name)

Secondary Character(s) (Relationship to Main Character)

Problem

Supernatural Helper

Means of Recognition

Conclusion

Postreading strategies

• Using a Venn diagram and/or the class-made charts, have students compare and contrast the stories. Possible discussion questions can include the following:

Is there a similar theme across the stories?

How are the main characters similar? Different?

How do the stories differ from one another?

Which is your favorite one? Why? Have the students vote on their favorite versions, and compile the results in graph form.

• Students can respond through writing, whether individually or in small groups, some confessions of the evil characters, Cinderella's journal, dialogues among the princes, or newspaper reports. Students can update the story, telling it from the point of view of the prince, the fairy godmother, the father, or another character.

• Folk tales often contain vivid, evocative images. Students could choose to transform some of those scenes into poetry or to write an original poem of their own for a pivotal scene or moment. Students can work individually or in groups. Some possible verse forms include found poetry, free verse, and cinquain. The story of Cinderella and its themes have appeared in literature and other forms of art, such as film and music. For music, film, and drama references (including finger puppets), check out the SurLaLune Fairy Tale Pages website (www.surlalunefairytales.com). And, of course, there are many animated and live-action films based on the Cinderella story available on video and DVD, including Disney's animated *Cinderella* (1950) as well as the Rodgers & Hammerstein musical version (1965 and 1997) or a contemporary remake, *Ever After* (1998). Other websites that offer Cinderella resources are as follows:

www.acs.ucalgary.ca/~dkbrown/cinderella.html
www.nationalgeographic.com/grimm/cinderella.html
www.northcanton.sparcc.org/~ptk1nc/cinderella
www.pitt.edu/~dash/grimm.html

Cinderella vs. Cinderella

A literary approach to the Cinderella tale is simply to take two or more examples of the tale and read, analyze, and compare them. Modern versions of "Cinderella," such as the novels *Ella Enchanted* by Gail Carson Levine (1997) or *Just Ella* by Margaret Peterson Haddix (1999), could be read and compared to more traditional folk tale picture book Cinderella tales with older students. Or younger students could read several picture book versions of "Cinderella," such as *Princess Furball* by Charlotte Huck (1989) or *Cinderella* by K.Y. Craft (2001), and look for similarities and differences in both the narrative and the illustrations in these picture book versions. They may be surprised to discover that in some Cinderella tales, there is no glass slipper or fairy godmother (Stewart, 2000). Nevertheless, the story is considered a version of the Cinderella story. You and the students can work together to generate a list of story characteristics and decide which or how many elements must be present in order to say, "That's a Cinderella story." Then, once a clear understanding of "Cinderella" elements is in place, students can apply their knowledge by reading and responding to other variants from a variety of world cultures. Figure 14.1 presents a list of Cinderella books to use with your students in comparing story variants.

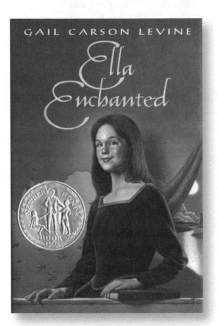

Book cover from *Ella Enchanted*, written by Gail Carson Levine, illustrated by Mark Elliot. Copyright © 1997. Used by permission of HarperCollins Publishers.

To conclude their study of Cinderella, students can create their own version of the Cinderella tale or a sister tale. They should follow the basic outline of the other Cinderella variants and versions they have read and discussed, but they can change the elements of the story, such as the setting, names, and conclusion. This also provides an excellent opportunity to point out the difference between a fictional story with an author (e.g., their own stories) and a preexisting story that an adapter has retold authentically (a folk tale). This also may lead to further folk tale reading, writing, and research including multicultural variants of "Cinderella," gender-bending versions, and humorous Cinderella stories and parodies (see the following sections of this chapter).

Figure 14.1
Cinderella Picture Books: European Variants and Cinderella Novels

European Variants

Brown, M. (1954). *Cinderella, or the little glass slipper*. New York: Scribner's.

Craft, K.Y. (2001). *Cinderella*. New York: Seastar.

Daly, J. (2000). *Fair, brown, and trembling: An Irish Cinderella story*. New York: Farrar, Straus & Giroux.

Huck, C. (1989). *Princess Furball* (A. Lobel, Illus.). New York: Greenwillow.

Huck, C. (1996). *Toads and diamonds* (A. Lobel, Illus.). New York: Greenwillow.

Jaffe, N. (1998). *The way meat loves salt: A Cinderella tale from the Jewish tradition* (L. August, Illus.). New York: Henry Holt.

Jeffers, S. (1990). *Cinderella*. New York: Dial.

Karlin, B. (1989). *Cinderella*. Boston: Little, Brown.

Mayer, M. (1994). *Baba Yaga and Vasilisa the brave* (K.Y. Craft, Illus.). New York: Morrow.

Silverman, E. (1999). *Raisel's Riddle* (S. Gaber, Illus.). New York: Farrar, Straus & Giroux.

Steel, F.A. (1976). *Tattercoats: An old English tale*. New York: Simon & Schuster.

Cinderella Novels

Burnett, F.H. (1886). *Little lord Fauntleroy*. New York: Scribner's.

Haddix, M.P. (1999). *Just Ella*. New York: Pocket.

Levine, G.C. (1997). *Ella enchanted*. New York: HarperCollins.

Maguire, G. (1999). *Confessions of an ugly stepsister*. New York: HarperCollins.

White, T.H. (1938). *Sword in the stone*. London: Collins.

Cultural Diversity and Cinderella Variants

Norton (1990) proposes using traditional literature as the first step in weaving culture into the usual curriculum. Folk tales provide many benefits for developing cultural identity and cultural sensitivity, as well as for literacy instruction. Using folk tales from a child's native culture gives him or her something to identify with and can lead to a heightened self-concept for those whose culture is being represented. It provides windows into unfamiliar cultures for the other students. Comparing variants from various countries helps children see their common heritage with the rest of humankind. Folk tales also offer better understanding of dialects and languages of various countries because idiomatic expressions often are used in the storytelling. And finally, folk tales extol the qualities of goodness, mercy, courage, love, and industry, which children can see are valued in all cultures, as well as the relatedness of various story types and motifs among the peoples of the world. Studying folk tale variants from a variety of cultures opens an avenue to understanding basic human characteristics underlying the simple folk story. Folk tales can help children understand the personal dimension and the standards of behavior of a culture (Bosma, 1992).

However, Tunnell and Jacobs (2000) remind us of the importance of going beyond using only traditional literature and folk tales to teach children about culture. Contemporary realistic literature (as well as other genres) also is needed to provide a well-rounded picture of the "parallel cultures" of our world. Otherwise, children can grow up thinking Japanese people lived "once upon a time" instead of down the block. We also need to teach students to read critically, looking for cultural details that add authenticity to the folk tale and avoiding those that reflect negative or inaccurate stereotypes.

You can begin by choosing a Cinderella story that may be somewhat familiar to the students, such as *Cinderella* by Susan Jeffers (1990), and then comparing it with another less-familiar tale from a non–European culture, such as *Mufaro's Beautiful Daughters*, retold and illustrated by John Steptoe (1987). (See Figure 14.2 for a selection of multicultural Cinderella stories.) To understand the new story better, stu-

Figure 14.2
The Multicultural Cinderella

Latin American

Coburn, J.R. (2000). *Domitila: A Cinderella tale from the Mexican tradition* (C. McLennan, Illus.). Arcadia, CA: Shen's.

Hayes, J. (2000). *Estrellita de oro/Little Gold Star: A Cinderella cuento* (G.O. Perez & L.A. Perez, Illus.). El Paso, TX: Cinco Puntos.

San Souci, D. (1998). *Cendrillon: A Caribbean Cinderella* (B. Pinkney, Illus.). New York: Simon & Schuster.

San Souci, R.D. (2000). *Little Gold Star: A Spanish American Cinderella tale* (S. Martinez, Illus.). New York: HarperCollins.

Native American

Martin, R. (1998). *The rough-face girl* (D. Shannon, Illus.). New York: Philomel.

Pollock, P. (1996). *The turkey girl: A Zuni Cinderella* (E. Young, Illus.). Boston: Little, Brown.

San Souci, R.D. (1997). *Sootface: An Ojibwa Cinderella story* (D. San Souci, Illus.). New York: Bantam.

Rural American

Hooks, W. (1987). *Moss gown* (D. Carrick, Illus.). New York: Clarion.

San Souci, R.D. (1998). *The talking eggs: A folktale from the American south* (J. Pinkney, Illus.). New York: E.P. Dutton.

Schroeder, A. (2000). *Smoky Mountain Rose: An Appalachian Cinderella* (B. Sneed, Illus.). New York: Puffin.

African

Climo, S. (1992). *The Egyptian Cinderella* (R. Heller, Illus.). Minneapolis, MN: Econo-Clad.

Onyefulu, O. (1994). *Chinye: A West African folk tale* (E. Safarewicz, Illus.). New York: Viking.

Sierra, J. (2000). *The gift of the crocodile: A Cinderella story* (R. Ruffins, Illus.). New York: Simon & Schuster.

Steptoe, J. (1987). *Mufaro's beautiful daughters: An African tale*. New York: Lothrop, Lee & Shepard.

Asian

Climo, S. (1996). *The Korean Cinderella* (R. Heller, Illus.). New York: HarperTrophy.

Coburn, J.R. (1998). *Angkat: The Cambodian Cinderella* (E. Flotte, Illus.). Arcadia, CA: Shen's.

Coburn, J.R., & Lee, T.C. (1996). *Jouanah: A Hmong Cinderella* (A.S. O'Brien, Illus.). Arcadia, CA: Shen's.

Louie, A. (1996). *Yeh-Shen: A Cinderella story from China* (E. Young, Illus.). New York: Puffin.

Lum, D.H.Y. (1994). *The golden slipper: A Vietnamese legend* (M. Nagano, Illus.). Memphis, TN: Troll.

Middle Eastern

Climo, S. (1999). *The Persian Cinderella* (R. Florczak, Illus.). New York: HarperCollins.

Hickox, R. (1999). *The golden sandal: A Middle Eastern Cinderella story* (W. Hillenbrand, Illus.). New York: Holiday House.

dents can research the following story components, concluding with a comparison and contrast of the two stories. Older students can work in groups to read and research several variants, coming together to share multiple variants from several cultural groups.

Researching and responding to cultural variants

- Students can research social studies–related topics relevant to the story, such as geography, climate, or flora and fauna (begin by studying the book illustrations closely).

- Students can investigate some aspect of the culture that emerges in the story, such as courtship and weddings, holidays, religion, clothing, or food.

- Compile a list of Cinderella stories from around the world. After reading various Cinderella stories, students can locate each country of origin on a map.

- Students may create a database or comparative graph reflecting information for each variant. Some possible fields may include the following:

    Type of community (rural, urban, etc.)

    Foods mentioned in the story

    Buildings or homes in the story

    Clothing of the characters

    Gender of main character; role in society

- Students who have proficient computer skills may create a webpage consisting of a world map with links to information on each country and its Cinderella story.

- Students can research and create their own versions of "Cinderella," based on their own family or neighborhood cultures.

What Makes a Hero?

Once students have encountered a variety of Cinderella tales from several cultural contexts, they also may begin to notice the different ways the heroine herself is portrayed. In some Cinderella tales, such as those of Catskin and Cap o' Rushes, the Cinderella protagonist takes responsibility for herself and doesn't look to external parties for help. This is in direct contrast with the classic Perrault heroine waiting for the prince to find her, and it also differs markedly from the Disney Cinderella with whom children are usually most familiar. This basic attribute of Cinderella as an active or passive figure can be a subtle and interesting area to address with students and can be explored by comparing and contrasting different variants of stories with

Figure 14.3
Male Cinderellas

d'Aulaire, I., & d'Aulaire, E.P. (1969). The maid on the glass mountain. In *East of the sun and west of the moon: Twenty-one Norwegian folktales*. New York: Viking.

Greene, E. (1994). *Billy Beg and his bull: An Irish tale* (K.B. Root, Illus.). New York: Holiday House.

Martin, C. (1992). *Boots and the glass mountain* (G. Spirin, Illus.). New York: Dial.

Philip, N. (1991). Cinder Jack. In *Fairy tales of eastern Europe* (L. Wilks, Illus.). New York: Clarion.

San Souci, R.D. (1995). *The little seven-colored horse: A Spanish American folktale* (J.T. Dicks, Illus.). San Francisco: Chronicle.

Sierra, J. (1984). *How the cowherd found a bride in "Cinderella"* (J. Caroselli, Illus.). Phoenix, AZ: Oryx.

---

male and female protagonists. Traditional stories can be useful tools for learning about gender roles. Studying "Cinderella" versions and variants that have male protagonists can lead students to discuss their understanding of the usual role played by protagonists, whether male or female, in Cinderella stories of all kinds.

Mello (2001) reports on a study of children's responses to gender roles in fairy tales, focusing on students ages 9–11. Mello recommends using these stories to help children develop an understanding of the value, power, and authority of gender relationships. When students are presented with a variety of gender roles from disparate cultural texts, they begin to examine their own understanding of how to assign value to gender roles and gendered relationships. Several modern interpretations of "Cinderella" offer heroines with attributes usually credited to male heroes. These characters are not modern revisionist creations by contemporary authors but rather authentic folk heroines of the past whose stories are finally being put in book form. And casting Cinderella as a boy with stepbrothers helps put the usual submissive female role in stark relief. Like modern writers, students also can transform the traditional Cinderella into an action hero by rewriting the stories in which she is more passive or by creating new endings that empower her. These rewritings can take the form of a cartoon strip, a ballad, or a dramatic skit. Figure 14.3 presents a list of books with male Cinderella figures.

The Humorous Cindy

To bring the "Cinderella" study into the present, it can be very appealing to share versions of "Cinderella" that parody the traditional story elements. This requires of students both a familiarity with the older story versions as well as higher level thinking to catch the puns and irony often present. Over the years, modern authors have had great success adapting the Cinderella formula to create new stories. New picture book versions loosely based on the Cinderella tale appear often. Many of the more current versions use parody or humor to reinvent the Cinderella tale. Cinderella thus becomes a dog, penguin, dinosaur, Halloween witch, or even skeleton. The lan-

Figure 14.4
The Humorous Cindy

Buehner, C. (1996). *Fanny's dream* (M. Buehner, Illus.). New York: Dial.

Cole, B. (1999). *Prince cinders*. Minneapolis, MN: Econo-Clad.

Dematons, C. (1996). *Looking for Cinderella*. Chicago: Front Street.

Edwards, P.D. (1999). *Dinorella: A prehistoric fairy tale* (H. Cole, Illus.). New York: Hyperion.

Holub, J. (2001). *Cinderdog and the wicked stepcat*. Morton Grove, IL: Albert Whitman.

Jackson, E. (1998). *Cinder Edna* (K. O'Malley, Illus.). London: Mulberry.

Johnston, T. (2000). *Bigfoot Cinderrrrella*. New York: Puffin.

Ketteman, H. (2001). *Bubba, the cowboy prince: A fractured Texas tale* (G. Brian Karas, Illus.). New York: Scholastic.

Lattimore, D.N. (2002). *Cinderhazel: The Cinderella of Halloween*. New York: Scholastic.

Lowell, S. (2001). *Cindy Ellen: A wild western Cinderella* (J. Manning, Illus.). New York: HarperTrophy.

Minter, F. (1999). *Cinder-Elly* (J. Warhola, Illus.). Minneapolis, MN: Econo-Clad.

Perlman, J. (1993). *Cinderella penguin or, the little glass flipper*. New York: Viking.

San Souci, R.D. (2000). *Cinderella skeleton* (D. Catrow, Illus.). San Diego: Harcourt.

Takayama, S. (1997). *Sumorella: A Hawai'i Cinderella story* (E. Szegeky, Illus.). Mercer Island, WA: Island.

Yorinks, A. (1993). *Ugh*. Pleasantville, NY: Sunburst.

Cinderella poems:

Dahl, R. (2002). Cinderella. In *Revolting rhymes* (Q. Blake, Illus.). New York: Knopf.

Silverstein, S. (1981). In search of Cinderella. In *A light in the attic*. New York: HarperCollins.

Viorst, J. (1981). ...And then the prince knelt down and tried to put the glass slipper on Cinderella's foot. In *If I were in charge of the world and other worries*. New York: Atheneum.

guage is full of puns and riffs on traditional character names, dialogue, and story-telling motifs.

For older students, in particular, these versions make the story fresh and interesting again. But understanding the humor depends on some degree of familiarity with some version of the root story. Children who are new immigrants to the United States or who are not well versed in European/Western traditional tales may not "get" it. But for students who have the background and skills, contrasting modern parodies (see Figure 14.4) with classic European (or even non–European) Cinderella tales can lead to a deeper understanding of the story itself as well as of storytelling devices. And you can use a few of these books to let students explore the lighter side of the classic characters. Follow up with humorous poem versions of the Cinderella story written by Roald Dahl (2002), Shel Silverstein (1981), and Judith Viorst (1981). Then students also can turn their favorite version into their own poem or into a Readers Theatre presentation, or they can use this as inspiration for creative versions of their own.

Conclusion

The process of listening to and reflecting on traditional stories can be an important component of literacy instruction. Teachers can use these stories as models for building literacy skills, encouraging critical thinking and reflection, as well as for presenting multicultural and equitable perspectives. Folk tales grew out of the basic human need to explain our world and ourselves. Why are we here? What is our destiny? Cinderella and her sisters (and brothers) around the world continue to speak to us across the generations about those basic questions. Their themes are as relevant to young people today as they were in the past. Life still can be full of neglectful parents, personal challenges, and unkind strangers hiding treacherous hearts. Literature today continues to address people's concerns about human strengths and weaknesses and our relationship to the world and other people.

REFERENCES

Bettelheim, B. (1989). *The uses of enchantment*. New York: Vintage.

Bosma, B. (1992). *Fairy tales, fables, legends, and myths: Using folk literature in your classroom*. New York: Teachers College Press.

Cox, M.R. (1891). *Cinderella: Three hundred and forty-five variants of Cinderella, Catskin, and Cap o' Rushes*. London: Folk-Lore Society.

Datlow, E., & Windling, T. (2000). *Black heart, ivory bones*. New York: Avon.

Dundes, A. (Ed.). (1988). *Cinderella: A casebook*. Madison, WI: University of Wisconsin Press.

Huck, C., Hepler, S., Hickman, J., & Kiefer, B. (2001). *Children's literature in the elementary school* (7th ed.). New York: McGraw-Hill.

Jameson, R.D. (1988). Cinderella in China. In A. Dundes (Ed.), *Cinderella: A casebook* (pp. 71–97). Madison, WI: University of Wisconsin Press.

Lukens, R. (1999). *A critical handbook of children's literature* (6th ed.). New York: Addison-Wesley.

Mello, R. (2001). Cinderella meets Ulysses. *Language Arts, 78*(6), 548–555.

Norton, D. (1990). Teaching multicultural literature in the reading curriculum. *The Reading Teacher, 44*(1), 28–40.

Philip, N. (1990). *Cinderella story*. New York: Penguin.

Stewart, M. (2000). How can this be Cinderella if there is no glass slipper? Native American "fairy tales." *Studies in American Indian Literatures: The Journal of the Association for the Study of American Indian Literatures, 12*(1), 3–19.

Tatar, M. (1987). *The hard facts of the Grimms' fairy tales*. Princeton, NJ: Princeton University Press.

Tatar, M. (Ed.). (1999). *The classic fairy tales*. New York: W.W. Norton.

Taylor, A. (1988). The study of the Cinderella cycle. In A. Dundes (Ed.), *Cinderella: A casebook* (pp. 115–128). Madison, WI: University of Wisconsin Press.

Tunnell, M., & Jacobs, J. (2000). *Children's literature, briefly* (2nd ed.). Upper Saddle River, NJ: Merrill.

Warner, M. (1996). *From the beast to the blonde: On fairy tales and their tellers*. New York: Noonday.

Worthy, M.J., & Bloodgood, J.W. (1993). Enhancing reading instruction through Cinderella tales. *The Reading Teacher, 46*, 290–300.

Yamate, S. (1997). Asian Pacific American children's literature: Expanding perceptions about who Americans are.

In V.J. Harris (Ed.), *Using multiethnic literature in the K–8 classroom* (pp. 95–125). Norwood, MA: Christopher-Gordon.

Zipes, J. (2002). *Breaking the magic spell: Radical theories of folk and fairy tales* (2nd ed.). Lexington, KY: University Press of Kentucky.

CHILDREN'S BOOKS CITED

Alexander, L. (1999). *Chronicles of Prydain* (5 vols.). New York: Yearling.

Brown, M. (1954). *Cinderella, or the little glass slipper*. New York: Scribner's.

Cooper, S. (1993). *The dark is rising* (5 vols.). New York: Pocket.

Craft, K.Y. (2001). *Cinderella*. New York: Seastar.

Dahl, R. (2002). *Revolting rhymes* (Q. Blake, Illus.). New York: Knopf.

Haddix, M.P. (1999). *Just Ella*. New York: Pocket.

Huck, C. (1989). *Princess Furball* (A. Lobel, Illus.). New York: Greenwillow.

Jeffers, S. (1990). *Cinderella*. New York: Dial.

LeGuin, U.K. (1984). *Earthsea* (3 vols.). New York: Bantam Spectra.

Levine, G.C. (1997). *Ella enchanted*. New York: HarperCollins.

Pullman, P. (2001). *His dark materials*. New York: Ballantine.

Sierra, J. (1992). *Cinderella*. Phoenix, AZ: Oryx.

Silverstein, S. (1981). *A light in the attic*. New York: HarperCollins.

Steptoe, J. (1987). *Mufaro's beautiful daughters: An African tale*. New York: Lothrop, Lee & Shepard.

Tolkien, J.R.R. (1954a). *The Fellowship of the Ring: Being the first part of The Lord of the Rings*. London: George Allen and Unwin.

Tolkien, J.R.R. (1954b). *The Two Towers: Being the second part of The Lord of the Rings*. London: George Allen and Unwin.

Tolkien, J.R.R. (1955). *The Return of the King: Being the third part of The Lord of the Rings*. London: George Allen and Unwin.

Viorst, J. (1981). *If I were in charge of the world and other worries*. New York: Atheneum.

CHAPTER 15

Starting at the Roots: Collecting Folklore in the Home, School, and Community

Nancy L. Hadaway

The word *folk* refers to any group linked by at least one common factor (Carthy, 2002). Each of us belongs to many groups—family, ethnic, regional, occupational, language, etc. As members of these groups, we share with each group's other members a common body of traditional knowledge, skills, and behaviors (Bartis & Bowman, 1994), and this universal core of understandings shapes our language, our ways of seeing life, and our ways of doing things. Human lore encompasses the traditional stories, customs, beliefs, and sayings that emerge from such groups.

From generation to generation, this lore, or the knowledge and stories of our ancestors, spreads by word of mouth (or through action and observation, in the case of nonverbal behaviors or customs) long before it is recorded in written form. These stories, traditions, customs, and sayings may be of long duration and cannot be traced to one single person. In the chain of transmission, the story, saying, or custom is altered somewhat as each performer leaves an imprint, crafting the folklore to fit the audience and the setting.

All cultures participate in this type of folklore through storytelling, children's chants, gestures, rhymes, riddles, proverbs, and so on. According to Carthy (2002), people carry along this oral tradition as part of their cultural freight. "No group of people, however remote or however simple their technology, has ever been discovered which does not employ some form of folklore.... [It] is a bridge between literate and non-literate societies" (Bascom, 1965, p. 26). Teachers often are unaware of this breadth of the genre of folklore, but it is exactly this scope that offers a rich source of literacy possibilities. The purpose of this chapter is to explore this level of folklore and teachers' awareness of it, along with its instructional potential for literacy development. In the chapter, the following issues will be addressed:

- What is the oral tradition or folk culture level of folklore, and how does it relate to folk literature (the written version of folklore)?
- What are the functions of folklore?
- What are the various subcategories that exist within the larger genre of folklore?
- What is the general level of teacher awareness and use of various types of folklore?
- How can folklore be used for literacy instruction and across the curriculum (i.e., what are its classroom applications)?
- What types of folklore projects connect the school with students' home and community?
- What is the influence of technology on folklore?

The Oral Tradition and Literacy Instruction

Folklore survived for hundreds of years in oral form only. Although traditional oral lore may gain such widespread recognition that it moves beyond the folk culture and into the popular culture with printed or broadcast versions, much of our oral tradition never is institutionalized via print or media. For several hundred years, however, researchers have attempted to record the oral traditions and stories of various groups before that information was lost (Becker, Beyers, & Miller, 1997). Anthropologists and linguists often spend years studying groups and gathering their folklore. For instance, Brunvand interviewed respondents across the United States, recording versions of contemporary or urban legends such as the vanishing hitchhiker (1989a, 1989b), and Hastings (1990) spoke to children all over New England, collecting their rhymes and chants.

The importance of preserving and disseminating the oral tradition, or the folk culture level of folklore in the United States, was underscored by the passage of Public Law 94-201, the American Folklife Preservation Act of 1976, and the creation of the American Folklife Center of the Library of Congress (see www.loc.gov/folklife). Such traditional expressive culture includes custom, belief, technical skill, language, architecture, music, play, dance, drama, ritual, pageantry, handicraft, and so on (Bartis & Bowman, 1994). However, this is exactly the type of folklore that teachers tend to overlook. Most teachers gravitate toward folk literature derived not from the folk culture but from the popular culture—in other words, published folklore.

In a survey of 60 teachers involved in a literacy workshop, almost all the teachers defined folklore as traditional stories passed down by word of mouth (Hadaway, 2002). However, when reporting the types of folklore they used in the classroom, virtually none of the teachers noted this oral tradition. Instead, they listed various authors associated with folk literature (e.g., Steven Kellogg) as well as published works including *Lon Po Po* (Young, 1989), *How the Camel Got His Hump* (Kipling, 1991), and *Why Mosquitoes Buzz in People's Ears* (Aardema, 1975). In addition, they noted other examples of folk literature commonly found in written form and used in classrooms, including tall tales such as those highlighting Paul Bunyan and John Henry, trickster tales such as those about Anansi, fables with talking animals, myths, fairy tales, and folk tales.

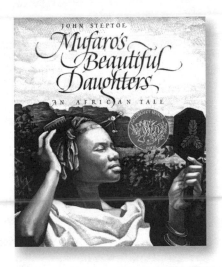

Book cover from *Mufaro's Beautiful Daughters: An African Tale* by John Steptoe. Copyright © 1987. Used by permission of HarperCollins Publishers.

This instructional omission of the roots of folklore not only provides a limited perspective of the genre, but it also fails to tap into many children's backgrounds. For instance, some African American students may come from a rich oral tradition using verbal performance to achieve recognition within their group in the community (Anokye, 1997). Other children may come from homes with a low level of family literacy or an absence of print materials but where storytelling and verbal play may be a common occurrence. Emphasizing the oral tradition can serve to level the literacy playing field for students from diverse backgrounds and to validate their cultural roots.

Functions of Folklore

When students' exposure to folklore focuses on the published versions of folk literature, as noted by the survey responses discussed previously, they miss out on exposure to the powerful role that the oral tradition has played throughout history. When we follow the roots of folklore, we discover that it taps into the most basic human needs and offers an inside view of diverse groups of people. Over time, folklore has been used to instruct, to amuse, to bond together, and to create boundaries. On the light side, for instance, jokes, riddles, and puzzles serve to entertain. At the other extreme, folklore offers relief from troubling matters. Folk sayings such as "every cloud has a silver lining" are meant to comfort, and ventures such as the Vietnam Veterans Oral History and Folklore Project (Fish, 2000) help to heal wounds and validate individuals. The familiarity of folk songs creates a sense of togetherness among group members, and other types of folklore may be shared as a means of social control to keep people in line (e.g., what happens to children who disobey their parents). Finally, one of the most important functions of folklore is to introduce and indirectly teach the rules of society; it impresses upon individuals specific values, attitudes, and beliefs. Greatly influenced by this function of folklore, two recent projects reflect the direct use of traditional oral lore and formats to inform. In Ghana, Africa, an innovative project involves folk performers using puppetry, storytelling, proverbs, role-play, drumming, and dance to communicate vital information for HIV/AIDS prevention (Panford, Nyaney, Amoah, & Aidoo, 2001). A second program in remote eastern Uganda uses the teaching power of songs and stories to train traditional birth attendants to address serious health problems (Silver, 2001).

Categories of Folklore

The functions of folklore—to entertain, to teach, to validate or bond together—are accomplished through an assortment of media. This range of folklore can be classified from major to minor, from oral lore to nonverbal varieties, as social/folk customs and material culture, and as folk and popular culture examples (Carthy, 2002; Dundes, 1965; Gonzalez, 1982; Lutz, 1986; Morain, 1970, 1971; Renner & Carter, 1991). Each type of folklore offers teachers wonderful opportunities to engage students in the full scope of language—listening, speaking, reading, and writing. Figure 15.1 supplies a quick reference for the many forms of folklore. A brief examination of this table will help you understand the variety of possibilities that a broader approach to folklore offers.

Teacher Awareness and Use of Folklore

Folklore is easily integrated into any language arts program and across the curriculum at any grade level, yet it is not necessarily a strong component in most curricula. According to a survey of 120 teachers working in grades K–12, one third noted that they never included folklore with their classes (Hadaway, Vardell, & Young, 2002). The other two thirds used folklore sometimes. When asked what type of folklore they included in the classroom, they all cited only folk literature (e.g., stories about Lon Po Po, John Henry, Three Little Pigs, Johnny Appleseed, Aesop's fables, etc.), and, in general, they used the selections located within the class basal or anthology, or more well-known published works such as *Mufaro's Beautiful Daughters* (Steptoe, 1987), a Cinderella variant.

Most classroom instruction centers on the major types of folklore or oral lore (in published form), including epics, myths, legends, fairy tales, and fables, and only occasional reference is made to minor forms of folklore such as proverbs, riddles, songs, jokes, insults, toasts, nursery rhymes, or partly verbal and nonverbal formats such as folk dance or games (see Figure 15.1 for these categories and some examples). Still less emphasis is given to social and folk custom and material culture. This instructional tendency was verified in a survey of 60 teachers, grades K–12, in a

Figure 15.1
Folklore in a Variety of Forms

Oral Lore includes the stories of the "folk." The key characteristic of this type of folklore is its oral transmission. Once folklore is published, it enters the popular culture and may lose much of the authenticity for a particular culture/group (Hadaway, Vardell, & Young, 2002). Types of oral lore include the following:

Epics
Myths, legends, and fables
Pourquoi tales
Folk tales and fairy tales
Tall tales
Trickster and animal tales
Personal experience narratives
Hero tales
Local character anecdotes
Contemporary/urban legends
Horror and ghost stories

Material Culture includes items of folklore that we can touch or hold:

Folk costumes
Folk crafts
Folk art
Architecture

Verbal and Partly Verbal

Jokes, pranks, practical jokes
Toasts and insults
Proverbs, prayers, and blessings
Jingles, riddles, and rhymes
Puzzles and folk games
Folk songs, yodels, and chants
Stories behind place names
Oral histories

Nonverbal

Folk dance
Games
Quilt designs
Festivals
Gestures, kinesics, and body language

Social and Folk Custom includes folklore that reflects our actions:

Recipes, food lore, and table manners
Beliefs and superstitions
Traditional or folk medicine
Folk ways regarding pregnancy, birth, baptism, rites of passage, courtship, betrothal, weddings, and death
Traditional festivals and celebrations

Sources: Carthy, 2002; Dundes, 1965; Gonzalez, 1982; Lutz, 1986; Morain, 1970, 1971; Renner & Carter, 1991

literacy workshop (Hadaway, 2002). Teachers were given a survey and asked to rank 22 varieties of folklore, from major types of oral lore to more minor varieties of verbal/nonverbal folklore. They ranked each topic according to use in a lesson or as a discussion topic, from frequent or occasional use to never used. The teachers were not informed that these topics were categories of folklore, however.

The results, outlined in Table 15.1, demonstrate that few of the topics are used or discussed in classrooms on a frequent basis. Furthermore, when the oral lore often found in published versions in basals and anthologies is eliminated from the "occasional use" category, this column shrinks by five topics (animal tales, fairy tales, folk songs, myths/legends, and tall tales). The "never used" response was reported predominantly for folklore topics that are part of the folk culture and not emphasized in textbooks and other written material. As a follow-up to the teachers' rankings, respondents were asked what the general curricular category was for all these topics. They were unable to respond to this question. When the group discussed that all these items could be a part of the genre of folklore, the teachers were surprised by this idea and noted that they had never considered the larger picture of folklore, from oral traditions to published works.

Table 15.1
Rankings of Folklore Categories as Topics for Lessons or Class Discussion (60 Respondents)

Frequent Use (Includes items ranked by 40% or more of participants as frequently used/discussed)	Occasional Use (Includes items ranked by 40% or more of participants as occasionally used/discussed)	Never Used (Includes items ranked by 40% or more of participants as never used/discussed)
Children's games (46%) Fairy tales (46%) Gestures (72%) Personal experience narratives (59%) Puzzles (46%)	Animal tales (50%) Beliefs/superstitions (50%) Children's games (46%) Fairy tales (46%) Folk songs (46%) Handicrafts (54%) Jokes (41%) Myths/legends (54%) Oral histories (73%) Puzzles (46%) Rhymes (59%) Riddles (68%) Stories about courtship/weddings (49%) Stories behind place names (49%) Tall tales (41%) Traditional celebrations (60%)	Customs concerning baptism (100%) Folk songs (50%) Horror/ghost stories (82%) Jokes (50%) Proverbs (54%) Stories about courtship/weddings (51%) Stories behind place names (40%) Tall tales (41%) Traditional medicine (68%)

Benefits of Folklore

The absence of the rich oral roots of folklore from most classroom instruction is indeed unfortunate, as Krogness (1987) and Wilson (1988) have noted the many benefits of folklore study. First, folklore exposes students to the universal human experience. Through folklore, all students come to a greater understanding of the similarities and differences across groups, as well as an appreciation of their own cultural heritage and that of others (Gonzalez, 1982; Lutz, 1986). For instance, a project to collect and share family folklore fosters students' pride and helps them to see their uniqueness and the distinctiveness of others (Renner & Carter, 1991). A study of family history also can draw the parent(s) into a child's literacy experience and help validate the home culture.

As part of the Maryland Arts Council Folklife Program, Kotkin and Baker (1977) produced a brief guide for collecting a family history. The final section of this publication is a questionnaire with prompts that can be used as listening, speaking, reading, and writing activities in the classroom as well as serving as a structured interview guide for collecting family lore. The Grand Generation Website of the Smithsonian Institution (http://educate.si.edu/migrations/seek1/grand1.html) has another interview guide to assist in collecting folklore from family members and older tradition-bearers in the community. A thematic unit could easily evolve from any section of these guides. Kotkin and Baker suggest the following areas of emphasis:

- Family names
- Traditions and customs
- Stories of childhood, adolescence, school, work, religion, politics
- Recreation and games
- Tales of the "black sheep" of the family
- Courtship, betrothal, weddings, and marriage
- Historical events associated with weather or nature phenomena
- War or immigration experiences
- Financial sagas (e.g., "rags to riches")
- Family expressions and phrases
- Holidays and celebrations
- Reunions and family gatherings
- Recipes, cooking, and food taboos
- Extended family
- Funeral and burial customs
- Stories behind family heirlooms, photos, or memorabilia

The Kotkin and Baker guide was the impetus for my work with a secondary ESL class (Hadaway & Mundy, 1992). The teacher and I planned a family folklore unit beginning with an emphasis on oral folklore and personal experience stories, with a move to folk literature later. We began with a study of names and naming practices. Students created illustrations using the letters of their names, then shared these with a partner, discussed whether they liked their names, and noted any stories behind their names. Especially for students who may have names that are quite unusual, the discussion of names can be a rich cultural experience. Simons (1990) devotes a chapter to "The Folklore of Naming" in her book *Student Worlds, Student Words: Teaching Writing Through Folklore*, which is an excellent professional resource for a teacher embarking on a project such as this. Other resources that address naming practices across cultures include *Do People Grow on Family Trees? Genealogy for Kids and Other Beginners* (Wolfman, 1991) and *Multicultural Teaching: A Handbook of Activities, Information, and Resources* (Tiedt & Tiedt, 1995).

Later in my folklore unit, students interviewed family members about how their parents met and, for immigrant family members, about their personal experience stories from the journey to the United States. For younger students, a folklore study devoted to recreation and children's games might be an engaging focus. The class can compare and contrast traditional pastimes across cultures and generations.

To provide a background for a family history/folklore study, teachers can use many excellent books. Carol Otis Hurst (1999) suggests several books related to family stories on her children's literature website (www.carolhurst.com/subjects/history/local.html). For instance, Lois Lowry's *Looking Back: A Book of Memories* (2000) is a memoir that uses family photographs to both illustrate and inspire memory. Using this as a model, children can bring their own family photos to class and share the stories behind them. Another possibility is Betsy Byars's story of her first day of school in *The Moon and I* (1996).

Young children might enjoy interviewing family members about their experiences with their first day of school, and then they can do oral retellings in class or written ones with illustrations. In the secondary folklore unit with English-language learners noted earlier, I found that students needed to rehearse their questioning and interviewing techniques prior to trying them in a real situation. After the teacher and I engaged in a mock interview, we had students practice with each other. They alternated asking each other questions and answering, taped the interview, and then listened and evaluated their techniques. You also can draw in members of the larger community, inviting a variety of family members or city officials for possible guest interviews. Once information is collected, Hurst (1999) suggests a variety of formats to showcase the stories, including a class book, a bulletin board display, an annotated timeline, a newsletter, or an oral history day.

A second benefit of folklore is that it allows students to examine the artistic and creative efforts of all human beings, not just the elite. Wigginton (1972, 1985, 1991) demonstrated the power of using folklore for this purpose when his students interviewed and collected folk ways within their communities in the U.S. Appalachian Mountain region so that information regarding the local customs and traditions (e.g., spinning and weaving, midwifery, etc.) could be preserved. Numerous projects that highlight the traditions and lore of everyday communities are available via the Internet; one of the most comprehensive is the American Folklife Center. The center has 11 collections online as part of the American Memory project. They range from fiddle tunes of the old frontier to Omaha Indian music to the landscapes of southern West Virginia to blues and gospel songs from the Fort Valley Music Festivals in Georgia. These collections are "a rich combination of sound recordings, photographs, field

Book cover from *Family Pictures/Cuadros de familia* by Carmen Lomas Garza. Copyright © 1998. Used by permission of Children's Press/Scholastic Library Publishing.

notes, artifacts, and manuscripts that serve as living histories for a new generation" (Library of Congress, 2002). Other websites highlight the traditional culture of the southern United States (Southern Council for Folk Culture, http://personal.cfw.com/~dday/#contact) as well as urban life (Citylore, www.citylore.org) and more rural, natural areas (Montana Heritage Project, www.edheritage.org).

The potential for folklore to cross disciplinary lines is a third benefit. For a geography class, a survey of any U.S. map yields countless place names highlighting the influence of various ethnic groups on U.S. history. In science, a survey of folk medicine demonstrates that many traditional herbal cures are valid medicine in today's world. Further information regarding a host of topics concerning traditional or folk medicine is available at the Online Archive of American Folk Medicine at www.folkmed.ucla.edu/advanced.html (UCLA, 2001). Working collaboratively, history and science classes can collect the personal stories surrounding historical events such as floods, hurricanes, or tornadoes. Family recipes can be collected and used in mathematics to teach measurements along with the differences in measuring systems among different countries. A language arts or social studies class, on the other hand, might research the roots of folk sayings over time. As an informational example and model for a history class, students might check out The Suffragists Oral History Project, a collection of interviews, tape recorded and transcribed in the early 1970s, with 12 leaders and participants in the woman's suffrage movement (University of California, Berkeley, 1998). Or students might read one of the interviews such as "Wife, Homemaker, and Civil Defense Volunteer" in the oral history project *What Did You Do in the War, Grandma?* (Wood, Scott, & Brown University, 1997).

Finally, a study of folklore holds great promise for developing communication skills and writing (Bartis & Bowman, 1994; Simons, 1990). Before the media barrage of recent decades, storytelling was a common pastime. Many evenings and weekends were passed sharing folk stories such as hero tales or character anecdotes. Indeed, some individuals were regarded as gifted storytellers and were respected in the community for their oral skills, their knowledge of local lore, and their performance abilities. Current research indicates that children involved in storytelling programs exhibit improved listening skills, better sequencing abilities, increased language appreciation, and more thoughtful organization in their own writing (Speaker, 2000). Carthy (2002) concurs, noting that beyond an emphasis on basic skills such as separating main ideas from details, recognizing fact from opinion, and summarizing, students studying storytelling also gain experience in higher level skills such as comparing and contrasting, tracing patterns and motifs, making inferences, recognizing cause and effect relationships, and expressing individual interpretations.

Although the benefits of storytelling are numerous, however, most schools do not employ or have students study storytelling techniques. Therefore, Speaker (2000) linked elementary students and preservice student teachers for a shared experience in storytelling. Her study demonstrates how the experience helped to change children's reading habits and encouraged them to read more frequently. Story Arts Online (www.storyarts.org; Forest, 2000) is one useful resource for teachers who wish to include a storytelling emphasis in their classrooms. This website provides a handbook for storytelling, along with lesson suggestions and rubrics to assess students' efforts. There is also a section titled "Exploring Cultural Roots Through Storytelling," which includes interview questions. For students' first attempts, Buchoff (1995) recommends that children begin their storytelling work in familiar territory by interviewing adults at home and then retelling the story to the original respondent as a means to practice. In order to collect personal experience narratives on the home front, Buchoff suggests a series of "tell me about" prompts such as the following:

Tell me about something I did when I was little.

Tell me about a time when I got lost.

Tell me about the neighborhood where you lived as a child.

Tell me about someone who used to come and visit at your house when you were growing up.

Tell me about your favorite relative when you were a child.

Oral history, like storytelling, is another opportunity for an authentic language workout as students are involved in speaking, listening, reading, and writing. While storytelling may include fact and fiction, oral history is focused on the factual representation of information. "Oral histories are people's stories about events in their lives or the life of their community. The gathering of these stories requires respectful listening and a willingness to interact and learn from individuals" (Stasz, 2000, p. 560). What is generated goes well beyond an individual or community history. Using an oral history approach, students practice their oral communication skills and hone their writing skills. Students have opportunities to accomplish a myriad of literacy tasks (Lutz, 1986; Renner & Carter, 1991; Wigginton, 1991), including the following:

- Interview and take notes
- Read, define, and organize topics
- Compose and edit
- Present orally and listen
- Learn about the relationships between oral and written literature
- Work with primary source material
- Gain an understanding of how folklore develops, is gathered, and is recorded

As a professional resource for lesson planning, you can refer to guides for interviewing and field work such as *Folklife and Fieldwork: A Layman's Introduction to Field Techniques* (Bartis, 1979). *Like It Was: A Complete Guide to Writing Oral History* (Brown, 1998) is also an excellent reference tool. Stasz (2000) notes, "the skills required for folklore and oral history projects provide students with almost limitless opportunities to practice authentic reading and writing" (p. 561). In addition, such projects allow students to meet individuals from diverse backgrounds—different ages, occupations, and ethnicities—thus expanding students' awareness of not only language but also the world (Penyak & Duray, 1999; Pile, 1992; Steinberg, 1993). For instance, as students interact with diverse individuals, they must adjust to different accents, styles of speech, and language abilities.

As noted previously, collecting local history can engage students in authentic language and link classrooms to the community. Hurst (1999) recommends several books that provide a framework for oral history projects that showcase the community. For instance, *Letting Swift River Go* (1992) by Jane Yolen tells the story of a WPA (Works Progress Administration) project of the 1930s that created the water supply for Boston. There are countless stories such as this. Hurst also suggests that you have the class brainstorm a list of landmarks in the community and then do research via old newspapers and maps of the area to uncover their stories.

To summarize, including the oral roots of folklore as a part of classroom instruction affords students an opportunity to engage in meaningful language work. A folklore study exposes students to the universal human experience, allows them to examine the creative efforts of all humans, enables them to work across interdisciplinary boundaries, and helps them to develop communication skills. The next section of this chapter continues to highlight the many instructional possibilities of folklore and offers suggestions for reaching out to the home and community through a variety of activities.

Connecting the School to Home and Community Through Folklore

In many communities, there is a growing divide between the way the school looks in terms of teachers, curriculum, and textbooks and the makeup of the community, the students, and their families. To bridge this gap, relevant materials and activities are needed. Folklore serves as an ideal link between the school and the home/community. Rather than beginning with published materials that might not accurately reflect the students' backgrounds, teachers can create projects highlighting the oral traditions, customs, and history of children's homes and community.

As stated earlier, folklore includes the knowledge and stories of a people. This lore is just what Wigginton (1972) and his students from Appalachia collected in the several volumes of the Foxfire project cited earlier. They set out to record how the local folk performed certain tasks, used language, entertained themselves, etc. Classroom teachers can use this same idea by shaping class activities around several folklore themes, such as how to make or do something, how to educate, how to communicate without words, and how to entertain. Following are a variety of classroom activities for students of all ages and all language abilities.

How to Make or Do Something

Studying everyday processes such as cooking or working can yield fascinating results. This topic can yield not only oral and written results but also ideas for classroom demonstrations. As a start, students can talk to family members to collect any of the following (Hadaway, Vardell, & Young, 2002):

- Home remedies and cures, for the common cold or the not so common illness—folk maladies such as *mal de ojo* (evil eye, an ailment caused by simply looking at an individual)
- Procedures for crafts such as origami and paper cutting, or for gardening and canning
- Traditions and preparations for family celebrations (e.g., birthdays) and traditional holidays such as Passover
- Ways to predict the weather or someone's fortune

- Food ways and recipes for traditional dishes (e.g., menudo, latkes, etc.)
- Stories behind family recipes and actual instructions for making and serving a dish
- Directions for making a traditional holiday ornament or decoration, or for playing games such as hide-and-seek or tag
- The process for various recreational activities such as square-dancing

As an introduction to this type of study, you can again turn to literature. The theme of everyday processes is touched on in many trade books. Carmen Lomas Garza provides illustrations and text in both English and Spanish to describe traditional holidays and family celebrations, as well as folk illnesses and cures, in her books *In My Family/En mi familia* (1996) and *Family Pictures/Cuadros de familia* (1998). *Grandma's Latkes* (Drucker, 1992) furnishes an excellent example of the way that folk ways are shared and passed along within families. In this story, the grandmother teaches her granddaughter to make the traditional dish of latkes (potato pancakes) while sharing the origin of Hanukkah. Once these books are shared, students can contribute their own family traditions for a variety of celebrations.

How to Educate

One of the most powerful functions of folklore is to educate, specifically to teach manners and social behaviors (Simons, 1990). Knowing how to treat one's elders or how to behave toward strangers is important in any group. Another area, eating customs, also makes an interesting cross-cultural study. We don't all eat the same things, use the same types of utensils, or even eat at the same times of day. Given such diversity in the dining experience, how do we learn the correct way to eat in our cultures, and how easy is it to adapt to another eating style? Friedman's *How My Parents Learned to Eat* (1984) highlights the cultural differences that come into play as a U.S. sailor courts a Japanese girl and they adjust to each other's way of eating. For background information, James Cross Giblin offers a fascinating nonfiction look at eating across time in *From Hand to Mouth, Or, How We Invented Knives, Forks, Spoons, and Chopsticks, and the Table Manners to Go With Them* (1987). As a starting point, students can share not only typical foods and traditional recipes from their homes but also the customs surrounding food preparation, table setting, and serving. In some cultures, for instance, the family or group serves the meal from a common dish or pot on the table, and only one hand is used for reaching into that container. To touch the food with the other hand (reserved for hygiene purposes) is not an acceptable behavior.

Another educational tool from folklore is the proverb or folk saying (e.g., "pretty is as pretty does"). Such sayings have been used throughout time for the purpose of indoctrinating individuals with certain cultural messages and taboos. One interesting aspect of proverbs is their similarity across cultures and languages. The translations may vary somewhat, but the message is the same. The Golden Rule about how we should treat others as we wish to be treated, for example, exists in all the major religions of the world. Among the many books that provide an overview of common proverbs, *First Things First* (Fraser, 1990) and *A Word to the Wise and Other Proverbs* (Hurwite, 1994) are a great beginning, as they combine strong visuals linked to each saying. *And the Green Grass Grew All Around* (Schwartz, 1992) also offers many amusing folk sayings. Once each proverb is shared with the class, the students can discuss together the "value message" behind the saying. As an extension of the activity, students can collect and illustrate common proverbs and sayings used in their own families.

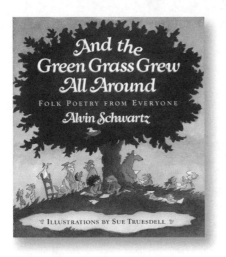

Book cover from *And the Green Grass Grew All Around: Folk Poetry From Everyone* by Alvin Schwartz, illustrated by Susan G. Truesdell. Copyright © 1992. Used by permission of HarperCollins Publishers.

How to Communicate Without Words

The folklore of gestures, greetings, symbols, and signs across cultures furnishes a fascinating glimpse of nonverbal language. The study of communication without words also offers an engaging opportunity to physically participate in a classroom activity. One very basic difference across cultures occurs when we greet one another. Some cultures shake hands, others kiss or bow, etc. In her book *Greetings!* Karen Luisa Badt (1994) provides an informative survey of the many methods of greetings. After you read aloud this book, students can role-play some typical greeting styles. In addition, students might interview workers in various occupations (e.g., construction workers, airport crews, sports officials) about the signals they use to carry out their jobs. Then, they can demonstrate the signals for the class, and students can guess the meanings of the symbols. Students can even devise their own signals for the classroom environment.

How to Entertain

Beyond teaching people the do's and don'ts of a culture, one of the main functions of folklore is to entertain. Tall tales, jokes, riddles, games, songs, and storytelling all serve this purpose. For example, Mexican American students may be familiar with the corridos, or ballads, often sung to report actual events. Paredes (1958) researched the history behind a popular ballad concerning a border hero from the Mexican American community. This ballad was the impetus for the 1982 movie *The Corrido of Gregorio Cortez*. Other folk songs provide a glimpse into a specific historical period or group of people. Songs sung by African slaves in the United States, as an example, sometimes provided clues to the route along the Underground Railroad.

Certainly, young people are familiar with the storytelling sessions as family members gather for the holidays, or they may have experienced parties or gatherings where ghost stories were the expected fare. Many of the ghost or horror stories shared in these settings are urban legends, as in the story of the Kentucky Fried rat or the vanishing hitchhiker. Indeed, these tales often are offered as true stories. Brunvand (1989a, 1989b), cited earlier, has two books that provide different versions of the most popular urban legends, and these would be excellent resources to use when planning such a unit with intermediate and middle school students. You can check out the latest tales on the Urban Legends Reference Pages at www.snopes2.com (Mikkelson & Mikkelson, 1995). This site is full of information about and examples of urban legends.

The purposes of folklore in explaining how to make or do something, how to educate, how to communicate without words, and how to entertain offer a framework for teachers to integrate the full range of verbal and nonverbal folklore into literacy instruction. With this as a beginning, students are more aware of the original roots of folklore and how traditional literature emerged from the oral culture of a group.

The Influence of Technology on Folklore

Unlike the general emphasis in classrooms on the written body of folklore through traditional literature, folklore research has focused on the oral transmission of stories, jokes, etc., and emphasized the traditions of the past and the folk culture. Although this oral tradition is still an important area of inquiry, the increasing influence of technology, particularly of access to the Internet, has shifted the focus of folklore. Technology provides folklore with a wider audience and range of influence than ever before. Photocopiers, fax machines, e-mail, and electronic newsgroups spur the distribution of "modern" folklore and make it possible for urban legends, folk sayings, stories, and such to reach more people. Particularly in the electronic format of e-mail, folklore is subject to the same kind of variations as the oral stories of the past.

In addition to disseminating folklore rapidly across geographic, cultural, and socioeconomic boundaries, technology helps connect students with folklore in other ways. There are countless websites (see Figure 15.2) with background information

Figure 15.2
Folklore-Related Websites

The Library Workplace Folklore Page
    http://alexia.lis.uiuc.edu/~lis405/folklore/folk.htm

A Teacher's Guide to Folklife Resources for K–12 Classrooms
    http://www.loc.gov/folklife/teachers.html

Library of Congress Learning Page: Using Oral History
    http://rs6.loc.gov/ammem/ndlpedu/lessons/oralhist/ohstart.html

Integrating Folklore, Music, & Traditional Culture Into K–12 Education
    http://www.edu-cyberpg.com/Teachers/folk.html

Early Life in Our Area and Veterans' Accounts
    http://users.owt.com/rpeto/early.html

Voices From the Thirties: Life Histories From the Federal Writers' Project
    http://memory.loc.gov/ammem/wpaintro/exhome.html

American Life Histories: Manuscripts From the Federal Writers' Project, 1936–1940
    http://memory.loc.gov/ammem/wpaintro/wpahome.html

California Heritage Project
    http://sunsite.berkeley.edu/calheritage/k12project/index98.html

Folklore: A Tapestry of Life
    http://www.infotoday.com/MMSchools/nov01/cybe0111.htm

Oral History & Interviews
    http://www.cyndislist.com/oral.htm

Doing Oral History
    http://www.gcah.org/oral.html

Ethnographic Collections in the Archive of Folk Culture: A Contributor's Guide
    http://www.loc.gov/folklife/cg.html

International Folk Culture Center, San Antonio
    http://www.n-link.com/~ifccsa

Carol Hurst's Children's Literature Site: Local History and Family Stories
    http://www.carolhurst.com/subjects/history/local.html

Miami Valley Cultural Heritage Project
    http://www.georgetown.edu/crossroads/innovistas/miami.html

Suffragists Oral History Project
    http://sunsite.berkeley.edu:2020/dynaweb/teiproj/oh/suffragists

Southern Council for Folk Culture
    http://personal.cfw.com/~dday

Western Folklife Center
    http://www.westfolk.org

What Did You Do in the War, Grandma?
    http://www.stg.brown.edu/projects/WWII_Women/tocCS.html

Southern Council for Folk Culture
    http://personal.cfw.com/~dday/#contact

Citylore
    http://www.citylore.org

Montana Heritage Project
    http://www.edheritage.org

Story Arts Online
    http://www.storyarts.org

Urban Legends Reference Pages
    http://www.snopes2.com

and actual examples—both written and recorded—of urban legends, oral histories, etc., that can help teachers and students in their research efforts. In addition, technology can serve as a data-gathering tool for students collecting information for oral history projects and the like. With e-mail contacts, students can extend their geographic reach and easily and effectively interview subjects around the world. Or students can use electronic bulletin boards or chat rooms to post surveys and questions regarding class or individual folklore projects.

One interesting type of folklore that the advent of technology has encouraged is occupational or workplace folklore, the stories and traditions of a work or corporate culture. The Library Workplace Folklore Page (Becker, Beyers, & Miller, 1997) serves as a great introduction to students about this type of folklore. Moreover, as schools have their own unique culture as well, students can transfer the idea of workplace folklore to the school setting and collect their own school lore.

Technology has extended boundaries in many ways. The Foxfire projects beginning in the 1960s and 1970s exemplified one effort to keep the roots of folklore alive through oral history projects and printed text. Technology is providing yet another means of informing us of the traditions of the past and of preserving them for generations to come.

Conclusion

The oral and nonverbal traditions, or folklore, within any culture include the stories that have been passed down from generation to generation. These traditions, such as jokes, riddles, and oral histories, are naturally motivating to students but often are neglected by teachers who tend to focus on published traditional literature. Yet, folklore not only involves students in language study but also unlocks an understanding of our own and others' cultures, values, and motivations. The breadth of possibilities is what makes folklore study so effective in the classroom. You can find engaging content for a diverse student audience. In addition, folklore study that centers on oral traditions holds great promise for connecting the school with students' home and community, from family history projects to oral histories of a local area.

Finally, while oral traditions and customs were preserved through verbal transmission in previous times, current and future technology may hold the key to preserving much of the traditional wisdom and customs of our past. Our electronic communication network has had a profound impact on folklore, preserving the folk culture through informational websites and contributions to the transmission of folklore as more and more individuals use electronic mail and discussion forums.

REFERENCES

Anokye, A.D. (1997). A case for orality in the classroom. *Clearing House, 70,* 229–232.

Bartis, P. (1979). *Folklife and fieldwork: A layman's introduction to field techniques.* Washington, DC: American Folklife Center, Library of Congress.

Bartis, P., & Bowman, P. (1994). *A teacher's guide to folklife resources for K–12 classrooms.* Publications of the American Folklife Center, no. 19. Washington, DC: American Folklife Center, Library of Congress, http://www.loc.gov/folklife/teachers.html

Bascom, W.R. (1965). Folklore and anthropology. In A. Dundes (Ed.), *The study of folklore,* pp. 25–33. Englewood Cliffs, NJ: Prentice-Hall.

Becker, V., Beyers, L., & Miller, J. (1997). The library workplace folklore page. Accessed June 20, 2003, at http://alexia.lis.uiuc.edu/~lis405/folklore/folk.htm

Brown, C.S. (1998). *Like it was: A complete guide to writing oral history.* New York: Teachers & Writers Collaborative.

Brunvand, J.H. (1989a). *Curses! Broiled again! The hottest urban legends going.* New York: W.W. Norton.

Brunvand, J.H. (1989b). *The vanishing hitchhiker: American urban legends and their meanings.* New York: W.W. Norton.

Buchoff, R. (1995). Family stories. *The Reading Teacher, 49,* 230–233.

Carthy, J. (2002). *Folklore in the oral tradition, fairytales, fables, and folk-legend.* Yale–New Haven Teachers Institute. Retrieved June 20, 2003, from http://www.yale.edu/ynhti/curriculum/units/1984/4/84.04.01.x.html#a

Dundes, A. (1965). *The study of folklore.* Englewood Cliffs, NJ: Prentice Hall.

Fish, L. (2000). Vietnam Veterans Oral History and Folklore Project. Accessed June 20, 2003, at http://facstaff.buffalostate.edu/fishlm/folksongs

Forest, H. (2000). Story Arts Online. Accessed June 20, 2003, at http://www.storyarts.org

Gonzalez, R.D. (1982). Teaching Mexican American students to write: Capitalizing on culture. *English Journal, 71,* 20–24.

Hadaway, N.L. (2002). *Survey of teacher awareness and use of folklore.* Unpublished data.

Hadaway, N.L., & Mundy, J. (1992). Crossing curricular and cultural boundaries: A study of families and family folklore. *English Journal, 81,* 60–64.

Hadaway, N.L., Vardell, S.V., & Young, T.A. (2002). *Literature-based instruction with English language-learners, K–12.* Boston: Allyn & Bacon.

Hastings, S.E. (1990). *Miss Mary Mac all dressed in black: Tongue twisters, jump-rope rhymes, and other children's lore from New England.* Little Rock, AR: August House.

Hurst, C. (1999). Local history and family stories. In Carol Hurst's Children's Literature Site. Retrieved June 20, 2003, from http://www.carolhurst.com/subjects/history/local.html

Kotkin, A.J., & Baker, H.C. (1977). *Family folklore interviewing guide and questionnaire.* Baltimore: Maryland Arts Council Folklife Program.

Krogness, M.M. (1987). Folklore: A matter of the heart and the heart of the matter. *Language Arts, 64,* 808–817.

Library of Congress. (2002). American Folklife Center of the Library of Congress. Retrieved June 20, 2003, from http://www.loc.gov/folklife

Lutz, E. (1986). Using folk literature in your reading program. *Journal of Reading, 30,* 76–78.

Mikkelson, B., & Mikkelson, D.P. (1995). *Urban legends reference pages.* Retrieved June 20, 2003, from http://www.snopes2.com

Morain, G. (1970). Cultural pluralism. In D.L. Lange (Ed.), *Britannica review of foreign language education* (Vol. 3). Chicago: Encyclopedia Britannica.

Morain, G. (1971). Teaching for cross-cultural understanding: An annotated bibliography. *Foreign Language Annals, 5,* 82–83.

Panford, S., Nyaney, M.O., Amoah, S.O., & Aidoo, N.G. (2001). Using folk media in HIV/AIDS prevention in rural Ghana. *American Journal of Public Health, 91,* 1559–1562.

Paredes, A. (1958). *With a pistol in his hand: A border ballad and its hero.* Austin, TX: University of Texas Press.

Penyak, L.M., & Duray, P.B. (1999). Oral history and problematic questions promote issues-centered education. *Social Studies, 90,* 68–72.

Pile, S. (1992). Oral history and teaching qualitative methods. *Journal of Geography in Higher Education, 16,* 135–144.

Renner, S.M., & Carter, J.M. (1991). Comprehending text—Appreciating diversity through folklore. *Journal of Reading, 34,* 602–604.

Silver, D. (2001). Songs and storytelling: Bringing health messages to life in Uganda. *Education for Health: Change in Learning & Practice, 14,* 51–61.

Simons, E.R. (1990). *Student worlds, student words: Teaching writing through folklore.* Portsmouth, NH: Boynton/Cook.

Smithsonian Institution. *The grand generation: Interviewing guide and questionnaire.* Retrieved June 20, 2003, from http://educate.si.edu/migrations/seek1/grand1.html

Speaker, K.M. (2000). The art of storytelling: A collegiate connection to professional development schools. *Education, 121,* 184–188.

Stasz, B. (2000). The road to Chiliseni: Collecting stories to read by. *The Reading Teacher, 53,* 560–564.

Steinberg, S. (1993). The world inside the classroom: Using oral history to explore racial and ethnic diversity. *Social Studies, 84,* 71–73.

Tiedt, P., & Tiedt, I. (1995). *Multicultural teaching: A handbook of activities, information, and resources* (4th ed.). New York: Allyn & Bacon.

University of California, Berkeley. (1998). Oral history online: Suffragists oral history project. Retrieved June 20, 2003, from http://sunsite.berkeley.edu:2020/dynaweb/teiproj/oh/suffragists

University of California, Los Angeles (UCLA). (2001). Online Archive of American Folk Medicine. Retrieved June 20, 2003, from http://www.folkmed.ucla.edu/advanced.html

Wigginton, E. (Ed.). (1972). *The foxfire book: Hog dressing, log cabin building, mountain crafts and foods, planting by the signs, snake lore, hunting tales, faith healing, moon-*

shining, and other affairs of plain living. New York: Doubleday.

Wigginton, E. (Ed.). (1985). *Sometimes a shining moment: The foxfire experience*. Garden City, NY: Anchor/Doubleday.

Wigginton, E. (1991). Culture begins at home. *Educational Leadership, 49*, 60–64.

Wilson, W.A. (1988). The deeper necessity: Folklore and the humanities. *Journal of American Folklore, 101*, 156–167.

Wolfman, I. (1991). *Do people grow on family trees? Genealogy for kids and other beginners*. New York: Workman.

Wood, L., Scott, J., & Brown University's Scholarly Technology Group. (1997). *What did you do in the war, Grandma? Teaching English via oral history*. Retrieved June 20, 2003, from http://www.stg.brown.edu/projects/WWII_Women/TeachingEnglish.html

CHILDREN'S BOOKS CITED

Aardema, V. (1975). *Why mosquitoes buzz in people's ears* (L. Dillon & D. Dillon, Illus.). New York: Dial.

Badt, K.L. (1994). *Greetings!* Chicago: Children's Press.

Byars, B.C. (1996). *The moon and I*. New York: Beech Tree.

Drucker, M. (1992). *Grandma's latkes* (E. Chwast, Illus.). New York: Trumpet.

Fraser, B. (1990). *First things first: An illustrated collection of sayings useful and familiar for children*. New York: HarperCollins.

Friedman, I.R. (1984). *How my parents learned to eat* (A. Say, Illus.). New York: Houghton Mifflin.

Garza, C.L. (1996). *In my family/En mi familia*. Chicago: Children's Press.

Garza, C.L. (1998). *Family pictures/Cuadros de familia*. Chicago: Children's Press.

Giblin, J.C. (1987). *From hand to mouth, or, how we invented knives, forks, spoons, and chopsticks and the table manners to go with them*. New York: Crowell.

Hurwite, J. (1994). *A word to the wise and other proverbs* (R. Rayevsky, Illus.). New York: Morrow.

Kipling, R. (1991). *How the camel got his hump* (K. Motoyama, Illus.). New York: Simon & Schuster.

Lowry, L. (2000). *Looking back: A book of memories*. New York: Delacorte.

Schwartz, A. (1992). *And the green grass grew all around: Folk poetry from everyone* (S. Truesdell, Illus.). New York: HarperCollins.

Steptoe, J. (1987). *Mufaro's beautiful daughters*. New York: Lothrop, Lee & Shepard.

Yolen, J. (1992). *Letting swift river go* (B. Cooney, Illus.). Boston: Little, Brown.

Young, E. (1989). *Lon Po Po: A Red Riding Hood story from China*. New York: Philomel.

CHAPTER 16

"I'll Be the Monster!" Folk Tales and Classroom Drama

Judy Sierra

It is the story...that saves our progeny from blundering like blind beggars into the spikes of the cactus fence. The story is our escort; without it we are blind. Does the blind man own his escort? No, neither do we own the story; rather it is the story that owns and directs us. (Chinua Achebe, *Anthills of the Savannah*, p. 114)

My first experience teaching drama in the classroom remains a vivid memory. I visited an eighth-grade class with a puppeteer friend who was working as a resident artist. I was only there as an observer, or so I thought. He told the students to gather in small groups and create a script for a puppet play of "Cinderella," and then he assigned me to assist a group of eight young ladies. My heart sank. "Oh no," I thought. "First I have to remember the story, then I have to tell it to them. After that, I have no idea what I'll do."

As I approached their table, the girls were huddled together. One spoke in a disapproving tone. "I know *just* how that stepmother talked," she said. "When the father was around, she was *so-o-o* nice to Cinderella. Then when he was gone, it was 'Cinderella-do-this' and 'Cinderella-do-that.'" The others nodded their heads in solemn agreement. I didn't remember this from any version of "Cinderella" I knew. Had they made it up? Whether they had or not, it was quintessentially dramatic—a perfect way to let an audience know just how cruel and devious Cinderella's stepmother was. I jumped in. "Let's pretend that Cinderella and her father and the stepmother are in the kitchen talking, and then her father walks out of the room. What would they say?" I scribbled notes as quickly as I could. To my surprise, these girls had a sort of generic Cinderella story in their heads—formed, no doubt, by the Walt Disney movie, combined with assorted book and media versions and their own life experiences. No one girl could recall all the details, but collectively and most enthusiastically they pieced it together. My job that day turned out to be little more than writing down their words and ideas. The folk tale fired their imaginations and sustained their interest over many weeks of scriptwriting, puppet making, and, finally, performance.

Not all playwriting sessions proceed quite so smoothly, of course. Every teacher and group leader develops strategies to jump-start drama projects and keep students moving along. However, I made an important discovery that day, one that would be reinforced time and again during my years as an artist in the schools: There was nothing like a folk tale (the *right* folk tale—more about that later) to inspire performances so fresh and interesting that I never grew tired of the core group of stories I used in my work. Whether a tale is familiar to the group or brand new, whether it is from their culture or a remote one, the right folk tale allows children and young adults to take the lead in interpreting it through drama while the teacher coaches, makes suggestions, and supports their efforts. I found the power of folk tales so intriguing yet elusive that I went on to pursue graduate studies in folklore in hopes of discovering the secret of their magic.

The Memorable Nature of Folk Tales

Folk tales are tales from the oral tradition. Unlike myths and legends, which are regarded as true (or as having once been true), folk tales are acknowledged as fictional, yet as providing access to another reality—a symbolic reality. (For a general discussion about folk tales and some information about the different types of stories available, see chapter 2.)

Folk tales are inherently memorable. In contrast to original authored tales (those with a specific, acknowledged author), folk tales can be remembered and told by ordinary people who have no specialized theater training. Nor is painstaking rote memorization required in order to tell a folk tale. Like plants and animals that have evolved to survive in a special niche, folk tales are adapted to survive in the unique terrain of human memory. They do so (if we can, for a moment, suspend disbelief and imagine that a folk tale evolves like a living organism) through a combination of memorable plot structure, compelling theme, vivid imagery, stock character types, and generous use of repetition. Although each of these components contributes to the memorable nature of folk tales, I will focus on the two that I believe contribute most to their success as classroom drama—plot structure and the use of repetition.

Plot Structure

Because folk tales are memorable, drama leaders can begin a performance project without a script. I chose to work this way because of the greater sense of ownership and empowerment it gave students. After students hear a folk tale several times, they are able to call up a mental storyboard that they can access and manipulate. I have found that when I work with folk tales, all or nearly all students in a group can imagine and discuss possible variations in plot, dialogue, setting, and so forth, whereas when I have used a literary tale, or even one created by the children themselves, only the more gifted students have been able to retain it in memory.

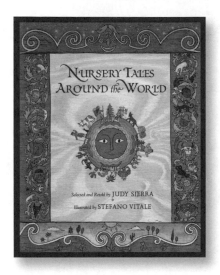

Book cover from *Nursery Tales Around the World* by Judy Sierra, illustrated by Stefano Vitale. Jacket copyright © 1996 by Stefano Vitale. Reprinted by permission of Clarion Books/Houghton Mifflin Company. All rights reserved.

One of the first researchers to recognize the memorable qualities of folk tales in contrast to original authored narratives was the British psychologist Frederic Bartlett. He was investigating human memory for stories in general, using Cambridge University students as research subjects. Neither Bartlett's subjects nor his laboratory methods were quite like the oral storytelling model, yet he unexpectedly discovered a striking difference in subjects' memory for folk tales versus literary tales. All his experiments were conducted in writing. A student would read a story, for example, then recall and rewrite it many times over intervals of days, months, and even years. In another type of experiment, a subject would read a tale, then write it down from memory, and then that version would be read and remembered by a second subject, and so on along a chain of up to 20 individuals. Bartlett found that when he used folk tales, subjects' retellings would actually become longer over time as they rationalized the tales (i.e., changed them to make them more coherent) and added their own morals. Nonfolk narratives, in contrast, quickly lost all sense "so that nobody, seeing only the first and last versions, would be inclined to connect them in a continuous series" (Bartlett, 1920, p. 165). When Bartlett tested subjects' memory for logical arguments, "every bit of general reasoning...disappeared" (p. 171). He found that of all folk tales, cumulative tales were remembered best, and he speculated that the characteristic repetition in these tales aided retention.

My research with librarian storytellers supports Bartlett's findings. Folk tales are not simply memorable; they are productive. That is, they encourage creativity on the part of storytellers, and this creativity is a source of pleasure. I believe that a large part of folk tales' appeal to traditional and modern storytellers is, in fact, the amount of individual expression they accommodate. As a Tuscan proverb reminds us, "The tale is not beautiful if nothing is added to it" (Calvino, 1980, p. xi).

Bartlett did not investigate why folk tales are more memorable than authored tales. Folklorists have speculated on the reasons folk tales survive in oral tradition, but few have actually conducted experiments. In my doctoral dissertation, I hypothesized that the episodic structure of folk tales was fundamentally different from that of authored tales. Psychologists Jean M. Mandler and Nancy Johnson, in studies of children's memory for stories, found that a memorable plot consisted of a nested series of goal-oriented episodes and that memorable tales (which I took to mean folk tales) are about characters pursuing goals (Mandler & Johnson, 1977). The episodes of memorable stories are tightly bound together: The end of one episode becomes the beginning of the next, culminating in the main protagonist's success or failure at achieving the original goal.

I applied Mandler and Johnson's story grammar (a method of parsing a story somewhat like sentence diagramming, based on the work of Russian folklorist Vladimir Propp [1968] in *Morphology of the Folktale*) to two sets of stories. I asked experienced storytelling teachers and librarians to name their most successful tales for telling and also the stories they liked but found difficult or impossible to remember and retell. Predictably, the second group was made up of literary creations such as Hans Christian Andersen's "The Ugly Duckling" (cf. Owens, 1993) and Rudyard Kipling's "The Elephant's Child" (1996). These stories share some features with folk tales—verbal style, types of characters and settings, repetition—yet I could not parse them into goal-oriented episodes using Mandler and Johnson's model. The storytellers' most successful tales, in contrast, were all folk tales (the two top favorites were "Mollie Whuppie" and "Wiley and the Hairy Man") that fit the story grammar almost perfectly (Sierra, 1993).

Characters' goals in a folk tale may be stated or inferred. The minor characters can be pursuing the same goal as the protagonist, like the birds who join Henny Penny in her questionable quest to tell the king that the sky is falling, or they can seek competing goals, like the wolf and the pigs in "The Three Pigs." Children are more likely to become interested in tales that feature goals they can understand, especially if these reflect their own hopes and fears. They enjoy laughing at characters who pursue goals in inappropriate ways, or rooting for the victory of the small and weak over the large and powerful.

The goal orientation of folk tales helps children improvise drama. If one character is pursuing a goal and another resists or pursues a competing goal, interesting dialogue will almost always ensue. Scenes such as one in which the wolf tries to convince a pig to let him into his house, or the little billy goat attempts to convince a troll to allow him to cross the bridge, can be expanded in rehearsal if the teacher encourages children to have their characters refuse (initially) to give in to threats or persuasion or have them use deception, flattery, or logic—in other words, to bring the tale to life and make it uniquely theirs.

Repetition

Repetition is a pleasurable aspect of all works of art, from the refrain of a song to the recurring patterns and forms in the visual arts. In children's folk tales that have been collected in authentic storytelling sessions, one encounters abundant repetition of sounds, words, word groups, chants, and rhymes. The episodes of a folk tale are similar, often with only minor changes or substitutions from one to the next. Folk tale dialogue may predict or recapitulate plot; for instance, one character may advise another to perform a series of actions and the second character follows those instructions. Or a character may summarize the preceding action, as the Gingerbread Man does each time he meets a new character ("I've run away from an old man, and an old woman, and a pig..."). Plot structures, themes, and characters are repeated across groups of related tales from the same culture region, such as Anansi tales from West Africa, or Brer Rabbit tales from the African American tradition (see chapter 7). Taken together, the repetitious elements of folk tales make it easy for a storyteller to reconstruct an extended narrative from just a few remembered elements.

A teacher can use folk tales' repetitious patterns to inspire the creation of lively and distinctive characters by encouraging students to vary similar actions and verbatim dialogue. This might create distinctive styles of movement for each character in a tale such as "Henny Penny" or "Momotaro" that features a lot of "walking along," or unique voices for characters, such as the three pigs, who have repetitious dialogue. Repetition also helps the youngest audience members recall what has already happened in a play and to predict what will happen next, and it thus keeps their attention from wandering.

Folk Tales as Drama in the Oral Tradition

In traditional settings, have folk tales been dramatized either by or for children? Myth has been acted out on ritual occasions using costumes, masks, and puppets. Folk tales, on the other hand, are typically told by one person. The style of folk tale telling is often very dramatic: Storytellers sing traditional refrains, engage audiences in call and response, and portray characters with exaggerated voices, gestures, and facial expressions.

Children's folk tales are not the fictional material children tell one another or the preferred material for their spontaneous dramatic play, although traditional children's games such as the Anglo-American "Old Witch" and "What Time Is It, Mister Wolf?" have story structures that resemble those of folk tales. Children's folk tales are very much adult messages *to* children. They have been shaped by child audiences' developmental stage, interests, and receptivity, but they are not often told *by* children. These folk tales are didactic. Adults use them to teach children lessons that adults think are important. The Gingerbread Man, for example, willfully disobeys the first rule of toddlerhood ("Don't run away") and is punished. Goldilocks violates the rules of visiting: "Ask first before you help yourself, and don't break anything." At around the age of 7 or 8, children realize that these folk tales are didactic, and they will usually choose to parody them in drama unless they are intentionally creating entertainment for an audience of younger children.

Finding Tales to Dramatize

The tales chosen for classroom drama must meet three criteria: They must appeal to the group leader, they must appeal to the students, and, because folk tales were never intended to be acted out by a group, they must be selected for their adaptability to the limitations of theater. Tales that require elaborate scenery or many changes of scenery, for example, are usually more trouble than they are worth. Tales with too few characters will not satisfy enough children's desire to play a part. Finding tales that meet all three criteria is time-consuming, so I recommend beginning with anthologies of folk tale texts or scripts chosen by experienced classroom drama leaders, such as those listed in Figure 16.1. I also recommend that new drama leaders begin with the very simplest folk tales, ones that have traditionally been told to children at ages 3–7. Familiar folk tales such as "The Three Billy Goats Gruff" and "The Three Pigs" are perfect choices for dramatization by children new to the English language. For native English speakers, though, these tales and their innumerable variations and parodies are much too familiar, and lesser known tales that are reminiscent of old favorites will be more stimulating. I have included many of these tales in my published anthologies, such as the Italian folk tale "Buggy Wuggy"

Figure 16.1
Anthologies of Folk Tales to Dramatize

Korty. C. (1975) *Plays from African folktales, with ideas for acting, dance, costumes, and music.* New York: Scribner. (scripts)

Mahlmann, L., & Jones, D.C. (1980). *Folk tale plays for puppets: 13 royalty-free plays for hand puppets, rod puppets, or marionettes.* Boston: Plays. (scripts)

Sierra, J. (1996). *Multicultural folktales for feltboard and reader's theater.* Phoenix, AZ: Oryx. (texts and scripts)

Sierra, J. (1996). *Nursery tales around the world* (S. Vitale, Illus.). New York: Clarion. (texts)

Sierra, J. (1997). *Flannel board storytelling book.* New York: H.W. Wilson. (texts and patterns)

Sierra, J. (2002) *Silly and sillier: Read-aloud tales from around the world.* New York: Knopf. (texts)

Sierra, J., & Kaminski, B. (1989). *Twice upon a time: Stories to tell, retell, act out, and write about.* New York: H.W. Wilson. (texts)

Sierra, J., & Kaminski, B. (1996). *Multicultural folktales: Stories for young children.* Phoenix, AZ: Oryx. (texts and patterns)

(in *Silly and Sillier: Read-Aloud Tales From Around the World*, Sierra, 2002), a funny tale with a strong resemblance to three better-known stories, "Henny Penny," "The Three Pigs," and "The Fat Cat."

Dramatizing Tales Through Puppetry

As a performer, puppetry was my chosen means of dramatizing folk tales, and it proved to be a perfect medium for the classroom as well. There are compelling reasons to use puppets rather than costumed actors to bring folk tales to life. For one, the relative size and appearance of puppet characters can be more true to the tale.

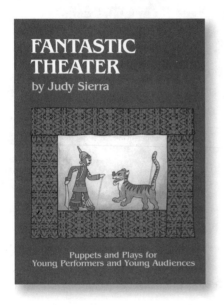

Book cover from *Fantastic Theater: Puppets and Plays for Young Performers and Young Audiences* by Judy Sierra. Copyright © 1991. Used by permission of The H.W. Wilson Company.

With a little ingenuity, puppeteers can make their creations seem to fly, to magically appear and disappear, or to transform into another shape entirely. Puppetry offers every child a chance to contribute to a successful dramatic production, from puppet making, to creating and playing music and sound effects, to acting, to selling tickets, to managing properties, to directing. It is an ideal medium for engaging and honoring multiple intelligences.

I once encountered a boy in a fifth-grade class who was unable to draw or use scissors. His friends pitched in to make a shadow puppet for him. Later, as his group performed its play, I was surprised by improvised dialogue far more clever and rapid-fire than usual, and by characters that had wonderfully varied, cartoon-like voices. I peeked backstage. That same boy had commandeered all the puppets and was performing the entire play by himself—just like a traditional shadow puppet performer from Bali or Java.

During the years my husband, Bob Kaminski, and I worked as artists in the schools, the amount of time we were given to work in a single classroom slowly dwindled, due to budget cuts, from several weeks to several hours. We had to find a way to quickly move a group from reading or listening to a folk tale, to making puppets, to presenting a play. We would begin by telling a story, or several stories from which the students would choose a favorite. Then we divided the class into small groups, each of which would perform the same story. After the students had made simple puppets and props, we coached them on how to enter and exit and how to manipulate the puppets, then sent one group at a time backstage. Bob or I told the story, pausing for the students to improvise dialogue, or coaching them when dialogue wasn't forthcoming. We also provided simple music and sound effects with a kazoo, slide whistle, and tambourine. There would be three to five groups in a class acting out the same folk tale, and after the first group's performance, we would pass along the roles of narrator and musician to willing students.

After a group of fourth, fifth, or sixth graders has assimilated the basics of puppetry (especially shadow puppetry), they often can take over the whole process, calling on the teacher as an advisor. When a play is ready to be shown to outsiders, it is wise to choose a director to be in charge of rehearsals and to make sure that performances run smoothly and make sense to the audience.

The Fat Cat: A Favorite Type of Folk Tale

One of our favorite folk tale types for acting out and for storytelling is "Fat Cat" tales, officially known to folklorists as Aarne-Thompson Tale Type 2027—The Cat Who Was a Glutton (for more information about this official folklore classification system, see Aarne & Thompson, 1961). Published versions of this tale type from several cultures are highlighted in Figure 16.2, including *The Fat Cat* from Denmark (Kent, 1971) and "The Cat and the Parrot" from India (Sierra, 1996). For a book of puppet plays, *Fantastic Theater* (Sierra, 1991), I adapted an Anglo-American variant of the tale "The Greedy Old Fat Man" (Galdone, 1983), calling my version "The Hungry Monster." Elementary and even middle school students love to perform this deceptively simple tale (see Figure 16.3 for a synopsis), and I am always surprised by the rapt attention with which both children and adults listen to this and other "Fat Cat" stories.

Folklorist Bengt Holbek (1990) compared 19 versions of "The Cat Who Was a Glutton" collected from oral storytellers in Denmark, and he provided a fascinating example of how much a tale type varies in actual storytelling situations, even within a small geographical area. Holbek noted that in these tales, the cat eats a series of five to eight animals, objects, or people (seven plus or minus two is, not coincidentally, the number of items that people are able to store and quickly access from short-term memory). Another constant feature of the tale is that the cat recites a complete list of his previous victims before devouring the next one, and this list has a catchy,

---

Figure 16.2
Tales of the Fat Cat

"The cat and the parrot." (1996). In Sierra, J. (Ed.), *Nursery tales around the world*. New York: Clarion. (India)
The fat cat: A Danish folktale by Kent, J. (1971). New York: Parent's Magazine. (Denmark)
The greedy old fat man: An American folk tale by Galdone, P. (1983). New York: Clarion. (United States)
"The hungry cat." (1991). In Sierra, J. (Ed.), *Multicultural folktales: Stories to tell young children*. Phoenix, AZ: Oryx. (Norway)
"Kuratko the terrible." (2002). In Sierra, J. (Ed.), *Silly and sillier: Read-aloud tales from around the world*. New York: Knopf. (Czech Republic)
"Sody Sallyratus." (1948). In Chase, R. (Ed.), *Grandfather tales: American-English folk tales*. Boston: Houghton Mifflin. (United States)

Figure 16.3
"The Hungry Monster": A Synopsis

A monster gets up in the morning and eats one hundred pancakes and drinks one hundred glasses of milk, but he is still hungry. He goes out for a walk and he meets a little boy and a little girl who greet him, saying, "Hello, Mister Monster. How did you get to be so fat?" "Well," said the monster, "I'll tell you. I ate one hundred pancakes and I drank one hundred glasses of milk, but I am still hungry. I think I will eat you, too!" And he did.

The monster walked a bit further and he met a dog. "Ruff! Hello, Mister Monster," said the dog. "How did you ever get to be so fat?" "Well," said the monster, "I'll tell you. I ate one hundred pancakes and I drank one hundred glasses of milk, and I ate a little boy and a little girl, but I am still hungry. I think I will eat you, too!" And he did.

The monster walked a bit further and he met a cat. "Meow. Hello, Mister Monster," said the cat. "How did you ever get to be so fat?" "Well," said the monster, "I'll tell you. I ate one hundred pancakes and I drank one hundred glasses of milk, and I ate a little boy and a little girl and a dog, but I am still hungry. I think I will eat you, too!" And he did.

The monster walked a bit further and he met a squirrel. "Hello, Mister Monster," said the squirrel. "How did you ever get to be so fat?" "Well," said the monster, "I'll tell you. I ate one hundred pancakes and I drank one hundred glasses of milk, and I ate a little boy and a little girl, and a dog, and a cat, but I am still hungry. I think I will eat you, too!"

"First, you will have to catch me," said the squirrel, and she ran up a tree, singing, "You can't catch me! You can't catch me!" "Oh yes I can," said the hungry monster, and he started to climb the tree, but his belly was so big and he was so heavy, he fell to the ground. His belly burst open and out came the little boy saying, "I'm out!" Out hopped the little girl saying, "I'm out!" Then the dog jumped out saying, "I'm out!" And the cat climbed out saying, "I'm out!"

The squirrel said, "I'm out, because I was never in." Then the hungry monster's mother came along and took her needle and thread and sewed up the monster's belly, and after that, he never ate anybody ever again.

---

rhythmic, or rhyming form. The types of animals, objects, or people eaten by the cat vary from teller to teller, although the cat always goes after progressively larger and more powerful prey. Finally, each Danish cat meets someone who is capable of cutting open his belly and releasing his victims, an action that can happen from inside or outside his belly. He might meet a billy goat or a ram who tears him with his horns, a sharp-toothed dog, a boy with a sword, or a man with an ax.

In my script for "The Hungry Monster," I allowed the monster to live—his mother comes along just at the right time and sews up the hole in his belly. In most folk variants, the glutton does not survive, but I preferred not to leave a dead body onstage at the end of the puppet play. This highlights another interesting feature of the folk tale. In most tale types, there is a certain obligatory climax (e.g., in "Fat Cat" tales, the glutton bursts, and everyone inside escapes unharmed). The denouement of the tale, however, varies. It appears that storytellers (with the approval of their listeners, of course) retain the right to divvy up rewards and punishments at the end of a tale, and to add their own moral. This storytellers' choice can be seen in the two best-known versions of the Cinderella story, Charles Perrault's "Cinderella" (cf. Philip, 1992) and the Grimms' "Aschenputtel/Cinderella" (cf. Stern, 1976). (In each, the heroine marries the prince—the obligatory climax—however,

Perrault's Cinderella chooses noble husbands for her two stepsisters, but in the Grimms' tale, birds peck out the stepsisters' eyes. These are both literary retellings of oral tales, yet one finds similar variations in oral versions.)

An ESL Performance of "The Hungry Monster"

My most memorable experience with "The Hungry Monster" was as an observer of performances by my husband's class of fourth through sixth graders, all recent immigrants to the United States who were at the beginning level of English comprehension. With this particular class, the narration-improvisation method was not an option. Bob gave each child a script, and he read it to them and with them, over and over. He also instructed them to read their lines aloud as homework. The group rehearsed often, perfecting stage business and sound effects as well as dialogue. In performance, the play was remarkably lively and entertaining. Although some of the puppeteers were difficult to understand, no one could doubt that their characters were fully engaged in the play. Their voices were perfect, from the monster's cruel boasting to the "I-told-you-so" attitude of the squirrel. The students performed "The Hungry Monster" for many appreciative groups of native English speakers. Some of the students even began to improvise and add small bits of dialogue, especially taunts, which they had probably learned recently on the playground. After each performance, the students would come out from behind the shadow puppet stage to tell the audience their names and the roles they played, radiating pride and confidence. Several of them were so pleased with their success that they decided on their own to enter a storytelling competition at the local public library, presenting other simple folk tales with a flannel board.

As in other classes, the qualities of folk tales that make them memorable also make them perfect for ESL dramatic productions. Repetitious dialogue allows children to play important roles just by learning a few words or phrases. Most of the uncomplicated character types who populate folk tales transcend culture, and the basic structure of children's folk tales is similar from culture to culture, providing a reassuring sense of familiarity to second-language learners.

Writing Scripts From Folk Tales

Developing a script presents children with an enjoyable challenge. Scripts follow a standard format that combines creative writing (dialogue and monologue) with precise technical writing (stage directions). When students create scripts *after* developing a play in rehearsal, they are writing from personal experience, which facilitates the process. Postproduction scriptwriting can be a way of documenting a group's work, or it can be a step toward a more formal performance for outside audiences. This is, in fact, how much professional playwriting is done: The script is changed and polished in rehearsal.

Other forms of writing can be successfully incorporated into a drama project based on folk tales: creating short rhymes and chants for the characters (these are especially effective preceding a character's entrance, or as the character travels), making up songs for characters to sing (perhaps based on well-known tunes), writing promotional material such as news releases and posters, and creating theater reviews.

Conclusion

When dramatizing folk tales, students practice reading, writing, oral comprehension, and oral expression while they develop performance and visual arts skills. Because tale-based drama can be initiated easily, and because it encourages cooperation, it is especially recommended for teachers who see a particular group infrequently— music, art, and drama teachers, for example, or substitute teachers. When children dramatize folk tales, they bring traditional stories full circle, coaxing them off the printed page and back into oral culture. The changes that children make in folk tales are part of the ongoing process of narrative tradition.

REFERENCES

Aarne, A., & Thompson, S. (1961). *The types of the folktale: A classification and bibliography*. Helsinki, Finland: Academia Scientiarum Fennica.

Achebe, C. (1987). *Anthills of the savannah*. Portsmouth, NH: Heinemann.

Bartlett, F.C. (1920). *Remembering: A study in experimental and social psychology*. Cambridge, UK: Cambridge University Press.

Calvino, I. (1980). *Italian folktales*. San Diego: Harcourt.

Holbek, B. (1990). The big-bellied cat. In M. Nøjgaard (Ed.), *The telling of stories: Approaches to a traditional craft* (pp. 57–70). Odense, Denmark: Odense University Press.

Mandler, J.M., & Johnson, N.S. (1977). Remembrance of things parsed: Story structure and recall. *Cognitive Psychology, 9*, 111–151.

Propp, V. (1968). *Morphology of the folktale* (2nd ed.). Austin, TX: University of Texas Press.

Sierra, J. (1993). *What makes a tale tellable? Narrative and memory process*. Unpublished doctoral dissertation, University of California, Los Angeles.

CHILDREN'S BOOKS CITED

Galdone, P. (1983). *The greedy old fat man: An American folk tale*. New York: Clarion.

Kent, J. (1971). *The fat cat: A Danish folktale*. New York: Parent's Magazine.

Kipling, R. (1996). *Just so stories*. New York: Morrow.

Owens, L. (1993). *The complete Hans Christian Andersen fairy tales*. New York: Grammercy.

Philip, N. (Trans.). (1992). *The complete fairy tales of Charles Perrault* (S. Holmes, Illus.). New York: Clarion.

Sierra, J. (1991). *Fantastic theater: Puppets and plays for young players and young audiences*. Bronx, NY: H.W. Wilson.

Sierra, J. (1996). *Nursery tales around the world* (S. Vitale, Illus.). New York: Clarion.

Sierra, J. (2002). *Silly and sillier: Read-aloud tales from around the world*. New York: Knopf.

Stern, J. (Ed.). (1976). *The complete Grimm's fairy tales* (Pantheon Fairy Tale & Folklore Library) (J. Scharl, Illus.). New York: Random House.

CHAPTER 17

Transforming Fairy Tales to Inspire Young Authors

Laura Tuiaea

airy tale...the term has an inherent mystique, a draw to both one's own cultural heritage and the global community at large. Fairy tales are found all over the world and written from many time periods—present-day to long, long ago—yet they are often intensely personal. Who doesn't know of the naive girl in the red hood who struggles past the wolf and his evil plans? We root for her just as we root for the detours around roadblocks in our own lives. We cheer for those three pigs as they find sanctuary, just as we cheer for our personal attainment of goals. We pull for Cinderella to win her prince and any other rewards she can for her endearing perseverance. Within the justice of her life is the potential justice in ours. In such stories it is clear that hard work really does pay off, that good thinking solves problems, that those who are unselfish are rewarded. Good readers are constantly making connections between text and self. Within these connections, and the awareness of theme beneath them, lies the foundation for transformation of text. We can tweak the story a bit and make it ours, make it something new and unique with a personal slant. Voila! But what value is there in doing so?

First, let us consider what we mean by transforming text. In the most basic definition, it relates a change in words. Moffett and Wagner state, "To transform a text is to take the essence of what it expresses and transfer it to another form of writing or to another medium altogether" (1992, p. 164). For our purposes, we will suggest taking an initial step to the side. We will address first adapting a story element, and then examining a wide range of possibilities for change of genre, form, or medium. These transformations, then, begin with an intentional bit of elemental adaptation such as a change in setting or point of view, followed by the possible transformation into other modes. Such stories are called fractured, twisted, tweaked, newfangled, revisited, or topsy-turvy fairy tales. Some are pure parody, with a desired comic effect as part of the change. So, it is clear that there are several options for the writer of a transformed tale; let's return to the why of it.

Exploring the Study of Fairy Tales

The rationale for fairy tale study itself is clear. In addition to a universal appeal and the widespread availability of such tales, it is great fun. All students enjoy comparing versions of traditional stories, contrasting what they know about the wolf or fairy godmother or magic wand with what others know. Most students reach school age with some knowledge of fairy tales, and many with quite an extensive background in them. Parents and grandparents often have their own joyous experiences with fairy tales, which they pass on to their children and grandchildren. Some students, however, do not have this prior introduction. For these students, exposure to the traditional tales is even more important. Many references to fairy tales appear in our current world of newspapers, public speakers, political cartoons, and so on. Our society presumes that we all have this common background. Being part of the fairy tale "in" group helps us establish a place in the general community. The work of a young author to transform such a story, moving around, within, and through the writing process, certainly solidifies his or her grounding in that particular story as well as in others of the genre.

In addition to the sheer fun and common background are the valuable lessons within these traditional stories. Routman (1991) speaks to the benefit fairy tales have as an "acceptable way for children to deal with violence" (p. 77b). These tales offer clearly defined differences between good and evil and help students make connections to problems in society that are not so clear. Assertiveness, wit, and planning ahead pay off in many cases, as in *Ruby* by Michael Emberley (1990), in which both a street mugger and a devious, hungry cat are foiled by savvy little red-hooded Ruby and her friends. Calling on others, being patient, and taking action oneself are all good solutions found in fairy tales. The inspiring and consistent message is that good triumphs over evil. Bosma (1992) addresses the fairy tale lessons that can be found for use in character building and social development. Such lessons can occur "through humor rather than didactic teaching" (p. 5). As an illustration of social awareness and development, consider how current events could provide intriguing problems, characters, or other bases for change within a story. Imagine a daring young princess on a quest to rescue the falling stock market, or an endangered turtle/enchanted prince who saves a beached pod of whales and is returned to his true form. Gleaning articles and photos from local newspapers may generate a wealth of possibilities. Social tie-ins abound for both structuring the story and supporting changes within it.

There are also multiple opportunities within all kinds of fairy tales for students to practice basic skills of comprehension. Certainly all the strategies of good readers—predicting, visualizing, questioning, and inferring, for instance—have a fine arena for practice within such tales. Why? Because both the original stories and their many variations are open to multiple interpretations depending on factors such as the reader's point of view or culture. There is probably no gift quite so fine as to tap into understanding the common heritage of these tales with their connections to past generations, global diversity, and the positioning of self within worlds.

Once the understanding of and the appreciation for the traditional tales are established, benefits accrue from studying versions that have a twist. Offerings in bookstores and catalogs continue to multiply rapidly. Some are written for adult or more sophisticated child audiences. For instance, James Garner's *Politically Correct Bedtime Stories* (1994) claims to be free from bias and cultural stereotypes. The stories allow readers to "slip into a liberated land" as they read the many amusing stories with updated characters, as in "The Three Codependent Goats Gruff." There are also sequenced novels such as Adele Geras's (1992) trilogy about three English girls, which mixes concepts from "Rapunzel," "Sleeping Beauty," and "Snow White." In the second book of the series, *Watching the Roses*, the sleeping heroine withdraws to avoid abusive memories, and she must, this time, free herself. Jane Yolen's *Briar Rose* (1992) takes the old German tale of "Sleeping Beauty" (originally called "Briar Rose") and sets it in the German forests of World War II for an absorbing tale with Holocaust references, strong on both social implication and the power of love.

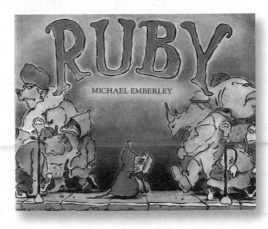

Book cover from *Ruby* by Michael Emberley. Copyright © 1990. Used by permission of Little, Brown and Company.

For younger readers, there are several short story collections that merit a visit. An all-time favorite of both elementary and middle school students is the collection, written by 13 award-winning fantasy and science fiction authors, titled *A Wolf at the Door and Other Retold Fairy Tales* (Datlow & Windling, 2000). Picture, if you will, a large and strong Cinderella, or Hansel lured into a witch's shop full of PlayStations and snacks. Another sure favorite is *The Rumpelstiltskin Problem* by Vivian Vande Velde (2000), which holds six surprising versions of the tale of the odd little man who spins straw into gold. Also, the Starbright Foundation for ill children has prompted 21 celebrity authors and 21 renowned illustrators to create *Once Upon a Fairy Tale* (Kushell, 2001). This exceptional collection retells four traditional tales from varied points of view and is accompanied by a CD of the authors reading their contributions. For instance, in "Little Red Riding Hood," Robin Williams (alias Wolf von Big Baden) shares the wolf's take on things, and in "The Frog Prince," Martha Stewart fills us in on what the rather pompous pillow of the princess has to say. There is also a collection edited by Bruce Lansky titled *Newfangled Fairy Tales* (1997), which contains lots of surprises, such as the three bears who invade Goldy's home to escape a superhighway under construction. A final collection for younger readers is the wacky medley by Allan Ahlberg and Andre Amstutz called *Ten in a Bed* (1990). All of these collections hold a wealth of examples and enjoyment for students.

In addition to the short story, there is the "transformed" novel. *Just Ella* by Margaret Haddix (1999) tells the unexpected story of a Cinderella who was not so happy in her ever after. For a bit shorter read, Gail Levine has created a series titled

The Princess Tales with four delightfully transformed tales, each in its own chapter book. How about having a new kind of "glass slipper"—a hill of slippery glass for the inventive hero to climb to win the princess—as in Levine's *Cinderellis and the Glass Hill* (2000). All these engaging volumes promote a stream of ideas for story tweaking. (For an in-depth discussion of "Cinderella" and its variants, see chapter 14.)

The preponderance of twisted fairy tale offerings, however, is found in the ever-popular picture book. There are dozens. From *Dinorella: A Prehistoric Fairy Tale* by Pamela Edwards and Henry Cole (1998) to Marilyn Tolhurst's *Somebody and the Three Blairs* (1990), a treasury of parody awaits the reader. These stories beg to be read aloud, and students beg to hear them or tell them, as the wordless picture book *Deep in the Forest* by Brinton Turkle (1976) invites. In this book, a mischievous bear cub puts a reverse on the Goldilocks story by invading a pioneer family's home. One classic transformation of point of view is Jon Scieszka's *The True Story of the 3 Little*

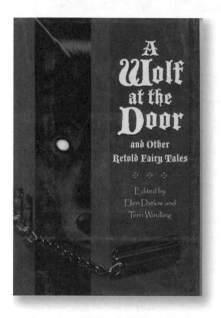

Book cover from *A Wolf at the Door and Other Retold Fairy Tales* edited by Ellen Datlow and Terri Windling. Jacket illustration copyright © 2000 Tristan Ellwell. Used with the permission of Simon & Schuster Books for Young Readers, an imprint of Simon & Schuster Children's Publishing Division.

Pigs by A. Wolf (1989). Writing educator Ralph Fletcher (1993) speaks to the fun of using an "unreliable narrator" to change stories. He credits Scieszka's Alexander T. Wolf using all the tricks of the unreliable narrator, including humor, logic, appeals to sympathy, and chumming up to the reader as the wolf tells his side of the story. It is a charming adaptation to share and discuss. A final delight is the gender-switched story *Prince Cinders* by Babette Cole (1987). References to muscle building and disco dancing only enhance the lively action. Picture books are indeed one of the best sources of transformation surprises.

Treasures also can be found in the supporting artwork of picture books. For example, Fiona French's *Snow White in New York* (1990) is a wonder of striking design and perspective with its bold and elegant pages. Bosma (1992) reminds us of the value of illustration. She states that children "cannot create in a vacuum, and should not be limited to television images as models for creating their own imaginative worlds" (p. 21). The illustrated book reigns supreme in appeal to the right-brained reader and writer and as inspiration for the spatial learner/artist. Illustrations can complement any student's text changes. In fact, developing the mood of a picture to match the mood of the transformed setting or character is a challenge many students enjoy, and it makes a wonderful topic for direct instruction. Whether or not students illustrate their own writing, awareness of such varied art possibilities and their impact on the reader is well worth a discussion in the classroom.

In addition to the novels, short story collections, chapter books, and picture books, there are more finds for the true transformations collector. There are books of fairy tales presented as poetry, rap, and song. There are cassette tapes, CDs, video-tapes, DVDs, and websites dedicated to them. Indeed, the expanding mountain of available resources speaks clearly to the wide appeal of the transformed fairy tale.

The close relationship between the reading of text and the writing of it provides additional pluses for learners with differing literacy skill levels. Reading and writing are interactive, and story lies firmly at the foundation of both language and learning. In using a fairy tale as a core and in first being able to comprehend it, then transform it, much of the brain is engaged; higher level thinking flourishes. Fairy tales themselves have many layers of meaning. The unpeeling of those layers provides an automatic differentiation among learners of varied developmental levels; some will unpeel more than others. A parent once asked Albert Einstein how to create genius within his child. Einstein's purported reply was "Read fairy tales to him." In other words, levels of analysis are fully engaged with such timeless stories, be it with the youngest bedtime listener or the child much more skilled at discerning the complexities of the text. As a young author takes on the task of writing a transformation, the analysis level is bumped up first into evaluation, as decisions of adapting *what* and *how* arise, and then is boosted into full-blown synthesis as the new tale is constructed. These new layers of meaning are being created by the writer at his or her discretion and are thus at the perfect developmental level for each student.

A final benefit of transforming fairy tales in the classroom is the positive emotional experience for the student. The validating feedback to the student writer that can come from conferencing about such a compelling work in progress is perhaps one of the best payoffs a teacher can put in place. Hearing about what is working well for an audience, both adult and peer, is instrumental in a young author's motivation and excitement for improving his or her draft. There is something about taking a time-tested structure and personalizing it with your own slant that ensures success. Susan, a sixth grader, commented after a peer response session for her transformed tale "The Three Nasty Coyotes," "I am really clever!" The next section of this chapter will set forth one way to structure an activity on the transformation of a fairy tale.

Writing a Transformed Tale: A Suggested Learning Sequence

The basis for a transformed fairy tale study must be the common grounding of students in traditional tales. Figure 17.1 captures a quick look at the sequence of the learning activities presented here. There is likely no better way to begin than by finding out what students already know about fairy tales, and what they have questions

Figure 17.1
Suggested Learning Sequence of Activities

Fairy Tale Transformation

1. **KWLH chart** to activate prior knowledge and clarify direction

2. **Reading aloud** traditional and twisted tales to establish common background
   Before: retelling story as known or introducing characters
   During: questioning, predicting, graphic organizers
   After: responding through discussion, writing, art, drama

3. **Exploration time** to allow for individual interests and abilities

4. **Direct instruction** leading to general understandings (literary terms, fairy tale indicators, modes of writing)

5. **Ongoing sharing of learning** structured into class time

6. **Transforming assignment** presented, including assessment

7. **Direct instruction** for specific assignment (note-taking, quality parameters, text examples, and analysis)

8. **Prewriting**, as with story map

9. **Drafting, collecting response, revising, editing** via workshop

10. **Publishing** from read-around circles to performing to festivals

11. **Reflecting**, as with KWLH chart, paragraph frame, or learning log entry

---

about. A large KWLH chart for the class on butcher paper (adapted from Ogle, 1986) can be a strong first step. KWLH stands for **K**now, **W**ant to Know, **L**earned, and **H**ow We Learned. The example in Figure 17.2, developed by one class, points out some interesting directions for the teacher. Students in this group know many of the characteristics of fairy tales (magic, talking animals, princes and princesses, castles, happily-ever-after endings). Others could be taught and added, such as actions (or items) occurring in threes.

This class is interested, as all classes seem to be, in the very first fairy tale. An Internet search by one student led to Cinderella references from the ninth century in China—recorded in the L and H columns on the chart shown here. (The rest of the L and the H columns will be filled in during and after the study.) This chart is also a handy spot for the teacher to plant a reference or two (see final entries in the K and W columns) toward the ultimate goal—the creation of a transformed fairy tale. Whatever the objectives, it is important to share them with the students as the lessons begin. Awakening prior knowledge and setting some avenues for learning establish a strong foundation for any study.

After determining what is already known among your students, you will next need to make sure all students have some background in traditional fairy tales. An easy and reliable way to accomplish this "backgrounding" is to read aloud. There are many collections and exquisite picture books that are primary in language and

Figure 17.2
Fairy Tales KWLH Chart by Sixth-Grade Class

Fairy Tales

K We **K**now or Think We Know...	W We **W**ant to Know...	L We **L**earned...	H **H**ow We Learned...
Can do supernatural things (fly)	How old are they?	Cinderella in China, 800s	Sean— http://members.aol.com/surlalanefrytale.index.htm
Animals can talk	What was the first one?		
Has a plot, something happens	Is one most common?		
	Why called "fairy tales"?		
Has a moral, lesson	Do they all have evil?		
Can have a prince/ princess	Are families important in fairy tales?		
Characters in the story sometimes tell the story	What do they center around?		
	Where did they come from?		
Live "happily ever after"	Are they based on real things? Were they ever believed?		
Can have castles, woods, candy cottage, plants, jungles, dungeons, witches, dwarfs	How do we "fracture" a fairy tale?		
Make into movies sometimes			
Begin "once upon a time"			
Objects can be magic			
Some have versions like 3 wolves and big bad pig			

L and H columns are filled in during and after the study.

concise in story. Good-sized illustrations easily seen from the back of the room are another plus. One collection that lends itself to the read-aloud is titled *A Treasury of Fairy Tales* by Annie-Claude Martin (1995); it has large print and also large-scale drawings. It is easy to show the pictures to a class, especially if students are gathered in one area of the room sitting on the floor. Even middle school students will respond well to such an arrangement. Many other picture books are equally effective.

If your main objective is to move rapidly into working with the changed versions of fairy tales, this exposure to the traditional ones needs to be a fairly quick process. It is sufficient to lay such groundwork by reading aloud only a few stories. Students usually seem to gravitate toward "Little Red Riding Hood," "The Three Little Pigs," "Cinderella," and "Snow White and the Seven Dwarfs" as primary choices for their own transformations. These four are enough to get things rolling. Some classes, depending on ages and backgrounds of students, may prefer to hear only one or two stories. Other stories to share, less often used by student writers but still popular, include "Sleeping Beauty," "Rapunzel," "Rumpelstiltskin," "The Three Billy Goats Gruff," "Goldilocks and the Three Bears," and "Hansel and Gretel." These may be read to the class or read individually by interested students. With all stories, be they traditional or twisted, read aloud or read by students, an active approach has big payoffs in greater interest and understanding. The following suggestions center around active learning on the part of the student.

Before the read-aloud, a quick and effective strategy to involve students and activate prior knowledge is an oral retelling. Younger students may contribute to a whole-class retelling as one student after another tells an event. With students who are a bit older, teams of four can help each other by adding a thought or two in a round-robin retell as they speak around and around their small circle until the tale is told. Minidiscussions inevitably erupt, as known versions tend to vary. Another related activity is the alphabet retell: Pairs list a sequence of perhaps 8 to 10 letters in alphabetical order down the left side of a sheet of paper. Then they proceed to write a retelling of the story with sentences or phrases, each starting with the letter on the given line, in the manner of an acrostic poem. Students enjoy working with the structure of the alphabet in this activity, counterbalanced by the correct order of the events. A third way to get students sharing their knowledge is to focus in on what they already know about the fairy tale characters. For example, a pair of students could create a quick advertisement or interview telling about the role the character plays in the story. Any prereading strategy that engages prior knowledge and calls for students to do something (as opposed to only listening) will add greatly to the reading.

Some interaction *during* the read-aloud is also important. The simplest way is to throw out a question or prediction for student response when a good moment in the story presents itself: "What about Little Red Riding Hood is revealed during this conversation with the wolf?" or "Do you think we'll hear from this character again?" Giving pairs a chance to quickly share ("You have 15 seconds to talk with your partner") keeps student involvement high. A more involved activity for use while reading is the graphic organizer, which has visual appeal. There are many choices. Feature analysis charts that compare different fairy tales and their parts give a clear purpose for listening. (An example of a completed feature analysis chart is shown in Figure 17.3.) These can be large wall versions for the class to complete or desk copies for each student. The chart itself can address several levels of sophistication, depending on the column headings you choose. Choosing areas, for example, of stereotyping or motif (and offering direct instruction on them) keeps the challenge level high.

Figure 17.3
Feature Analysis Chart

Comparing Several Different Fairy Tales

Title/ Author	Setting (time/place)	Prota- gonist	Anta- gonist	Magic	Impt. Item	Motif (reappears)	Resolution	Theme/ Lesson	Stereotypes?
Little Red Riding Hood Grimm	past forest	Little R.R.H.	Wolf	wolf talks	basket of goodies	big eyes big ears big mouth	woodcutter kills wolf	respect others	wolf evil man strong old lady-feeble
Ruby Emberly	present big city	Ruby	lizard cat	animals talk	pay phone	cheese pies	Mrs. Mastiff ate the cat	be honest	cats hate mice dogs hate cats
Ugh Yorinks	prehistoric island	Ugh	siblings	—	Ugh's bike	inventing	Ugh became king	inventing brings fame	mean brothers and sisters
The Princess and the Pea Tharlet	past kingdom	Princess	fake princesses	feel pea through 20 mattresses	The Pea	prince meets a person	Prince + Princess get married	Don't lie	weak girl
Frog Prince Continued Scieszka	past forest, castle	Frog Prince	desires to be frog again	enchanted spells witches	clock strikes midnight	witches	both turn into frogs	be glad for what you have	evil, selfish witches

The Venn diagram is another classic graphic organizer to use for comparison between two stories, especially between two versions of the same story. In Figure 17.4, Aaron has picked *Bubba the Cowboy Prince* by Helen Ketteman (1997) to compare with a classic version of "Cinderella." Students can deepen their understandings of both the similarities and differences between tales by thinking through a chart like this. These graphic organizers can improve students' understanding during the readings and aid retention afterward.

Primary students enjoy drawing their favorite part of a story they have just heard. An effective way to share such artwork is the Community Circle (Curran, 1990): As students sit in a large circle on the floor with their drawings placed in front of them, each in turn holds up his or her work and tells about it. The inclusion of some teaching about a social skill such as active listening is a natural fit here. The Community Circle may be followed with a sequencing activity when all artwork is eventually posted on the wall or in a booklet. The potential for responding to a story through artwork should not be ignored with older students, either, as such right-brained activities are powerful, often accessing unusual facets of a tale. There is also a novelty about pulling out the watercolors, or tearing paper, or even using black markers, that adds great fun to the responding process.

If one of your objectives is using literary terms such as *setting*, *character*, *plot*, *problem*, *climax*, *resolution*, and *theme*, then listing story specifics to match the terms can be a quick way to introduce or review them. You could assign each small group

Figure 17.4
Venn Diagram Comparing Two Fairy Tales

Name _Aaron_

Compare/Contrast Chart

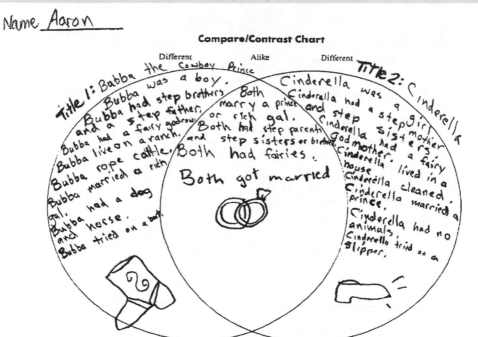

Different   Alike   Different

Title 1: Bubba the Cowboy Prince
Bubba was a boy.
Bubba had step brothers
and a step father.
Bubba had a fairy godmother.
Bubba live on a ranch.
Bubba rope cattle.
Bubba married a rich gal.
Bubba had a dog and horse.
and Bubba tried on a boot.

Both marry a prince or rich gal.
Both had step parents and step sisters or brothers.
Both had fairies.

Both got married

Title 2: Cinderella
Cinderella was a girl.
Cinderella had a step girl
Cinderella had step sisters
Cinderella had a fairy God mother.
Cinderella lived in a house
Cinderella cleaned.
Cinderella married a prince.
Cinderella had no animals.
Cinderella tried on a slipper.

---

of students their own fairy tale. The job of each group is to list and share who or what fits each literary term: Who is the protagonist in "Cinderella"? What is the climax in "The Three Little Pigs"? Even a flow chart or story map of some kind that refers to the terms makes a natural follow-up to the read-aloud. Caution, however, is needed to make sure such activities are not too time-consuming. The purpose of this suggested sequence is to lay the foundation for students to appreciate the transformed tales they hear and read, and then eventually to create one of their own. These literary terms activities work well as simple group events, quickly done and quickly shared.

Other follow-ups to the read-aloud that drive home the story line may involve drama. One that requires minimal preparation is the tableau, a freeze frame from the tale. Small groups of students choose or are assigned a section of the story. They meet for a short time to pick a specific scene, plan their group pose, select individual roles, and develop character thoughts. In only five or so minutes, it's time to perform. The students in the audience close their eyes, or a bed sheet is held in front of the actors as they assume their positions. The curtain falls. The frozen stance is revealed. Then the audience makes inferences about the still scene before them.

What is happening? What came before or after? What makes this scene important? Some or all of the performers may next be tapped on the shoulder to reveal what they are thinking.

In an Appalachian version of Cinderella, *Smoky Mountain Rose* (Schroeder, 1997), a thoughtful hog gives Rose a high-heeled "sparklin' glass slipper" on each foot. One group of students froze this scene as the onlookers guessed what was being shown. Once the scene itself was confirmed, there came the taps on the shoulders. Rose, when tapped, thought aloud, "I might fall on my face square-dancing, but they sure are purty!" The slippers thought, "These feet are dirty, all right; where's the Lysol?" And the snortin' hog thought, "Git home from this shindig by midnight—or you're a goner!" The other six or seven scenes "enacted" by the groups combined with this one to make a fine retelling of the story as well as reflection on the characters and their actions.

Once the traditional fairy tales and some transformed ones have been explored by the class, the students will be eager to explore more on their own. Some students will move right into the fractured versions, but others, perhaps students from other cultures or with less family literacy involvement, or those with non–English native languages, may choose to explore the originals a bit more. Some kind of a record is helpful, be it a simple list with title, author, and a short response, or something more elaborate like the chart shown previously in Figure 17.3. This may be the time for you to invite an individual study of multiple versions of a specific title. In addition, the students could be scouting for the methodology of the authors: "What element did this author change? Was it the character? Setting? Point of view?" Techniques for transformation can be identified and recorded.

This also may be a fitting time to look at other formats. Have some varied books such as *Roald Dahl's Revolting Rhymes* (Dahl, 1986), David Vozar's rap *Yo, Hungry Wolf!* (1993), and the letters collection of Janet and Allan Ahlberg's *The Jolly Postman, or Other People's Letters* (1986) on hand. Scholastic Press has a series titled Rap Tales with accompanying cassettes, which appeals to all ages (see Chardiet, 1993). This is a perfect time to invite students to join you in the choral reading of a fractured fairy tale poem, or to share any other assorted pieces that may have been collected or created. You might try creating a Poem for Two Voices for students (see Fleischman, 1985), based, perhaps, on "Little Red Riding Hood." Students could then practice in pairs and perform their poems to another pair. Barry Lane will "sing" to a class from his CD *Recycled Fairy Tales* (1999), wherein the pigs are not so nice. Watching any of the fractured fairy tales from *The Adventures of Bullwinkle and Rocky* (Ward, 1961; some also available on DVD) will inspire and delight the class. Other video hits include *Muppet Classic Theater: Where 6 Fairy Tales Take a Wacky Twist* (Hensen, 1994), *Faerie Tale Theatre—Little Red Riding Hood* (Clifford, 1990), or any of the HBO Family series *Happily Ever After: Fairy Tales for Every Child*.

Students also enjoy reading scripts such as "The Trial of Jack and the Beanstalk" by Keith Polette (1994). The message becomes clear that varied formats for transformed fairy tales are both novel and fun.

Structuring in a time and method for students to share what they are spotting is vital after such exploration. Both oral reporting and written reflections in a notebook or learning log are helpful. Students can find many possibilities to list on a class chart for future reference; several examples are listed in Figure 17.5. This comprehension list may be useful as a teacher resource for encouraging findings or preparing an assignment. Sharing in pairs, a small group, and with the whole class not only builds the community of fairy tale experts but also generates many possibilities for an approaching goal: the writing of a transformed tale.

You design the specific writing assignment, depending on the needs of the curriculum and your class's composition; many options are possible. Here are some considerations:

> Have literary elements been taught? What are the possible literary elements for transformation? Are there any that will be required or strongly suggested?

> Of the possible modes (narrative, persuasive, expository, descriptive, creative, reflective), which should be emphasized? It is likely that narrative will be a main focus, but are there others to present to students?

> What formats are acceptable (e.g., picture books, scripts, news reports, comics)?

Figure 17.5
Possibilities for Transformation

Elements to Adapt	Forms	Media/Formats
Character—gender	Narrative story	Audio/videotape
Character—change into animals/ objects	Tableau series	Pop-up folder
Character—personality	Script—drama/Readers Theatre	Diorama/mobile
Stereotyping	Newscast of an incident	Power point slides
Narrator—point of view	News article	Illustration series
Setting—location	Choral reading	Collage
Setting—time	Story poem, ballad, sonnet	Sequence map
Problem	Trial script	Symbolic art
Solution	Rap, chant, song	Musical instrument
Ending	Monologue	Cartoon/comic strip
After the ending	Dialogue	Big Book
Important item (glass slipper)	Diary, series of letters	Puppetry
Motif (what reappears/repeats)	Debate	Photo journal

Are there fairy tale indicators such as magic or sets of three to require or suggest?

How will the piece be assessed?

Follow both your own objectives and the cues you receive from students to tailor the best writing assignment for your situation. This shaping of requirements is where the art of teaching resonates.

Sample Assignment

The rest of this chapter will follow the path of a particular assignment that is integrated with a social studies unit on global studies. For this assignment, the common requirement for all students is to include a transformation of setting. Some fairy tale characteristics also are expected, although exactly which ones will be each student's choice. Other adaptations of story elements or format are optional, but it is required that students include at least five references to culture or geography, initiated from the shift in setting. An assignment sheet, such as the one shown in Figure 17.6, will be useful if there are several considerations, as in this example.

One of the most effective ways to introduce such an assignment is to share assessment plans with students. Shown in Figure 17.7 is a Performance Task Assessment List (PeTAL) that specifies the traits of writing, fairy tale characteristics, and social studies tie-ins that will be scored. The PeTAL is given to students to help clarify the assignment expectations. The "possible points" column is negotiated, together, usually totaling 100. At the end of the assignment, students will score their own work before the teacher does. Students can become remarkably adept at accurate self-scoring when clear expectations and practice with assessment lists and/or rubrics are provided.

With this emphasis on setting, there are some fabulous transformed tales to read aloud. A prime example is *The Three Little Javelinas* by Susan Lowell (2003), a transformation of "The Three Little Pigs" that takes place in the southwestern United States. Sixth graders collected 19 examples of ideas that matched the shift in setting established by Lowell. From the javelinas replacing the original three little pigs, to saguaros, to cowboy spurs, to dust storms, to Native American dress, to Spanish chili sauce, the clues to the blending of cultures and geography in this area are intriguing to identify. Creating such a list of an author's altered choices to support a new, nontraditional setting gives clarity as to story detail as well as a "handle" for students on how such substitutions lead to transformed tales. Other favorites for new locales include Tony Johnston's *Bigfoot Cinderrrrrella* (1998), set in the forests of the Pacific northwest; Lisa Ernst's *Little Red Riding Hood: A Newfangled Prairie Tale*

You are to write your own story by transforming a well-known fairy tale. You will begin by doing some research into another geographic area and its cultures. This will be a basis for your story, although you also may choose other changes such as

- time changes (past? present? future?)
- gender twists or other stereotype reversals
- updates—where are the characters now?
- ending changes
- point of view changes

You also have a wide variety of choices for the form of your written fairy tale parody. The mode will be narrative (telling a story), but the tale may be told in many ways. Here are several examples:

- story
- picture book
- poem, rap, or song
- news report or series of news reports
- script for dramatizing as a play or Readers Theatre
- series of letters
- diary
- photo journal
- interview or debate

Your story needs all the literary elements (setting, character, plot, problem, climax, resolution) as well as the elements present in fairy tales (magic, evil versus good, a moral, etc.). Most of all, your story will showcase your skills as a writer; be sure to review your organization, content, style, and conventions to create your fairy tale transformation masterpiece.

To help you think through possible fairy tale motifs (subjects that keep reappearing in a story), here are some ideas:

- events in threes
- the wise and the foolish
- supernatural gifts
- a test or series of tests
- seemingly impossible tasks
- changes in appearance

LET THE WRITING FUN BEGIN!

(1995); Michael Emberly's *Ruby* (1990), set in the big city; and Susan Lowell's *Cindy Ellen: A Wild Western Cinderella* (2000). The prehistoric setting for *Ugh* by Arthur Yorinks (1990) not only gives a new location and gender reversal for "Cinderella" but also carries a message about invention. All these books excel at showcasing the changes that can occur when setting is shifted. Small groups can read the books and sleuth for setting changes and indicators to share with the class. Students who are heading toward adapting stories to new locations of their own now have a compelling purpose for careful listening—to consider how ideas heard from classmates can assimilate with their own thinking process and their developing story.

Figure 17.7
Fairy Tale Transformation Assessment Form

PETAL
PERFORMANCE TASK ASSESSMENT LIST
TRANSFORMING A FAIRY TALE

	ASSESSMENT POINTS		
	Points Possible	Points Earned (Student)	Points Earned (Teacher)
1. The written piece is well organized with a strong beginning, a clearly sequenced middle, and a solid ending. Transitions are used.	_____	_____	_____
2. The fairy tale has a clear, logical plot that is well developed, with sufficient detail.	_____	_____	_____
3. In the introduction, the setting and characters are described vividly and the problem is revealed.	_____	_____	_____
4. The ending resolves the problem with a satisfactory conclusion.	_____	_____	_____
5. There are at least three characteristics of fairy tales in the story (examples: magic, good versus evil, a moral, use of motif).	_____	_____	_____
6. There is strong style; that is, words are carefully chosen for effect, there is variety in sentence length and structure, and we can hear the author's voice.	_____	_____	_____
7. There are at least five references made to the culture or geography of the area where the fairy tale takes place.	_____	_____	_____
8. The writing is neat and mechanically correct with good spelling, punctuation, grammar, and usage.	_____	_____	_____
TOTAL:	_____	_____	_____

If you have access to previous student papers, now is an ideal time to share them. (If you do not have any previous papers, be sure to save some of these for next time.) In one student's (Christina's) story "Snow White and the Seven Eskimos," there are puffins, Siberian huskies, harpoons, Northern Lights, and a game of ring around the totem pole. This student author tells us that inside an igloo a special song breaks the curse of the tainted salmon, and all is well again with Snow White and her Eskimo Prince. When a student piece resonates with fitting location tweaks such as Christina's, the process of transforming is perceived by others as being manageable.

As you employ student-made samples, try to show your students some strong examples and some weaker ones. After the whole class has studied an example or two, students might be given a set of three other papers and asked to rank order them. The discussions about which are stronger pieces of writing and why are very enlightening for students and are a great indicator of student understanding for teachers. The targets become more and more sharply defined.

Once the assignment and standards of quality have been clarified, have students choose a region of the world to study. They can collect information about the history, flora and fauna, and cultures of their region. Note-taking skills can be taught or revisited here. The more complete the bank of facts a student compiles and the more expert he or she becomes in the subject, the better the chance of engaging his or her future readers with interesting specifics.

One of the greatest adventures, of course, is in the drafting of the transformed tale. A workshop approach is recommended, in which students are encouraged to share emerging pieces with peer, adult, small-group, and whole-group audiences. The first activity may well be a prewriting one for the whole class. A story map, such as the one shown in Figure 17.8, is very useful to ensure that all elements are in place. Direct instruction is likely to be needed in the form of minilessons on including setting indicators and revising by adding detail, as well as instruction in the continued revisiting of published twisted pieces for leads, endings, and character development.

Also, if students have not learned to begin a conference by pointing out what they like about a piece, this is an imperative lesson to teach them at this point. Questions and suggestions should follow after your praise. Moffett and Wagner (1992) tell us, "Peer feedback may vastly improve drafts even when no members are more skilled than others" (p. 203). Students who are new to writing workshops will need to see such feedback in action. In the earlier suggestions for direct instruction, there is no replacement for the teacher as a model. Here is true mentorship at work, as you show your "apprentices" what mental processes are going on in the head of a writer at work. A visual showing of such material—perhaps using an overhead projector—is vital also.

It is a fine idea to draft a complete piece along with the students. If the piece happens to be a script, you are then creating a wonderful resource for future use as Readers Theatre or full-blown drama. In the drafting and revision of the script "Dizzy Mae and the Seven Bumpkins," one class had many good ideas. Students suggested the magic mirror should be called a lookin' glass, and the hunter should be named Mighty Abner. The first scene evolved from "This is a tale from the backwoods called 'Dizzy Mae and the Seven Hillbillies'" to one that begins,

> Howdy folks. Well, for this here tale 'bout Dizzy Mae and the Seven Bumpkins you got to think yoreself to a big forest way back in the Appalachian Mountains. For it waren't too many years ago that this story actually took place in them there backwoods.

Figure 17.8
Story Map Used for Prewriting

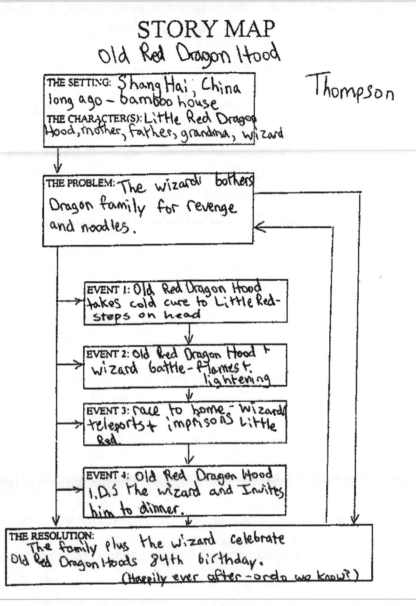

STORY MAP
Old Red Dragon Hood

Thompson

THE SETTING: Shang Hai, China
long ago – bamboo house

THE CHARACTER(S): Little Red Dragon
Hood, mother, father, grandma, wizard

THE PROBLEM: The wizard bothers
Dragon family for revenge
and noodles.

EVENT 1: Old Red Dragon Hood
takes cold cure to Little Red-
steps on head

EVENT 2: Old Red Dragon Hood +
wizard battle- flames +
lightening

EVENT 3: race to home - wizard
teleports + imprisons Little
Red.

EVENT 4: Old Red Dragon Hood
I.D.s the wizard and Invites
him to dinner.

THE RESOLUTION:
The family plus the wizard celebrate
Old Red Dragon Hoods 84th birthday.
(Happily ever after - or do we know?)

Dialect reigned supreme in this tale. Students realized that Granny's devious personality could be shown through her choice of words as she delivered her poisoned Hillbilly bread: "Jest mind yer own business and eat that bread! Ah...that is...I'm jest trying to lose a little weight, my dear." And the search for humor led to Happy's repetitive words, "She's in the well! That's where she is! She thinks she's drowned!

That's what she thinks!" capped by Grumpy's reply, "I think you're an idiot! Now shut up and get her out!" This was one of the students' favorite parts of the piece. It spoke to and through them. Remember that as young writers develop characterization and a sense of order and style with your help, they learn lessons to apply in their own pieces.

Once the final drafting is complete, it is time to publish, to take the final step in the writing process, to share the work with an audience. Here are six all-time favorite story-sharing methods of students:

1. Have students share their stories around a circle with three to five writers. All group members are expected to give a positive response to each author. Have each group pick one story and create a tableau (a freeze frame or a series of frames as described earlier in this chapter) to share with the class.

2. Authors can read a few stories each day in a large Share Circle with the whole class. Each audience member jots a strength (as simple as a really juicy word) on a sticky note, which you screen and then pass along to the author.

3. Some authors may write their pieces purposefully for a choral-type read or a Readers Theatre; performance is then an obvious choice. (See "The Seven Stage a Comeback" in *A Wolf at the Door* [Datlow & Windling, 2000] for a several-voice read-aloud delight.)

4. Create a three-ring binder for the classroom with a snazzy title chosen by the class, such as *Fabulous Fairy Tales*, and ask each student to submit a story. Make it available to all during silent reading. You also can read aloud some stories at times for a real community builder.

5. Leave a collection of the stories in your local doctor's or dentist's office, with a comment sheet for the public in the front. You might even get a comment from the mayor, as one fifth-grade class did!

6. The grandest and most memorable way to highlight the transformed tales is to have a "Fairy Tales Festival" during an afternoon or evening. Try some of these:
   • Design invitations and send them to families or a neighboring class.
   • Have students come dressed as one of their characters.
   • Serve snacks that are themed with the stories and labeled as such.
   • Give out student-designed bookmarks about the transformed tales.
   • Have an entertainment schedule. Include dramatizations, songs, selected readings, chants, Readers Theatre, and spoken dialogues. Have a mix of solo, small-group, and even whole-group presentations.

- Make it a "Tableau Festival" with two or three frozen scenes from each of six or so stories. Practice slow motion shifts from one scene to the next.
- Have displays of artwork students have made to go with their stories, or a display of the publishing binder or of individual books.

It is the publishing or presenting of the work in some way to an audience, be it large or small, that ultimately gives purpose to the creating of it. There is certainly no finer feeling of accomplishment for students than that of a job well done, and well shared.

The last step in any lesson or unit of study is to reflect on its original objectives. This debriefing clarifies the new understandings, shifting them into students' longer term memory. Of course, the completion of the L and H columns of the KWLH chart is a natural fit here. An alternative possibility is a KWL Paragraph Frame, which includes blanks for students to fill in. Figure 17.9 shows what one student had to say.

Figure 17.9
KWL Paragraph Frame

Although I already knew _that there were many versions_

of Cinderella,

I learned _that there is a Bigfoot version, and a 60s version,_

and a penguin version too!!

I still would like to know _HOW MANY VERSIONS ???_

Some new words I picked up when I learned about fairy tales were _motif,_

stereotypes, and _antagonist._

Overall, I think the study was a _fun_ experience for me because

we got to make our own fractured fairy tale.

Another student wondered why he had never heard of "Puss in Boots" before. Yet another was pleased to have revisited tales he first encountered at age 5 and to now be able to recognize the motif of the spinning sequences in "Rumpelstiltskin." This debriefing time is equally effective if students record their final thoughts in a learning log, responding to a question such as, What are the most important things you learned about fairy tales and their transformation? Individual think time leads well into a class discussion during which questions calling for comparison, evaluation, and elaboration evoke high levels of thought. This time to reflect is time well spent; it encourages metacognition and awareness of growth.

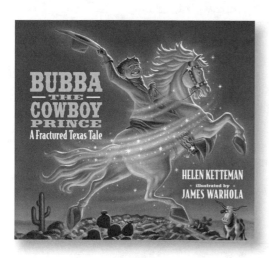

Illustration by James Warhola from *Bubba the Cowboy Prince: A Fractured Texas Tale* by Helen Ketteman. Published by Scholastic Press, a division of Scholastic, Inc. Illustration copyright © 1997 by James Warhola. Used by permission.

The validation of any directed writing assignment is obvious when students choose to write again in the genre or form presented. One student, Jamie, wrote "Bully," about three brothers on a venture for Mother's Day gifts outwitting the trollish bully under the bridge. Derek found great amusement in his story "The Sleeping Schizophrenic White Blood Cell" who received "big, wet, auntie kisses" at birth, along with auntie-predictions of fame and talent. Not to be outdone in wacky takeoffs is Michael's adventure inside a computer with "Brain, Brightless, Brainless, and the Normal-Sized Tricky Virus." Brain was finally too fast for Virus and "CRASH!!! The computer was destroyed and everything inside it. The virus was gone."

A final example of the continued life of these lessons comes from a middle school student. Laura chose a European location for "The Tale of Allerednic: A Norwegian Cinderella." She selected it as her best piece for evaluation during the quarter following the fairy tale study. Near the beginning, Allerednic's "last glimmer of hope died. Literally" as his mother took ill, with fatal results. His life "would be nothing but pure misery...scrubbing, cleaning fish, cooking, catching fish, and whatever his stepfather's sick, twisted mind felt like." Then one night before a fishing competition Allerednic was "wallowing in self-pity" when a "large sturgeon wearing a tutu" proclaimed itself the "Fairy Fish-Mother" and changed his shirt and pants from their "ragged tatters to their original mother-sewn glory." Allerednic proceeded to land the largest amount of salmon in the fishing tournament, have his boot lost and found, and win the role of "King's Advisor of Fishing." All's well that ends so very well. It is clear that Laura has taken the fun of creating parody into her writing realm.

Conclusion

Fairy tales in and of themselves make for a compelling study. In his classic work on enchantment, literary analyst and psychiatrist Bruno Bettelheim (1976) says that if we are to live in "true consciousness of our existence, then our greatest need and most difficult achievement is to find meaning in our lives" (p. 4). He goes on to say that with the exception of parental influence, our cultural heritage is the strongest guide in this search. Bettelheim claims that for children, "it is literature that carries such information best" (p. 4). This is certainly a valid argument for reading and writing within the cultural domains of the fairy tale.

The characters in fairy tales illuminate our own desires and shortcomings and strengths in a most vibrant and entertaining fashion. We thrill to Goldilock's assertiveness in entering off-limit territory and her rash actions as well as her guilt and ensuing flight from consequences. We can easily connect such traits and events with those in our lives or the lives of others we know. To take such lively and familiar characters and tweak their stories in a way that is personally meaningful is inherently engaging to students of all ages and abilities. According to Tomlinson (2001) and her widely accepted ideas on differentiation, "Engagement is a nonnegotiable of teaching and learning" (p. 52) and comes from the two powerful motivators of student interest and student choice. She also tells us that a "developed interest in one area is almost inevitably a route to learning about many other things" (p. 55). That is precisely what the classroom should be about.

As a doorway into topics of current events, global settings, social issues, and personal concerns, fairy tales reign supreme. They provide one of the most universally understood and joyful entries. In addition, the built-in community and audience within a classroom provide a near-perfect arena for writing growth and a springboard for inspiring gains from personal reflection along the way. Teachers have a rich field to mine for the development of critical thinking. As the variety of transformed fairy tale resources continues to explode in the world of trade books and media offerings, the ease of sparking the imagination of students also multiplies. It's just plain fun to step into that creative domain.

The opportunities after the writing itself for reading, drama, or even a full-fledged festival are important in embedding the power and worth of the study. Most of us can look back on certain memorable lessons from our schooling and recognize them as extremely good ones. Having an assignment that promotes personal decisions and thus allows for the investment of self is a key factor in such long-lasting memories. Jensen (1998) suggests that it's "smart teaching" (p. 94) for educators to purposely engage emotions, as through novelty, drama, peer collaboration and support, or the high stakes of public presentation in some form. In his considerations of teaching with the brain in mind, he states that "Emotions drive the threesome of attention, meaning, and memory" and that orchestrating to engage emotions productively will do 'triple duty' to capture all three."

The study of traditional and transformed fairy tales is one of the most flexible and rewarding for teachers and their students. Based on tradition, backed with individual choice, lending itself to different levels of learners, and infused with excitement all the way, it is a study well worth bringing to life in a classroom.

REFERENCES

Bettelheim, B. (1976). *The uses of enchantment*. New York: Knopf.

Bosma, B. (1992). *Fairy tales, fables, legends, and myths: Using folk literature in your classroom*. New York: Teachers College Press.

Curran, L. (1990). *Cooperative learning lessons for little ones*. San Juan Capistrano, CA: Resources for Teachers.

Fleischman, P. (1985). *I am phoenix: Poems for two voices*. New York: Harper & Row.

Fletcher, R. (1993). *What a writer needs*. Portsmouth, NH: Heinemann.

Jensen, E. (1998). *Teaching with the brain in mind*. Alexandria, VA: Association for Supervision and Curriculum Development.

Moffett, J., & Wagner, B.J. (1992). *Student centered language arts, K–12*. Portsmouth, NH: Boynton/Cook.

Ogle, D. (1986). K-W-L: A teaching model that develops active reading of expository text. *The Reading Teacher, 39*, 564–570.

Routman, R. (1991). *Invitations: Changing as teachers and learners K–12*. Portsmouth, NH: Heinemann.

Tomlinson, C. (2001). *How to differentiate instruction in mixed-ability classrooms* (2nd ed.). Alexandria, VA: Association for Supervision and Curriculum Development.

NOVELS, CHAPTER BOOKS, AND SHORT STORY COLLECTIONS CITED

Ahlberg, A., & Amstutz, A. (1990). *Ten in a bed*. New York: Penguin.

Datlow, E., & Windling, T. (Eds.). (2000). *A wolf at the door and other retold fairy tales*. New York: Simon & Schuster.

Garner, J.F. (1994). *Politically correct bedtime stories*. New York: Macmillan.

Geras, A. (1992). *Watching the roses*. New York: Harcourt Brace Jovanovich.

Haddix, M.P. (1999). *Just Ella* (R. Milot, Illus.). New York: Aladdin.

Kushell, K. (Ed.). (2001). *Once upon a fairy tale*. New York: Penguin Putnam.

Lansky, B. (Ed.). (1997). *Newfangled fairy tales: Classic stories with a funny twist*. New York: Meadowbrook.

Levine, G.C. (2000). *Cinderellis and the glass hill* (The Princess Tales series; M. Elliott, Illus.). New York: Scholastic.

Martin, A. (1995). *A treasury of fairy tales*. Oxfordshire, UK: Transedition.

Vande Velde, V. (2000). *The Rumpelstiltskin problem*. Boston: Houghton Mifflin.

Yolen, J. (1992). *Briar Rose*. New York: Tom Doherty Associates.

PICTURE BOOKS AND POETRY/RAP BOOKS CITED

Ahlberg, J., & Ahlberg, A. (1986). *The jolly postman, or other people's letters*. Boston: Little, Brown.

Chardiet, J. (1993). *The rough, gruff goat brothers* (Rap Tales series with accompanying audiocassette tapes). New York: Scholastic.

Cole, B. (1987). *Prince Cinders*. New York: G.P. Putnam's Sons.

Dahl, R. (1986). *Roald Dahl's revolting rhymes* (Q. Blake, Illus.). New York: Bantam.

Edwards, P.D., & Cole, H. (1998). *Dinorella: A prehistoric fairy tale*. New York: Scholastic.

Emberly, M. (1990). *Ruby*. Boston: Little, Brown.

Ernst, L.C. (1995). *Little Red Riding Hood: A newfangled prairie tale*. New York: Scholastic.

French, F. (1990). *Snow White in New York*. New York: Oxford University Press.

Johnston, T. (1998). *Bigfoot Cinderrrrella* (J. Warhola, Illus.). New York: Puffin.

Ketteman, H. (1997). *Bubba the cowboy prince: A fractured Texas tale* (J. Warhola, Illus.). New York: Scholastic.

Lowell, S. (2000). *Cindy Ellen: A wild western Cinderella* (J. Manning, Illus.). New York: Joanna Cotler Books.

Lowell, S. (2003). *The three little javelinas* (J. Harris, Illus.). New York: Scholastic.

Schroeder, A. (1997). *Smoky mountain Rose: An Appalachian Cinderella* (B. Sneed, Illus.). New York: Puffin.

Scieszka, J. (1989). *The true story of the 3 little pigs by A. Wolf!* (L. Smith, Illus.). New York: Puffin.

Tolhurst, M. (1990). *Somebody and the three Blairs* (S. Abel, Illus.). New York: Orchard.

Turkle, B. (1976). *Deep in the forest*. New York: Dutton.

Vozar, D. (1993). *Yo, hungry wolf!* (B. Lewin, Illus.). New York: Bantam Doubleday Dell.

Yorinks, A. (1990). *Ugh* (R. Egielski, Illus.). New York: Michael di Capua.

TAPES, CDs, AND SCRIPTS CITED

Clifford, G. (Director). (1990). *Faerie tale theatre—Little Red Riding Hood* [Videotape]. Twentieth Century Fox Studio.

HBO Family. *Happily ever after: Fairy tales for every child* [Television series].

Hensen, J. (Producer). (1994). *Muppet classic theater: Where 6 fairy tales take a wacky twist* [Videotape]. Jim Hensen Video.

Lane, B. (1999). *Barry Lane's recycled fairy tales* [Compact disc]. Shoreham, VT: Discover Writing.

Polette, K. (1994). The trial of Jack and the Beanstalk [Script]. *Middle Years, 4*(2), 38–41.

Ward, J. (Producer). (1961). *The adventures of Bullwinkle and Rocky* [Television cartoon series]. Jay Ward Productions.

RECOMMENDED WEB RESOURCES

Fairy Tale Resources, Ideas and Assessment
http://tlc.epsb.ca/aauthor/horrocksactivities/page8.html

PBS Kids: A Mixed-Up Fairy Tale
http://pbskids.org/zoom/playhouse/amixedupfairytale.html

SurLaLune Fairy Tale Pages
http://www.surlalunefairytales.com

CHAPTER 18

Timeless and Timely Fairy Tales, Ideologies, and the Modern Classroom

Jane E. Kelley

airy tales appeal to readers of all ages because they purport wish fulfillment and desires, and they portray the battle between good and evil with good usually being triumphant. Although fairy tales are entertaining, these stories of enchantment also instruct readers about values, beliefs, and social practices collectively known as ideologies (Stephens, 1992). As these ideologies often correspond to a given time and place, fairy tales also evoke a given time or place. Therefore, in order to fully understand and implement them in a modern classroom, teachers must consider fairy tales in historical perspective or must alter fairy tales to fit modern and current times.

In this chapter, I will examine three variants of the fairy tale "Rumpelstiltskin," which was first recorded by the Brothers Grimm nearly two centuries ago. This tale intrigues me because of its seemingly antisocial message that the only character who tells the truth is the villain, and he is the only one who is punished in the end. I will examine how the fairy tale has changed over time by identifying the ideology embedded in the fairy tales. I will speculate why the fairy tales have been adapted in different ways and discuss teaching approaches for how to incorporate fairy tales that are centuries old into your modern teaching.

When comparing fairy tale variations, folklorists often rely on a classification system identifying fairy tales by Tale Type—a complete tale that "is made up of a number of motifs in a relatively fixed order and combination" (Thompson, 1946, p. 415). "Rumpelstiltskin" is categorized as Tale Type 500 or The Name of the Helper. Tale Type 500 has three key elements: (1) an impossible task, (2) a bargain with a helper, and (3) overcoming the helper. Folklorists also consider motifs, the smallest distinguishable element in a tale, when studying fairy tales. Two of the motifs of Tale Type 500 include the task of spinning gold and guessing the name of a supernatural creature in order to have power over him (Thompson, 1993).

Although "Rumpelstiltskin" is the most well-known version of Tale Type 500, the oldest known written version is "Ricdin-Ricdon," written by Mademoiselle Jean-Marie L'Héritier and published in France in 1696. European versions of Tale Type 500 later became popular, such as the British "Tom Tit Tot" (e.g., Arbuthnot, 1952; Jacobs, 1967; Ness, 1997) and "Duffy and the Devil" (e.g., Phelps, 1981; Zemach, 1973) and the Scottish "Whuppity Stoorie" (e.g., White, 1997). This shows how the same fairy tale is interpreted and retold according to different ideologies, even on a local level. In North America, Tale Type 500 is adapted in picture books that include *Tucker Pfeffercorn* (Moser, 1994), set in Appalachia, and *The Girl Who Spun Gold* (Hamilton, 2000), set in the West Indies. Both Moser and Hamilton include dialect and incorporate aspects from the respective cultures in which they write, such as clothing, occupation, and the like. It is important to note that the aforementioned Tale Type 500 versions take for granted that Rumpelstiltskin is evil.

In several Tale Type 500 modern retellings, the authors significantly alter the fairy tale. All of these reconstructed versions explain why Rumpelstiltskin is evil, is perceived to be evil, or the character of Rumpelstiltskin is omitted from the story altogether. (Note: I prefer to use the word *reconstructed* to describe a fairy tale that is written in a different way. Often the word *fractured* is used for rewritten tales that significantly modify a fairy tale; however, to fracture means to break, to damage, to destroy, to cause great disorder in, to go beyond the limits of, or to violate. To reconstruct, on the other hand, means to construct again, reestablish, or reassemble.) Two reconstructed Tale Type 500 picture books include *Rumpelstiltskin/A Deal Is a Deal* (Granowsky, 1993) and *Rumpelstiltskin's Daughter* (Stanley, 1997). Older readers may find short story variations of Tale Type 500 in anthologies such as *Truly Grim Tales* (Galloway, 1995) and *The Rumpelstiltskin Problem* (Vande Velde, 2000). Some authors expand the fairy tale in a novel such as *Spinners* (Napoli & Tchen, 1999) and *Straw Into Gold* (Schmidt, 2001). Generally, the authors created reconstructed versions of Tale Type 500 because they found the traditional fairy tale to be confusing.

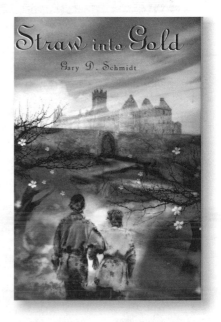

Book cover from *Straw Into Gold* by Gary D. Schmidt. Jacket illustration copyright © 2001 by Cliff Nielson. Reprinted by permission of Clarion Books/Houghton Mifflin Company. All rights reserved.

I will compare three versions of Tale Type 500—L'Héritier's "Ricdin-Ricdon" (1991), the Brothers Grimm's "Rumpelstiltskin" (1987), and Stanley's *Rumpelstiltskin's Daughter* (1997)—to demonstrate the evolution of a fairy tale. I selected "Ricdin-Ricdon" because it is the oldest written version, "Rumpelstiltskin" because it is the most well-known version, and *Rumpelstiltskin's Daughter* because it is gaining popularity in and out of the classroom. Recently a theater company adapted the story as a musical (Marshall & Battle, 2001/2002), and Macmillan/McGraw-Hill includes the story in its Reading and Language Arts Program (see www.mhschool. com/teach/reading/index.html). Further, these three fairy tales were written nearly 150 years apart and will provide an interesting contrast in regard to the time era.

In order to compare the ideologies in "Ricdin-Ricdon," "Rumpelstiltskin," and *Rumpelstiltskin's Daughter*, I will summarize each story. Then I will provide a comparison among four aspects (see Table 18.1): (1) how the girl/protagonist got into her predicament, (2) the bargain between Rumpelstiltskin/Ricdin-Ricdon and the girl, (3) why Rumpelstiltskin/Ricdin-Ricdon wanted this bargain, and (4) how the story concludes. Last, I will include historical information and perspectives showing that as the ideology changed, the tales changed with it.

Three Variants of the Rumpelstiltskin Tale

"Ricdin-Ricdon" by Jean-Marie L'Héritier

(My retelling and discussion of "Ricdin-Ricdon" are based on Jack Zipes's 1991 translation of the French version, originally published in 1696. This story is very long and complex; I provide a condensed version here.)

Rosanie is a young, beautiful, kind, and intelligent girl. Rosanie's father loves her dearly. He is a peasant whose honesty, intelligence, and integrity allow him to be chosen as an arbitrator for nearby villagers. In contrast to her father's pampering, Rosanie's mother often complains because of her slow spinning. When Rosanie's father leaves on a journey and does not return as scheduled, he is presumed dead. The mother's berating for insufficient spinning increases and intensifies in the father's absence.

One day, while Rosanie picks flowers in the garden rather than attending to her spinning, her mother becomes enraged and drags the girl back to the cottage to work. While the mother scolds the girl, a prince, who happens to be passing by, overhears the yelling. The prince questions the mother's actions. Realizing that she is in the presence of royalty, the mother explains that she is upset because her daughter works too hard. The prince convinces the mother that if Rosanie is as much of a diligent worker as she claims, the daughter should accompany him to the castle. He explains that his mother, the queen, values hard-working and industrious spinners. Wanting to rid herself of the girl, the mother consents to this arrangement, and Rosanie goes to live in the castle.

Table 18.1
Comparison of the Three "Rumpelstiltskin" Versions

	"Ricdin-Ricdon"	"Rumpelstiltskin"	*Rumpelstiltskin's Daughter*
The Predicament	Rosanie has difficulty with menial tasks. Her mother lies about Rosanie's spinning ability.	The girl's father boasts that his daughter can spin straw into gold.	Meredith's father likes to make up stories. A palace servant overhears him say that his daughter can spin straw into gold.
The Bargain	Rosanie bargains her soul for the magic wand.	The miller's daughter bargains her jewelry and her firstborn child for Rumpelstiltskin's help with spinning straw into gold.	Meredith bargains jewelry for Rumpelstiltskin's help with spinning straw into gold. However, Meredith refuses to bargain for her firstborn child.
Ricdin-don and Rumpelstiltskin's Desires	Ricdin-don wants to be master of Rosanie's destiny.	Rumpelstiltskin wants the girl's firstborn child; however, the reader does not know the reason he wants the child. As Rumpelstiltskin is described as an evil little man, it could be assumed by the reader that he will harm the child if he takes possession of it.	Rumpelstiltskin wants the girl's firstborn child so that he can become a father and have a child to love.
Conclusion	The prince tells Rosanie the name Ricdin-don. She discovers she is of noble birth, and she marries the prince.	The miller's daughter becomes queen. Rumpelstiltskin comes to claim the child unless she can guess his name. The girl/queen enlists help from servants to find Rumpelstiltskin's name. With the help of others, the girl "guesses" the name.	Meredith and Rumpelstiltskin elope and raise a daughter, Hope. As a young adult, Hope initiates positive change in the kingdom by helping the peasants.

At first, Rosanie is able to defer spinning for the queen by feigning rheumatism. However, when she can no longer hide the fact of her slow spinning, she plans to end her life. (At this point in history, fairy tales were written and published for adults, to reinforce the mores and values of the French aristocratic class [Zipes, 1994]). On her way to a tall tower to throw herself from it, she encounters a tall, dark man. This stranger queries Rosanie about her tears of anguish. Feeling that all will end soon anyway, Rosanie shares her sorrowful story with the stranger. The man says that he can help and offers her a magic wand that can swiftly spin flax into yarn, as well as create elegant embroidery. In return for this favor, all Rosanie needs to do is remember his name in three months. He willingly shares his name, Ricdin-don. If she does not remember his name, then Rosanie must forsake her soul. Contemplating the situation, Rosanie feels confident that she will surely remember his name and willingly accepts the help of his magic.

Rosanie returns to the palace and enjoys the pleasures of good food and fine clothing. The beautiful needlework and abundance of spinning impress the queen, who showers Rosanie with attention and gifts. The prince falls in love with Rosanie, but she feels she is unworthy of his love because of her low social status. When Ricdin-don returns for the magic wand, Rosanie does not remember his name, but he allows her a couple of days to try to remember.

In addition to Rosanie's anxiety in not remembering Ricdin-don's name, her guilty conscience wins out and she decides to own up to her facade and face any consequences for her deceitful actions. Before Rosanie discloses her secret, she meets the prince by chance and he recounts a story from one of his travels. The prince explains that while hunting, he walked through a secluded area of the forest. There he spied a group of people with hideous faces and strange clothing. They were encircling a dark, scary-looking man who was singing, dancing, and saying his name, Ricdin-don. When Rosanie meets Ricdin-don again, she says the name she learned from the prince.

> The evil spirit, who had not expected to hear this, disappeared while uttering terrible howls. And thus he was duped, something that happens to him when he tries to ensnare the innocent, who do not realize he is after their soul. (p. 83)

As it turns out, Rosanie's father was not her biological father, but was entrusted by her biological father, a king, to keep Rosanie in secret because her life was in danger had she stayed with her own royal family. In the end, Rosanie and the prince marry.

"Rumpelstiltskin" by the Brothers Grimm

(My retelling and discussion of "Rumpelstiltskin" here are based on Jack Zipes's 1987 translation of the German version, originally published in 1812.)

One day a miller boasts to the king that his beautiful daughter can spin straw into gold. The greedy king wants more gold, and he commands that the girl be brought to the castle. The king imprisons the girl in a room full of straw with a spinning wheel and insists that the girl spin the straw into gold by morning or die. Locked in the room full of straw, the miller's daughter begins to weep, for she cannot spin straw into gold. Mysteriously, a tiny man appears at the door and inquires about her crying. The girl tells him that she must spin the straw into gold but she does not know how to do so. The tiny man offers to spin the straw into gold if the girl pays him. All that she has to offer is her necklace; the little man accepts this payment and begins to spin.

The next morning, the king is overjoyed with the room of gold. Greedily, he imprisons the girl with more straw and informs her that she must spin or perish. Again, the tiny man appears and offers to spin straw into gold in exchange for payment. The miller's daughter offers her ring, and the spinning begins.

The next morning, the king is so delighted he tells the girl that if she can spin straw into gold one more night he will make her his bride. When the tiny man appears on the third night, the girl is distressed because she has nothing to offer in payment this time. The tiny man says that he will spin a third time if she promises to give him her first child when she is queen. The girl considers Rumpelstiltskin's deal and thinks, "Who knows whether it will ever come to that?... And since she knew of no other way out of her predicament, she promises the little man what he had promised" (p. 211). Therefore, the miller's daughter agrees to the bargain as she cannot think of an alternative solution. The tiny man spins straw into gold. When the king enters the room, he is excited about the gold; as promised, he marries the miller's daughter, and she becomes queen.

A year later, Rumpelstiltskin returns and demands that the queen fulfill her promise. The queen laments her promise and offers the little man the riches of the kingdom. He refuses the queen's gift, but he is moved by her tears and grants her three days to guess his name.

For two days, she tries to remember all the names she has ever heard. Each time she guesses a name, the little man says, "That's not my name." On the eve of the third night, the queen's loyal messenger spies Rumpelstiltskin in the woods. The messenger sees him dance and sing around the fire as he proclaims his name, Rumpel-Stilts-Kin. The next day the queen "guesses" his name. Upon hearing his name, he stomps his foot into the floor so forcefully that it becomes wedged there, and it takes both hands to remove his foot. Rumpelstiltskin flees the castle (in some versions, he flies away on a ladle or tears himself in two) and the queen is able to keep her child.

Rumpelstiltskin's Daughter *by Diane Stanley*

This story begins like the traditional Brothers Grimm "Rumpelstiltskin" folk tale; however, on the third night of straw spinning, the story takes a spin in another direction. When Rumpelstiltskin bargains for the firstborn child because he wishes to be a father, the miller's daughter, Meredith, offers him an alternative solution. She affirms that she is fond of short men, she likes his ideas on parenting, and she would rather marry Rumpelstiltskin and not the king.

Years later, they have a daughter, and together they have a quiet life on a farm. Rumpelstiltskin spins straw into gold only when the family needs money. Over time, the goldsmith whom they sell the gold to becomes curious and asks their daughter about the strange gold. Word about the gold reaches the king, and he says, "I once knew a miller's daughter who could make gold like that" (p. 9). The king, thinking that the girl can spin straw into gold, captures and locks her in a room full of straw.

The girl does not request help from her father, Rumpelstiltskin, because she realizes the king would make her father a prisoner and force him to spin gold. Rather, the next morning the daughter informs the king that she cannot spin gold, but she thinks she remembers how her grandfather did it. The girl explains that her grandfather grew the gold, and she convinces the king to use some of his money to make more gold: She advises him to give money to the poor farmers to buy seeds. During the summer months, the king impatiently waits while the "gold" is growing. When Rumpelstiltskin's daughter declares that the gold is ready, the king returns to the fields and sees the gold everywhere (fields of golden wheat). The jubilant farmers shower the king with provisions from their harvest such as wheat, apples, and pumpkins as tokens of their appreciation.

The king is pleased with the people's admiration, but he is dissatisfied with golden wheat. He wants real gold, and he pleads with the girl to remember if her grandfather did it another way. The girl reconsiders and tells the king she thinks that her grandfather knitted gold. She persuades the king to provide golden knitting needles and yellow yarn for the grannies in the countryside. Together they take the supplies to the grannies, and the girl advises the king to give the grannies some gold coins for their troubles. Weeks later, they return to the grannies, and the king is deluged with knitted socks, sweaters, and other articles of clothing. Again, the king is delighted with his people's veneration, but he wants gold.

The girl admits to the king that she does not know how her grandfather spun straw into gold. Although the king is disappointed in the news, he announces that he will marry the girl and make her his queen. The girl declines his proposal but suggests that he appoint her prime minister. The king grants her this position, and whenever he is feeling low, the girl organizes a goodwill tour. At the end of the story, the reader learns that the girl's name is Hope.

Ideologies Embedded in the Rumpelstiltskin Variants

Late 17th-Century France and Jean-Marie L'Héritier

France adopted the fairy tale as an artistic and social creation during the late 17th century. Similar to folk tales from the oral tradition, fairy tales became a narrative tactic, working on the one hand to promulgate correct behavior and demeanor. On the other hand, fairy tales were a subversive avenue in which to question the standards of taste and behavior that were considered the norm (Zipes, 1994).

Louis XIV (1638–1715) ruled France during the Baroque era. During this time, some French aristocratic women wanted to raise their intellectual status in society, and they organized gatherings known as salons. Women and men, from both aristocratic and bourgeois standings, gathered in the houses of wealthy women to discuss topics such as science, philosophy, art, and literature. The telling of fairy tales became a game, and the challenge for storytellers involved embellishment and improvisation of traditional folk tales. Within these tales, the female tellers represented their interests and the interests of the aristocracy.

Jean-Marie L'Héritier was a fairy tale storyteller who frequented the salons in Paris. L'Héritier was the niece of Charles Perrault, who himself wrote fairy tales "to provide some quaint amusement for the royal court of Louis XIV, of which he was a member" (Hallett & Karasek, 1991, p. 4). In L'Héritier's tales, her female characters were depicted as strong, determined, and being from an aristocratic background. In "Ricdin-Ricdon," Rosanie ponders how she will rise above dishonesty according to the standards of the French aristocracy. In the end, Rosanie learns of her noble birth and "this discovery only reinforces the notion that there is a natural hierarchy and proper manner of behavior that is best exemplified by the aristocracy" (Zipes, 1994, p. 67). In other words, Rosanie was born to rule, not to spin.

18th-Century Germany and the Brothers Grimm

Jacob Grimm recorded the first version of "Rumpelstiltskin" in 1808, supposedly from an anonymous oral tale. However, there is evidence that the Grimms were aware of the "Ricdin-Ricdon" version (Zipes, 1994). (More about the Grimms and their work can be found in chapter 9.) The Grimm Brothers' tale titled "Rumpenstünzchen" was later recorded in the Ölenberg manuscript in 1810 (Zipes, 1994). "Rumpenstünzchen" depicts the dilemma of a girl who could only spin flax into gold, therefore incorrectly performing her job. (Zipes [1994] asserts, "Her value was measured by her industriousness and yarn, and gold would have been a preposterously ironical symbol of her clumsiness and inability to learn to spin correctly..." [pp. 56–57].)

The Grimms rewrote "Rumpelstiltskin" in 1857. Here, the maiden's father brags that his daughter can spin straw into gold. Zipes (1994) notes that whether this difference is conscious or unconscious, "The Grimms were making a social-historical statement about the exploitation of women as spinners and the appropriation of the art/craft of spinning by men" (pp. 55–56). It is also interesting to note that in the later version, Rumpelstiltskin gains a level of masochism; rather than departing on a ladle as he did in the 1810 version, he tears himself in two.

Book cover from *Rumpelstiltskin* by Paul O. Zelinsky, copyright © 1986 by Paul O. Zelinsky. Used by permission of Dutton Children's Books, A Division of Penguin Young Readers Group, A Member of Penguin Group (USA) Inc., 345 Hudson Street, New York, NY 10014. All rights reserved.

Did the Grimms change their tales to accommodate their more middle class background and Calvinist outlook? Rather than have the miller's daughter come from royalty as in "Ricdin-Ricdon," the girl was really the miller's daughter. This change in the story may be based on the Grimms' own challenges of dealing with injustices while in school. The Grimms' father died when they were young, and their family suffered financial hardships. "They were treated by some teachers as socially inferior to the other 'highborn' students" (Zipes, 1988, p. 3). In their version of the story, someone not born into royalty outsmarted a king and a so-called helper (both men, by the way) and entered into a position of wealth and power. Maybe this is what the Grimm Brothers hoped for themselves as they, too, encountered inequities because of their lineage. Sometimes it is difficult to pinpoint the implied ideology of an author, but what is demonstrated by these two versions of Tale Type 500 is that the story has changed and a different ideology is presented in each one. The differences outlined here demonstrate how the tales changed and incorporated their authors' values.

SOME PROBLEMATIC ASPECTS OF THE GRIMMS' "RUMPELSTILTSKIN." Folklorists, psychologists, and other interpreters of tales have long been fascinated with "Rumpelstiltskin." In most versions of the story, there are four major characters: the miller, the miller's daughter, the king, and Rumpelstiltskin. Russell (2001) uses this familiar folk tale to demonstrate reader-response criticism. He asks his students to rank order the characters "according to their ethical behavior" (p. 71), and it is through sharing and respecting others' responses that individuals come to a deeper understanding of the text and possibly a deeper understanding of themselves.

Russell's use of the reader-response theory to rank order the characters in "Rumpelstiltskin" can be used to make students consider who they think is the most honest or upstanding character. So, who is the most honest character? The daughter lets Rumpelstiltskin do her work and marries the king under false pretenses. The miller lies about his daughter's talent and does nothing to save her life. The king is so greedy that he would kill an innocent girl when she cannot make him more money. And Rumpelstiltskin blackmails the daughter and insists that she give up her child. This exercise highlights why folklorists and readers have found "Rumpelstiltskin" so problematic.

Jane Yolen, a prolific writer who is the author of more than 200 books for children and adults, also has wondered about the moral center of the Rumpelstiltskin story. Yolen believes that her scrutiny of the tale has uncovered hidden messages in the Grimm version and that the Rumpelstiltskin tale has anti-Semitic elements. Yolen's (2000) afterword for her story "Granny Rumple" brings the possible religious connotations of "Rumpelstiltskin" to the foreground:

> I was considering the moral center of the story. Something was horribly wrong. Here was a miller who lies, his daughter who is complicitous in the lie, a king only interested in the girl if she can produce gold. And the only upright character in the tale is sacrificed in the end.
>
> So I looked more carefully at the little man, Rumpelstiltskin, himself. He has an unpronounceable name, lives apart from the kingdom, changes money, and is thought to want the child for some unspeakable blood rites. Thwack! The holy salmon of inspiration hit me in the face. Of course. Rumpelstiltskin is a medieval German story. This is an anti-Semitic tale. Little man, odd name, lives far away from the halls of power, is a moneychanger, and the old blood rites canard. (p. 288)

Yolen's reaction does highlight what could be interpreted as anti-Semitic overtones; for instance, Rumpelstiltskin's physical description, as given in this version of the story, resembles some anti-Semitic illustrations that depict Jews as short devils with long ears. The notion that Jews wanted children for "blood rites" is an example of stories that Christians have in past times propagated to create ill will against the Jewish people. The most obviously anti-Semitic depiction of Rumpelstiltskin, though, is as a money-changer. (A money-changer—also known as a moneylender or a usurer—is a person who loans money for interest. Many Jewish people worked at this occupation in the past.) During the Middle Ages, some clergy reminded "their flocks that usurers were invented by the Devil" (Wistrich, 1991, p. 27), which often reinforced the image of Jews as moneylenders: "The Jew as Satan's partner in all his financial dealings, fleecing poor Christians without mercy through this devilish practice" (Wistrich, 1991, p. 27). Did Rumpelstiltskin consider his magical ability as a loan and the firstborn as interest? These anti-Semitic images in literature are in direct conflict of the teachings of Judaism, which supports agrarian socialism and rejects the seeking of money and luxury items for their own sake. However, a paradox was created by this in the society of the time, because laws prohibited Jews from buying land and forced them to become city dwellers. Handling money was often the only trade available to Jewish people, despite their religious doctrine promoting agrarian socialism (Glassman, 2000).

Another aspect that could support Yolen's anti-Semitism theory is the payment of jewelry for spinning straw into gold. In L'Héritier's version, Rosanie did not have to offer a necklace or ring in exchange for Rumpelstiltskin's help. Conversely, the miller's daughter owned two valuables that she used as payment for Rumpelstiltskin's help. Some Christians of past times believed that amulets or magical charms, such as jewelry, could keep a Jewish person from harming them. After the girl forfeited these items, Rumpelstiltskin aided her. Is it possible that the jewelry was a symbol for such amulets?

In the Grimms' story, Rumpelstiltskin offers help in hopes of obtaining the girl's first-born child; however, the reader does not know the reason Rumpelstiltskin wants the child. As Rumpelstiltskin is described as an evil little man, it could be assumed by a reader that he might harm the child if he takes possession of it; Yolen speculates that Rumpelstiltskin is accused of wanting the child for blood rites. Also, in "Ricdin-Ricdon," Rosanie was able to overcome the devil because she was innocent. Was Rumpelstiltskin also seen as the devil in the Grimms' tale, and the girl/queen seen as an innocent victim? If this is so, and if, as Yolen contends, Rumpelstiltskin was meant to represent a Jewish person, then it is possible that the Grimms were representing Jewish people as devils.

The Present Time and Diane Stanley

There are many issues at the forefront of the 21st century such as gender roles, corporate raiding, business ethics, diversity, socioeconomic class division, poverty, and familial roles. Even though the illustrations in *Rumpelstiltskin's Daughter* appear medieval, a careful inspection reveals more modern artifacts, such as pens and a portrait painted in Picasso's style. Also interwoven into this fairy tale are modern issues and concerns. (For more discussion about transformed fairy tales, see chapter 17.)

Diane Stanley was born in 1943 and did not realize that she wanted to create children's books until she began to raise children. When her daughters were young, she visited the library regularly to find books to read to them. She became interested in nonfiction picture books for children and found them to be both entertaining and a teaching tool. Stanley acquainted herself with the business by researching bookmaking and experimenting with illustration techniques. At the first showing of her portfolio, the editor from Little, Brown immediately gave her an assignment. Stanley began illustrating books in 1977 and later worked as the art director at Putnam before she began writing her own books (Gale Research Company, 2000).

Meredith Charpentier at Macmillan encouraged many of Stanley's book ideas and accepted Stanley's first book, *The Conversation Club* (1983), for publication. The women developed such a close relationship that the miller's daughter in *Rumpelstiltskin's Daughter* was given the name Meredith. In writing this reconstructed fairy tale, Stanley wondered, "Why would the miller's daughter marry the king who had been tormenting her?" (Stanley, 1997). Admittedly, Stanley enjoys creating humorous stories, and she states, "My unabashedly feminist fairy tale was sheer pleasure" (Contemporary Authors Online, 2003). Stanley continues to write and illustrate books, mostly picture book biographies, because she finds the work both challenging and satisfying.

In *Rumpelstiltskin's Daughter*, Meredith's father likes to fabricate stories. One day, he makes up the story that his daughter can spin straw into gold. A servant of the kingdom overhears this story and tells the king. This is different from the Grimms' version in that the father does not purposely lie about his daughter; also, he does not directly tell the king or the king's servant. We can assume that the father in *Rumpelstiltskin's Daughter* is a loving father and would not deliberately put his daughter's life in danger.

Meredith gladly accepts Rumpelstiltskin's help of spinning straw into gold in exchange for her jewelry. However, Meredith refuses to bargain for her firstborn child, and she offers an alternative solution: She prefers to marry Rumpelstiltskin instead of the king. Meredith recognizes the king for what his is, greedy and selfish. She prefers a husband who likes children and is kind-hearted. This reflects the fact that, in current times, many people who have the ability to make large amounts of money may actually choose to live more simply. They believe that they will be happier if they can spend time with family. In addition, familial roles are very different than they were even 30 years ago. Fathers often are more involved with their children than in the past, and society generally values and accepts a father who is an active parent.

Rumpelstiltskin offers help in hopes of obtaining the girl's firstborn child so that he can become a father and have a child to love. The illustrations in this book depict Rumpelstiltskin as a kind little man; he is shown smiling, and his features are gentle. When pre-

Book cover from *Rumpelstiltskin's Daughter* by Diane Stanley. Copyright © 1997. Used by permission of HarperCollins Publishers.

sented with Rumpelstiltskin's bargain to take the child, though, Meredith declines. She does not want to marry a man, even a king, who would kill her because she cannot spin straw into gold. Thus, Meredith resists a place in royal society. Later, Meredith and Rumpelstiltskin raise a daughter who in turn initiates change that benefits the peasants of the kingdom. Hope helps the peasants to become more self-sufficient. The prime minister replaces the all-powerful king, and now the systemic hierarchal structure more closely reflects modern society.

Classroom Applications and Concluding Thoughts

Are fairy tales timeless or timely? Both. Fairy tales are timeless because stories of enchantment satisfy the soul. Justice is served in fairy tales, and everyone enjoys a happy ending. Fairy tales are timely because these stories have evolved over time. What is considered fair and just changes as ideologies change. For example, in "Ricdin-Ricdon," it was considered fair and just that Rosanie came from royalty. Who else would be worthy of the queen's admiration and the prince's love?

For readers in the elementary classroom, I recommend that educators read similar fairy tales and include traditional, reconstructed, and multicultural versions. By focusing on shared story elements and common motifs of a given fairy tale, young readers will learn that folk literature is an important aspect in all cultures. It is important for young readers to be familiar with fairy tales, as the motifs are embedded in many movies, stories, and books. Because some fairy tales may not match current ideologies, initiate discussions that can get young students thinking—ask, for example, "Do we have kings and queens in the United States?" Time is limited, and teachers cannot read everything to children. Read some traditional fairy tales from various cultures so that children have the background knowledge to enhance the reading of modern tales. Children often gravitate to the modern versions, not only for the bright pictures but also for the current themes.

For readers in the middle school classroom, I recommend that educators present fairy tale versions within a historical context. Remind the students that the ideology portrayed in the text is based on the time and place in which the story was written and that it incorporates an author's beliefs, values, and assumptions. The students will benefit from your guidance in understanding how people's thinking changes over time. To bring ideological differences to the surface, juxtapose traditional literature with reconstructed fairy tales. By comparing tales from different centuries, as I did here, students can learn about historical facts.

Fairy tales are based on the oral tradition and for generations were retold by storytellers and changed to meet the audience's or storyteller's beliefs and values. That oral tradition allowed for an amalgamation of a group's reflective and reimagined beliefs. As stories were told orally, storytellers could easily modify the stories as the culture modified its ideologies. Just as folk tales evolve over time, so do ideologies. When a story is frozen in print, it somewhat freezes the ideology.

I urge educators to remember that all written fairy tales were written during a certain time in history. The ideology within the text may or may not represent the present-day beliefs and attitudes of the culture from which the story originated. Remind students that fairy tales are not static. By reading many fairy tales, you teach your students that fairy tales are timeless; by discussing fairy tales in a historical setting, you teach your students that fairy tales are timely.

Portions of this chapter are based on Critical Multicultural Analysis of Folk Tales: Rumpelstiltskin Is My Name, Power Is My Game *(forthcoming), my unpublished doctoral dissertation, University of Massachusetts, Amherst.*

REFERENCES

Contemporary Authors Online. (2003). *Biography Resource Center: Diane Stanley*. Retrieved January 29, 2003, from http://www.galenet.com/servlet/BioRc

Gale Research Company. (2000). Diane Stanley. In *Something about the author* (Vol. 115, pp. 191–198). Detroit, MI: Gale Research.

Glassman, R.M. (2000). *Caring capitalism: A new middle class base for the welfare state*. New York: St. Martin's.

Hallett, M., & Karasek, B. (1991). *Folk & fairy tales*. Peterborough, ON: Broadview Press.

Russell, D.L. (2001). *Literature for children: A short introduction* (4th ed.). New York: Longman.

Stanley, D. (1983). *The Conversation Club*. New York: Macmillan.

Stephens, J. (1992). *Language and ideology in children's fiction*. New York: Longman.

Thompson, S. (1946). *The folktale*. New York: Dryden.

Thompson, S. (1993). *Motif-index of folk-literature: A classification of narrative elements in folktales, ballads, myths, fables, mediaeval romances, exempla, fabliaux, jest-books, and local legends* [CD]. Bloomington, IN: Indiana University Press & IntelLex Corporation.

Wistrich, R.S. (1991). *Antisemitism: The longest hatred*. New York: Pantheon.

Zipes, J.D. (1988). *The Brothers Grimm: From enchanted forests to the modern world*. New York: Routledge.

Zipes, J.D. (1994). *Fairy tale as myth/myth as fairy tale*. Lexington, KY: University Press of Kentucky.

RUMPELSTILTSKIN TALES

Arbuthnot, M.H. (1952). Tom Tit Tot. In M.H. Arbuthnot (Ed.), *Time for fairy tales, old and new* (Rev. ed., pp. 21–23). Chicago: Scott Foresman.

Galloway, P. (1995). The name. In *Truly grim tales* (pp. 1–15). New York: Delacorte.

Granowsky, A. (1993). *Rumpelstiltskin/A deal is a deal: A classic tale* (L. Graves & T. Newbury, Illus.). Austin, TX: Steck-Vaughn.

Grimm, J., & Grimm, W. (1987). Rumpelstiltskin. In J.D. Zipes (Ed. and Trans.), *The complete fairy tales of the Brothers Grimm* (pp. 209–212). New York: Bantam.

Hamilton, V. (2000). *The girl who spun gold* (L. Dillon & D. Dillon, Illus.). New York: Blue Sky.

Jacobs, J. (1967). Tom Tit Tot. In J. Jacobs (Ed.), *English fairy tales* (pp. 1–8). New York: Dover Publications.

L'Héritier, M.-J. (1991). Ricdin-Ricdon. In J.D. Zipes (Ed. and Trans.), *Spells of enchantment: The wondrous fairy tales of Western culture* (pp. 48–84). New York: Viking.

Marshall, R.N., & Battle, T. (2001/2002). *Rumpelstiltskin's daughter: A musical*. Retrieved January 28, 2003, from http://www.rumpelstiltskinsdaughter.com

Moser, B. (1994). *Tucker Pfeffercorn: An old story retold*. Boston: Little, Brown.

Napoli, D.J., & Tchen, R. (1999). *Spinners*. New York: Dutton.

Ness, E. (1997). *Tom Tit Tot: An English folk tale*. New York: Aladdin.

Phelps, E.J. (1981). Duffy and the devil: A Cornish tale. In E.J. Phelps (Ed.), *The Maid of the North: Feminist folk tales from around the world* (pp. 119–127). New York: Holt, Rinehart and Winston.

Schmidt, G.D. (2001). *Straw into gold*. New York: Clarion.

Stanley, D. (1997). *Rumpelstiltskin's daughter*. New York: Morrow.

Vande Velde, V. (2000). *The Rumpelstiltskin problem*. Boston: Houghton Mifflin.

White, C. (1997). *Whuppity Stoorie: A Scottish folktale* (S.D. Schindler, Illus.). New York: Putnam.

Yolen, J. (2000). Granny Rumple. In *Sister Emily's lightship and other stories* (pp. 44–55). New York: Tor.

Zelinsky, P.O. (1986). *Rumpelstiltskin*. New York: E.P. Dutton.

Zemach, H. (1973). *Duffy and the devil* (M. Zemach, Illus.). New York: Farrar, Straus & Giroux.

ADDITIONAL RECOMMENDED RESOURCES

Canepa, N.L. (1997). *Out of the woods: The origins of the literary fairy tale in Italy and France*. Detroit, MI: Wayne State University Press.

De Vos, G., & Altmann, A.E. (1999). *New tales for old: Folktales as literary fictions for young adults*. Englewood, CO: Libraries Unlimited.

Harries, E.W. (2001). *Twice upon a time: Women writers and the history of the fairy tale*. Princeton, NJ: Princeton University Press.

Afterword

Susan Hepler

There is no doubt, as you read this wonderful collection of chapters, that traditional literature is alive and thriving as the 21st century takes wing. The book in your hand contains the keys to the world's wisdom. That is, the authors of *Happily Ever After* encapsulate the many possibilities that traditional literature has to offer on what different cultures and traditions have valued throughout their histories.

Why is traditional literature important? Authors here have reiterated the many uses to which folk tales have been put. For listeners and readers, stories entertain, reflect values, explain natural phenomena, pass on shared history, and link the hearers or readers into a community. Stories also enable both tellers and listeners to make sense of enormous or seemingly incomprehensible events. Witness the power to an apprehensive child of a reassuring story in which a clever little character like Flossie conquers the fox, Rabbit uses wit and cunning to trick Coyote, or Clever Beatrice outwits the giant.

Stories, or their tellers, take joy in words. Within the spare tellings of many folk tales, actions repeat (Doc Rabbit challenges the Tar Baby and gets his four feet stuck, one at a time); words and phrases escalate ("big, bigger, biggest," whether it's Billy Goats Gruff or the Three Bears) and encapsulate ("Long ago in India, there lived a raja who believed that he was wise and fair, as a raja should be"; Demi, 1997). Listeners delight in these repetitions and anticipate the next use while enjoying the economic descriptions that keep the story moving. Many traditions make use of onomatopoeia, and readers hear in their mind's ear the sounds of the weaver at work, *shu-sha*, *shu-sha*, or the *clomp-clomp* of the giant that approaches. They tuck away the openings and closings of traditional stories ("Once there was and was not" or "Snip, snap, snout. My tale's told out"). Several articles note that many folkloric traditions encourage group participation, like the Haitian inquiry, "Crik?" to which the audience answers "Crak!" if they are ready to hear a story. Thus, these chapters point out, the love of words is passed along to the next generation.

Folk literature and its many subgenres have distinctive features, which are helpfully explored and explained throughout *Happily Ever After*. It is often a challenge for readers to sort out the qualities of a genre that distinguish a fable from a moral tale, for instance, or to separate a modern literary folk tale from a traditional one. These chapters provide examples to help us through these definition swamps. As these chapters indicate, the boisterous and blustery energy of the tall tale genre did not, as many think, originate in America; the fable is one of the oldest genres around, but moral stories probably preceded this tidily told genre. Headlines confuse legends and myths. What are the connections between these two genres? And there's some debate over whether a Native American tale from an oral tradition that depends on a performance context can ever be written down. Select any chapter in this book and discover not only a scholarly discussion with references to help define the markers of each subgenre but also a refreshing acknowledgment of the places where scholars, teachers, tellers, and writers overlap or take odds.

While each genre has distinctive features, there are patterns across all genres. Characters repeat. Look at some of the tricksters across cultures mentioned in this book: The African and Caribbean Anansi the Spider, the German Tyll Eulenspiegel, the southwest Native American Coyote, and the Chinese Monkey King all share a common theme, that of being tricked even as they are being tricky. In folk literature across cultures, clever characters outwit the king, the rich, the landowner, the slave owner, and the greedy. The Puerto Rican Juan Bobo, the Jewish people of Chelm, and the Arab Nasruddin share moments of pure confusion and misunderstandings that encourage us to laugh at ourselves.

Themes and morals repeat, too. Each tradition—whether it be from the Arab or Hopi or Jewish cultures; from Japan, Tanzania, Bolivia; or from the Taíno or Muslim world—has its own distinctive characters, themes, and ways of telling, as well. As many writers here have pointed out, cultures may be studied according to the folklore they have told. Some writers also have provided curriculum support with nonfiction or fiction that augments or illuminates the resource folk tales.

This collection also provides valuable insight into the changes in children's literature over the years. The authors of these chapters show that there are more and more tales that feature strong women. An increasing number of single tales and collections from Central and South American heritage, distinct Native American populations, the Middle East, and the countries of south Asia indicate other exciting trends. And while tellers have always played with traditional stories, how delicious it is to mix up a traditional tale's ingredients and make a whole new recipe. Hence, we have numerous new "fractured fairy tales," a genre all its own that uses such techniques as changing settings, switching points of view, or converting the folk tale form to rhyme, a novel, or an intermingling of several forms.

The useful and complete bibliographies that follow each chapter indicate how many fine selections are available for teachers to use in exploring traditional literature. And nearly all selections from the last decade heed Betsy Hearne's (1993a, 1993b) long-ago warning that folklore without some indication of its provenance or origin is not a book worthy of study. Thus, today's folk literature has fascinating notes, author information, illustrator sources, or other material to indicate how the author shaped the story. Readers may note, too, the many new illustrators whose work in this collection draws on well-researched visual material in creating pictures or who are themselves of the culture they paint or sketch.

This unique collection provides many opportunities for teachers to plan activities to help children explore a subgenre. No longer is the "folk tale unit" the way to begin. It is, instead, with one of these subgenres or with selections from a particular culture that children can discover the unique patterns found within. The authors throughout point to multiple ways of learning that play to our knowledge of "multiple intelligences." The fourth section opens the reader to replicable ideas while suggesting that any teacher can make a start.

This essential resource for understanding traditional literature provides curriculum builders with the information they need to meet a classroom of learners with exciting books and vibrant ways of exploring them. To paraphrase the famous dance instructor Arthur Murray's motto, "Put a little fun in your life. Try folk tales."

REFERENCES

Hearne, B. (1993a). Cite the source: Reducing cultural chaos in picture books, part one. *School Library Journal*, *39*(7), 22–27.

Hearne, B. (1993b). Respect the source: Reducing cultural chaos in picture books, part two. *School Library Journal*, *39*(8), 33–37.

CHILDREN'S BOOKS CITED

Demi. (1997). *One grain of rice: A mathematical folktale*. New York: Scholastic.

Author Index

Note. References followed by *t* or *f* indicate tables or figures, respectively.

GLASSMAN, R.M., 325
GLIMM, J.Y., 110
GOFORTH, F.S., 6, 10, 111
GOLDBERG, H., 241
GONZALEZ, R.D., 266, 267f, 269
GREENE, E., 171
GREENE, J., 8
GREEVER, E.A., 170
GUREWITSCH, M., 71

H

HADAWAY, N.L., 3, 11, 12, 264, 266, 267f, 268, 270, 274
HALLETT, M., 323
HAMILTON, E., 70
HAMILTON, M., 106
HAMILTON, V., 7
HASTINGS, S., 8, 264
HEARN, M.P., 114, 115
HEARNE, B., 84, 164, 165, 236, 237, 332
HEINIG, R., 171
HEPLER, S., 10, 13, 87, 236, 237, 241, 250, 252
HEWETT, C.J., 176
HICKMAN, J., 10, 13, 87, 236, 237, 241, 250, 252
HILL, P.L., 139, 142, 143
HIRSCHFELDER, A.B., 233, 238
HOLBEK, B., 289
HONKO, L.K., 224
HORNING, K.T., 106
HOXIE, F.E., 239
HUCK, C., 2–3, 10, 13, 87, 111, 236, 237, 241, 250, 252
HURST, C.O., 270, 273
HURSTON, Z.N., 143

I – J

INGRAM BOOK GROUP, 143
JACOBS, H., 142
JACOBS, J.S., 83, 248, 257
JACOBS, M., 209
JAMESON, R.D., 249
JANISCH, H., 8
JENDRESEN, E., 8
JENSEN, E., 313
JOHNSON, N.S., 285
JOHNSON, T.D., 147
JONES, G., 244
JONES, M.B., 129
JONES, S.S., 38, 46

K

KARASEK, B., 323
KIEFER, B., 10, 13, 87, 92, 236, 237, 241, 250, 252
KOTKIN, A.J., 269
KRAUS, A.M., 19, 23, 24, 30, 31, 38, 42, 50
KROGNESS, M.M., 269
KUSKIN, K., 8

L

LANDIS, B., 239
LEACH, M., 31, 46
L'ENGLE, M., 13

LEPP, B., 120
LEPP, P., 120
LEVINE, L.W., 139, 145
LEVI-STRAUSS, C., 69
LEVSTIK, L., 92
LEWIS, A.C., 193
LI, S., 94
LIBRARY OF CONGRESS, 271
LIGOURI, O., 195
LIMA, C.W., 116
LIMA, J.A., 116
LOUIS, D., 147
LUKENS, R., 6, 250, 252
LUTHI, M., 169
LUTZ, E., 266, 267f, 269, 273
LYNCH-BROWN, C., 87

M

MACDONALD, M.R., 13, 106
MAGGI, M.E., 8
MALVASI, M.G., 144
MANDLER, J.M., 285
MARSHALL, H., 142
MARTINEZ, M., 83, 111, 239
MAY, G.S., 127
MAYER, M., 8
MCCARTHY, M., 8
MCCASLIN, N., 80
MCCONNELL, M.L., 115
MCDERMOTT, G., 146
MCKAY, N.Y., 139, 142, 143
MEDICINE, B., 235
MELLO, R., 260
MENDOZA, J., 239
MIKKELSON, B., 277
MIKKELSON, D.P., 277
MILLER, J., 264, 279
MILLER-LACHMANN, L., 195
MIRANDA, D., 239
MITTEN, L., 238
MOFFETT, J., 69, 293, 308
MOLIN, P.F., 238
MOOMAW, S., 244
MOONEY, M., 83, 86, 87, 106
MORAIN, G., 266, 267f
MORPURGO, M., 8
MUNDY, J., 270
MUSLEAH, R., 183

N

NARAYAN, K., 223
NAYLOR, A., 83, 111, 239
NESSEL, D.D., 129
NIETO, S., 195
NORTON, D., 4, 192, 205, 257
NOY, D., 182
NYANEY, M.O., 266

O – P

OFFODILE, B., 139
OPPENHEIM, S.O., 8

ORTIZ-CASTRO, V., 193
PANFORD, S., 266
PAPPAS, C., 92
PAREDES, A., 277
PATRISSI, N., 209
PATTON, J., 149
PAVONETTI, L.M., 114
PBS ONLINE, 194
PENYAK, L.M., 273
PEREZ-STABLE, M., 193
PHILIP, N., 249
PILE, S., 273
PRESTON, E.Y., 222
PRICE, A., 116
PROPP, V., 168, 222, 285

R
RALPH, K.S., 192
RANDOLPH, V., 120
REARICK, J., 80
REDDISH, P., 209
REESE, D., 239, 241
RENNER, S.M., 266, 267f, 269, 273
ROGERS, D.L., 113
ROHMER, H., 215
RONEY, R.C., 171
ROSENBERG, D., 2, 7, 83
ROSS, K., 37, 42
ROUTMAN, R., 294
RUSH, J.C., 176
RUSSELL, D.L., 3, 5, 13, 324

S
SALAS, L., 195
SAN SOUCI, R.D., 8
SAVAGE, J.F., 5
SAWYER, R., 229
SCHICKEL, R., 170
SCHON, I., 195
SCHULTZ, F., 192
SCHWARTZ, H., 182
SCOTT, J., 271
SEALE, D., 82, 238
SHOR, R., 116
SIERRA, J., 229, 285
SILVER, D., 266
SILVEY, A., 167, 168
SIMONS, E.R., 270, 272, 275
SIMS BISHOP, R., 237
SLAPIN, B., 82, 238
SMITH, L., 70
SMITHSONIAN INSTITUTION, 269
SMOLEN, L.A., 193
SPATZ, J., 209
SPEAKER, K.M., 272
SPILLMAN, C.V., 6, 10
STANLEY, D., 326
STASZ, B., 273

STEINBERG, S., 273
STEPHENS, J., 316
STEWART, M., 256
STEWIG, J.W., 175, 176, 177
STONE, K.F., 170
STOODT-HILL, B.D., 83
STURM, B.W., 13
SUBJECT GUIDE TO CHILDREN'S BOOKS IN PRINT, 70
SUTHERLAND, Z., 111, 196, 236
SWAIN, G., 42

T
TALBOTT, H., 8
TATAR, M., 169, 249, 250, 252
TAYLOR, A., 248, 250
TEMPLE, C., 83, 111, 239
THOMPSON, S., 168, 222, 235, 289, 316
TIEDT, I., 270
TIEDT, P., 270
TOMLINSON, C., 87, 313
TUNNELL, M., 83, 248, 257

U–V
UNIVERSITY OF CALIFORNIA, BERKELEY, 271
UNIVERSITY OF CALIFORNIA, LOS ANGELES, 271
VARDELL, S.M., 3, 11, 12, 266, 267f, 274
VIDAURE, M., 215
VILLEGAS, A.M., 192

W
WAGNER, B.J., 172, 174, 293, 308
WAKIM, Y., 238
WARD, V., 118
WARD, W., 79
WARNER, M., 165, 166, 168, 169, 170, 249
WEISS, M., 106
WEST, D.H., 115, 116
WHITE, C.S.J., 224, 225
WIGET, A., 234
WIGGINTON, E., 271, 273, 274
WILSON, W.A., 269
WINDLING, T., 249
WISTRICH, R.S., 325
WOLFMAN, I., 270
WOOD, L., 271
WORTHY, M.J., 253, 254

Y–Z
YAAKOV, J., 116
YAMATE, S., 248
YOKOTA, J., 83, 111, 195, 239
YOLEN, J., 12
YOUNG, J.D., 131
YOUNG, R., 131
YOUNG, T.A., 3, 4, 9, 11, 12, 31, 210, 266, 267f, 274
ZIPES, J., 31, 164, 165, 166, 167, 168, 169, 249, 323, 324
ZUNI PEOPLE, 240

Folk Literature Author Index

Note. References followed by *t* or *f* indicate tables or figures, respectively.

D'Aulaire, E.P., 73, 260f
D'Aulaire, I., 73, 260f
Dawood, N.J., 220
Day, N.R., 21, 41
Deedy, C.A., 4, 105
Delacre, L., 76, 84, 97, 193, 194, 206
Delessert, E., 33t
Dematons, C., 261f
Demi, 4, 6, 59, 229, 331
De Montano, M.K., 243
Denise, C., 45
dePaola, T., 28, 89, 96, 226
De Sauza, J., 204
DeSpain, P., 27, 29, 30, 207
Dewey, A., 86, 124
Doherty, B., 10, 32, 33t, 44
Dolan, T., 244
Doucet, S., 29, 144
Drucker, M., 189
Drummond, A., 103
Duntzee, D., 171
Dupre, R., 88
Dwyer, M., 27

E

Early, M., 93, 100
Echewa, T.O., 141
Edens, C., 93
Edmonds, I.G., 86, 97
Edwards, P.D., 261f, 296
Egielski, R., 47
Emberley, B., 121
Emberley, M., 11, 34t, 174, 176, 294, 306
English, K., 231
Epstein, S., 157
Ernst, L.C., 35t, 305
Esterl, A., 47
Evetts-Secker, J., 45

F

Farley, C., 10, 22, 158
Farmer, N., 102, 118
Felleman, H., 62
Felton, H.W., 122
Finkel, I., 98
Fisher, L.E., 8, 73, 100
Fleischman, S., 123, 125, 131
Fletcher, S., 229
Foster, K., 98
Fraser, B., 276
Frazee, M., 49
Freedman, F.B., 187
Freedman, R., 159
French, F., 11, 174, 176, 296
Friedman, I.R., 275
Fritz, J., 92
Furlong, M., 93

G

Gaber, S., 227
Galdone, P., 49, 227, 289, 289f

Gallenkamp, C., 209
Galloway, P., 317
Gantschev, I., 33t
Garland, S., 20, 22, 25
Garner, J., 295
Garza, C.L., 275
Geras, A., 189, 295
Gershator, P., 20, 47
Gerson, M.-J., 141, 145, 197, 207, 211, 214
Gerstein, M., 8
Gibbons, G., 91
Giblin, J.C., 275
Gilchrist, C., 74, 222
Gilmore, R., 230
Glass, A., 123, 124, 127
Glubok, S., 209
Goble, P., 22, 70, 78
Goldin, B.D., 27
González, L.M., 12, 203, 204, 205
Goode, D., 175
Gorham, M., 129
Granowsky, A., 317
Greene, E., 260f
Greene, J., 8, 225
Greger, C.S., 196, 211
Griesser, J., 224
Grimm, J., 10, 34t, 38, 39, 316, 317, 320–321, 323–324
Grimm, W., 34t, 38, 39, 316, 317, 320–321, 323–324
Grindley, S., 37t
Guy, R., 140, 141

H

Haddix, M.P., 256, 257f, 295
Haley, G.E., 139
Hamanaka, S., 158
Hamilton, M., 20, 44, 46
Hamilton, V., 9, 12, 20, 28, 35t, 72, 74, 143, 144, 145, 148, 317
Han, S.C., 153
Harris, J.C., 10, 44
Harris, R.J., 77
Harrison, M., 39
Hartman, B., 11
Haskins, J., 144
Hastings, S., 8, 90, 92
Hausman, G., 70
Hausman, L., 70
Hayes, J., 202, 235, 258f
HBO Family, 303
Heaney, M., 76, 89, 90
Hearne, B., 84
Heins, P., 174
Hensen, J., 303
Herzog, G., 141
Hettinga, D.R., 177
Hickox, R., 258f
Hicks, R., 44
Hillenbrand, W., 49, 50
Ho, M., 153, 155
Hoberman, M.A., 49
Hodges, M., 91, 95, 96, 99, 123, 154
Hoffman, M., 7, 29, 48

HOFMEYR, D., 71, 73
HOGROGIAN, N., 175
HOLT, K.D., 159
HOLUB, J., 261*f*
HONG, L.T., 10
HOOKS, W.H., 143, 144, 170, 258*f*
HOPKINS, J.M., 39
HOVEY, K., 7
HOWE, J., 177
HOWLAND, N., 47
HOYT-GOLDSMITH, D., 230
HUCK, C., 35*t*, 175, 256, 257*f*
HULL, R., 77
HURWITE, J., 276
HUTH, H., 21, 25
HYDE-CHAMBERS, A., 72
HYDE-CHAMBERS, F., 72
HYMAN, T.S., 12, 34*t*, 172, 175

I–J

ISAACS, A., 9, 126, 131
JACKSON, B., 34*t*
JACKSON, E., 72, 170, 261*f*
JACKSON, S.L., 101
JACOBS, J., 317
JAFFE, N., 155, 188, 197, 209, 210, 257*f*
JANISCH, H., 8
JARRELL, R., 140, 177
JEFFERS, S., 257*f*, 258
JENDRESEN, E., 8, 225
JIANG, J.L., 154
JOHNSON, P.B., 44, 124
JOHNSTON, T., 203, 261*f*, 305
JONES, C., 47
JONES, D.C., 287*f*
JONES, M., 142
JOSEPH, L., 146

K

KAJIKAWA, K., 155
KAMINSKI, B., 287*f*
KARAS, G.B., 49
KARLIN, B., 257*f*
KEAMS, G., 23
KEATS, E.J., 102, 122
KEENAN, S., 73
KEILLOR, G., 103
KELLOGG, S., 9, 33*t*, 45, 49, 101, 121, 122, 123, 126, 127, 128, 129
KENNARD, E.A., 243
KENT, J., 289*f*
KETTEMAN, H., 125, 261*f*, 301
KIMMEL, E.A., 10, 21, 22, 26, 27, 30, 33*t*, 45, 47, 49, 62, 140, 148, 183, 187, 188, 198, 221
KING, S., 244
KIPLING, R., 265, 285
KITE, P., 20, 25
KNUTSON, B., 73
KORTY, C., 287*f*
KRACH, M.S., 158
KRAUS, R., 34*t*, 154

KRISHNASWAMI, U., 223
KUNSTLER, J., 101
KURTZ, J., 47, 199
KUSHELL, K., 295
KUSKIN, K., 8

L

LANE, B., 303
LANGLEY, J., 173, 174
LANSKY, B., 295
LASH, D., 76
LASKY, K., 11
LATTIMORE, D.N., 261*f*
LEAVY, U., 39
LE CAIN, E., 173
LEE, T.C., 258*f*
LEGUIN, U.K., 252
LELOOSKA, C., 72
LELOOSKA, D., 20, 28, 40
LERCH, M., 228
LESSER, R., 172
LESTER, J., 9, 28, 59, 73, 101, 102, 122, 131, 141, 142, 144
LEVINE, G.C., 178, 256, 257*f*, 296
LEWIN, T., 221
LEWIS, J.P., 39, 45
LEXAU, J., 27, 30
L'HERITIER, M., 317, 318–320, 322–323
LIND, M., 3, 23
LINDAHL, C., 225
LINDBERGH, R., 123
LIONNI, L., 60
LIPPERT, M., 63, 73
LJUNGKVIST, L., 33*t*
LOBEL, A., 59
LONDON, J., 23
LONG, J.F., 156
LOUIE, A., 258*f*
LOURIE, P., 74
LOWELL, S., 33*t*, 261*f*, 305
LOWRY, L., 270
LUM, D.H.Y., 258*f*
LUNGE-LARSEN, L., 23
LUPTON, H., 48
LYNCH, T., 5
LYONS, M.E., 144

M

MACDONALD, A., 145
MACDONALD, M.R., 29, 30, 49
MACGILL-CALLAHAN, S., 39
MADDERN, E., 72
MAGGI, M.E., 8, 72
MAGUIRE, G., 257*f*
MAHLMANN, L., 287*f*
MAHY, M., 9
MANS, R., 75
MARCELLINO, F., 176
MARCHANT, K., 230
MARK, J., 7
MARSHALL, J., 33*t*

MARSHALL, R.N., 318
MARTIN, A.-C., 299
MARTIN, C., 36, 260*f*
MARTIN, R., 6, 22, 41, 71, 74, 154, 258*f*
MARTORELL, A., 201
MATHEWS, M., 230
MAYER, M., 8, 85, 88, 90, 99, 257*f*
MAYO, M., 21, 85, 96
MCBRATNEY, S., 39
MCCARTHY, M., 8
MCCASLIN, N., 80
MCCAUGHREAN, G., 22, 70, 75, 95, 98, 99, 100
MCCORMICK, D.J., 120, 127
MCCULLY, E.A., 156
MCCUNN, R.L., 102
MCDERMOTT, G., 6, 10, 27, 28, 75, 139, 140, 145, 197, 212, 240
MCKINLEY, R., 178
MCKISSACK, P.C., 34*t*, 144, 148
MCLELLAN, J., 243
MCLELLAN, M., 243
MEDEARIS, A.S., 143, 144
MEDLOCOTT, M., 76
MEEKER, C.H., 155
MELTZER, M., 90
MERCREDI, M., 244
MEYER, C., 209
MINTER, F., 261*f*
MOHR, N., 201
MOLLEL, T., 30, 41, 140, 141, 148
MONTES, A., 204, 205
MONTES, M., 46
MONTRESOR, B., 36
MOONEY, M., 86
MORA, P., 7, 61, 65
MORIMOTO, J., 157
MORPURGO, M., 8, 93
MOSER, B., 33*t*, 35*t*, 317
MOSES, W., 101, 123
MULDAUR, S., 104
MUSGROVE, M., 22
MYERS, C., 74
MYERS, T., 3
MYERS, W.D., 64

N
NAPOLI, D.J., 178, 317
NESS, E., 317
NEURATH, M., 209
NIXON, J.L., 125, 131
NOLEN, J., 117, 125, 126
NORDENSTROM, M., 21
NORMAN, H., 30, 40

O
OBER, H., 197
O'BRIEN, J., 48
OGLE, D., 298
O'HARA, C., 89
OHMI, A., 158
ONISH, L.B., 173

ONYEFULU, O., 258*f*
OODGEROO, 73
OPPENHEIM, S.O., 8
ORGEL, D., 5, 7
OSBORNE, M.P., 7, 9, 44, 45, 76, 102, 117, 118, 127
OWENS, L., 285

P
PALACIOS, A., 197, 209, 210
PANDYA, M., 230
PARKINSON, K., 49, 50
PARKS, V.D., 142
PAYE, W., 63, 73
PEABODY, J.P., 79
PECK, J., 49
PERLMAN, J., 261*f*
PHELPS, E.J., 317
PHILIP, N., 7, 33*t*, 70, 74, 76, 260*f*, 290
PILEGARD, V.W., 153
PILLING, A., 7
PINKNEY, J., 5, 58, 131
PINOLA, L., 23
PITRE, F., 204, 205
PITTMAN, H., 230
PLUME, I., 172, 174
PODWAL, M., 185
POLETTE, K., 304
POLLAN, M., 101
POLLOCK, P., 240–241, 258*f*
POOLE, A.L., 10, 62
POULAKIS, P., 118
POWELL, P., 23, 41
PREUS, M., 23
PROSE, F., 183, 186
PULLMAN, P., 176, 252

R
RAY, J., 32
REARICK, J., 80
RENEAUX, J.J., 28
REPCHUK, C., 60
RINGGOLD, F., 143
RIORDAN, J., 21
ROBERTS, L., 175, 176
ROCKWELL, A., 7, 22, 25
ROGASKY, B., 173, 184
ROHMER, H., 196, 201
ROOT, P., 142
ROS, S., 153, 155
ROSALES, M., 36
ROSENTHAL, P., 11
ROSS, G., 10, 27, 237, 242, 244
ROSS, T., 44
ROSSI, J., 117
ROUNDS, D., 125
ROUNDS, G., 33*t*, 117, 121, 129, 130
ROWLING, J.K., 77, 87
RUMFORD, J., 226
RUSH, B., 182, 185, 186, 188

S

SALLEY, C., 45
SANFIELD, S., 143, 144
SAN JOSE, C., 176
SAN SOUCI, D., 28, 258*f*
SAN SOUCI, R.D., 8, 9, 20, 25, 28, 29, 35*t*, 39, 40, 41, 45, 91, 92, 117, 124, 125, 126, 143, 144, 145, 147, 148, 154, 202, 258*f*, 260*f*, 261*f*
SANTORE, C., 175
SCHAEFER, L.M., 49
SCHANZER, R., 9, 86
SCHMIDT, G.D., 317
SCHROEDER, A., 258*f*, 303
SCHWARTZ, A., 49, 118, 129, 276
SCHWARTZ, H., 182, 185, 186, 188
SCIESZKA, J., 11, 60, 170, 173, 296
SEKAQUAPTEWA, E., 242
SHAH, I., 222, 227, 228
SHANNON, G., 34*t*
SHAPIRO, I., 114
SHELLEY, M., 95
SHEPARD, A., 9, 25, 39, 41, 125, 222, 224, 228
SHULMAN, L., 49
SIDDIQUI, A., 228
SIERRA, J., 4, 12, 27, 28, 32, 34*t*, 35*t*, 36, 45, 47, 49, 251, 258*f*, 260*f*, 287*f*, 288, 289, 289*f*
SILVERMAN, E., 188, 257*f*
SILVERSTEIN, S., 121, 261, 261*f*
SIMON, T., 110
SINCLAIR, M., 228
SINGER, I.B., 185, 189
SINGH, R., 22, 25, 45, 76
SLOAT, T., 49
SOGABE, A., 64
SOUHAMI, J., 28, 34*t*
SPENSER, E., 99
SPIRES, E., 76
SPIRIN, G., 39
STAMM, C., 9, 157
STANLEY, D., 11, 95, 173, 317, 321–322, 326–327
STEEL, F.A., 257*f*
STEIG, J., 7, 76
STEIG, W., 92
STEIN, J., 85
STEPTOE, J., 5, 147, 258, 258*f*, 266
STERN, J., 290
STEVENS, J., 10, 28, 60, 61, 65, 143, 144
STEWART, B., 90
STEWIG, J.W., 36, 174
STOUTENBURG, A., 101, 102, 118, 123, 129
STOW, J., 49
STRAUSS, G., 175
STRAUSS, S., 198
STROUD, V., 244
STUART-CLARK, C., 39
SUTCLIFF, R., 84, 90, 91, 92
SWANSON, D., 25
SWENTZELL, R., 244
SYNGE, U., 99

T

TABACK, S., 49

TAKAYAMA, S., 261*f*
TALASHOEMA, H., 242
TALBOTT, H., 8, 91
TARNOWSKA, W., 225
TCHEN, R., 317
TOLHURST, M., 296
TOLKIEN, J.R.R., 87, 252
TOLSTOY, A., 49
TOMLINSON, T., 93
TOMPERT, A., 97, 99
TRAN, N.D., 159
TURKLE, B., 296

U – V

UNTERMEYER, L., 121
VAN LAAN, N., 199
VANDE VELDE, V., 295, 317
VELARDE, P., 244
VERNIERO, J.C., 76
VIDAL, B., 200
VIDAURE, M., 201
VIORST, J., 173, 261, 261*f*
VOGEL, C.G., 20, 22, 25
VOZAR, D., 303
VUONG, L.D., 156

W

WAHL, J., 28, 144
WALDHERR, K., 74
WALKER, B., 222, 228
WALKER, P.R., 9, 117
WALKER, R., 30, 44
WALLNER, A., 49
WANG, R.C., 156
WARD, J., 303
WARGIN, K., 20, 21, 25
WATTENBERG, J., 49
WEISS, M., 20, 44, 46
WESTCOTT, N.B., 49
WHATLEY, B., 33*t*
WHELAN, G., 229
WHITE, C., 35*t*, 317
WHITE, T.H., 257*f*
WIESNER, D., 33*t*
WILDSMITH, B., 6
WILFORD, J.N., 71
WILLEY, M., 29, 30, 126
WILLIAMS, J., 87
WILLIAMS, L.E., 154
WILLIAMS, M., 75
WILLIAMS, S., 144
WILSON, T., 206
WINDLING, T., 295, 310
WINTER, J., 49, 50
WINTER, M., 5
WINTHER, B., 207
WISNIEWSKI, D., 89, 94, 185
WOLFSON, M.O., 41, 74
WOLKSTEIN, D., 21, 25, 36
WOOD, A., 11, 121
WOODS, D., 237

WOOLDRIDGE, C.N., 124
WRIGHT, C., 126
WYNDHAM, R., 156

Y
YEE, P., 154
YEOMAN, J., 49, 220
YEP, L., 35*t*, 77, 157
YOHANNES, G., 45
YOLEN, J., 5, 26, 39, 77, 92, 125, 133, 170, 273, 295, 325, 326

YORINKS, A., 261*f*, 306
YOUNG, F., 12, 34*t*, 40, 48, 62, 63, 154, 155, 150, 265

Z
ZELINSKY, P.O., 35*t*, 36, 173
ZEMACH, H., 317
ZEMACH, M., 189
ZEMAN, L., 78, 87, 98, 225, 226
ZHANG, S.N., 84, 94
ZIEFERT, H., 49
ZIMMERMAN, M., 71

Subject Index

Note. References followed by *t* or *f* indicate tables or figures, respectively.

EL CID (RODRIGO DIAZ DE VIVAR), 99–100
ELIJAH THE PROPHET: stories of, 185
ENGLISH AS A SECOND LANGUAGE (ESL) CLASSES: drama with, 291
ENTERTAINING: collecting folklore on, 276–277
EPICS: Indian and Middle Eastern, 223–226; versus legends, 87
EUROPEAN STORIES, 164–180; Celtic, 28, 89–93; Czech Republic, 95; development of, 164–168; France, 95–96; Germany, 96; Switzerland, 100; United Kingdom, 89–94. *See also* fairy tales
EXTENDING, 173–174

F

FABLES, 5–6, 6t, 56–68; definition of, 57; Middle Eastern, 227; original, 59–60, 64; persistence of, 58; retold, 58–63; student, 66f
FAIRY TALES, 10–11, 31–37; benefits of, 294–297; classification of, 316; fractured, 11, 170; ideologies of, 316–329; reconstructed, 317; scrambled, 37t; term, 165; transforming, 293–315; variants of, 33t–35t
FANTASY: versus legends, 87–88
FAT CAT TALES, 289–291, 289f
FEBOLD FEBOLDSON, 124
FINN MACCOOL, 89–91
FLAG BOOK: with transformation tales, 42
FLANNELBOARD: with cumulative tales, 50
FOLK: term, 18, 263
FOLK LITERATURE, 2–16; benefits of, 3–5, 331–333; definition of, 2; functions of, 2–3; subgenres of, 5–12
FOLKLORE: benefits of, 269–274; categories of, 266, 267f; collecting, 263–281; definition of, 263; functions of, 265–266; as lesson topics, rankings of, 268, 268t; study of, 165–169, 177–178, 235
FOLK SONGS, 48, 49t
FOLK TALES, 6t, 9–12, 18–55; collectors of, reading about, 177–178; definition of, 51; memorable nature of, 283–286; versus myths, 70; versus tall tales, 111; variants, comparison of, 147, 148t
FOLLY: in Asian stories, 157–158
FRACTURED FAIRY TALES, 11, 170; term, 317. *See also* transformed fairy tales
FRANCE: legends, 95; Rumpelstiltskin variant from, ideology of, 322–323

G

GAWAIN, 92
GENDER ROLES: in Cinderella, 259–260
GENRE ASSESSMENT, 104–105
GENRE STUDY: tall tales, 126–132
GEOGRAPHY: folklore and, 271
GERMANY: legends, 96; Rumpelstiltskin variant from, ideology of, 323–326
GILGAMESH, 98, 225–226
GINGERBREAD MAN, 47, 47t
GOALS: in folk tales, 285
GODS AND GODDESSES, 73–74
GOLEM, 95, 184–185
GREEK MYTHS, 7, 70, 73, 79–80

GRIMM, JACOB AND WILHELM, 165–166, 177–178, 320–321, 323–326
GRIOTS, 139
GUANINA, 97
GUINEVERE, 91–92

H

HANS COBBLER, 96
HEATHCOTE, DOROTHY, 174–175
HERDER, JOHANN GOTTFRIED, 165
HEROISM: characteristics of, 259–260
HIEROGLYPHICS, 211, 212f
HIGH JOHN, 143
HISTORICAL FICTION: versus legends, 87
HOLIDAYS: in Indian stories, 230; in Jewish stories, 188–189
HOME-SCHOOL CONNECTIONS: collecting folklore, 269–270, 272–277
HUMOR: in Asian stories, 157–158; in Cinderella stories, 260–261, 261f; in Jewish stories, 187–188; in Middle Eastern stories, 227–228
HUNGRY MONSTER TALES, 289–291, 290f

I

IDEOLOGIES: in fairy tales, 316–329; in folk literature, 4
INCAS, 194
INDIA: stories of, 219–232; study of, 230–231
INDIANS. *See* Native American stories
INSECTS: pourquoi tales on, 19–20
ISLAMIC TRADITION, 8, 220, 230

J

JACK TALES, 44
JAPAN: legends, 97
JATAKA TALES, 6
JEWISH STORIES, 181–191; characteristics of, 181–183; legends, 95; and Rumpelstiltskin, 325–326
JIM BRIDGER, 123–124
JOAN OF ARC, 95
JOHN CHAPMAN, 101, 122–123
JOHN HENRY, 101–102, 122
JOHNNY APPLESEED, 102–103, 122–123
JUAN BOBO, 204–205
JUDAH LOEW BEN BEZALEL, 94–95

K–L

KINDNESS: in Asian stories, 154–156
KWLH CHART, 298, 299f
KWL PARAGRAPH FRAME, 311, 311f
LA FONTAINE, JEAN DE, 6
LANDFORMS: pourquoi tales on, 20–21
LANG, ANDREW, 167
LATIN AMERICA: legends, 97–98; study of, 209
LATINO STORIES, 192–218; cautions with, 195; collections of, 206–208; criteria for, 195–196; historical perspective on, 194–196
LEARNING SEQUENCE: for Cinderella unit, 297–305, 398f
LEGENDS, 6t, 8–9, 82–109; characteristics of, 83–84;

definition of, 83; knowledge of, assessment of, 104–105; Latino, 199–201; Middle Eastern, 226–227; versus other genres, 86–88; term, 84–86; urban, 106, 277

LESSON PLANS: for Cinderella unit, 253–261; on tall tales, 126–132; writing transformed fairy tales, 297–312. *See also* activities

L'HERITIER, JEAN-MARIE, 318–320, 322–323

LITERACY INSTRUCTION: oral tradition and, 264–265

LITERARY PASSPORT, 147, 147*t*

LITERARY TALES, 11

LONG BOOKS, 178

M

MAGIC: in Latino stories, 201–203

MAHABHARATA, 223–225

MASKS: with Asian stories, 158; with Latino stories, 214

MAYA, 194; myths of, 7

MELLA, 88

MIDDLE EAST: legends, 98–99; study of, 230–231

MIDDLE EASTERN STORIES, 219–232; formulas in, 220–221; preservation and transmission of, 221–222

MIDRASH: stories from, 183–184

MIKE FINK, 123

MOE, JORGEN, 166

MONOGENESIS, 13

MORALS: in African stories, 140–141; in fables, 56–68; in fairy tales, 294; in Jewish stories, 182; in Latino stories, 208

MOSE HUMPHREYS, 102, 118

MOTIFS, 13; in Tortoise and the Hare, 65*t*

MULAN, 94

MULTIMEDIA ACTIVITIES: with Latino stories, 209

MYTHS, 6*t*, 7–8, 69–81; collections of, 75–76; definition of, 69–70; versus legends, 87; relevance of, 70–72; sources of, 72–76

N

NANABOSHO, 243

NASRUDIN, 227–228

NATIVE AMERICAN STORIES, 233–246; cautions with, 233–237; selection of, 237–244; transformation tales, 39–40; trickster tales, 27–28

NIZAMI, 225

NONVERBAL COMMUNICATION: collecting folklore on, 276

NOODLEHEAD TALES, 43–46; definition of, 43; Jewish, 186–187; Latino, 204–205

NORSE MYTHS, 7, 73

NOVELS: from folk tales, 178; of transformed fairy tales, 295–296

O

OOKA TADASUKE, 97

OPEN SESAME, 219–221

ORAL INTERVIEWS: on folk tales, 172

ORAL RESPONSE, 174–175

ORAL TRADITION, 264–265; collecting, 272–273; drama in, folk tales as, 286–287; in Latin

America, 194; preservation of, 221–222, 264–265

OSSIAN, 89

OVID, 71

OYATE, 82, 238, 243

P

PAUL BUNYAN, 120–121, 127

PECOS BILL, 121–122

PENTAMERONE, 164

PERFORMANCE TASK ASSESSMENT LIST (PeTAL), 305, 307*f*

PERRAULT, CHARLES, 164–165, 249, 323

PICTOMAPS, 78

PICTURE BOOKS, 171

PIE-BITER, 102

PLOT STRUCTURE: of folk tales, 283–286

POINT OF VIEW, 172–173

POLYGENESIS, 13

POSTREADING STRATEGIES: for Cinderella unit, 255–256

POURQUOI TALES, 10, 19–25; definition of, 4, 19; Latino, 196–199; versus myths, 70

PREREADING STRATEGIES: for Cinderella unit, 254

PUEBLO TRIBE, 240–241

PUPPETS, 288–289; with Asian stories, 158; with Latino stories, 213, 214*f*

Q–R

QUILTS: with fables, 67, 67*f*

RAMAYANA, 223, 225

READ-ALOUDS: myths, 77; in writing transformed fairy tales, 300

READERS THEATRE: with Latino stories, 212

READING STRATEGIES: for Cinderella unit, 254–255

RECONSTRUCTED FAIRY TALES, 317

RED RIDING HOOD: variants of, 34*t*

RELIGION: myths and, 8

REPETITION: in folk tales, 286

RETELLING, 171; in different time, 174

ROBIN HOOD, 93–94

RODRIGO DIAZ DE VIVAR (EL CID), 99–100

ROMAN MYTHS, 7

RUMPELSTILTSKIN: variants of, 35*t*, 316–329, 319*t*

S

SAINT FRANCIS, 96–97

SAINT GEORGE, 99

SAINT MARTIN DE PORRES, 97–98

SAINT NICHOLAS, 99

SAINT PATRICK, 91

SALLIE ANN THUNDER ANN WHIRLWIND CROCKETT, 126

SANTA CLAUS, 99

SCHOOLCRAFT, HENRY ROWE, 235

SCIENCE UNITS: folklore and, 271; with pourquoi tales, 25

SHADOW PUPPETS: with Latino stories, 213, 214*f*

SHAPESHIFTERS, 38

SHEHEREZADE, 220, 229

SILK ROAD, 222–223

SINBAD, 220–221

SKY: pourquoi tales on, 21–22
SNOW WHITE: variants of, 33t
SOCIAL STUDIES: and writing transformed fairy tales, 305–312
SOTOMAYER, 97
SOURCE NOTES: with legends, 84; with Native American stories, 236–237
SOUTH AMERICAN STORIES: African, 145–146
SPAIN: legends, 99–100
SPEECH-TEACH, 155
SPELLS: in transformation tales, 38–39
SPIRITS: activities with, 158–159; in Asian stories, 153–154
STEREOTYPES: in Native American literature, 234–235, 238; in Rumpelstiltskin, 324–326
STORIES: functions of, 237; sharing methods, 310–311; similarities across cultures, 12–13
STORY GRAMMAR, 285
STORY MAP: circular, 212, 213f; for writing transformed fairy tales, 308, 309f
STORYTELLING, 77–78; African, 139; with Latino stories, 214; Middle Eastern, 221–222; by students, 160, 272
SUNDIATA KIETA, 89
SURLALUNE FAIRY TALE PAGES, 255
SWITZERLAND: legends, 100

T

TAÍNOS, 194
TALE TYPE, 316
TALL TALES, 6t, 8–9, 110–135; cautions with, 120; characteristics of, analyzing, 132–133; characters in, 116–117, 120–124; collections and anthologies of, 117–120; commercialization of, 115; definition of, 111; history of, 111–113; versus legends, 86; library holdings of, 116, 116t; literary, 124, 125t; popularity of, 113–116
TALMUD, 182; stories from, 183–184
TAYLOR, EDGAR, 167
TECHNOLOGY: and folklore, 277–279
TEXTS: comparing, 175–176
THOMPSON, STITH, 31
THOUSAND AND ONE NIGHTS, 219–221
THREE LITTLE PIGS: variants of, 33t–34t
TORTOISE AND THE HARE: variants of, 65t
TRADITIONS: pourquoi tales on, 22
TRANSFORMATION TALES, 37–43; definition of, 38
TRANSFORMED FAIRY TALES, 293–315; assignment,

306f; possibilities for, 304f
TRAVEL BROCHURES, 211, 211f
TRIBES: in Native American stories, 235–236; study of, 244
TRICKSTER TALES, 10, 25–31, 74–75; African, 139–140; African American, 142–143; definition of, 26; Latino, 203–204; Middle Eastern, 227–228; Native American, 242–243; writing, 146–148, 146t

U

ULSTER CYCLE, 89
UNITED STATES: European stories in, 169–171; legends, 100–103; Native American stories, 27–28, 39–40, 233–246; tall tales, 110–135
URBAN LEGENDS, 106, 277

V

VALUES: books of, 159; transmission of, folk literature and, 3, 4
VARIANTS: of Cinderella, 12, 202, 248–262, 257f; comparing, 175, 210, 210t, 255–256; of cumulative tales, 49t; of fables, 65t; of fairy tales, 33t–35t; of Rumpelstiltskin, 316–329, 319t
VENN DIAGRAMS, 301, 302f; on pourquoi tales, 24
VIOLENCE: in fairy tales, 294
VISUALS: with myths, 78; responding to, 176–177
VRINDAVAN, 229

W–Z

WEATHER: pourquoi tales on, 22
WEBSITES: Cinderella resources, 255–256; folklore resources, 269, 271, 278f; Native American resources, 238–239; From Remus to Rap, 12
WILLIAM TELL, 100
WIT: in Asian stories, 153
WOMEN: in Asian stories, 94, 156–157; in Celtic legends, 90; in Cinderella variants, 259–260, 260f; in Disney movies, 170; in Indian stories, 223; in Rumpelstiltskin variants, 326–327; in tall tales, 124–126
WONDER TALES: Latino, 201–203
WORKING: collecting folklore on, 274–275
WORKSHOP: on transformed fairy tales, 308
WRITING: dramatic, 291–292; responses, 174–175; transformed fairy tales, 297–305
ZUNI TRIBE, 241–242